GENESIS

Cover image: *Forms of English Red* by Christian Hugo Martin
http://www.christianhugomartin.com/
Cover design: Laurie Ingram
Book design: PerfecType, Nashville, Tenn.

Library of Congress Cataloging-in-Publication Data
Genesis / Athalya Brenner, Archie Chi-Chung Lee, and Gale A. Yee, editors.
    p. cm. — (Texts@context)
Includes bibliographical references and index.
ISBN 978-0-8006-5999-8 (alk. paper)
1. Bible. O.T. Genesis—Criticism, interpretation, etc. I. Brenner, Athalya.
II. Lee, Archie Chi-Chung. III. Yee, Gale A., 1949-
BS1235.52.G47 2009
222'.1106089—dc22   2009029714

Manufactured in the U.S.A.

15 14 13 12 11 10   1 2 3 4 5 6 7 8 9 10

CONTENTS

Part Two
Redreaming with Joseph and Others

Part Three
Issues of Gender, Family, and Class

ABBREVIATIONS

AB	Anchor Bible
ABD	*Anchor Bible Dictionary*, ed. D. N. Freedman (New York, 1992)
AJBS	*African Journal of Biblical Studies*
AJT	*Asia Journal of Theology*
AmJT	*American Journal of Theology*
ASV	American Standard Version
ATD	Das Alte Testament Deutsch
BBB	Bonner biblische Beiträge
BBE	Bible in Basic English
BDB	*The Brown-Driver-Briggs Hebrew and English Lexicon*
BibInt	*Biblical Interpretation*
BZAW	Beihefte zur Zeitschrift für die alttestamentliche Wissenschaft
CAH	Cambridge Ancient History
CBQ	*Catholic Biblical Quarterly*
CCIJ	*Corporate Communications, an International Journal*
CH	Code of Hammurabi
Dʙʏ	Derby Bible
DR	Douay–Rheims
FRLANT	Forschungen zur Religion und Literatur des Alten und Neuen Testaments
IB	*The Interpreter's Bible*
IDS	*In die Skriflig*
JAAR	*Journal of the American Academy of Religion*
JBL	*Journal of Biblical Literature*
JNES	*Journal of Near Eastern Studies*
JNSL	*Journal of Northwest Semitic Languages*

JPS	Jewish Publication Society
JSOT	*Journal for the Study of the Old Testament*
JSOTSup	Journal for the Study of the Old Testament: Supplement Series
KJV	King James Version
NAB	New American Bible
NASB	New American Standard Bible
NEB	New English Bible
NIB (NIV)	New International Bible (Version)
NIB	*The New Interpreter's Bible*
NIDB	*New International Dictionary of the Bible*
NJB	New Jerusalem Bible
NKJV	New King James Version
NLT	New Living Translation
NRSV	New Revised Standard Version
OBO	Orbis biblicus et orientalis
OBT	Overtures to Biblical Theology
OTE	*Old Testament Essays*
RelEd	*Religious Education*
RevQ	*Revue de Qumran*
RSV	Revised Standard Version
RWB	Revised Webster Bible
SBL	Society of Biblical Literature
SemeiaSt	Semeia Studies
TRu	*Theologische Rundschau*
TS	*Theological Studies*
TT	*Theology Today*
VT	*Vetus Testamentum*
VTSup	Supplements to Vetus Testamentum
WBC	Word Biblical Commentary
WEB	Webster Bible
WW	*Word and World*
YLT	Young's Literal Translation
ZAW	*Zeitschrift für die alttestamentliche Wissenschaft*
ZDMG	*Zeitschrift der deutschen morgenländischen Gesellschaft*

texts @ contexts
SERIES PREFACE

Myth cannot be defined but as an empty screen, a structure. . . .
A myth is but an empty screen for transference.

MIEKE BAL[1]

שבעים פנים לתורה

The Torah has seventy faces.

MEDIEVAL JEWISH TRADITION[2]

The discipline of biblical studies emerges from a particular cultural context; it is profoundly influenced by the assumptions and values of the Western European and North Atlantic, male-dominated, and largely Protestant environment in which it was born. Yet like the religions with which it is involved, the critical study of the Bible has traveled beyond its original context. Its presence in a diversity of academic settings around the globe has been experienced as both liberative and imperialist, sometimes simultaneously. Like many travelers, biblical scholars become aware of their own cultural rootedness only in contact with, and through the eyes of, people in other cultures.

---

1. Bal 1993: 347, 360.
2. This saying indicates, through its usage of the stereotypic number 70, that the Torah—and, by extension, the whole Bible—intrinsically has many meanings. It is therefore often used to indicate the multivalence and variability of biblical interpretation. The saying does not appear in this formulation in traditional Jewish biblical interpretation before the Middle Ages. Its earliest appearances are toward the end of the medieval commentator Ibn Ezra's introduction to his commentary on the Torah, in midrash *Numbers Rabbah* (on 13:15-16), and in later Jewish mystical literature.

The way one closes a door in Philadelphia seems nothing at all remarkable, but in Chiang Mai, the same action seems overly loud and emphatic—so very typically American. In the same way, Western biblical interpretation did not seem tied to any specific context when only Westerners were reading and writing it. Since so much economic, military, and consequently cultural power has been vested in the West, the West has had the privilege of maintaining this cultural exclusivity for over two centuries. Those who engaged in biblical studies—even when they were women or men from Africa, Asia, and Latin America—nevertheless had to take on the Western context along with the discipline.

But much of recent Bible scholarship has moved toward the recognition that considerations not only of the contexts of assumed, or implied, biblical authors but also the contexts of the interpreters are valid and legitimate in an inquiry into biblical literature. We use *contexts* here as an umbrella term covering a wide range of issues: on the one hand, social factors (such as location, economic situation, gender, age, class, ethnicity, color, and things pertaining to personal biography) and, on the other hand, ideological factors (such as faith, beliefs, practiced norms, and personal politics).

Contextual readings of the Bible are an attempt to redress a previous longstanding and grave imbalance. This imbalance rests in the claim that says that there is a kind of "plain," unaligned biblical criticism that is somehow normative and that there is another, distinct kind of biblical criticism aligned with some social location: the writing of Latina/o scholars advocating liberation, the writing of feminist scholars emphasizing gender as a cultural factor, the writings of African scholars pointing out the text's and the readers' imperialism, the writing of Jews and Muslims, and so on. The project of recognizing and emphasizing the role of context in reading freely admits that we all come from somewhere: no one is native to the biblical text, no one reads only in the interests of the text itself. North Atlantic and Western European scholarship has focused on the Bible's characters as individuals, has read past its miracles and stories of spiritual manifestations or "translated" them into other categories, and has seen some aspects of the text in bold and other aspects not at all. These results of Euro-American contextual reading would be no problem if they were seen as such; but they have become a chain to be broken when they have been held up as the one and only "objective," plain truth of the text itself.

The biblical text, as we have come to understand in the postmodern world and as pre-Enlightenment interpreters perhaps understood more clearly, does not speak in its own voice. It cannot read itself. *We* must read it, and in reading it, we must acknowledge that our own voice's particular pitch and timbre and inflection affect the meaning that emerges. In the past, and to a large extent still in the present, Bible scholars usually read the text in the voice of a Western Protestant male. When interpreters in the Southern Hemisphere and in Asia began to appropriate the Bible, this meant a recognition that the Euro-American male voice is not the voice of the text itself; it is only one reader's voice, or rather, the voice of one context—however familiar and authoritative it may seem to all who have been affected by Western political and economic power. Needless to say, it is not a voice suited to bring out the best meaning for every reading community. Indeed, as biblical studies tended for so long to speak in this one particular voice, it may be the case that that voice has outlived its meaning-producing usefulness: we may have heard all that this voice has to say, at least for now. Nevertheless we have included that voice in this series, in part in an effort to hear it as emerging from its specific context, in order to put that previously authoritative voice quite literally in its place.

The trend of recognizing readers' contexts as meaningful is already recognizable in the pioneering volumes of *Reading from This Place* (Segovia and Tolbert 2000; 2004; Segovia 1995), which indeed move from the center to the margins and back and from the United States to the rest of the world.[3] More recent publications along this line also include *Her Master's Tools?* (Penner and Vander Stichele 2005), *From Every People and Nation: The Book of Revelation in Intercultural Perspective* (Rhoads et al. 2005), *From Every People and Nation: A Biblical Theology of Race* (Hays and Carson 2003), and the *Global Bible Commentary* (*GBC*; Patte et al. 2004).

The editors of the *GBC* have gone a long way in the direction of this shift by soliciting and admitting contributions from so-called Third, Fourth, and Fifth World scholars alongside First and Second World

---

3. At the 2009 Annual Meeting of the Society of Biblical Literature, the Contextual Biblical Interpretation Consultation held a joint special session with the Asian and Asian-American Hermeneutics Group to commemorate the fifteenth anniversary of this three-volume project.

scholars, thus attempting to usher the former and their perspectives into the *center* of biblical discussion. Contributors to the *GBC* were asked to begin by clearly stating their context before proceeding. The result was a collection of short introductions into the books of the Bible (Hebrew Bible/Old Testament and New Testament), each introduction from one specific context and, perforce, limited in scope. At the Society of Biblical Literature's annual meeting in Philadelphia in 2005, during the two *GBC* sessions and especially in the session devoted to pedagogical implications, it became clear that this project should be continued, albeit articulated further and redirected to include more disparate voices among readers of the biblical texts.

On methodological grounds, the paradox of a deliberately inclusive policy that foregrounds interpretative differences could not be addressed in a single- or double-volume format because in most instances, those formats would allow for only one viewpoint for each biblical issue or passage (as in previous publications) or biblical book (as in the *GBC*) to be articulated. The acceptance of such a limit might indeed lead to a decentering of traditional scholarship, but it would definitely not usher in multivocality on any single topic. It is true that, for pedagogical reasons, a teacher might achieve multivocality of scholarship by using various specialized scholarship types together: for instance, the *GBC* has been used side by side in a course with historical introductions to the Bible and other focused introductions, such as the *Women's Bible Commentary* (Newsom and Ringe 1998). But research and classes focused on a single biblical book or biblical corpus need another kind of resource: volumes exemplifying a broad multivocality in themselves, varied enough in contexts from various shades of the confessional to various degrees of the secular, especially since in most previous publications, the contexts of communities of faith overrode all other contexts.

On the practical level, then, we found that we could address some of these methodological, pedagogical, and representational limitations evident in previous projects in contextual interpretation through a book series in which each volume introduces multiple contextual readings of the same biblical texts. This is what the Society of Biblical Literature's Consultation on Contextual Biblical Interpretation has already been promoting since 2005. The Consultation serves as a testing ground for a multiplicity of readings of the same biblical texts by scholars from different contexts.

These considerations led us to believe that such a book series would be timely. We decided to construct a series, including at least eight to ten volumes, divided between the Hebrew Bible/Old Testament (HB/OT) and the New Testament (NT). Each of the planned volumes will focus on one or two biblical books: Genesis, Exodus and Deuteronomy, Leviticus and Numbers, Joshua and Judges, and early Jewish novels (such as Judith, Susanna, and Tobit) for the HB/OT; Mark, Luke-Acts, John, and Paul's letters for the NT.[4] The general HB/OT editor is Athalya Brenner, with Archie Lee and Gale Yee as associate editors. The general NT editor is Nicole Duran, with Daniel Patte and Teresa Okure as associate editors.

Each volume will focus on clusters of contexts and of issues or themes, as determined by the editors in consultation with potential contributors. A combination of topics or themes, texts, and interpretive contexts seems better for our purpose than a text-only focus. In this way, more viewpoints on specific issues will be presented, with the hope of gaining a grid of interests and understanding. The interpreters' contexts will be allowed to play a central role in choosing a theme: we editors do not want to impose our choice of themes upon others, but as the contributions emerge, we will collect themes for each volume under several headings.

While we were soliciting articles for the first volumes (and continue to solicit contributions for future volumes), each contributor was asked to foreground her or his own multiple "contexts" while presenting her or his interpretation of a given issue pertaining to the relevant biblical book(s). We asked that the interpretation be firmly grounded in those contexts and sharply focused on the specific theme, as well as in dialogue with "classical" informed biblical scholarship. Finally, we asked for a concluding assessment of the significance of this interpretation for the contributor's contexts (whether secular or in the framework of a faith community).

Our main interest in this series is to examine how formulating the content-specific, ideological, and thematic questions from life contexts will focus the reading of the biblical texts. The result is a two-way process of reading that (1) considers the contemporary life context from the perspective of

---

4. At this time, no volume on Revelation is planned, since Rhoads's volume, *From Every People and Nation: The Book of Revelation in Intercultural Perspective* (2005), is readily available, with a concept similar to ours.

the chosen themes in the given biblical book as corrective lenses, pointing out specific problems and issues in that context as highlighted by the themes in the biblical book; and (2) conversely, considers the given biblical book and the chosen theme from the perspective of the life context.

The word *contexts*, like *identity*, is a blanket term with many components. For some, their geographical context is uppermost; for others, the dominant factor may be gender, faith, membership in a certain community, class, and so forth. The balance is personal and not always conscious; it does, however, dictate choices of interpretation. One of our interests as editors is to present the personal beyond the autobiographical as pertinent to the wider scholarly endeavor, especially but not only when grids of consent emerge that supersede divergence. Consent is no guarantee of "truth speak" (Bal: 2008, 16, 164–6 and elsewhere); neither does it necessarily point at a sure recognition of the biblical authors' elusive contexts and intentions. It does, however, have cultural and political implications.

Globalization promotes uniformity but also diversity, by shortening distances, enabling dissemination of information, and exchanging resources. This is an opportunity for modifying traditional power hierarchies and reallocating knowledge, for upsetting hegemonies, and for combining the old with the new, the familiar with the unknown—in short, for a fresh mutuality. This series, then, consciously promotes the revision of biblical myths into newly reread and rewritten versions that hang on many threads of transference. Our contributors were asked, decidedly, to be responsibly nonobjective and to represent only themselves on the biblical screen. Paradoxically, we hope, the readings here offered will form a new tapestry or, changing the metaphor, new metaphorical screens on which contemporary life contexts and the life of biblical texts in those contexts may be reflected.

Athalya Brenner
Nicole Wilkinson Duran

Introduction

Athalya Brenner

This volume on Genesis is the first in the Texts @ Contexts series from Fortress Press. As such, it stands on its own as a multivocal volume on several significant issues in Genesis, but it also serves as a model for what we intend to achieve with this series. Here we have gathered essays from very different perspectives and life contexts; the diverse readings produced by those contexts in turn illuminate biblical themes and passages in new ways. Contexts are complex, as are the dynamic identities they help create. It is customary for biblical interpreters to privilege geophysical contexts as factors in identity formation. This is understandable: where we live is a major variable for successful or failed globalization today, as well as for issues in cultural hegemony, economy, and politics. The same goes for social, religious, and ethnic contexts. However, at a given moment in life or in one's research, a reader may wish to favor a certain component of her or his complex context out of personal concern, or as a response to social or personal events, or simply as a response to a chance encounter or coincidence. Such choices may either underscore or minimize difference; they may produce shared insights or disagreements. In any event, personal concern—whatever the dominant component of a person's context that comes into the foreground—will color the questions asked and hence the answers attempted.

In this sense, as already mentioned in the series preface, our quest for contexts addresses the unique, the personal, the autobiographical, the social, and the geographical and goes beyond them as well to include what may be called the global. Consequently, insights reached from one metaphorical "place" may not answer concerns that stem from another—or again, paradoxically, they may. This remains to be seen in each case.

Three clusters of issues in Genesis, chosen in consultation with the contributors, are addressed here. Part One, "Beginnings," covering Genesis 1–11, is divided into two subsections: "The Creation Revisited" and "Flood and New Order." Part Two addresses "Redreaming with Joseph and Others," and part Three, "Issues of Gender, Family, and Class." These textual and thematic clusters by no means cover all or even most of the issues in Genesis that can be profitably taken up by other readers in specific contexts. Rather, they were chosen for availability as well as centrality of concern to the contributors, whether or not they have been central to more "classical" modes of Bible interpretation.

Part One: Beginnings: The Creation Revisited

Amadi Ahiamadu, David Tuesday Adamo, Athalya Brenner, Philip Venter, Edwin Zulu, and Yan Lin write about various aspects of Genesis 1–3. Archie Chi Chung Lee, Mark Rathbone, and Yael Shemesh write about the flood narrative in Genesis 6–9 and the new cosmic order that ensues after it.

Ahiamadu attempts to assess the creation mandate in Gen. 1:26-28, which positions human beings as partners of God in creation and stewards over the physical earth. Stewardship has been exercised either in a domineering manner over nature or in a caring partnership with nature. Ahiamadu considers the forces that corroded natural rights in Nigeria and critically assesses how the Genesis pericope might enhance a new sense of human rights culture in the distressed Niger Delta region.

Adamo works from a Christian Nigerian perspective. He compares the biblical creation myths with African ones, especially but not only creation myths from Nigeria. Finding many similarities (as well as differences), Adamo argues that although there is a scholarly consensus that the biblical creation myths were influenced by Mesopotamian literature, examination of additional accounts should be carried out in search of a possible ultimate source of the Genesis creation account. The several African myths that he presents show that Africans have abundant myths similar to those of the

Mesopotamians and Israelites. In the light of the similarities in content, motifs, and theology, the issue of cultural contact should be investigated as well.

Brenner looks at an academic book containing a collection of women's embroidery that harks back to very early times and ancient civilizations. Some of the symbols used in the embroidery certainly stood originally for goddess images, especially the tree of life cluster associated with goddesses. The women whose embroidery is shown in the book hardly recognized the ancient symbols they used for what they were, although they had a strong notion of their being associated with female experience and the female life cycle. This usage, coupled with lack of consciousness about the symbols' origin, together with the writer's personal experience as a native-born Israeli and the daughter of immigrants from Eastern Europe, serve as incentive for reexamining the tree of life trope in Genesis 2–3.

Venter investigates the category of gender in the ideology of the body that infuses the Bible's history of origins. Operating from the premise that Genesis 1–3 is, for his South African and church context, an authoritative history, he focuses on the creator God Elohim. This figure stands at the highest hierarchical point of a system of value and power that the community that gave birth to the text perceived as threatened by circumstances. Venter concludes that the text was written by priests during and after the exile, in the attempt to reintegrate the battered community and with an eye toward restoration.

To gain new insights into matters of sin, gender, and responsibility, Zulu interprets Genesis 3 from a particular context as a Christian of the Ngoni people of Eastern Zambia. He states that the text of Genesis 3 is often interpreted with a gender bias against women, which overshadows the significant place a woman has in many communities such as his. Traditional interpretation does not reflect the Ngoni and other African societies where the responsibility for sin cannot be heaped on the community of women, because in these societies the men undertake leadership and responsibility for everything that happens within the homestead. A critical analysis of the passage then points to the man's failed responsibility and cover-up. Therefore, the blame game that follows plays out at the expense of the woman, who in an African context always enjoys respect and honor due to the various roles she plays in the community.

Yan Lin is a Chinese scholar who explores the meaning of Genesis 1–3 in the light of creation myths from ancient Chinese texts. The method she uses is cross-textual reading. Focusing on cosmology, cosmogony, the origin of human beings, and divine–human relationship, she attempts to understand Hebrew creation myths from the Chinese cultural context and vice versa. Among her insights are the notion that in Chinese cosmology, time coordinates with space, whereas in Genesis 1, the time system is just a sequence of narrative instead of real time; that chaos is a basic matter in Chinese creation myths, but the antithesis of creation in Genesis 1; that there is no sacred dimension in human beings in ancient Chinese texts, in contrast to Genesis and ancient Mesopotamian texts; and that in both Chinese and Hebrew literatures, there appear the themes of creation, the created, and salvation.

Lee looks at the biblical flood narratives from the context of the numerous flood myths in China. In a cross-textual reading, the chief myths he presents are those of the Naxi, an ethnic minority of China. The text, a well-known literary work of Dongba literature entitled *Record of Genesis,* contains quite a few motifs common to the biblical flood narrative and also other Chinese flood myths. Two issues are especially highlighted: the mythic themes in the structure of flood stories, and the conception of relationship between the divine and the human in the religious world of the biblical flood narrative and of the Naxi Genesis. Lee's aim is to show how, in the cross-textual reading process, Chinese readers receive and appropriate the biblical flood narrative along with the Naxi flood myth and how the Naxi text contributes to the understanding of the biblical flood narrative.

Rathbone begins by stating the context for his work on Gen. 11:1-9, the story of the city and the tower. In South Africa, neocolonial readings of Gen. 11:1-9 played a major role in justifying apartheid, formalized even in a document released by the Dutch Reformed Church (1976). This reading gave priority to the scattering of the people gathered in Shinar. Desmond Tutu responded by providing an anticolonial reading of Gen. 11:1-9 that leans on Western scholarship, a reading that favors unity in a critique of apartheid. Rathbone rejects both readings on the grounds that a resolution of the unity/scattering dichotomy by favoring a particular side of the dichotomy may end in racism (for the former) or cultural relativism (for the latter). He argues instead that the unity/scattering dichotomy is kept in a critical tension through the holistic cultural matrix that operates in the interpretations of nonscholarly African readers of this text. These are specifically reflected in readings of African Initiated Churches in which Moya, or the Spirit, plays a critical role. These readings provide a noncolonial alternative for the interpretation of Gen. 11:1-9.

After the flood, as part of the new world order, humans were allowed to consume meat. Yael Shemesh is a believing and observant Jew and a confirmed vegetarian/vegan. She points out that although Judaism is not a vegetarian religion, the Jewish sages in general wanted to restrict meat consumption. The classical Jewish texts include voices that praise meat abstention or condemn its consumption, explaining that meat eating is damaging to the human body and even more so to the human soul. The dominant view among the talmudic sages and traditional commentators was that vegetarianism is an ideal that existed before the flood. Several also suggest that the primeval vegetarian diet will be restored in the messianic era. Her aim, therefore, is to bring distant realms—religious faith and vegetarianism, both ways of life—closer together.

Part Two: Redreaming with Joseph and Others

Dreams are considered meaningful, one way or another, in most human societies and cultures. They certainly feature largely in Genesis 12–50, serving as pivotal literary devices in the unfolding of plot as well as offering content in human-human and human-divine mutual relationships. Therefore, dreams were chosen as one of the central themes for this volume. Carole Fontaine, Meira Polliack, and Gerald West and Thulani Ndlazi write about Joseph's dreams. Wai Ching (Angela) Wong writes about Genesis dreams other than Joseph's.

Fontaine reads Joseph "in company with" and for two distinct groups: Iranian refugees, students, and friends who are dispossessed and even enslaved; and secular human rights defenders and policy makers. Her experience in childhood and her work later on have shaped her standpoint in these multicultural "foreign courts," sharing her texts and daring to dream of them in a way that might lead to a world better fed and less violent than the one we have now. In the story of Joseph, Fontaine sees at least two tales. Joseph is seen as a survivor of human trafficking, and he becomes a successful state food aid distributor, who then himself colludes to enslave people in their own lands in return for the bread he has stored up with God's help. Can modern human trafficking shed any light on the cloaks of many colors that interest scholars in Joseph?

Polliack examines Joseph's dreams and his actions before and after Egypt against the backdrop of biblical exegesis, including medieval Jewish exegesis. She looks at Joseph's dreams and his story in the context of personal trauma and in the light of current theories of trauma and trauma resolution by recourse to memory. From Joseph's initial dreams to his self-revelation in front of his brothers and beyond, he has to go through a journey of remembering the trauma of being sold to Egypt, performing the trauma again by reenacting the event against his brothers, and finally performing it again by being able to speak to his brothers. Healing and resolution begin with memory and continue with reenactment, in stages, until a harmony of sorts is achieved.

For the past three years, West and Ndlazi have participated in a series of contextual Bible studies for the tripartite alliance of the Church Land Programme, the Ujamaa Centre for Community Development and Research, and a network of church- and community-based organizations working with land issues throughout the KwaZulu-Natal province of South Africa. In their workshops, they have created a series of four studies under the following themes: "Land Possession and Land Dispossession," "Women and Land," "Food Security and Land," and "Leadership and Land." The fourth theme is the topic of their essay here, which charts the study and its results from the level of reading to that of the political. They describe how contextual Bible study—in this case, of Genesis 37–50—can be used for empowering and for changing hegemonies. They write with the aim not to remain on the level of words alone but also to move into works.

Wong reads the patriarchal stories in Genesis, especially dream stories outside the Joseph pericope, together with literature and films that tell the stories of migrants, mostly women, in Hong Kong and against the backdrop of dreams and divination that are popular in her culture. By moving back and forth between then and now (or nearly now), she shows how cultural praxis, biblical interpretation, and psychological analysis can work together to illuminate Genesis figures, especially the women, as migrants whose status colors their lives, behavior, hopes, and action. Wong analyzes dreams of the patriarchs but also pays special attention to women's dreams, or rather the lack thereof in Genesis, a lack that stands in contrast with the way women's dreams feature largely in women's experience in her own culture. Her question—What would a Leah, or a Rachel, or a Sarah have dreamed?—remains pertinent and unanswered, a glaring literary gap. However, the migrant Chinese women's dreams may supply some pointers in the right direction across distances, cultures, and time frames.

Part Three: Issues of Gender, Family, and Class

Feminist scholarship has repeatedly shown that gender issues are bound up with and have bearing on other social issues, such as class, poverty or wealth, and family hierarchy. Genesis is presented by its writers and families as a book of history—of the world, of the human race, of a family that becomes God's nation. It is therefore not surprising that many of the Genesis texts can be read for those issues and that their presentation has had an authoritative influence on disparate life contexts. Here essays by Yairah Amit, Cheryl A. Kirk-Duggan, Kari Latvus, and David Tuesday Adamo and Erivwierho Francis Eghwubare illustrate how such issues can be read in and into the Genesis texts, on the one hand, and be inscribed onto life situations, on the other hand.

Amit rereads Genesis 38, the story of Tamar and Judah that ostensibly intrudes on the plot of the Joseph cycle. Her discussion is divided into two parts. The first part deals with Genesis 38 as textual interpolation; the second part discusses the story's relevance to the contemporary Israeli context. The story's placement between Genesis 37 and 39 is traced for its possible history and meaning within the present textual context, before the implications of the story itself are discussed. Amit concludes that Genesis 38 serves as a platform for two subjects: marriage with non-Jewish women and levirate marriage. Ultimately, she wishes to emphasize that the need for interpolation in the past is relevant also today.

Kirk-Duggan reads the stories found in Genesis 1–9 from a womanist interdisciplinary context, as a scholar, musician, pedagogue, athlete, quilter, and lover of rose gardens, for characterizations of the divine and of related human couples. These stories unfold with two genealogies: of the Adam (earth creature) and Eve, and of Noah and "Mrs. Noah." Kirk-Duggan explores the contexts and dynamics of divine sensibilities, instances of comedy, and the impact of tragedy. Her reading is designed to hold together scholarship, faith, and commitment to contemporary social issues, among other things, through rereading and posing to the texts questions that are, perhaps, considered less relevant to "classical" biblical scholarship.

According to Latvus, the story of Hagar in Genesis 16 and 21 illustrates both classical exegetical and recent contextual questions. His article covers the major exegetical results and aims to read the stories using the method referred to here as intercontextual analysis. The analysis offers a tool to connect past text with present reality and to read the Hagar story in both contexts. Thus, Hagar, an Egyptian slave, becomes in the analysis a forerunner and companion to all immigrant women who live and work in forced reality. In this multilayered analysis, focusing on the positions of the poor, Latvus advocates a timely reminder that the current social location of many poor immigrant females, similar to Hagar's, is not over yet. Marginal voices still cry for refuge and protection and are still in danger of being expelled. The question of the ancient writers' morality is relevant and requires both ethical and practical actions.

Adamo and Eghwubare proceed from the twin notion that whereas the tendency of Euro-American Old Testament scholars has been to deny or dilute African influence upon Scripture (that is, to de-Africanize it), recent efforts of Afrocentric scholars have helped to establish the African presence in the Bible. Yet there remains the problem of inadequate attention to the status and role of African biblical women. Adamo and Eghwubare's study examines Hagar's story in order to demonstrate the position of Hagar, an African woman, in the biblical text, in light of the customary marriage law of the Urhobo, a Nigerian tribe. The essay is written from the faith position that God's option is for the oppressed and disinherited. It therefore points to God's work in the world for all of humanity, with the hope that contemporary African women will find in it a useful resource when confronted with religious, social, and cultural problems in their faith journeys.

So What? Instead of Concluding Remarks

If we trace the similarities and differences of the essays just summarized, the following picture emerges.

First is the prominence of location, location, location—that is, geographic location. Eight of the contributors are from sub-Saharan Africa: three from Nigeria, one from Zambia, four from South Africa. Three are from Hong Kong/China. Two are from the United States; one is from Finland; four are from Israel. (The African contributors are all male, as is the Finnish contributor. Of the Chinese contributors, one is a male, and two are females. All the Israeli contributors are females.)

It would seem that the positions of the African and American contributors and the questions they ask are strongly informed by a Christian faith context together with a strong social commitment related to the awareness and pain of past colonial and ethnic wrongs, from without or within. The Chinese contributions, by and large, are more informed by cultural factors than by faith factors. This is not to say that the Chinese contributors are less socially, politically (in the wider sense), or religiously committed, but that their angle of view is different. Of the Israeli contributors, only one has a Jewish faith context. The other three focus on the biblical text itself and its cultural significance for their contemporary lives in their own cultural and geographical setting. It is therefore hardly surprising, yet worth noting, that terms such as *the fall* (relating to Genesis 2–3) or *sin* will appear only in certain essays and that they will be of concern to people of Christian faith, but not to the other writers. This way of looking at the text—by affirming or negating blame, justifying or vilifying humans, reflecting on the figures of the divine—does not seem to stem from a single location, but from the confessional situation as well as from the contents of the Genesis texts themselves.

Another interesting feature is the space given to issues of gender, especially as these relate to class and economy. These issues are not limited to the essays in part three only but are omnipresent. (Is this a result of the contemporary *zeitgeist*?) Certainly much is to be gleaned from comparing the biblical text with current gender mores and customs, as illustrated by essays on African cultures.

We could go on to consider the gains for biblical studies from contextual studies, as argued practically by all the contributors and exemplified, for instance, by the Chinese contributions. An overriding concern in this book is the dual purpose of refreshing both biblical scholarship (which is certainly one of the contributors' contexts!) and current life situations. This concern produces an ethic that is both similar to the classic guild ethic and different from it: it is as deeply involved in local sociocultural issues as in the more global endeavor; and as committed to the historical custom of "living by the Bible" as to understanding it. We are beginning to understand that newer reading methods do not necessarily mean a wholesale denial of the old and that moving back and forth in time and space may be confusing but is also beneficial—or, at the very least, interesting. Promoting such variety and new insights is the mission of this volume and of the Texts @ Contexts series.

Part One

Beginnings: The Creation Revisited

CHAPTER 1

A Critical Assessment of the Creation Mandate in Genesis 1:26-28

and Its Human Rights Implications for Nigeria

Amadi Ahiamadu

Introduction

The creation ordinance in Gen. 1:26-28 reads

> *Then God said, "Let us make man in our image, after our likeness; and let them have dominion over the fish of the sea, and over the birds of the air, and over the cattle, and over all the earth, and over every creeping thing that creeps upon the earth. So God created man in his own image, in the image of God he created him; male and female he created them. And God blessed them, and God said to them, "Be fruitful and multiply, and fill the earth and subdue it; and have dominion over the fish of the sea and over the birds of the air and over every living thing that moves upon the earth."*

This passage has been given such an interpretation as to encourage Western explorers, entrepreneurs, and investors to engage in economic activities especially in a global quest for energy sources, which has resulted in latifundism or the act of grabbing more and more land, ecological destruction, environmental pollution, land degradation, deforestation, desertification, and impoverishment especially in oil mining within the Niger Delta (Butler 1991: 862; Wybrow 1991: 17; Primavesi 2000: 188; Dibeela 2001: 396). Some have misread the above-quoted creation or cultural mandate in Gen. 1:26-28 as portraying humanity in superlative terms and as pointing to human beings as the crown of creation. Others have traced these problems to Western political domination, economic conquest, and rule over various "native" territories in Asia, Africa, and the Americas during the eighteenth and nineteenth centuries especially. These developments and more have been traced to some prevailing Western philosophical definition of the concept of stewardship, including the present environmental and ecological disaster rocking our planet today. By contrast, there are those who point to African traditional worldviews or the lack of such worldviews as responsible for the recklessness of multinational oil companies in their industrial and chemical operations on the continent. Still others think the problems result from government's inability to enact appropriate environmental and ecological protection laws, which could serve as guides and checks on the multinational oil companies operating in Africa and especially Nigeria and Angola.

With respect to the earlier objection, certain misconceptions of humanity's role in creation are inherent even in the traditional African worldview. For instance, in some parts of Africa, including Nigeria, the human role in creation is seen as subservient not only to the spirits of the ancestors, but also to forests and wildlife,[1] thus placing humans at the mercy of creation (Parry-Davis 2004: 63). The role of the human is surrounded with various superstitious beliefs, which reduce him or her to the status of a servant to every created being on earth, and never a master. Acceptance of this role leaves Africa at the mercy of foreign explorers and investors who engage in vast land acquisition with purely economic motives.

An example is the practice of latifundism by multinational oil companies, which has turned out to be a potent means of mass impoverishment in the Niger Delta in particular and the developing countries in general with a severe circumscription of community and individual rights (Benhabib 2002: 61–62; Blum 1998: 73–99; Fager 1993: 27). Multinational oil companies' acquisition of more and more land is not a boost to individual freedom of worship, of association, of religion, of conscience, or of movement. Instead, latifundism has seriously compromised these eternal values as people are

---

1. The fear of nature and natural phenomena is usually a feature of primordial and pre-Christian societies. It was indeed during the Enlightenment in the Middle Ages that Europe was rid of morbid fears as a result of the work of the Scholastics and the mission of the Gothic cathedrals. See Wybrow (1991: 163–64).

progressively becoming landless, impoverished, and subservient (Hattingh 1997: 12; Amnesty 2005: 199–200). Another factor that has impoverished the people is crop failure resulting from land degradation and ecological disruptions. This impoverishment has also affected social values, so that all social regulations intended to protect the individual's rights to equality before the law—rights to life, to property, to liberty, and to the pursuit of happiness—have been distorted.

Constitutional Corrosion of Human Rights Culture in Nigeria

The issue of constitutional rights will require a dissertation of its own. Here only the salient issues will be touched upon. In 1960, when Nigeria gained political independence from the United Kingdom, it inherited a constitution with fundamental human rights. It introduced a plethora of rights, some of which transcended the natural rights of humans in gerontocratic cultures. A distinction can be made between natural and inalienable or special rights on the one hand and between these rights and what is generally termed "civil" rights. Natural rights are synonymous with moral rights, which in turn are limited to inalienable rights (Benhabib 2002: 18).

In Nigeria and perhaps continental Africa, the human rights culture emphasized more rights than duties in so-called "freedom clauses," which of course are considered fundamental to human survival and self-actualization in the new nations of Africa, Asia, and Latin America. In Nigeria, the right to life, rights to freedom of person, conscience, movement, association, speech, and opinion, and rights to personal safety and integrity or self-actualization are deeply entrenched in the postcolonial constitution. While this constitution does not deny anyone the right to property or land, it does not stress this natural right. It is in a secondary sense that the right to property was not included, because in a primary sense, nearly all Nigerian citizens have a customary and untrammeled right to property and to land in particular (Yakubu 1985: 126). The postcolonial erosion of gerontocratic land tenure systems in Nigeria, and particularly in the Niger Delta, affects the principle of equal rights of all Nigerian citizens, be they elderly or young, vis-à-vis the constitutional rights of individuals and corporate bodies to acquire land or property in any part of the country. Although land could not be acquired without the consultation of the elders and chiefs who are custodians of land in their respective territories and domain, in practice, the Land Use Decree of 1978 has tended to incapacitate such rights claims.

The land tenure situation in Nigeria has gradually been changing for the worse in the past two decades, particularly in the oil-bearing communities of the Niger Delta. To facilitate economic and social development, the federal military government under General Olusegun Obasanjo (who until recently has been the third republican civilian democratic president of Nigeria) in 1978 promulgated a decree tagged the Land Use Decree, which vested the title to all lands in Nigeria's urban areas in the hands of state governors, rather than in the eldest members and chiefs of local communities, contrary to what obtained from precolonial until recently in postcolonial times (1900–1976).

The law also defined some hitherto traditional communities and elevated them to "urban" status by law, bringing such areas under the government's radical land laws and facilitating both individual and corporate land acquisitions in such areas for social, agricultural, industrial, and economic development purposes (Evuleocha 2003: 328–40). This decree empowers corporate bodies and individuals to acquire land for developmental purposes in any part of the country, and the authority to make such land grants has been vested in state governors, no longer the gerontocrats of the traditional kinship groups, which may still hold such rights outside the urban areas (Yakubu 1985: 74–75, 257).

In principle, land ownership and use has by this decree been moved from the natural to the civil domain, and stewardship of land from the communal to the civil sector. In other words, all land ownership rights have been invested in the federal government of Nigeria with the state governments as its surrogates, instead of the usual communal ownership through a gerontocracy recognized by government, reflecting the tradition and customs of the people.

By attempting to make the ownership of land a "civil" rather than an inalienable or "natural" right,[2] the federal government of Nigeria in 1978 had

---

2. It has been a "successful" attempt from the perspective of multinational oil companies, as they now gain untrammeled access to land acquisition or latifundism in the Niger Delta, whereas it has been an "unsuccessful" attempt from the perspective of the general public, as the "decree" remains abhorrent and has not been endorsed by successive Nigerian parliaments either in the second republic (1979–1983) or in the present fourth republic (since 1999). Politicians have consistently contested the validity of the Land Use Decree of 1978. For a recent statement on it, see *Thisday*, November 5, 2006, in which the decree was referred to as marginal and irrelevant to the people of Nigeria.

constituted itself as the chief custodian of all land in Nigeria. So the government paved the way for the multinational oil companies in particular to collude with key government officials in "grabbing" large hectares of land in the Niger Delta and other parts of Nigeria,[3] but largely in areas richly endowed with huge deposits of hydrocarbon (Obi 2006: 59).

By virtue of that decree, the federal government withdrew the right of stewardship, land ownership, and land use from the gerontocrats, and vested such rights in the authority of state governors (Yakubu 1985: 263). Thus, the enjoyment of communal landholding or property rights is now relocated from the gerontocratic sphere to the sphere of corporate or civil authority (Ayandele 1969: 69). In that case, a special or natural right of custody and stewardship have been moved into a civil rights sector, with the implication that a primary right is being made civil or secondary from the point of view of the human rights debate (Blum 1998: 77). In other words, a right that inheres in one's status as a human being is being made dependent upon one's ability to assert or claim such rights without which state protection is denied or deferred. Yet God created human beings with certain natural and inalienable rights, which of course include stewardship, land ownership, and land use rights along with the norms, laws, and values that govern the use and enjoyment of such rights.

If anything, unilateral land decrees, especially as has been experienced in postcolonial Nigeria, have often been used to a great advantage by corporate bodies and multinational companies to the detriment of the elders and chiefs who still uphold the institution of gerontocracy in Nigeria. It has often resulted in an erosion of the stewardship, land ownership, and land use rights of the people in general and of gerontocracy in particular. Lawrence Blum (1998: 77) pointed out that the greatest challenge to the human rights debate is the issue of globalization (a euphemism for neocolonialism). Each human rights context faces a global challenge of economic and political subjugation by others who are wealthier and more powerful. Therefore, each global constituency must define its own predicaments and proffer its own solutions without, however, ignoring the collective experiences emanating from other contexts.

---

3. For rudimentary statistics on the various hectares acquired by MNOCs and their subsidiaries, see Ahiamadu 2003: 4–5.

A second issue is the scrapping of the "house of chiefs" on both federal and state parliamentary levels. Only a résumé of its salient features can be attempted. The postcolonial presidential constitution of 1979, which marked the beginning of the second republic in Nigeria, scrapped the house of "chiefs/elders" in the federal and state parliaments, and replaced them with a Western-type "Senate," whose composition is similar to the House of Representatives in Nigeria, consisting mainly of educated and young elites (Ahiamadu 1982: 67; Oyediran 1979: 43). The implication is that the elders had no formal forum in which to deliberate on sensitive issues such as stewardship of land as it is being practiced in postcolonial Nigeria.

The absence of a formal elders' forum paved the way for the erosion of gerontocracy along with the principles of justice and equity that it represented. As a result, inalienable rights to stewardship, land ownership, and land use by the senior members of the community are gradually being transformed into a civil rights exercise more or less at the discretion of governors. Their appointees are mostly "civil" servants not rooted in the customs and norms of the local cultures.

Little wonder then that the land decree that was enacted by military fiat in 1978 has never been endorsed by any of the successive federal parliaments marking Nigeria's wobbling democracy since 1979—not even by the parliament of 1999–2007, of which Olusegun Obasanjo himself served as incumbent president. The refusal to recognize or ratify the land decree is not unconnected with its alien and neocolonial character. Instead, it has created a restive civil society in which oil-bearing communities are engaging the federal police and army in an itinerant struggle for economic and social liberty—a struggle called "militancy" in those parts of Nigeria. It is nothing but the result of erosion of preexisting gerontocratic authority and of the principle of equity and justice underlying it (Obi 2006: 65). To what extent does Gen. 1:26-28 help matters?

A Critical Interpretation of "Dominion" and/or "Partnership" in Gen. 1:26-28

In Gen. 1:26-28, humans are identified as the finest species of the divine creative fiat. As part of creation, humans have a central role to play in superintending the earth and its vast natural land and marine resources. Let us begin with an assessment of Israelite conception of the creation of humans on the sixth day of creation. Similar concepts of creation can also be found in both Akkadian and Ugaritic literature (Van Seters 1992: 50). Those who managed God's creation were to observe the natural cycles of days, months, and seasons. In the case of a six-day creation, which idea pervaded the ancient Near East, it proves that a series of seven consecutive days was considered a perfect period in which to develop an important work, the action lasting six days and reaching its final conclusion and outcome on the seventh day (Cassuto 1978: 9–22). Cassuto's argument in support of humans as the apex of creation as well as of a six-day creation proves that even this was part of ancient Near Eastern traditions (13). It is remarkable to note, however, that creation stories of the ancient Near East such as the Babylonian creation story feature a succession of various rival deities. This is as far as comparison can go. Henceforth, the biblical version is dominated by the monotheistic concept of Deity which summons all humans to account as those who are responsible for the care and nurture of life on the earth.

Moreover, Van Seters (1992: 50) has shown that the narration of the creation of humankind in the *Enuma Elish*, the ancient Babylonian Story referred to earlier, has its parallels also in the epic of *Atrahasis* (that is, creation stories from ancient Near Eastern, especially Babylonian, sources), and that both accounts seem to run alongside similar details with the biblical account. This line of thinking runs parallel to that of Gunkel (1997: li), who literally assumes a Babylonian origin for most of the legends in Genesis. As in Genesis, both *Enuma Elish* and *Atrahasis* mention clay as the substance used in molding humankind, and creation was for the purpose of filling a gap existing in the service of the gods (Bosman 2006: 3).

The mention of clay as a substance from which humans were molded is one point of similarity, and the creation of humans for the purpose of filling a gap for the service of the gods is another (Van Seters 1992: 50). In the Mesopotamian *Enuma Elish*, for instance, human beings were created to provide the gods with food, clothing, and honor. There are also similarities of the creation of humans resulting from a great assembly of the deities in mutual consultation in which the gods were duly informed of the creation of humans (Schuele 2005: 2–3). This is perhaps the idea behind biblical references to the heavenly court summoned by God to witness the creation of humans (Gen. 1:26-28; Job 38:7).

In the *Epic of Atrahasis,* as in *Enuma Elish* and the Memphis creation story, stewardship as part of ancient Near Eastern cultures is embedded in expectations or requirements for the treatment of creation by humanity (Coats 1983: 46). All such accounts seem to run alongside similar details with the biblical account (Garr 1996: 22). The implication of this for the ancient Near Eastern concepts of human stewardship and accountability to the gods is that humans are not an autonomous entity but were made with a purpose of rendering services that the gods consider to be below their dignity (Bosman 2002: 4).

The clarity and conciseness of scholarly views can be further pursued from the perspective of Egyptian myths as well as African cultural observances in consonance with a positive role for humans in creation by adopting an ethical framework of humans in partnership with nature, as opposed to the present "domino" mind-set prevailing with multinational oil conglomerates. A gerontocratic culture resonating with the Genesis narratives does easily merge with a human rights culture and is capable of revamping some earth-keeping traditions in consonance with the present quest for clean air, green environment, freedom of movement, and sustainable development in parts of Africa, especially in the Niger Delta.[4] It is important to employ African lenses in correcting the misconceptions and indictments associated with a too literal and uncritical reading of Gen. 1:26-28 because of the inevitable challenges it poses to a critical hermeneutic, especially in the Nigerian context (Runzo and Sharma 2003: 61; Bryant 2000: 35).

There exists an African spiritual wisdom that is capable of correcting the environmental pressure and ecological distortion that the operations of multinational oil companies have caused in oil producing areas. This damage is inspired by a "scientism" born out of a "dominion" mind-set (DeWitt 1996: 19; Gitau 2000: 31). In critically assessing our pericope, the aim is to provide a redefinition of stewardship. While standing on a theological and ethical framework that Gen. 1:26-28 affords us in the wider context of the Old Testament, we may have to dig deep into the wisdom of our fathers, in critically assessing both the creation mandate and its reflection in a human rights culture capable of dealing with the ecological problems affecting nature and

---

4. The area, sometimes also refered to geographically as the Gulf of Guinea, runs from Bamenda in Cameroon to Dakar in Senegal, and covers all of the West African States of Nigeria, Ghana, Togo, Sierra Leone, etc.

the inhabitants of the oil-rich Niger Delta in Nigeria.[5] There is a conception in Africa of humans in partnership with nature which contrasts with the mentality of humans above nature, with the latter's implication that nature must be dominated, devastated, and destroyed to advance the human course. Although such a dominion mind-set has been adapted to the developmental economics of most modern societies in Africa, it has been the result of contact with such ideas floated through Western media and a mechanistic mind-set. Yet people of the continent have reacted to it negatively, particularly during the past three decades or more in what is today pejoratively labeled "militancy" in the Niger Delta (Eze 1997: 103).

In contrast, some have accused a Western interpretation of texts such as Gen. 1:26-28 and Ps. 8:4-8 as a possible source of a (mis)-definition that regards humans, instead of the whole earth, as the center or pivot of creation (Wybrow 1991: 48–49; Dibeela 2001: 396; White 1967: 1214). This interpretation creates a human rights problem of inequality of legal status, of incomes, and of abilities (Noebel 1999: 702). It denotes a dominion mind-set on the part of multinational oil companies and perhaps the government, and it tends to distort and even disparage the concept of stewardship in particular, and of responsible and accountable land ownership in general, invariably creating a problematic scenario in which humans are seen as ruling over all of God's creation on earth, with a view to using the earth's abundant resources in a practically unsustainable manner. At the center of the ancient Israelite conceptualization of stewardship is the theme of creation or of nature which is entrusted to humans as an inalienable patrimony (Brueggemann 2002: 191). For this reason, it might be necessary to keep the priestly creation narrative in Gen. 1:1—2:4a in mind as we critically assess scholarly views on stewardship.

Apparently, such a dominion mind-set has also influenced theological and ethical discussions of both priestly and Yahwist creation narratives in Genesis 1–3.[6] Due to (mis)-readings of biblical imperatives in

---

5. The term *nature* is used here to mean the created world in its entirety, the totality of physical reality exclusive of mental things.

6. The Bible has been translated into several African languages, and the first two Nigerian languages with translations of the whole Bible were Efik (1868) and Yoruba (1884). As of 2005, either the whole Bible or New Testament translations are read in 104 out of 432 languages in churches in the country, and scores of other translations are at different stages of completion. A New Testament translation into Ogba can be viewed online at http://www.ogba-obtlt.org. See Gordon (2005), available online at http://www.ethnologue.com/.

regard to subduing the earth, humans have tended to misuse that dominion. It does not, however, diminish the fact that in most parts of Africa, nature is considered sacred and worthy of responsible care and use, especially with respect to land owned. This also resonates with conceptions of nature prevalent in the ancient Near East that produced the Bible. As John S. Mbiti of Kenya has observed, traditional Africa is immersed in a religious environment where natural phenomena are intimately associated with one or another god (cf. Gitau 2000: 33). In a multicultural, multiethnic, and multireligious context such as Nigeria, one can see the theological and ethical implications of an erosion of preexisting ecology- and environment-friendly values.

Restoring and Enhancing a "Human Rights Culture" in Nigeria

To restore and/or enhance a human rights culture in Nigeria, there is a need to consider its theological and ethical dimensions from the perspective of the dominant religions in the country, without ignoring African traditional beliefs and values.

Theologically and from the perspective of Old Testament and Islamic laws, the concept of human rights is understood as pointing to the individual's rights to a share of and from the land, to a personal pursuit of happiness, and to life and liberty, which are in conjunction with numerous other rights deeply entrenched in the canons of Christianity, Judaism, and Islam. The Decalogue, for instance, protects individual human rights such as the rights to conscience, to recreation, to life, to family, to property, to a good association or reputation, and to liberty. In this way, the individual's relationship to God is protected, so that a violation of an individual's rights was considered an interference with that individual's commitment or devotion to God (Wright 1990: 136).

Such laws and the sanctions that went with them provided Israel with a social organization built upon a substructure of tribal or communal solidarity and mutual responsibility even at the level of the *bet ab* ("father's house"). The paterfamilias in resonance with gerontocracy is what made the relative strength of the tribe as a whole desirable. Not only were laws enforceable at various levels of kinship, but they also provided the moral resource for the retention of kinship wealth within a broader kinship group. Gerontocracy also made it possible for individual nuclear families to enjoy the ownership and use of property, particularly land (Fager 1993: 91).

In the context of ethics it will be appropriate to make a few observations about gerontocratic care and nurture of nature, which forms part of the norms and ethos in postcolonial communities in the Niger Delta in particular, and also generally in Nigeria and other parts of Africa. The Batswana of Botswana in Southern Africa and their Yoruba counterparts in West Africa, for instance, believe that the responsibility for earth keeping is a joint one between the living dead (the ancestors) and the living living (the elders). Consequently, the land is seen as sacred space that must neither be abused nor used to any advantage beyond the ordinary search for the means of economic, social, and cultural survival (Dibeela 2001: 395–96; Idowu 1969: 97). This means especially for the Batswana that the land has to lie fallow for a year after a year's use.

Such a time of rest for the land allows for the restoration of the earth after each year's use, similar to what is observed in the Niger Delta among, for example, the Ogba and Ekpeye (Amadi 1982: 55). Interestingly, this hallowing of land resonates remotely with the Judeo-Christian belief that land belongs to Yahweh and so must be left fallow each seventh year. In both African and Judeo-Christian understanding, the concept of rest for the land is considered an integral part of humans' responsible and accountable use of land. Experience has, however, shown that neither the government nor the multinational oil companies have paid attention to the Judeo-Christian and African traditional beliefs, which might have lessened the alarming destruction of the natural environment and the latifundism that has gone hand in hand with it in, for instance, the Niger Delta (Ahiamadu 2003: 11–18).

The erosion of such a stabilizing institution as paterfamilias or gerontocracy in the Nigerian context has tended to stultify the processes of accountable and responsible land ownership and use. Moreover, it has challenged, if not distorted, the congruity existing between a postcolonial interpretation of Gen. 1:26-28 and African culture, both of which enhance a mind-set of humans in partnership with nature, as well as a caring and nurturing attitude to creation. This congruity evokes a restoration and enhancement of a human rights culture, as already indicated.

Conclusion

Evidently, some Western interpretations of texts such as Gen. 1:26-28 and Ps. 8:4-8 can become possible sources of such a (mis)-definition of human stewardship of the earth's resources, when by such interpretations the impression is created that humans, instead of the whole earth, are the centerpiece or the pivot of creation (Wybrow 1991: 48–49; Dibeela 2001: 396; White 1967: 1214). In addition, it creates a human rights problem of inequality not only before the law, but also from rationalizing the inequities of incomes and abilities (Noebel 1999: 702). No degree of hermeneutical distortion of our pericope, however benign, can diminish the fact that in most parts of Africa, nature is considered sacred and worthy of responsible care and use, especially with respect to land owned. Such a high sense of responsibility toward nature and creation also resonates with conceptions of nature prevalent in the ancient Near East that produced the Bible.

In our critical assessment of the hermeneutics of Gen. 1:26-28, it can be seen that humans are created in the image of God and are therefore placed in personal relationships to God and as partners in ongoing creative works. Moreover, this relationship was protected in Genesis 1–11, so that a violation of an individual's rights was considered as interference with that individual's commitment or devotion to God (Wright 1990: 136).

In a cultural context such as has been known since precolonial times, there is a sense of stewardship, land ownership, and use that tends to emphasize a mind-set of humans in partnership with nature, rather than humans above nature (Aderibigbe 1999: 334–35). It behooves us, therefore, to frown at a reductionism that not only places humans at the apex and center of creation, but also drives a wedge between humans and nature, such that the former treats the latter as if it were an enemy to be mastered and subdued (Towner 2001: 28).

CHAPTER 2

The Genesis Creation Accounts
An African Background

David Tuesday Adamo

Introduction

For the ancient Israelites, the idea that God is the creator was not disputed.[1] It was presupposed and affirmed in their thought. In their thought, there could have been no other way in which the heavens and the earth originated. Therefore, we see in Genesis that "In the beginning God created the heavens and the earth" (1:1 KJV).[2] This idea of creation runs throughout the entire Old Testament. It was retold and contextualized over and over again. To emphasize the repetition of the idea of creation throughout the entire Bible, Martin Luther has said, "He who would understand the first chapter of Genesis needs to have studied and digested all sacred scriptures" (Smart 1952: 2–5).

Although creation faith holds a less important place in the Old Testament concept than salvation and election, the Christian church stood firmly with the biblical account of creation (with the affirmation in the Apostles' Creed "creator of heaven and earth") until the rise of natural sciences during the age of the Enlightenment, which brought serious opposition to the biblical ecclesiastical tradition. Like the ancient Israelites, practically all Africans

---

1. An earlier version of this article was formerly published in D. T. Adamo's *Exploration in African Biblical Studies* (Eugene, Ore.: Wipf & Stock, 2001), 95–106. Used with permission.
2. The King James Version of the Bible shall be used throughout this essay.

consider God as the creator of the world. Even in this technological age, it is beyond the imagination of an ordinary African who has not been brainwashed by the mentality of the West to consider any other way in which the world could have been created. This belief in God as the creator makes this one of the commonest attributes of God among Africans and is expressed in their different versions of myths, names given to God, prayers, and praises (Mbiti 1970: 49).

This essay is an attempt to understand the Genesis creation accounts in African context. This I hope to accomplish by a comparative study of the Genesis and African creation accounts, drawing implications from the similarities and differences.

Genesis and African Creation Myths

One of the most common ways of affirming God as the creator in Africa is by calling God various names. These names picture God as a carver, maker, originator, inventor, builder, and others. Apart from these names, myths are also a very strong vehicle by which Africans affirm their faith in God as the creator of the heavens and the earth. These myths are in different versions from one place to another and are contradictory at times. However, most of the time, they have common motifs, common theology, and common elements. Since the Genesis creation myth is indeed a very popular one, which I believe most of my readers are well acquainted with, I will not waste time describing the Genesis account, but rather will introduce some of the African creation myths, which may not be well known to some of my readers.

The creation myth of the Yoruba people of Nigeria has two versions. (Idowu 1962: 18–22). After the earth was created in four days, the fifth day was a day of rest and worship. The Supreme God (Olodumare) then sent his deputy (Orisanla), accompanied by a counselor (Orunmila),[3] to "embellish" the earth. Orisanla was given a primeval palm tree, silk rubber tree, white

---

3. Orunmila was the only being who know the secret of giving life, because he was with Olodumare from the beginning. He also knew the secret of the existence of all the divinities, endowed with unique wisdom and foreknowledge, and that is why he was able to be a counselor of Orisanla.

wood, and *dodo* to plant so that their seeds could be used for drink and food. After Orisanla had completed his job, Olodumare sent Oreluere, who led a party of beings to the earth. Orisanla was assigned another job: molding human beings from the dust of the earth into physical forms, but Olodumare alone was to give life.

Another version of the Yoruba creation myth says that the task given to Orisanla, who was Olodumare's deputy, was later accomplished by another agent of Olodumare, Oduduwa. This happened because Orisanla was drunk with palm wine and fell asleep on the way to the earth. God then reassigned his job to Oduduwa, who performed the task of planting the trees and molding man's physical being.

According to the creation myth of the Vugusa people of Kenya (Mbiti 1970: 48), after God had created the heavens (in two days), he created his dwelling place and that of his two assistants. He also created the moon, the sun, the stars, rain, rainbows, and then the earth with mountains and valleys for his two assistants. Then God created man and woman. Lastly, he created plants, animals, birds, and other creatures. All of these were completed in six days. He rested on the seventh day because it was a bad day.

The Ashanti creation myth of Ghana says that after God had created the sky, the earth, rivers, waters, plants, and trees, then he created humankind. He also made animals for humankind's use. God later made the spirits of the mountains, forests, and rocks to protect humanity (Mbiti 1970: 49).

According to the Bambuti of the Congo (Schebesta 1936: 168–69), the heavens above and the earth below were God's home until dust began to fall and God feared that his food might be contaminated. He then ordered the lightning to find him another abode above the earth. Lightning found God a new home in heaven, by dividing the earth from the sky. God and moon, his closest being, went upward to dwell. Then God created the chameleon, water, trees, humankind (woman first), and then the rest of the animals, the "celestial goat" being the ancestor of all animals.

The creation myths of the Azande of Sudan have many versions (Mbiti 1970: 49). The most prominent says that God put all creatures in a sealed canoe, leaving only a waxed hole on it. Then he set his sons—moon, sun, night, cold, and stars—the task of opening the canoe to discover what was inside it. The sun opened the canoe by heating it, because the secret had been revealed to him by God's messenger. Then all animals, rivers, trees, hills, and grass came out.

The Fon people of Dahomey say that sometime, somewhere, Da, God's assistant, appeared (Mbiti 1970: 50). Sometimes he is called the first created being, who set up four pillars to sustain the sky and caused his excreta to form waterways on earth. God, however, created vegetation, animals, and later humankind from the clay and water. God also created the divinities as his children and set all the universe in order.

Biblical and African Creation Myths: A Comparison

Differences

In African creation myths, almost all versions say God had an assistant who helped him in the work of creation. These are the divinities. The Yoruba version calls the assistant Obatala or Oduduwa. The Fon call him Da. However, in Genesis, God alone created not only the heavens and the earth, but also all that are in them. In Genesis, we have the record of all God's activities: "In the beginning God created the heavens and the earth" (1:1); "God's Spirit moved upon the face of the waters" (1:2). God alone created light (1:3-4), firmament (1:9-10), grass (1:11-12), and all creatures, animals and humans, without any help from another person (1:20-31).

In the African myths, there is no idea of chaos or the deep when the heavens and the earth were created by God. However, Gen. 1:2 says, "And the earth was without form, and void; and darkness was upon the face of the deep and the Spirit of God moved upon the face of the waters."

According to the African creation myths known to us so far, there is no idea of humankind created in the image of God, as in the biblical account in Gen. 1:26. This is a very remarkable difference between the African and biblical creation myths, because this enabled humankind to be the apex of creation and to be able to have fellowship with God. Genesis 1:26-27 says:

> And God said, Let us make man in our image, after our likeness: and let them have dominion over the flesh of the sea, and over the fowl of the air, and over the cattle, and over all the earth, and over every creeping thing

that creepeth upon the earth. So God created man in his *own* image, in the image of God created he him; male and female created he them.

While the seventh day of rest may be an evil day in African myth (Vugusu of Kenya), it is a holy day in the biblical myth: "And on the seventh day God ended his work which he had made; and he rested on the seventh day from all his work which he had made. And God blessed the seventh day and sanctified it because that in it he had rested from all his work which God created and made" (Gen. 2:2-3).

In the creation account of the African people, the moon and the trees are personified. According to the Azande of Sudan, God set his sons—moon, sun, stars, and others—the task of opening the sealed canoe where he put all the creatures. However, nowhere in Genesis is an inanimate object personified and a participant in the work of creation.

Finally, the African creation myths are polytheistic. There is always the account of the divinities present. But the biblical account is monotheistic, as far as the Genesis 1 account is concerned.

Similarities

As there are differences between the Genesis and African accounts of creation, so also are there some fundamental similarities that must not be ignored, because there are reasons for these similarities.

In both the African and the biblical creation accounts, God is regarded as the creator and the controller of the universe. According to the Yoruba, Vugusu, Ashanti, Bambuti, and the Azande, the supreme God is the creator of the heavens and the earth. This fact is not questioned or disputed. There might be some assistants who continued to create things on the earth, yet basically, God is the creator of the heavens and the earth and gives instructions to those divinities, in the case of the Yoruba and Fon myths in Nigeria and Dahomey, respectively.

In the order of creation, in both the African and the biblical accounts, the heavens and the earth are the first things to be created by God (Gen. 1:1). Then the rest of the inhabitants of the heavens and the earth were created in an ongoing process.

In almost all versions of the African accounts, the creation of humankind involved the creation of male and female, as in Gen. 1:27: "so God created man in his own image, in the image of God created he him; male and female created he them." However, in some cases (for example, Vugusu, Bambuti), man was not the first creature to be created. The Bambuti believe that woman was created before man.

In some African accounts of creation, the creation of man from the dust or clay of the earth is mentioned, as in Gen. 2:7: "And the Lord God formed man of the dust of the ground and breathed into his nostrils the breath of life; and man became a living soul." However, in the case of the Yoruba people of Nigeria, one version indicates that Obatala, God's deputy, was in charge of molding human beings, but God had the right and power of giving life to the molded humankind.

In both the African and the biblical accounts of creation, humankind was given power over all the rest of creation, as in Gen. 1:26: "And God said, let us make man in our image, after our likeness; and let them have dominion over the fish of the sea, and over the fowl of the air, and over the cattle, and over all the earth, and over every creeping thing that creepeth upon the earth."

The idea of God resting on the seventh day was present in both the African and the biblical ideas of creation. However, while the seventh day in Gen. 2:2-3 was a holy day because it was "sanctified and blessed by God," according to the Vugusu myths, God rested on the seventh day because it was a bad day.

The idea of the fall of humankind is present in African as well as the biblical creation myths. According to one version of the Yoruba myth, Obatala got drunk on his way to the earth and therefore could not perform the work of creation assigned to him; God then chose Oduduwa to perform the work. The Bambuti people of Ghana believe that God inhabited the earth and the heavens until dust began to fall and God feared contamination of his food. So he went far upward to dwell. Another version of the Yoruba myth says that the sky, God's abode, was originally closer to the earth than it is, until a woman who was pounding yam hit the sky with her mortar and God moved his abode (sky) upward far away from the earth.

Finally, one of the most important similarities lies in the myths' theological concepts. In the biblical account, before Israel could fully realize God's creative power, greatness, and lordship, the people had to first of all experience God's greatness in delivering God's people from bondage, preserving them, and making them a great nation (Dyrness 1979: 64). After all these experiences, Israel could then affirm clearly in the Genesis accounts of creation that Yahweh who redeemed us is the creator and the Lord of all that is. Both the Priestly and Yahwistic traditions expressed this affirmation.

A look at various African creation accounts reveals this same affirmation. According to the Yoruba people, Olodumare is always in control. He gives orders to all the divinities, who did not act in isolation. That is why they called him *Oluwa* (Lord) and *Olorun* (the owner of heaven). According to the Azande, God put all the world's creatures in a canoe; the Bambuti see the heavens and the earth as God's throne. The Lugbara see God as "the ultimate fountain head of all power and authority" (Mbiti 1970: 51).

Another theological affirmation in both the Genesis and the African creation myths is God's transcendence and immanence. In the Genesis account, God's transcendence is stressed by the creation by God's word, that is, the primacy of God's will and the ease of God's work. God's immanence is stressed in God's breath into man, which suggests God's intimate involvement in creation. That also becomes the basis for God's intimate relationship and communion with God's creation. In African myths, God's transcendence is affirmed not only in the ease with which he created the heavens and the earth but also in his abode in heaven and the order he gives to the divinities, God's assistants, who duly carry out his order on earth. God's immanence is affirmed by his breath of life, which only he has the right to give (according to the Yoruba account).

The Genesis account also stresses God's omnipotence. Both P and J consider God's ability to create out of nothing *(creatio ex nihilo)* as an expression of God's omnipotence. This *creatio ex nihilo* is also expressed among the Banyarwanda of Rwanda: God created the world out of nothing (Mbiti 1970: 50). Both the African and the Genesis creation myths affirm that absolute power belongs to God, the source of everything that exists.

God as creator of the world in both the African and the Genesis creation accounts means that God encompassed the complete time process, ruling, determining, and completing all ages.

Implications

The comparative study of the Genesis and African myths has some implications. After a comparative study of the Genesis and the Mesopotamian creation story, the most common conclusion by Eurocentric biblical scholars is that the source of the Genesis creation accounts is in Mesopotamia, with no regard to the possibility of other sources. So, among others, E. A. Speiser (1979: 19), on the basis of linguistic similarity between the Mesopotamian and the Genesis creation accounts, G. W. Coats (1983: 51), in his discussion of the literary forms of the Genesis creation account, and Claus Westermann (1984: 212–13), J. L. McKenzie (1954), and Morris Jastrow (1914: 5–7) all conclude, on the basis of recurring motifs in the cognate accounts, that the source of the biblical myth is Mesopotamian. However, it is time for a further examination of additional accounts for a possible ultimate source of the Genesis creation account other than Mesopotamia. The few African myths that have been presented here show that Africans have abundant myths similar to those of the Mesopotamians and Israelites. In the light of the similarities in content, motifs, and theology, there is the possibility of contact.

There are several suggested possibilities of how the Hebrews came into contact with the creation myths of Africa. The first possibility was during the sojourn in Egypt. The Hebrews lived in Africa for about 430 years (Exod. 12:44). During this period, they probably learned the myths but did not take them very seriously until they came across similar Mesopotamian myths that threatened their faith. They were then forced to reexamine their faith in terms of the African and Mesopotamian versions of the myths.

The second possibility is that the Mesopotamians had trade contacts with Africa as early as the third millennium BCE. According to the inscriptions of Sargon of Agade and Gudea of Lagash, the main items of trade between the Mesopotamians and the Africans—called Magan (Egypt) and Meluhhan (Ethiopia)—were "gold in dust form," logs, ivory, and more.[4] What probably happened was that the Sumerians perfected and localized the African myths. The Israelites then came into contact with these myths, which threatened their faith in Yahweh, and it was probably not until the period of the exile that the Israelites were able to contextualize the myths in the light of their experience and faith in Yahweh.

The third possibility is that both the Sumerians and Israelites came into contact with these myths in Africa, but Israel did not take them too seriously

---

4. Some scholars argue that Magan and Meluhhan cannot be Egypt and Ethiopia, respectively. However, C. J. Gad (1981: 453–54), George Rawlinson (1875), and S. N. Kramer (1970: 61) maintain that Magan and Meluhhan should be located in Africa.

until they came in contact with the Sumerian version of the African myth in Canaan, which threatened their faith in Yahweh.

One may then ask what is responsible for the differences. The reason for the difference is the nature of a floating oral tradition. When oral, a story is repeatedly told and diffused in different places, and it usually loses its original proper names and local color. It is therefore possible that the creation myths ultimately originated from Africa and, by the time they reached the Sumerians and Israel, they had lost their proper names and local color while still retaining their essential motifs and theology.

CHAPTER 3

The Tree of Life as a Female Symbol?

Athalya Brenner

My initial intention for this article, within this volume on Genesis, was to write about territory and identity in Genesis and beyond, substituting a notion of "Diaspora" for "exile," and problematizing the seemingly paradoxical biblical insistence upon "our" foreign descent as part and parcel of the ideological claim for owning the Promised Land even—or perhaps especially—in absentia. I thought my own experience as an Israeli foreign worker in European, American, and Asian universities, a person who for years has moved between work and Israel, would help me gain insights into the cluster of issues that are metaphorized by attitudes toward real or imagined territory.

But life intervened. In August 2008, a conference/seminar organized by Diana Lipton and Deborah Rooke under the title "Embroidered Garments" was to be held at Kings College, London. The subject was a gender assessment of women in positions of social power, such as priesthood, politics, prophecy and community leadership, in the Hebrew bible.[1] A volume of the "Embroidered Garments" papers will soon be published by Sheffield Phoenix Press (Rooke [ed.] 2009). I was invited to speak at the conference and did so with great pleasure.

---

1. In this article, the author does not capitalize the words *god, goddess,* or *bible,* and the Hebrew god's name is given as *Yhwh.* These forms represent the author's view that the commonly accepted usages (*God, Goddess, Bible, YHWH*) reflect a privileging of the words' referents, which the author does not share. Capitalization in quoted materials within the article, or its lack, follows the original materials exactly as they are.

A former student who became a dear friend, Mary Hill of Fort Worth, Texas (where I taught at the Brite Divinity School), wrote to me that her cousin, Mary B. Kelly, had written a book about goddess embroideries that might or might not have a bearing on the conference topic. Was I interested? Yes, I was. So Mary sent me the book (Kelly 1999), and it duly arrived in Israel as I was writing the paper for that conference. It was now mid-October 2007.

I took the book, *Goddess Embroideries of the Balkan Lands and the Greek Islands,* with me to a routine dental checkup. As it turned out, its topic was actual, rather than metaphorical, embroidered textiles made by women, unlike the King's College conference name. Almost immediately I sat up in the waiting room chair, with full attention.

To begin with, the embroidery patterns photographed and schematized in the book were intimately recognizable. My parents were *Ostjuden,* Jews from Poland and Lithuania, who immigrated to the British Mandate of Palestine/Eretz Israel in the late 1930s. They had friends from Romania, the former Yugoslavia, and other central and East European countries. We have all been wearing garments and using table runners and tablecloths and napkins and handkerchiefs with such patterns, embroidered on linen, as long as I can remember, without ever relating them to specific women's traditions.

A second detail was enlightening. Although the book's title has the word *goddess* in it, the author stipulates from the very start, already in her preface, that this is shorthand only. While she can, and does, point to many embroidery details as originating in goddess imagery and as having been transmitted for millennia (we shall return to this later), Kelly understands that for the women whose artwork she researches, the images are *not* necessarily known as divine female ("pagan") images; most of the women are devout Christians. What they see in the images, what they transmit according to their own understanding, are depictions of women's symbols, hopes, prayers, and traditions, in short—female concerns translated into artifacts.

Next, Kelly was able to show that the images, symbols, and so on have survived horizontally and vertically, that is, across places and times, in plastic art such as figurines, reliefs, and schematic paintings as well as embroidery.

Finally, a series of images that grabbed my attention in a special way, encapsulating the points just stated and propelling me strongly towards Genesis 2–3, show the female with raised arms that turn into leafy branches, or a female figure or figures that stand between or among trees, meaning trees of life. Figure 3.1 shows three of the images, works created by women in Bulgaria and Romania. More and similar images, schematic or more realistic, can be viewed in Kelly's book—or perhaps in a reader's wardrobe or linen closet.

Figure 3.1. Three examples of women's handiwork with female figures and tree branches, after Kelly: 1999

(a) *Apron from Tolbukhin. Ethnographic Museum, Sofia #11.915. After front cover photograph in Kelly: 1999.*

(b) *"Goddesses" between trees of life. Embroidered cloth. After Illustration 30 (p. 49) in Kelly: 1999. Used with permission.*

(c) *Metal belt buckle showing "goddess" figure with upraised arms/branches. Bulgaria. After Illustration 8 (p. 22) in Kelly: 1999. Used with permission.*

Now, the Eden tree of life happens to stand rather forlornly in Genesis 2–3, so to speak in the shadow of the central tree of knowledge, until god remembers it as an afterthought at the end of chapter 3 and bars the humans' access to it out of his own fear that, eating from it, they will acquire an unlimited life span. Let me hasten to add that I'm fully aware of the connection that has been made between that tree and the goddess Asherah, on the one hand, and Wisdom, or Knowledge, on the other. The logic goes like this. Female goddesses, especially as identified with Asherah, are graphically associated with vegetation (and animals, snakes among them; see, for example, Gimbutas 1991; Keel 1998; Hadley 2000). Wisdom and life/fertility are associated with femininity and femaleness, as in "She [wisdom personified as a female figure] is a tree of life to those who hold her" (Prov. 3:18, a verse discussed by, for instance, McKinley [1996: 141]), again through the link to the/a goddess. In other words, the two trees are collapsed into each other to form a whole, thus ostensibly solving the problem that the tree of life "in the middle of the garden" (Gen. 2:9) is marginal until the very end, even liminal, almost forgotten and ostensibly appended, deferred as an object of desire—and proscription.

Let me cite several more discussions of the matrix *tree of life/Asherah/ Wisdom* that have been advanced in recent years. At its bizarre apex, such assessments can metamorphose into a dual identification of the tree of life = Asherah and the tree of life = cannabis; first, Chris Bennet:

> Among her other titles, Ashera was known as "the Goddess of the Tree of Life," "the Divine Lady of Eden," and "the Lady of the Serpent." Ashera was often depicted as a woman holding one or more serpents in her hands. It was Ashera's serpent who advised Eve to disobey the male god's command not to partake of the sacred tree.
>
> The historical record shows that the Old Testament version of the myth of Eve, the serpent and the sacred tree was concocted as propaganda against pre-existing Goddess cults.
>
> Originally, the outcome of the Eden myth was not tragic, but triumphant. The serpent brought wisdom, and after the magic fruit was eaten, Adam himself became a god. What was originally involved was probably a psychedelic sacrament, like the [Eleusinian] festival in Athens, in which the worshipper ate certain hallucinogenic foods and became one with the Mother Goddess Demeter.

Like the Tree of Life, the Tree of Knowledge was a symbol associated with the Goddess. The rites associated with her worship were designed to induce a consciousness open to the revelation of divine or mystical truths. In these rites cannabis and other magical plants were used, and women officiated as priestesses. (Bennet 1998)

Next, H. N. Wallace, who sees strong associations between Eve, the tree of life, and Asherah: It is not impossible that a tree which is associated with fertility and the mother goddess figure on one level of a story could take on other life-giving aspects, also a divine gift at another level, especially when we remember the broad spectrum covered by the word "life" (1985: 114).

Asphodel Long cites Wallace in a lecture of 1996 called "The Tree of Life and the Menorah." Having reviewed also the Khirbet el-Qôm and Kuntillet 'Ajrud materials concerning Asherah, Long ultimately connects the tree of life with the Kabbalah's divine female principle, the Shekhinah, and also brings the menorah into the discussion, viewing it as a symbol of the divine goddess life tree, whose meaning was eventually forgotten. Her summary of her position is this:

I have suggested tonight that the Hebrew religion contains a female divine figure, Asherah, who may have been the consort of God, Yhwh, and also was interchangeable with the Tree of Life. This latter is represented by the Menorah, the seven-branched candlestick, a religious symbol in Judaism whose connection with the female aspect of divinity has been lost. Until the archaeological finds of this century it was generally supposed that the forty texts in the Hebrew bible concerning Asherah referred to wooden cult objects connected with earlier near eastern goddesses, associated with trees. To perceive in the biblical texts any reference to the figure of Asherah as a Goddess in her own right, and certainly as a goddess of the Hebrews, was condemned. . . .

Referring back to my original question: Was the story of the denial of the Tree of Life to humans in Gen 3:24 a prohibition of worship of the goddess Asherah? It is suggested that an affirmative answer may respectably be given. (Ashphodel Long 1996; italics added)

So far, I have quoted from studies of the/a goddess and the tree of life, to which I turned after looking at the *Goddess Embroideries* book. Now I wish to comment upon the connections between goddesses and trees, from my own particular context, and to apply the book's insights selectively to the Genesis Tree of Life, in my own way.

I am a secular person. I am a feminist. I can see that a female principle has been part of understanding or defining the divine in the Hebrew bible and beyond it, in the emerging Judaisms and Christianities, even if that principle was at times repressed only to reemerge, or to be refined, later. Remaining within the spheres of the bible and the Judaisms that surfaced out of it, and taking archaeological findings into account, I perceive that goddess images were there aplenty and that goddess figures were associated with, then later removed from connection with, the Hebrew god. Whether there ever was a *single* goddess attached to the single god of Hebrew monotheism is both far from certain and unprovable. Especially if you are secular, you have no need to postulate a single divine pair from Genesis 2 onward—even if Asherah seems a prominent goddess. The Queen of Heaven, after all, might have been someone other than Yhwh's consort. Even though Asherah was a prominent goddess, there is no historical reason to assume that there was at any time one single mother goddess. The need for a single "mother goddess" arises directly out of monotheism, be it male-centered or otherwise. Is there an Asherah in Genesis 2–3? My cautious answer is: I can't see her lurking in that text or in that textual tree, repressed or otherwise.

I can see that "life" is linked to Eve = *ḥawwāh*, as when Adam names his wife "the mother of all living" (3:20) just before the tree of life is barred to them and the two are expelled from the garden (3:22-24), so there must be a connection between the woman and the tree, a life connection. This is not necessarily a divine connection: Eve is no more and no less divine than (the) Adam. Declaring Eve to be divine arises, in my view, from an urge to deify her, or what she represents.

A well-known exegetical principle is that in the Torah (meaning actually in the whole bible), considerations of which text is earlier or later than another don't apply. One text can explain another even if they don't appear in a certain chronological order: literally, "There is no before and after in the Torah" (אין מוקדם ומאוחר בתורה).

This is a midrashic principle often used in confessional, early biblical exegesis to explain apparent lacunae, contradictions, and inconsistencies in biblical texts. It is often used nowadays to read the biblical text "as is," namely, as it appears in the massoretic library of texts (MT). In such an adoption of a midrashic principle, the tree of life can be equated with the tree of knowledge, as it is in Proverbs or further in Jewish literature (or myth), by claiming that the two distinct texts—Genesis and Proverbs—can and do complement each other—for the reader or perhaps even the author, as the Song of Songs complements the garden story, and so forth. In this way, or so it seems, biblical integrity and harmony will be retained. But I am a critic. For me, the mere idea that the bible does *not* contain disagreement, different opinions, disharmonies, or disagreements is preposterous. There is no need to harmonize the tree of Proverbs 3 and the tree of Genesis 3. Each of these is a distinct, independent text.

So where does this leave me? With the instinctive recognition that, although there is no "goddess" in Genesis 2–3, there is a female/feminine principle that is expressed somehow in the tree of life symbol. Please understand me: I don't deny this principle might have once—long before the text was written—belonged to some goddess talk. (Asherah? Or another goddess? Who? Who knows? Who can tell?) But this is no longer apparent in the Genesis text, as it is no longer transparent for the women who have continued to embroider goddess symbols for millennia while being devout practicing Communists and/or Christians; and like Jewish women in the British Mandate (Palestine/Eretz Israel) and after 1948 in the state of Israel, who continued to copy these patterns and use them with no thought for their undoubted original context. And if women don't remember the source of their traditions, why should men remember (if we agree that the bible was written, transmitted, copied, and studied mainly by males)? And if they don't remember, how can they "suppress" or "repress"?

Further, because the creation myths of the Beginning (Genesis 1 as well as 2–3) are binary in nature, it is possible to surmise that, if the Genesis tree of life is the feminine/female (F) essence, like in Proverbs, the tree of knowledge is the masculine/male (M) essence. (For the F/M definitions and theory see Brenner and Van Dijk-Hemmes 1993.)

This would problematize Genesis 2–3 anew, albeit in a different direction. Why, then, would masculine knowledge be initially and mainly forbidden to both genders, more specifically to the male partner, by god? A possible answer would be this: a jealous Father may be withholding the Phallus from his son (and eventually daughter) out of anxiety. It's a Lacanian situation (Aichele et al. 1995, 196–211) with a twist. The association of intellect with the masculine principle is indeed essentialistic here, but perhaps is "in the text" rather than in the eye of the beholder. In this reading, would we see that the woman hands the Phallus to the man? Freud would groan at the suggestion, but if we remember that the Adam does not start talking, really talking, using language and articulating before he gets his female companion, this is worth a thought.

Now to the next problem: Why withhold the tree of life, the essential F principle, from the couple, M/male and F/female together, forever? Here, too, there are possibilities. Can we detect some male (authorial) anxiety here? In Genesis 1, both male and female are given the option, actually the command, to reproduce themselves, unproblematically so; at the end of Genesis 3, the woman is given that option, but as accompanied with pain (v. 16a). In 4:1 Adam is certainly involved—he "knows" his wife, she conceives—but the event is related, in the explanation of Cain's name, directly to Yhwh. Should we imagine that had they—had she—had access to the banned tree of life, her role as mother would have been redundant? Or different? Or unnecessary?

Be that as it may, I'm not at all sure of the preliminary reflections that I'm offering here regarding the two trees standing in the middle of the garden, in a grammatically awkward sentence (2:9) and in what seems like opposition and apposition to one another. The two trees may or may not represent or symbolize gender essences. How such a reading may affect another understanding of a foundational text I'm not at all certain at this point, but this is hardly the issue for me. What matters is that certain elements of my own contexts are at play here. "Only connect," to follow the famous motto in E. M. Forster's 1910 novel, *Howards End*. As a feminist, I look for gender issues. As a secular person, I do not need to find in the bible references to gods and goddesses at every turn; I can live with the notions that divine elements may metamorphose into forgotten patterns. I don't feel an urge to always find a single consistent god and to supply him with a single, consistent, named female consort. This may help me understand a world of a long time ago—or will it?

CHAPTER 4

History or His Story?

Ideology of the Body in the First Creation Narrative

Philip Venter

Introduction

J. Wentzel van Huyssteen (2004: 118) refutes Brueggemann's description (2003: 30)[1] regarding Gen. 1:1—2:4a when he says, "Yet, in spite of its present literary context, it is anything but a liturgy, but is presented rather as a movement of history: not in any modern or literal sense, but as history nonetheless: the creation of the human is presented simply as an event in the distant past. As such, it forms the beginning of the so-called primeval history, the early history of humanity as presented in Genesis 1–11."

Together with this rather authoritative typification of the first creation narrative, the motivation for this study of Genesis 1 lies deep in my own religious traditions. I grew up with a Bible, the Afrikaans 1953 version, in which Gen. 2:4a was translated as "Dit is die *geskiedenis* van die hemel en die aarde toe hulle geskape is" ("This is the *history* of the creation of heaven and earth"; italics added).

Nowadays the scientific discrepancies within the first creation narrative are explained away with the literary term *cosmogony*, that is, a theory about the coming-into-existence, creation, and origination of the universe. The Western world, however, with its history of value systems pervaded by

---

1. "Gen 1 is a solemn, stately, ordered, symmetrical text, like a liturgical antiphon."

dichotomies regarding, inter alia, gender, did not and does not regard the biblical creation narrative as simply a theory. There is more to this text than can be explained with categories such as mythology or cosmogony. It is firmly rooted in the historical traditions of the Israelite nation in exile, a time when the most foundational of values were threatened. At its origin, and even in its postmodern application, the biblical creation narrative represents a discourse category that performs a greater role than an isolated indication of identity. It strives to inform, reform, and transform politically and ideologically the regulatory body of those who regard this text as normative. At the time of its origin, in Israel, this was absolutely necessary because the *torso* (to use a phrase coined by Gerstenberger 2002: 207) that remained after the fall of Judah, the end of the monarchy, and the destruction of the temple was hardly recognizable as Israel, that is, the historical nation and people of God.

The purpose of this study is to investigate the category of gender as it features in the ideology of the body that infused this history of origins. The focus will be on the creator God, Elohim, because it was precisely this hierarchical highest point of value and power that was threatened by the circumstances in which the community that gave birth to Genesis 1 found itself. Neither Habel (2000) nor Van Heerden (2005) identifies the real victim of the exile, by regarding either *Earth* as threatened or *man* as in dire straights. In fact, God—that is, the God construct as regulatory body that gave solidity to the social practices of a nation—was threatened. The polemic rhetoric of Genesis 1 performs the personification of a creator God in order to counteract the God constructs in the dominant discourses of other cultures, with which Israel now came into close contact. The rhetorical purpose is to restore stability and solidarity in a community in which the ultimate values that constitute its very existence are challenged (Vorster 2002: 14). It became vitally important that the integrity, eminence, and sanctity of the social, regulating body of the community, as personified in its God construct, be restored.

The superiority of the community's bodily constructs had to be reconfirmed by embodying the realities of that community's very existence. This was attempted by resorting to the age-old tradition of, in the words of Walter Brueggemann,[2] "creative remembering": a story of origins, a history of

---

2. Brueggemann (2003: 24) defines the Torah as "a normative act of imagination that serves to sustain and legitimate a distinct community of gratitude and obedience."

beginnings, in which the personification of the regulating body features prominently.

It remains, however, an empowering exercise for a privileged group in order to give stability to their wisdom values, and to draw the boundaries between the wise in the group and foolish outsiders. That this privileged wise group was constituted in terms of, and empowered by, a regulatory body or God construct that was strictly masculine will be shown in the following critical analysis concerning the body.[3] In moralizing about the body and bodily parts in order to confirm and enforce the ideal, the regulatory body had a massive impact upon traditions and communities that took this text to heart—which is borne out by the tragic effects of gender dichotomies and dualisms based on this God construct, as seen in a history of discrimination against women and a disregard for Earth and nature.

Structure of the Text and Evolutionary Epistemology

The structure of Gen. 1:1—2:4a enhances the interdependence, symmetry, completeness, and apparent perfection of the creation, as stated by the narrative. Modern cognitive science proved the bodily foundation of these constructs, so the structure of the text itself represents an extension of the body in terms of the metaphorical and cognitive schemata inherent to it.

In his expansion upon the concept of evolutionary epistemology, J. Wentzel van Huyssteen (2004: 312) confirms that "we humans are, first of all, embodied beings, and as such what we do, think and feel is conditioned by the materiality of our embodiment." Acknowledging the validity of his statement that "our beliefs and convictions are not always explained by biological factors," I will nevertheless regard the cosmogony of Genesis 1 as an extension of bodiliness that can be explained by "naturalness" to religious imagination and the human quest for finding meaning in evolutionary epistemology.

The universe of Genesis 1 is a system, analogous to the body of an organism, a network in which elements are organized hierarchically and infused

---

3. The priestly origins also account for the fact that neither Asherah nor the Queen of Heavens, important goddesses in the Israelite tradition, were considered empowering and integrating god constructs at this time. The new or restored torso will be constructed in the image of the god of the kingdom tradition by the male elite of Israel.

with value (Clifford 1994: 143). Therefore, the text must be handled as a unity, a coherent whole, and the (gender) values underpinning the hierarchical formation in the narrative must be deduced from the metaphors that function in the representation of creation and creator entities.

Regarding those metaphors, their interpretation will be guided not by so-called objectivism, but by the philosophical departure point termed "embodied realism," in which it is recognized that our common capacity for metaphorical thought arises from the neural projections from the sensory and motor parts of our brain to higher cortical regions responsible for abstract thought. Whatever universals of metaphor there are arise because our experience in the world regularly makes certain conceptual domains coactive in our brains, allowing for the establishment of connections between them. The commonalities of our bodies, brains, minds, and experience make much meaning public.

The first striking public meaning extolled by the structured and symmetrical text of Genesis 1 already points to masculinity as an important value, since in ancient societies, wholeness and completeness were characteristics of the male body, in contrast to the fluidity and imperfection of female bodies. The whole of creation, as well as the process by which it came into being, forms a rounded, symmetrical, and closed gestalt. It is characterized by a hierarchical structure, with Elohim at the top of the pyramid and humanity in mimetic format on a second level of domination over all creatures.

The one explicit reference to gender, namely in Gen. 1:27, forms part of a larger engendered whole, and will be regarded as such, in contrast to the suggestion by Trible (1988) that in this unique pinnacle of the creation narrative, a human point of reference is found for metaphors of God in terms of sexuality. Trible regards the sexuality of the created humans as the basic metaphor for the transcendent God in terms of masculinity and femininity—in contrast to metaphors in which explicit maleness or femaleness is attributed to God, as in Ps. 103:3 (father), Hos. 2:6 (husband), Isa. 42:14 (pregnant woman), and Ps. 22:9 (midwife). Instead of deducing so-called gender equality from this metaphor, as suggested by Trible and other feminist scholars, we should read it as part of a hierarchical engendered whole that represents an orientation toward a one-sided bodily image of God.

Which brings us to the essential question: What does the ideal typical body of Elohim in Genesis 1 look like? Is it a male, controlled and controlling godly body, or are there instances of femininity? It is important to realize, from the historical and societal context that gave birth to this text, that the possibility of having a complete, balanced, and self-supporting body functions in Genesis 1 as a rhetorical strategy of empowerment. With this body and through this body, it becomes possible to resist dysfunctional and foreign bodies, as personified in the foreign God constructs of the exilic world. This whole body, the telos or hierarchical pinnacle in the form of a God construct (Elohim), is depicted in its interaction with "lower levels" of reality. In the process, "things" are empowered, an empowering that will be reinscribed upon the bodies of a community in exile, in order to resist the dangers of the historical time and circumstances in which they find themselves. That is why a proper ideological analysis of Genesis 1 will incorporate a good look at the person of Elohim as a constructed entity, filled with strategic ideological values, a regulatory body and embodied telos. In that way, the world vision from which a text that had a massive influence upon Western society and its value systems originated can be revealed as a rhetorical strategy.[4]

Aspects of the Embodied Personification of Elohim

From the very fiber of the narrative, it is clear that Elohim has a body. He is like a "human" that performs human actions and displays human characteristics. He speaks and orders, sees and looks, evaluates, divides, names, fertilizes, orders, blesses, considers, represents, feeds and nurtures, completes, rests, sanctifies. He takes up space, desires, wants order, experiences day and night. He knows of seasons, light, and darkness. He has an ecological awareness, wants to be perpetuated, knows sexuality, knows about hunger and food, has an aesthetic awareness, becomes tired, and can distinguish between sacred and profane. From this embodiment of the God character Elohim in human terms, the ideological purpose of the rhetoric shines through: identification with the ideal or regulatory body must be possible so that this body can reinscribe upon the bodies of the Israelites in exile. Exactly what type of body in terms of Elohim's gender, form, and type can be found between the lines in the metaphorical constructions of the creation process needs to be investigated.

---

4. "As symbols are the key to the *Weltanschauung* of a culture, the available specimens of language may not adequately reflect the level of symbolism" (Malul 2002: 11).

A Male Presence

The components that represent the existential crisis of the community already exist when everything starts. The infertile earth and the unruly waters with—under the darkness—the coldness and concealment thereof, represent the chaos from which Elohim will construct a cosmos. With chaos, the femininity of the threatening forces is implied, analogous to the *Enuma Elish* discourse and Tiamat, as well as to other myths of dominant femininity. Yet Elohim is actively and spatially present from the very beginning. In fact, the *ruach Elohim* (breath? wind? of Elohim) is positioned above the chaotic forces, an active presence with generative capacity. As Schroer and Staubli (2001: 214) put it, "Ruach creates room, puts in motion, leads out of narrowness into broad space, and gives life."

In the connection with *hover* in Genesis 1:2 in the New International Bible (Heb. *merachefet*), *ruach Elohim* is confirmed as the life-giving, creative, godly power, not immobile and receptive or passive and enduring, but an active, producing dynamism. The maleness of the metaphor is pronounced by the typical male characteristic of activity versus typically female passivity[5] positioned above the female chaotic forces. The effect of the dynamic presence of the god construct in the form of the *ruach Elohim* is expounded in the rest of the narrative. It will produce light and heat, give orders, see and evaluate (judge), divide, name and order, fertilize and systematize, perpetuate and fix boundaries, and eventually sanctify. The building blocks of this whole process are entities to which typically feminine characteristics are attributed—namely, chaos, infertility, uncontrollability, cold, darkness, and fluidity, waters or moisture. From the outset, femininity has no right to existence outside the male domain. Everything comes from the man. The man in his fertilizing, controlling essence is present from the start. This is the consolation presented to the exile community. Stability will replace instability, control will replace chaos, honesty will replace temptation, and courage in the place of humility will empower the community, just as darkness

---

5. An authoritative and profound exposition of the ancient perception regarding differences between males and females, an exposition that resonates even with our own dualities regarding gender, is given by Malul (2002: 319). Males are holy, living and fertile, active, powerful, good, healthy creatures of the upper regions (air) and the east (where the sun lives). Females are profane, deathly, passive, weak, evil, and unhealthy creatures of the lower regions (earth) and the west (where the sun dies).

and secrecy, infertility and desolation, and the chaotic masses of water were replaced by their very antitheses.

Phallogocentric Transformation

Elohim as a personalized construct, "the culmination of a culture's linguistic hierarchy" (Vorster 2002: 11), produces the seed of transformation in the form of that self-same *lingua verba*, words. From the male domain of oratory, the producing dynamisms that gave birth to, for example, light come forth. Furthermore, since the woman's speech was considered but idle chatter (Eilberg-Schwartz 1995a: 6), the creative and transforming character of Elohim's words clearly denotes a male creator. The creation by way of speech has even more profound roots within the culture of Ancient Israel's monotheism, and is as such a clear indication of a particular bodily image. The male mouth was metaphorized as an organ of reproduction and dissemination (Eilberg-Schwartz 1995a: 6). In various ways, the mouth serves as replacement (sublimification) for the phallus. Thus, as an example of phallogocentrism, the words of Elohim in the creation narrative represent the generative creative fertilization by a man. The depiction of creation by way of the mouth also conceals the problem about God's gender that developed with the advent of monotheism as a cultural system. The depiction of God as having genitalia was unthinkable; being an only god, what would he do with it? Therefore, the organ of male procreation is concealed behind the veil of the face, the mouth. That the face replaced the Phallus is also suggested by the importance of God's words in later priestly narratives. The words of God replaced the generativity of the phallus (Eilberg-Schwartz 1995b: 179).

Whether this *creatio per verba* served to illustrate the sovereignty and effectiveness of God's directive dominion over everything that was created (Van Till 1990: 218), or was an extrapolation of the edicts of human rulers such as in 2 Kings 12, or was deduced from other ancient Near Eastern mythopoetic models, such as the Egyptian god Ptah that created by first speaking "in the heart" and then by mouth, or whether it refers to the god Marduk in *Enuma Elish* (Middleton 2005: 66), it is clear that a man creates. The bodily image of Elohim confirms it and is confirmed by it. To depict the words of Elohim as transforming power is to state the body ideology in clear male terms.

Foundation: Light and Heat

A superior element of the macrocosmos—namely, light/heat—forms the foundation upon which the rest of creation was based. This was an element associated with masculinity in metaphorical terms, as shown by Vorster (2002: 12) and Rouselle (1988). The connection with the inside of Elohim from which these elements come forth confirms what Ruether (1982: 58) said: "The characteristics of sovereign maleness are seen as essential to the nature of God." Prioritizing the creation of light right at the outset of the creation process represents a power play against femininity and a manifestation of a male bodily image as far as the person of the creator is concerned.

Partition, Separation, and Control

The process by which entities are created is one of separation, partition, and naming. In this regard, Butler's statement (1993: 8) is important: "The naming is at once the setting of a boundary, and also the repeated inculcation of a norm." This process of differentiation is characterized by the hierarchizing inherent to it. Light rules over darkness, earth rules over the waters, sacred rules over profane, and so on. The initiative for this process comes from Elohim, and there is no participation and reciprocity from creatures. Even the living beings produced by the earth only appear by the grace of Elohim, to which the credit for this creation is attributed in Gen. 1:25. The division of the creation process into separate days (a system of seven days to legitimate the whole process in terms of the covenant theology) represents the activity of intellectual, ordered, analytical, dominating, and male capacity. As shown by Gerstenberger (1997: 374), the process lacks any reference to metaphors humanly associated with the creation of new life, namely, pregnancy and birth. This is no coincidence.

Evaluation

The expression "and God saw that it was good" represents, according to Malul (2002: 147), a value judgment from the observer's subjective viewpoint. Although the Hebrew *tov* (translated "good") probably also denotes aesthetic value, the value is found in analytical and linear terms and stated as such. Furthermore, value is attributed with the incorporation of male values—as, for example, the statement in verse 4: "God saw that the light was good, and he separated the light from the darkness." "Good" meant conformation to the inherent characteristics of masculinity, and in a world where femininity is characterized by inter alia secrecy, being unfathomable and uncontrollably in darkness cannot be "good." The creator's subjective viewpoint is elitist, not context-sensitive, context-dependent or sympathetic.

Blessing: Perpetuation

The blessing Elohim bestows upon the creatures of the sea and upon the humans is not motivated by an interdependent wish for care and nurturing, but a penetration that denotes fertility (multiply and fill) in order to subjugate and dominate. The motive for the blessing of the sea creatures implies final subjugation of the waters, and the blessing for humanity has a direct reference to man's mimetic representation of the ruler Elohim in domination over all creatures.

Procreation: Resemblance (Imago Dei)

After all is said and done regarding the concept of *imago Dei*, there remains but one perspective that can withstand the tests of literary honesty and evolutionary epistemology: the *imago Dei* concept is a fascinating anthropomorphism (Moore 1996: 93; Hiebert 1996: 21; Sawyer 2002: 18). I concur with Robert Jenson's view as it is reflected in the argumentation by van Huyssteen (2004: 145–62) of "The *Imago Dei* as Embodied Self." In Genesis 1, the body of Elohim is absorbed and internalized and lives on through the body of the man created according to his image. Despite attempts by feminist writers such as Trible (1978: 80–140) and scholars like Moore (1996: 87–115) to argue for bisexuality or androgyny in the depicted body of God in Genesis, femininity within the creator God is not to be found in the body of the God imaged in the created man.

Consultation: Sexuality

Woman appears in the order of creation only as supplementary to, and in relationship with, the man. Her existence is due to the necessity of procreation in aid of the domination of the other creation entities. Gerstenberger (1996: 88) states it as follows: "The younger report (Genesis 1) knows only a male-dominated humanity, divided into two sexes for the purpose of procreation and for reasons of purity (Gen 1:26-27). There is no syllable in either story describing a democratic equality of the sexes." Brown (1988: 17) describes the advent of man and woman in Genesis as a "reassuring microcosm of the social order." This relationship between man and woman is reflected in Elohim's consultation in verse 26. Along with the tradition of a female companion, as shown by Klopper (2002: 430), Schrey (1979: 229), Smith (1987: 333–40), and Du Toit (2005: 39), the strict gender exclusivity of monotheism distorted Elohim's procreative act into a consultation with a heavenly council. This suggests that Elohim was so exclusively and typically male that procreation necessitated some form of dependence on another (female?) party.

Sustenance and Care

Eilberg-Schwartz (1990: 151) has convincingly shown the symbolic relationship between fruit trees and the male sex organ. Trees serve as metaphors for the phallus. The association between the abundant harvest of fruit trees and the vitality of humans is more than "simply" metaphorical; it is a bodily metaphor that represents and promotes male gender superiority and dominance. The sustenance and care of creation entities, therefore, are not born from "God's wombliness," but dominated by the fertility motif. The abundant harvest of seed and fruit symbolizes male procreativity in line with the priestly obsession with the patrilineal family tree.

Aesthetic Appreciation

The aesthetic appreciation, a fleeting moment of emotionality and spontaneity in verse 31, leads us to deduce some instance of femininity within the creator God. This was shown to be the only (albeit important) expression within the first creation narrative that possibly lends itself to eco-just interpretation (see Venter 2006). This moment of emotionality and awe, however, is soon put aside in the urgency for completion, and the spatial metaphors that are used reveal once again the motive of subjugation and domination.

Rest

The purity laws connected with the spillage of semen configure the rest of Elohim in terms of equalization and purification. The restricted impurity and necessity to pause after a climax symbolize the male sex act and its consequences. The rest of a day is in accordance with the priestly laws applicable to men, not with the uncontrollable impurity associated with women, which necessitates longer terms of seclusion and rest. Elohim's rest is another male power mechanism.

Sanctification

In the act of sanctification as far as the day of rest is concerned, the relationship with the covenant and with circumcision becomes clear. Identifying Elohim as the agent of cultification confirms the identity of the nation as mimesis of the male god. The mutilated torso, with which the post-exilic community had to cope, is once again restored and empowered as—clearly—a male torso.

Conclusion

The question arises: Why was such a forceful and one-sided empowering exercise of masculinity in Genesis 1 necessary? Mieke Bal (1987: 110) explains it through the issue of the problematization of male domination. Sometimes the burden of domination becomes too heavy to bear. Dominators had to, somehow and sometimes, reconfirm and ensure their position. They had to ensure that the dominated, and themselves, still believed in their dominating position and role. A feeling of no safety, of instability, was not confined to the dominated only. The compilation of a justifying and confirming myth of origins, believable and realistic enough to comply with the general experience, is no simple exercise. The myths are inundated with the spores of pain inherent to the process of attaining power and control. Those spores serve to restrict the domination motives to near acceptable, performable proportions.

A very acceptable form is the creation of a bodily image of the creator God that conforms to ruling values and priorities. As such, Elohim is the perfect role model, a role model that, in its maleness, is virtually a perfect image of the male, intelligent, and virile priest. Genesis 1 is his story, not history.

CHAPTER 5

Sin, Gender, and Responsibility
A Contextual Interpretation of Genesis 3

Edwin Zulu

Introduction

Genesis 3 will be analyzed here from an Ngoni Christianity context.

The Ngoni of Zambia is a tribe found in the eastern part of the country. The Ngoni people have a Zulu origin and originally came from KwaZulu-Natal, South Africa, during the 1820s. They share similarities with the Swazi, Zulu, and Ngoni of Malawi and Tanzania. Christianity was introduced to Ngoni land around 1900, and the first mission of the Dutch Reformed Church among the Ngoni was established in 1903 at Madzimoyo. This mission station still remains as one of the major mission stations of the Reformed Church in Zambia, a church born out of the Dutch Mission Reformed Church of Free State, South Africa (Cronjé 1982: 135).

Although the Ngoni area is predominantly Christianized, traditional African cultural elements form part and parcel of Ngoni lives. A number of cultural elements have been incorporated into the Ngoni brand of Christianity. In this context, the people are mostly organized on family levels. It is a community that is strongly connected to family ideals and genealogies in that those ideals and genealogies define every person. In other words, there is great emphasis on family bonds, so much so that everyone is expected to belong to a family and clan. This clan in turn would join others to form a tribe.

Furthermore, the roles played by individuals are defined by gender, and all individuals are expected to play their roles accordingly. In addition, the place of a woman is significant, since she is the giver of life and, as such, has a unique role in the Ngoni community.

The interpretation of Genesis 3 here offered takes into account various contextual dynamics that are at play in this community, and attempts to present an alternative interpretative premise for this life context.

Life Context for the Interpretation of Genesis 3

In this life context, our context, that of the Ngoni people of Eastern Zambia, responsibility and roles played by individuals are clearly defined according to gender, and this has a bearing on interpreting Genesis 3. A man's specific responsibilities are different from those of a woman. This is the norm in most African communities (Oduyoye 2003: 48). In this context, which is decidedly patriarchal, men do play a dominant role: they are more important than women. In other words, one could say that everything centers on men. A man is in the forefront not only in decision making, food security, and performance of rituals, but also in taking responsibility for everything that happens in one's homestead. This means, for example, that if a child steals from the neighbors, the father—as the head of the household—is responsible. In case of any restitution to be paid, the head of the household takes full responsibility for the payment.

Another matter that needs to be pointed out is that much secrecy surrounds marriage. Partners in marriage are expected to keep family secrets to themselves and are not supposed to divulge them to third parties.

Furthermore, the woman (*Omama*) has a special place in this community. It is woman (*Mama*) who makes sure that the homestead lacks nothing in terms of food, although the men (*Madoda*) provide the food. The responsibility of preparing food and making sure that everyone has eaten and that all have eaten enough rests on the woman's shoulders. She is adored as the giver of life. In cases of wife abuse, a man is strongly rebuked for molesting *Mama*, and such a man is considered not responsible enough to head a homestead. Every woman assumes the role of *Mama* whether she has her own biological children or not. This is done even where women's rights are violated: "African women used traditional coping devices: they smiled at the insensitivity of husbands and brothers and sons and bosses; with equanimity, they went about their self-assigned jobs of ensuring life" (Oduyoye 2003: 3).

Some other factors have to be considered as well. Niara Sudarkasa (2005: 27) writes, "In an extended family, women occupy roles defined by consanguinity, as well as conjugality. They are mothers, and daughters, as well as wives and co-wives. The position of 'wife' refers not only to the conjugal relationship to a husband, but also to the affinal (or in-law) relationship to all members—female as well as male—of the husband's compound and lineage." In addition, the woman (*Mama*) is also expected to look up to the man, who is expected to secure the homestead in the sense of food security and physical security. As there is a strong belief in ancestors, every man (*Lidoda*) plays his role carefully and with great responsibility, so as to leave a legacy that will make him remembered as an ancestor after death.

Although the Ngoni have been influenced by Christianity, they have incorporated elements of their own culture into their faith. Concurrently, the Christian faith has influenced some of those cultural elements. For example, war mentality is eroded, although it is believed that once one is an Ngoni (warrior), one always remains an Ngoni (warrior).

For Ngoni people, the concept of sin against God is strange, as there is no direct relationship between God and the people except through intermediaries, that is, the ancestors (Read 1956: 158). However, with the influence of Christianity, the Ngoni people have come to understand sin from the perspective of the Christian faith's interpretation. All in all, sin is still understood as rebellion against God, which warrants punishment.

Having given the Ngoni context of our interpretation in general terms, we need to point out that there still remain many important issues to consider. First, because this context clearly defines responsibilities according to gender, sin or rebellion in Genesis 3 cannot be the responsibility of a woman. The man ought to take the responsibility as the head of the household. Nevertheless, both are collectively guilty, since each one of them had a part to play in the matter. Second, the man as the head of the household must take the responsibility and leadership. His defined role in a community gives him privileges to take a leadership role, and he had an opportunity to do something differently. Third, although the narrative depicts Eve as the initiator of evil, the same narrative gives a nuance of goodness in her (Gen. 3:20), for she is the mother of all the living. The unique position of the woman as giver of life in the Ngoni community is significant and cannot be underestimated. This has a bearing on reading the Genesis 3 text. In short, the issue of sin in Genesis 3 is basically not gender based.

The Ngoni community has not escaped the many issues of concern that can and should be highlighted, such as the following. First, issues of women abuse, wife battering, violence, and rape need to be effectively addressed in this community. Second, there are irresponsible heads of family who neglect their responsibilities and blame others for their failures. Third, gender and role imbalances do arise—for example, sometimes a woman is the only person expected to be morally right—and there is need for all people to play their roles effectively at all times. Fourth, women are mostly not considered as capable of occupying leadership positions, based on the assumption that they cannot keep a secret. This is based on a biased interpretation of Genesis 3. Consequently, this interpretation perpetuates the denial of the possibility for women to assume positions of leadership. And ultimately, there is a need to redefine the Ngoni context in the light of the influence of Christianity as far as sin, gender, and responsibility are concerned.

Text Analysis I: Overview of Genesis 3, Placing the Book in Perspective

The book of Genesis belongs to the Pentateuch. Genesis 1–11 is the first part of the primeval history. Our passage falls within the part of the book that talks of creation stories and the fall of humans, and ends with the tower of Babel (Genesis 11). The book has some narratives similar to other ancient Near Eastern narratives on the creation.

The context of the fall of humans in Genesis 3 needs to be understood in the macro context of Gen. 2:4b—3:24. This narrative starts with the creation of the man (Gen. 2:7) and later the woman (2:22), and consequently, they live together as man and wife. In this narrative, the Garden of Eden is the center of all activities. However, the center of life in the Garden of Eden is the tree of life (2:9), from which man is prohibited to eat (2:17). It is a beautiful place, and humans are placed there with the freedom to eat all except from the tree of life. There are many explanations for the meaning of this tree's placement being at the center. One of them is that of Atkinson, who argues that "the freedom of human life is limited by one prohibition.

Freedom for his life and conditions are given by God. Life and liberty are found only with God's gracious law" (1990: 62).

In this interpretation, the issue of the fall (3:2-24) is significant, as it has a contextual appeal in my community. Traditionally, the responsibilities that humans carry are related to gender, and in this context, the men take responsibility for whatever happens to their homestead. Many interpretations depict women as evil and not trustworthy. These interpretations have contributed to the ill treatment and abuse of women in most African communities. An alternative interpretation that takes into account the unique position of women in the traditional Ngoni community, and the responsibilities accorded to humans, gives space for women to discover themselves, to move out of stereotypes, and to view themselves in a positive light.

Text Analysis II: Contextual Analysis of Genesis 3

The chaotic events of Gen. 3:1-24 evolve from the harmonious scenario in 2:4b-25. All things seem to fall apart in Genesis 3. The narrative here starts with the description of the seducer, the serpent, as being more crafty (3:1), setting the scene for the later deception of Eve. Gaebelein (1990: 50) argues, "The description of the serpent as 'crafty' is in keeping with the fact that there are several features of this story that suggest that the author wanted to draw a relationship between the fall and man's quest for wisdom."

The issue of the serpent's nature needs elaboration. Sometimes the serpent has been depicted as a supernatural being. It has often been identified with Satan. However, most scholars argue that the notion of the serpent as being a supernatural being is debatable. Hamilton (1990: 188) argues, "The serpent was an animal made by God not a supernatural, divine force." Therefore, we support the view that holds that the serpent was one of the animals God had created (1:25; 2:19). The serpent tempted Eve by "emphasizing God's prohibitions, not his provision, reducing God's command to a question, casting doubt upon God's sincerity and defaming his motives, and denying the truthfulness of His threat" (Sproul 1995: 12). The serpent's words are tempting and seductive: "You will surely not die . . . , for God knows that when you eat of it your eyes will be opened and you will be like God, knowing good and evil" (Gen. 3:4-5).

The narrative continues by indicating that Eve ate the fruit and also gave some to Adam, who also ate (3:6). The result was regret, of realizing that they had disobeyed God at the expense of the outsider, the serpent who tempted them. "Temptation is not presented as a general rebellion of God's authority. It is rather portrayed as a quest for wisdom and 'the good' apart from God's provision" (Gaebelein 1990: 50). We agree with Atkinson (1990: 81) that "the freedom not to trust God becomes the doorway to the loss of freedom itself." He goes on to point out, "The snake does not feature in this story as the cause of human failure, but as that which faces human beings with the reality of their trust in God'" (81).

In our context, these verses (Gen. 3:4-5) are crucial because of the responsibility a man plays in his own household. It is expected that he would take leadership by rejecting the offer and putting his foot down, saying he has an obligation to remain obedient to God's command.

What comes thereafter is an embarrassment—trying to hide and the blame game that follows. The blame game starts with the man saying (3:12), "This woman you gave me!" He needed to own up and say, "I have failed you as the head of the household, as an individual and as a family."

As expected, the woman would not take it alone; she, too, blamed somebody: the serpent. (Maybe the serpent would also have blamed the devil if it were given an opportunity to exculpate itself, and the devil would have shifted the blame elsewhere.)

The consequence of this episode is punishment (vv. 14-19). Different punishments are meted out to the three characters in the narrative: Adam, Eve, and the serpent. However, what is significant is that, despite the curse, the woman becomes the mother of all living (v. 20), even though evil or sin is often attributed to her. According to Sproul (1995: 14), Adam's choice of the name Eve demonstrates his faith in God's promise that the woman would bear children, including the seed that would defeat Satan. The fact that Eve is depicted as the mother of all the living is significant in our context. She remains the most valuable human being, bringing life into this world and sustaining it. The value and importance of the woman is not overshadowed by whatever happens to her.

The narrative ends with the banishment from the Garden of Eden (v. 24) and prevention of returning by the flashing sword. The issue of banishment from the Garden of Eden is not a strange phenomenon in our context. In most African societies, when one does something outrageous in the community, one would be banished for life or for a limited period from that community, though there is always room for repentance and return. A return is facilitated subject to the performance of a cleansing ceremony.

This interpretation addresses a number of contextual issues such as the nature of the sin Eve committed in the Garden of Eden. There are many interpretations in our context of this passage. A common one is the strong belief that Eve committed adultery with the devil, who impersonated a serpent (most translations translate the word *serpent* as a snake; *Njoka*). The argument is that the fruit might have been used figuratively to mean adultery. Therefore, there is a general understanding that the first sin is adultery, but figuratively indicated as a fruit. Since in our context figurative language is employed in daily communication, such an explanation is acceptable though difficult to substantiate. The factor that authenticates this view is the nature of punishment Adam and Eve got just for tasting the fruit. There is a general view that the measure of punishment meted out cannot be justified, as it is not proportional to the sin committed.

However, by concentrating on other features of the narrative, one takes one's eyes off the ball; the cardinal issue in this narrative is that humans accepted the temptation due to their quest for more knowledge and for being like God. The consequences are clear from the passage: punishment (curses) and banishment from the Garden of Eden. Humans tend to place the blame elsewhere, as demonstrated in this narrative. It was expected that the man would own up and accept that there was failure of leadership and abrogation of responsibility. This is so because it was expected that the man, being in charge, would "overrule" his wife and not accept the temptation.

In our context, where patriarchy is prominent, it is inconceivable for Adam to act the way he did. This is so because for one to see or talk to someone's wife, even if the subject matter has nothing to do with the husband, one has to ask the man first. It is even more imperative if you are a man. In this instance, therefore, it was expected that the serpent would have first of all asked for the man's permission. In addition, under normal circumstances, Eve would have rejected the offer and referred the serpent to the man. In the event that Eve took the fruit, she would have kept it and shown it to Adam to seek his approval before she could eat the fruit. Furthermore, if the decision was reached to eat the fruit, it had to be made by Adam's authority and consent.

The other important issue in the household management dynamics of Ngoni society is that each house earns a name for itself through its conduct. The virtues of honor and shame are significant. Malina (1993: 31) describes honor and shame as "socially proper attitudes and behavior in the area where three lines of power, gender, status and religion intersect." This understanding stems from the belief that in sustaining society, morals and ideals are the responsibility and expectation of every individual, family, clan, and tribe. This explains why, at all times, one is expected to behave in such a way that one does not bring shame or ridicule to the family. This is so because honor can either be ascribed to a person or acquired by a person through excelling in one's society. Being shamed involves loss of reputation and worth in the eyes of others, especially one's peers (Zulu 1999).

Therefore, in this instance, Adam would not have accepted bringing a bad name and shame upon his family (household) by entering into a disastrous deal with the serpent. Responsibility lay with Adam, and here we see a failed household, a failed head of household, and a failed family leader who shifts the blame onto a woman (3:12). This failed state (household) of Adam is a product of his leadership failure. Man's disobedience is not so much depicted as an act of great wickedness or great transgression, as much as it is an act of great folly. He had all the "good" he would have needed, but wanted more—he wanted to be like God (Gaebelein 1990: 50).

Conclusions

To sum up our interpretation, we first need to indicate the teachings for today's believers in the Ngoni context. First, there is need to be obedient to God and trust God only. Second, what God has given us is enough; therefore, any attempt to have more may lead into sin. Third, we cannot shift the blame for our own mistakes onto others. Acceptance of wrongdoing is the beginning of inner renewal. Therefore, we cannot hide from God, and any attempt to do so is a futile exercise. Fourth, being tempted is not sin in itself, but when one yields to the temptation, that is sin. This is so because Satan will do anything he can to get us to follow his evil and deadly ways.

This interpretation of Genesis 3 addresses some issues important to the Ngoni context. First, woman is not evil or the source of evil. The source of evil is not woman, but both man and woman, since they collectively disobeyed

God in their selfish quest for wisdom and the wish to be like God. Second, sins are not gender related. The actors in this narrative act in the way they did not based on their gender orientation, but on their own judgments as human beings. Third, respect for women, the givers of life, is paramount. The abuse of women, violence against women, sometimes emanates from the interpretation that supports the view that women are more susceptible to sin than men. However, this passage illustrates that, despite the fact that the woman fell into sin, her special role and status did not change. Women remain givers of life and deserve the respect of the community. Fourth, room should be made for women to be able to stand on their own. The Bible can be a tool of liberation in their emancipation. The patriarchal nature of the Bible and the Ngoni context should not hinder women from self-determination. Instead, the Bible and the interpretive context should propel women to a better and balanced interpretation that opens opportunities for them to stand up.

Issues that are not addressed remain, such as the patriarchal system that is tribal based and difficult to do away with over a short period of time. However, what this interpretation calls for is a need to question issues that make women vulnerable to male abuse as justified by a biblical interpretation.

Lastly, we have argued that an interpretation that has the notion that Eve is the source of all evil has always been used as a basis for stigmatizing and persecuting women. Sometimes, in song and dance, Eve (figuratively woman) is still depicted as the source of all evil. Consequently, in most African communities, trusting a woman is always questionable. Unless there is an alternative interpretation, as suggested in this work, woman would continue to be subjected to all sorts of persecution, and mistrust.

CHAPTER 6

Re-reading Genesis 1–3 in the Light of Ancient Chinese Creation Myths

Yan Lin

Introduction: Subject and Personal Context

As many scholars have argued, Genesis 1–3 can be separated into two creation stories: the Priestly (P) creation story (Gen. 1:1—2:4a) and the Yawhistic (J) creation story (2:4b—3:24). The former was presumably written in the Babylonian exile, and the life context of this biblical text mainly concerns ancient Israelites' cosmology and their cosmogony. The latter was presumably written in the age of the Israelite monarchy, and its life context reflects a people's etiology for their own civilization, beginning with the origin of human beings. Both of these creation stories concern the relationship between God and human beings.

My starting point for reading the Genesis creation texts is rooted in an alienation, a "remoteness" complex that has enveloped me since I was born in Xinjiang Uygur Autonomous Region, a remote area in China. I can identify four bases for my complex: (1) Xinjiang is the hometown of the Uighurs (ethnic group) and the Han nationality is a minority here. I am a Han. When I was a young girl, I always wanted to go to places where Han people lived. (2) My mother became psychotic when I was eight months old, so my family became one of the poorest families in our factory. No one was willing to associate with me as an equal since that time. (3) In 1996, I was accepted as a student by Sichuan University after a brutal examination. Still, this could not change the complex because my major—philosophy—was seen as a cold subject by ordinary people. (4) I am now a teacher at Shenzhen University. Because of this and because I was awarded a Ph.D. degree by The Chinese University of Hong Kong, I am admired by most local women. However, and lamentably, my husband's mother wants to control her son and me arbitrarily, and I often feel alienated from my own family. The alienation, the "remoteness complex" inside me feels, perhaps, just like exile was felt by people of the Hebrew Bible. The relevance of this background will become clearer later.

Analysis: Text and Implications

The Priestly creation story can be read as a prayer that was initially used in the worship of God in exile (Westermann 1984: 92). There are at least two crises that the people of exile had to face. The first was a national crisis, and the priests hoped that their people could survive and flourish in Babylon. This biblical text can therefore be read as supporting the idea: "God blessed them, and God said to them, 'Be fruitful and multiply, and fill the earth and subdue it'" (Gen. 1:28). The priests in exile hoped their people could multiply in Babylon. This ideology was put into the text, and therefore we read that God let human beings fill the earth (not necessarily the land of Israel).

The second crisis was a crisis of faith. In the *Enuma Elish*, a Babylonian myth, there is a creation story about Marduk, who battled with Tiamat. This story has undoubtedly influenced Genesis 1; but in the biblical text, the priests demythologized it so that instead of gods, all we can find here is just one God.[1] At that time, the priests had to face the problem that the people exiled in Babylon had lost their faith in God, blaming the exile on the God who could not defeat Marduk, the god of Babylon (Hamlin 1979: 16–18, 42). Therefore, the priests had responsibilities to uphold their people's faith in God. What they had done was to present God as the creator who created everything, even his enemy Marduk. Thus, they bestowed onto God omnipotence and strengthened confidence in God on the part of their people, now exiled in Babylon.

---

1. However, we can still discover some vestiges of polytheism. For example, the word *Tiamat* has a linguistic resemblance to תהו (Heb. *tohu*; deep, primeval ocean), and God created the תנין (Heb. *tanin*; sea monster), which is a creature hostile to creation (Gen. 1:21). See Gunkel 1984: 25–52.

In my opinion, the two crises should be reconsidered. Compared with the often-miserable condition of people in exile, I find that the Judean exiles in fact lived more comfortably than could be expected.[2] These exiles lived in their own groups and they could have some right of autonomy. Some of them even owned real estate and, to some extent, they could also worship Yahweh (Hamlin 1979: 43). According to some scholars (von Rad 1966: 136, 142; Rendtorff 1990; Westermann 1969: 19, 24; Stuhlmueller 1970: 237; Clifford 1993: 5–10), the creation hymn of Genesis 1 conveys salvation theology. In fact, this salvation did not serve all ancient Israelites, and many exiled people may not have had strong motivation to return. This salvation theology just reflects the ideology of the priests, rather than of all the exiled people. The priests thought God built cosmic order within six days; but if we relate cosmic order to social order, as the biblical texts show, we will find it would be absurd for priests to imagine building a new social order in Babylon.[3] "Subdue it; and have dominion over the fish of the sea and over the birds of the air and over every living thing that moves upon the earth" (Gen. 1:28). It is obvious that "the earth" here is not Babylon. The priests were longing to govern those people who remained in Jerusalem, after returning, and they wrote:

> God said, "See, I have given you every plant yielding seed that is upon the face of all the earth, and every tree with seed in its fruit; you shall have them for food. And to every beast of the earth, and to every bird of the air, and to everything that creeps on the earth, everything that has the breath of life, I have given every green plant for food." (Gen. 1:29-30)

This biblical text clearly explains the destiny of the people who remained in Jerusalem. This will become clearer if we relate it to the second creation story. The Yahwistic story was written in the age of the monarchy, when farming was the main occupation. We can find this context in Genesis 2–3, since the first peasant in the Hebrew Bible is Adam (Yee 2003: 60–77). We also find that, according to the Hebrew Bible, Adam and the earth have a

---

2. In fact, Archie Lee does not totally agree with this pessimistic assessment, and he also believes the people of exile did have much freedom in Babylon. See Lee 1997: 22, 64.
3. The priests tried to build such an order in Jerusalem, their native locale, and we can see it in the books of Ezra and Nehemiah.

close relationship (*BDB*: 9). The Yahwistic author tried to liken peasants to beasts, birds, and creeping things, that is to say, the peasants are given the same food as these other creatures. On this score, the exilic priests reread the older Yahwistic story in a new light thus using it for interpreting their own ideology, which also encompassed preparing to govern the peasants who had remained in Jerusalem, by giving them some life status or guarantee.

The Yahwistic story is not a picture of humanity's original sin, but a story that can help people receive and resolve the realities of life. In such a story, people etiologically explain feasts, habits, customs, lifestyle, and the social systems in their life. And through such explanations, people can accept the imperfect reality in which they try to look for values and meaning. For example, the story explains the origin of marriage. Why can a man not live with his parents forever? The biblical text explains: "This at last is bone of my bones and flesh of my flesh . . . for out of Man this one [called Woman] was taken" (Gen. 2:23). Thus, there is also a blood relationship besides political and economic relations between a couple, and this relationship is no less than the bond between parents and their children. Only in this way can marriage be confirmed.

Another example concerns food. The woman ate the fruit not simply because it could help her to be wiser, but because it could become food. The woman ate the fruit following this order of thoughts: מַאֲכָל (food), תַאֲוָה (delight), נֶחְמָד (desirability), and לְהַשְׂכִּיל (becoming wise) (*BDB*: 16, 38, 326, 968). According to this order, the direct reason for the woman's eating of the fruit is not wisdom, but the desire for food. Thus, we can find here an idea similar to that of the Chinese saying, "People regard food as their prime want" (Ho 2006).

Text Analysis I

The creation myths in Genesis 1–3 convey ideas about God, the cosmos, and human beings. Therefore, in the next sections of my article, I would like to discuss cosmology, cosmogony, the origin of human beings, and the divine–human relationship. Moreover, since creation myths obviously embody the ideology of authors, editors, or readers, I will also show how ideology influences the formation of a text.

I am a Chinese Bible scholar, so cannot neglect my own cultural context when reading Genesis 1–3. I know that there are some creation myths in ancient Chinese texts that resemble those of Genesis 1–3, such as how

P'an-ku, a male god, separated the heaven and the earth; and Nu Kua, a goddess, made human beings by pinching clay. Therefore, when reading Genesis 1–3, I cannot prevent myself from interpreting Genesis 1–3 in the light of the Chinese stories and conversely, reviewing the ancient Chinese texts again using my new understanding back on Genesis 1–3. In other words, I read back and forth from the Chinese culture to the Bible, changing directions several times, as will be explained below.

Text Analysis II

The method that will be used for rereading Genesis 1–3 in light of Chinese creation myths is the cross-textual reading method, as developed by Archie Lee. Cross-textual reading is a method that juxtaposes two different texts by looking at them together, so that text A is read in the light of text B, and vice versa. We can understand text A more profoundly in the light of text B, and then reread text B using this deeper knowledge. The crossovers from text A to text B happen many times during the reading process, not only once. Of course, comparison/analogy is part of this process, but is not the final purpose. After the bidirectional crossovers, what we want to achieve is that both the cultural text and the biblical text seriously interact with each other in a creative and meaningful way so that both can be mutually enriched, transformed, integrated, and updated. In this article, then, I will regard Genesis 1–3 and some other related biblical texts as text A, and ancient Chinese creation myths as text B.

Cosmology

Separation is an important cosmological motif in the Priestly creation report. There are separations between light and darkness (v. 4), water above and water below (vv. 6-7), and dry land and the seas (v. 9).[4] Such a motif also appears in Chinese creation myths. The most important concepts, yin and yang, symbolize female and male. They can be applied to nearly every dualistic concept, such as earth and heaven, and darkness and light, which is very similar to the Priestly concept (Lee 1993a: 190). However, the yin–yang

---

4. In fact, the motif had appeared earlier in the texts of ancient Mesopotamia. There we can find the earth separated, high from below, and creation here means separating the earth and freshwater from saltwater. See Bottéro 2001: 78.

motif implies not only opposition but also harmony, complementarity, and amalgamation. Thus, Chinese cosmology indicates a cosmos that contains more self-management, self-sufficiency, and self-creation, and is embodied in the Tao (Ji 1986: 543).

When we return to Genesis 1 with this new understanding, we will be amazed to find that there is also a harmonious cosmos in the Priestly creation story, because God's creation is full of order, which explains why God said "good" (טוב) seven times within six days. Even though the flood (Genesis 6–9) threatened creation, it is only a temporary phenomenon. The order that God re-created after the flood parallels the created order in Genesis 1.[5] Therefore, I conclude that the priests longed for a harmonious cosmos even in the exile context, which corresponds to their ideology of social order. Certainly, as mentioned above, the priests also wanted to realize this harmonious social order in Jerusalem of the future.

An important characteristic of Chinese cosmology is that time coordinates with space. The English word *cosmos* corresponds to the Chinese term *yu-zhou*, in which *yu* denotes territory and the entire spacial world, and *zhou* means time immemorial to the present. That is to say, the term *yu-zhou* itself contains both meanings of time and space. There is a Chinese text on the Yellow Emperor and his chancellors:

> The East is Wood. Its god is Tai Hao. His assistant is Gou Mang. He grasps the compass and governs spring. . . . The South is Fire. Its god is Yan Di. His assistant is Zhu Ming. He grasps the balance-beam and governs summer. . . . The Center is Earth. Its god is the Yellow Torch. His assistant is Hou Tu [Sovereign of the soil]. He grasps the marking-cord and governs the four quarters. . . . The West is Metal. Its god is Shao Hao. His assistant is Ru Shou. He grasps the T-square and governs autumn. . . . The North is Water. Its god is Zhuan Xu. His assistant is Xuan Ming. He grasps the plumb-weight and governs winter. (*Huai Nan Zi*, chapter three). (Major 1993: 70–72)

The myth adequately expresses the idea of time coordinating with space—that is to say, in Chinese cosmology, the four seasons correspond to the four directions of the earth. The ancient Chinese believed that the Yellow

---

5. The parallelism that appears in these two texts can be arranged as follows: 1:20//8:17; 1:24//8:18; 1:26//9:6; 1:28//9:1, 7; 1:28//9:2; 1:29//9:3.

Emperor was the sun god; thus, they put forward that east corresponds to spring, south to summer, west to autumn, and north to winter, according to the orbit in which the sun remains in different times. Moreover, a concept of reciprocation clearly emerges from such a cosmology (Yang 2003).

When we view Genesis 1 on the basis of the coordination idea from Chinese cosmology, we will immediately notice there a time system (God created in six days and rested on the seventh day) and space system (sky-sea-land). Can we think this is similar to the coordination idea of Chinese cosmology? In my opinion, it is not, because the time system in Genesis 1 is a kind of framework or narrative sequence, not "real" time. Thus, there is no time corresponding to space in Genesis 1, and the priests just wanted to emphasize God's powers of creation. Time coordinates to space, which implies the cosmos can occur and survive by itself, but the ancient Israelites strongly believed that God created the cosmos, so there is a great and everlasting gulf between God and the things God created. Returning then to the Chinese creation myths, we will find that the Yellow Emperor is not only a supreme god, but also a forefather who is the greatest headman of the Chinese (Yuan 1998a). So there is less distance between god and human beings in the Chinese text, which is very different from the biblical texts.

Ancient Israelites used the Hebrew word 'et (עֵת) to indicate time; this word has several meanings and therefore is complex (*BDB*: 417).[6] If we put this word aside temporarily in order to look at Chinese texts, we find that the ancient Chinese paid close attention to the length of life. There are some strange Chinese myths, such as the "Ten Suns," "Kua Fu Chases the Sun," and "Chang Er Flies to the Moon."[7] Robert Shanmu Chen integrated these three creation myths. He thought the first myth expresses that the ancients profoundly realized that people were mortal; the second myth indicates that the ancients tried to rebel against time in order to change the destiny of mortality; and the last myth about Chang Er told the ancients that there was

---

6. See Neh. 9:28; Amos 5:13; Pss. 9:10, 37:39; and Eccl. 3:1-9.

7. The "Ten Suns" myth (Yuan 1998b: 308) tells that, long ago, there were ten sun-brothers who bathed every day. People could not live at that time, because the sun-brothers scorched the earth. A hero called Hou Yi shot nine suns and left only one. Henceforth, people could live and work in peace and contentment. "Kua Fu Chases the Sun" (Huang and Mei 1998: 68) has a giant called Kua Fu who conceives the vain ambition of overtaking the fleeting rays of the sun. "Chang Er Flies to the Moon" (Yuan 1998b: 434; He 1998: 501) has Hou Yi's wife, Chang Er, eating a cure by stealth and then fleeing to the moon.

no use rebelling against time, so they should reach harmony with time and realize their mortality (R. S. Chen 1992: 34, 36). Therefore, time in Chinese texts implies human beings' mortality.

Now we can learn more about עת and עולם in the light of Chinese thought. עולם means remote time, and it is only used by God. עת, as in Chinese thought, means mortality (Barr 1962: 117). Distinguishing between עולם and עת in fact reveals the difference between God and human beings.

Cosmogony

In the cosmonogy of Geneis 1, in which God created (ברא) the heavens, earth, and human beings. ברא was translated as *chuang zao* in the Chinese Bible. However, according to Chinese dictionaries, *chuang zao* has no meaning of creating, and it initially means people's invention, building, and making (Luo 1998: 253). Thus, the Chinese word *chuang zao* is similar to the Hebrew words עשׂה (to do, make) and יצר (to form, fashion). Afterward, scholars used *chuang zao* to translate the meaning of ברא, so that the Hebrew word ברא gave a new meaning to *chuang zao* when translated. Moreover, God is the subject of ברא. Thus, the term obviously displays the conflict between God's creation and human beings' making, which we cannot find in the Chinese term *chuang zao*.

There are four types of Chinese cosmogony. First, in a text written in the Three Kingdoms period, the whole cosmos was born from an egg:

> Before there were heaven and earth [the universe] was in Chaos (*huntun*) like a chicken's egg. At the time of dawn, when the darkness was about to dawn, P'an-ku was engendered within it. After 18,000 years Chaos split apart, what was bright and light formed the heaven, and what was dark and heavy formed the earth. P'an-ku had daily transformed nine times within the Chaos. He was more divine than the heaven and holier than the earth. Thereafter, during another 18,000 years, the heaven daily increased ten feet in height, the earth daily increased ten feet in thickness, and P'an-ku, between the two, also daily increased ten feet in size. This is how the heaven and earth came to be separated by their present distance of 90,000 li [roughly 30,000 miles]. (Chiu 1984: 123)[8]

---

8. For additional discussion, see Lee 1993a: 186.

In this myth, chaos was compared to an egg from which the giant P'an Ku was born, and he was the firstborn of the heavens and the earth. For some scholars, however, this is not a useful example, because it is too late to explain the myth from the Qin-Han period.

A second myth comes from *Huai Nan Zi*. It says that there were two essential elements, yin and yang, and they mixed together and then gave birth to the whole universe:

> Of old before Heaven and Earth even existed, there were only images and no physical shapes. It was dark, shapeless and abysmally still: so undifferentiated it was that no one knew its door. Then two divinities were born commingledly who were to supervise Heaven and regulate Earth. . . . They were divided into yin and yang, and separated into the eight extremes. (Fung 1952: 398)[9]

There are no creators, and every thing develops by itself. In fact, this kind of cosmogony had already appeared before the Qin period: "The Way (*Tao*) begets one; one begets two; two begets three, three begets the myriad creatures. The myriad creatures carry on their backs the *yin* and embrace in their arms the *yang*, taking the *ch' i* in between as harmony" (Lau 1982: 197; Lee 1993a: 192).

We can see that there is a binary and multiple process that can help us understand further the separation in Genesis 1. The differentiation of light/darkness, heaven/earth, dry land/waters, day/night, and then of "every kind," is similar to the idea of the latter Chinese text.

The third text is of the separation type, and the most famous myth also uses the one quoted in the first type. P'an-ku stood between yin and yang and then made Chaos split apart. God's creation in Genesis also uses the concept of "separate" (1:4, 7, 9-10). Thus, when we turn to inspect the Hebrew word בָּרָא, we will find it has not only the meaning of *create*, but also of *separate* (or cut) (*BDB*: 135).[10] Therefore, the creation type in the Priestly creation story is enacted not only through the word, about which scholars agree, but

---

9. Further see Lee 1993a: 189–90.
10. In fact, this creation tradition can be traced back to the Babylonian myth *Enuma Elish*. Marduk separated Tiamat's corpse into two pieces and let them become the heavens and the earth. See Pritchard and Albright 1969: 67.

also through actions similar to those in the Yahwistic creation story. To that extent, Genesis 1–3 is a unity.

The priests used תהו ובהו (formlessness and void) to describe the condition before creation, and we cannot guess whether the author has any positive or negative attitude toward this phrase. But when the Chinese Bible adopts the Hebrew terms *hun-tun*, we will find there is a deep theological meaning added to תהו ובהו. This story below will provide a ligament connecting the creation types previously mentioned:

> The Emperor of the South Sea was called *Shu* (Swift), the Emperor of the North Sea was called *Hu* (Sudden), and the Emperor of the Central Region was called *hun-tun* (Chaos). *Shu* and *Hu* from time to time came together for a meeting in the land of *hun-tun*, and *hun-tun* treated them generously. They said, "All men have several openings so they can see, hear, eat, and breathe. But *hun-tun* doesn't have any. Let's try to bore him some!" Every day they bored another hole, and on the seventh day *hun-tun* died. (Yu 1981; Lee 1993a: 189)

Zhuang Zi told us that an orderly cosmos would be born only after *hun-tun* died. However, Taoism favors *hun-tun*, because it symbolizes naturalness and spontaneity. Thus, Zhuang Zi did not appreciate what *Shu* and *Hu* had done to *hun-tun*. In fact, order is not good in Taoism, and Zhuang Zi felt sorry for *hun-tun*'s death. Turning back to תהו ובהו, we find that God's creation is a process that overcomes *hun-tun* step by step.[11] The appearance of cosmic order is the first step, with *hun-tun* as the hostile power to God's creation at this moment. *Hun-tun* is also the evil element that threatens the social order (Isa. 24:5, 10; 34:11; 45:18, 19).

The fourth type is incarnation, which refers to the body of a giant incarnating into everything on earth (Tao and Zhong 1989: 162). The most famous is the incarnation of P'an-ku 's body:

---

11. The Chinese word *hun-tun* can be translated into the English word *chaos*, and both words can be translated into the Hebrew phrase תהו ובהו. Chaos is "the confused unorganized state of primordial matter before the creation of distinct and orderly forms—contrasted with cosmos," in *Webster's Third New International Dictionary of the English Language* (Springfield, Mass.: Merriam, 1976), 375.

Pangu (P'an-ku), who was born before anything else, underwent great bodily changes when he was dying. His breath became winds and clouds, his voice thunder, his left eye the sun and his right eye the moon; his arms and legs the four poles of the earth and the five parts of his body the five mountains; his blood formed the rivers and his veins the roads; his flesh and skin became the soil of the fields and his hair and moustache the stars; the fine hair on his skin turned into grass and trees, his teeth and bones metals and rocks; his marrow changed to pearls and jade, and his sweat fell as rain that nourished all things; the insects on his body, caressed by the winds, took the shape of men and women. (Ding 1988: 5; Lee 1993a)

It is a basic theme in the Chinese creation myth that the giant P'an-ku incarnated into the cosmos, and that P'an-ku 's death made all life possible. In this sense, this type corresponds to the former three types that are based on *hun-tun* myth. And now we return to Genesis 1, where God at last creates a cosmos that is extrinsic to God's self. God was immortal and would perpetually participate in people's history. Reviewing P'an-ku's genesis in the light of Genesis 1, we will find that his incarnation is only a one-time occurrence, and after that, because of his mortality, he did not leave his mark on the world.

Origin of Human Beings

In the Yahwistic narrative, a story influenced by the ancient Sumerian myth, Yahweh makes a helper from the man's rib (Pritchard and Albright 1969: 40–41). The two words *life* and *rib* are a play on words in Sumerian, but we cannot find any relationship between the Hebrew words חוה (life) and צלע (rib) (Bechtel 1993: 97–98).

The most famous Chinese text on making human beings is Nu Kua's text on mending the sky:

It is said that when the heaven and the earth were separated there was no human being. It was Nu Kua who first created human beings by moulding yellow earth. The work was so taxing that she was very exhausted. So she dipped a rope into the mud and then lifted it. The mud that dripped from the rope also became human beings. Those made by moulding yellow earth were rich and noble, while those made by dripped mud were poor and low. (Bodde 1961: 389; Lee 1994: 312)

Nu Kua made human beings by herself, just as Yahweh did. We know that אדם (Adam) and אדמה (earth) are a pair, a pun (possibly on "red"), the latter suggesting the former's destiny (Gen. 3:19). In the Chinese text, Nu Kua also made human beings from yellow dust, but there is no linguistic relationship between human beings and dust. However, the Chinese always think their ancestor is the Yellow Emperor, so that they are of his yellow skin. In this sense, the Chinese are also related to the (yellow) dust. Thus, it is the essential existence of human beings to relate to dust, whether in ancient Israel or in China.[12]

Another Chinese myth about Nu Kua says that she also had the power of transforming and nourishing, and she could even transform seventy times (He 1998: 1186). We can be mindful from Nu Kua's character that Eve (חוה) was the mother of all living (חי), and both of the two Hebrew words come from the verb חיה (to live) (*BDB*: 310–12). So the biblical texts, much like the Chinese text, emphasize the relationship between women and life.

Jian Xian Chen (1994) assumes that Nu Kua is the Chinese Earth Mother, and her power of transforming and nourishing in fact means that living things come out of the earth. Taking up this idea and returning to Genesis 1–3, I assume there is a relationship between Eve and dust. Of course, we cannot find such ostensible relations in biblical texts, but we should not forget that the Hebrew word אדם (human being) also includes females (1:27-30). Since Yahweh formed אדם from אדמה (dust), woman also should have a relation to dust. However, the author of Genesis 1–3 does not show an interest in that; hence the author might have deleted some valuable contents available to him. Considering the tricks behind the biblical texts and by the same token, I also think the last sentence in Nu Kua's myth about the rich and the poor may have also been an addition. Indeed, the *Tai Ping Yu Lan* is a book initially written for kings, and the author distinguished the rich from the poor in order to look for a sacred foundation for a worldly social hierarchy. Reviewing Genesis 1–3, human beings there share the goodness of creation, and the creation had a strong divine dimension from the very beginning. By comparison, an important quality lacking

---

12. One Chinese text has it that Nu Kua was a chancellor in the court of the Yellow Emperor, who commanded her to descend and form a human being. So it is not strange that Nu Kua would make a human being who is like the Yellow Emperor (Le Blanc 1985: 162). See also Lee 1994: 312.

in the Chinese creation myths is a divine dimension, since the boundary between the divine and human beings is far from clear.

The Divine–Human Relationship

As far as the divine–human relationship is concerned, Genesis 1–3 shows there is a great perpetual gulf between God and human beings. Genesis 1–11 continuously narrates how God is totally different from human beings (3:22, 6:1-5, 11:1-9), but humans cannot always understand those differences. The most important reason leading to such a gulf is that God is the creator, and human beings are the created. Thus, compared with God, human beings are dust and flesh from the very start. But in Chinese texts, we can find that the divine (heavenly) and human beings become one. Turning back to *Zhuang Zi*, we will find that Zhuang Zi called into question the strict division between divine and human: "How do I know that the doer I call 'Heaven' is not the human being? How do I know that the doer I call the human being is not heaven?" (Graham 1981: 85; see also Lee 1995: 76). Zhuang Zi introduced the idea of "unity of divine and human," and he knew human beings cannot dominate heaven, because the wisdom of human beings is limited. This attitude is similar to that found in Genesis 2–3, which also denies the possibility that human beings determine their own destiny.

Whether we look at Chinese gods or at God/Yahweh in Genesis 1–3, they are not only the creators but also the redeemers. Genesis 1 tried to comfort the exiled people and confirm their faith in God by the Priestly creation story, and the biblical texts are saturated by the author's own ideology. If we read the Genesis 1 creation story with Second Isaiah, written in the same period, we will find a new creation theology: the themes of creation and redemption appear together (Clifford 1985: 520; 1993: 3–16). Of course, this new creation is not only the copy of the initial one, but also a re-creation. In fact, the Chinese Nu Kua's mending of the sky is also a reflection of the re-creation theme:

> Turning back to ancient times, the Four Pillars were shattered and the Nine Provinces dislocated. The sky did not cover [the earth] completely; nor did the earth uphold [all of the sky]. Fire roared with inextinguishable flames, and waters gushed forth in powerful and incessant waves. Ferocious animals devoured the good people, and birds of prey snatched away the old and weak. Thereupon, Nu Kua fused together

stones of the five colours with which she patched up the azure sky. She cut off the feet of the turtle with which she set up the Four Pillars. She slaughtered the black dragon in order to save the Land of Chi. She piled up reed ashes with which to check the flooding waters. When the azure sky was patched up, the Four Pillars set up straight, the flooding waters dried up, the Land of Chi made orderly and the cunning wild animals exterminated, the good people thrived. (Chiu 1984: 158–60; cf. Lee 1994: 313–14)

The cosmos was full of chaos, so Nu Kua rose to save her people. The biblical authors thought the exile was just like תֹהוּ וָבֹהוּ; it was hostile to creation:

> I looked on the earth, and lo, it was waste and void;
>> and to the heavens, and they had no light.
> I looked on the mountains, and lo, they were quaking,
>> and all the hills moved to and fro.
> I looked, and lo, there was no one at all,
>> and all the birds of the air had fled.
> I looked, and lo, the fruitful land was a desert,
>> and all its cities were laid in ruins
>> before the LORD, before his fierce anger. (Jer. 4:23-26; NRSV)

God created the cosmos to separate the primeval chaos, and God re-created the cosmos to overcome the threats that the chaos brought. Proceeding from this idea, I find Nu Kua's cosmic patching up a similar attempt to remove such a chaotic state.

God saved his people in history after fighting against the sea monsters, as in other biblical texts:

> Awake, awake, put on strength,
>> O arm of the LORD!
> Awake, as in days of old,
>> the generation of long ago!
> Was it not you who cut Rahab in pieces,
>> who pierced the dragon?
> Was it not you who dried up the sea,
>> the waters of the great deep;
> who made the depths of the sea a way
>> for the redeemed to cross over? (Isa. 51:9-10)

Nu Kua also eradicated dragons when the water was subdued but disappeared after that. In my opinion, ancient Chinese gods saved their people in history, but God/Yahweh participated in the history of the Israelites from beginning to end.

Conclusions

Creation myths are not only stories about the beginnings, as their authors claim, but also reflections of their authors' ideology. People recreate their own creation theology every time they face the same creation texts. Both the Priestly and Yahwistic authors had their own concerns, as apparent in Genesis 1–3. Genesis 1–3 was edited and reinterpreted by priests in exilic and postexilic times, when problems of returning had to be faced. Therefore, the creation stories in Genesis 1–3 have a relationship with the ideologies of the returnees. As a female scholar who suffers all kinds of remoteness/alienation complexes, I strongly wish I also could return to the center from remoteness, much the same as the returning exiles.

As a Chinese scholar, I use the cross-textual reading method to reread Genesis 1–3 in light of ancient Chinese creation myths. On the one hand, I hope this will help us understand Hebrew creation myths from a new angle and encourage cross-textual reading of the cultures. On the other hand, I find it important to retell creation myths in the age of Chinese transition and development. In fact, such attempts were already made by some famous scholars in the first half of the twentieth century: they worked diligently to arrange Chinese creation myths and got brilliant results (Lu 1979; Gu 1982; Wen 1947). In that period, China was cruelly invaded and exploited by the colonizers. Chinese scholars had a strong interest in creation myths in order to look for the core of the Chinese spirit and culture, hoping—by returning to the fountainhead—to encourage people with their reinterpretation of the myths. In my opinion, this is a historical junction similar to that of the author of Genesis 1, who, centuries and millennia ago, put the creation myth at the beginning of Hebrew Bible. Genesis 1–3 is, indeed, the root of the Holy Book.

China is gradually growing up now, but people have found she is losing some important and valuable things that construct a national character. We need to ask ourselves, within the context of globalization, should not a nation have exhaustless resources of strength, often referred to as time-spirit, creativity, enterprise, industry, bravery, and righteousness? How do we create those resources? These are serious questions that all Chinese people have to face. We need to turn back to the Chinese creation myths that are considered the earliest spiritual home of Chinese culture, and draw strength from them. I believe that rereading the Chinese creation myths will make the Chinese spirit glow again, advancing the development of the nation from her situation in the first half of the twentieth century.

CHAPTER 7

When the Flood Narrative of Genesis Meets Its Counterpart in China
Reception and Challenge in Cross-Textual Reading

Archie Chi Chung Lee

Introduction

This paper is an attempt to look at the biblical flood narratives (BFN) from the perspective of the numerous flood myths in China. It will adopt the cross-textual interpretive method,[1] reading the BFN in parallel with one of the myths of the Naxi, an ethnic minority of China. The chosen Naxi text is taken from a well-known piece of literary works of Dongba literature entitled *The Genesis Account,* which contains quite a few of the motifs common to the BFN and also other flood myths of China. One particular aspect will be highlighted for discussion in this paper: the conception of relationship between the divine and the human in the religious world of the BFN and the Naxi's Genesis. The aim of the paper is to see how Chinese readers appropriate the BFN in the cross-textual reading process with the Naxi flood myth and how the latter contributes to the understanding of the BFN. I will first investigate the historical encounters of the biblical Genesis with Chinese ancient history in the time of the Jesuit Mission in China in the seventeenth century. The investigation serves to highlight the contrast between the two traditions and sets the stage for a cross-textual reading

---

1. I have written on the method in a few articles: Lee 1993; 2002; and 2008. The research for this paper was partially funded by the Hong Kong Research Grants on biblical interpretation in China.

81

of the BFN and the Naxi flood myth. Since the Naxi myth is perhaps less known by most of my readers, more details will be provided in order to introduce it properly.

Historical Encounter of the Biblical Flood Narrative with China

When the Jesuits first brought the biblical stories of Genesis to China in the seventeenth and eighteenth centuries, very little cultural impact had been made on the Chinese audience. Instead, there were some unanticipated reactions and radical challenges back home in Europe. The issues of the authenticity and historicity of the Genesis stories of creation and the flood were debated among scholars in Europe. According to the reports of the Jesuits, there was in China an ancient history with a continuous chronology that had not been disrupted with the alleged universal flood destroying the whole world and the human race, leaving behind only a family of eight. If Noah's flood had occurred, the Chinese would have survived it or not been affected by it at all.

How to reconcile the conflict between a much longer Chinese chronology of the Chinese race, which even antedated Adam and Eve and survived the flood, is a great challenge to the Western church and serious readers of the Bible. The church has so far upheld the position that Genesis was basically historical in its account. It is obvious that the Chinese history, narrated and reported by the Jesuits back home, could not be accommodated into the history derived from the Bible. This presented a serious problem to the Christendom of Renaissance Europe.

The Italian Jesuit priest Martino Martini (1614–1661) came to China in 1643 and learned of the incredible early Chinese history that was claimed to have started with Fuxi, the founder of China, in 2952 BCE (4,595 years earlier).[2] Martini was convinced of the accuracy of ancient Chinese chronology and defended its credibility in his 1658 book *Sinicae historiae decas prima* (*The First Ten Divisions of Chinese History*) (Lust 1987).[3] The book's challenge

---

2. See the conference papers on Martino Martini edited by Franco Demarchi and Riccardo Scartezzini (1996).

3. See also the discussion on harmonizing Chinese history and the biblical record and symbolic interpretation in the so-called figurism in Mungello 2005: 93–94 and Lackner 1991, especially 132–33.

lies in its strong belief in the Chinese chronology, which clearly contradicted the commonly held biblical view of the world's age as dated to 4004 BCE and the year of Noah's great flood in 2348 BCE. Controversies centered on Fuxi's reign, which predated the flood by 600 years. There was no evidence of any destruction of China or any discontinuity of the long Chinese history since Fuxi's time. This experience, referred to as "Europe's discovery of China" (Van Kley 1971), had great impact on the church's strong conviction of the historicity of the BFN record. The image of China and its historical chronology, as presented by Martino Martini and others (Heyndricks 1990), were taken as credible and reliable, so the authenticity of the Bible was threatened with bankruptcy, and its authority drastically challenged.

As a matter of fact, the authority and historicity of the Bible had already been under attack in Europe for quite a while at the time, and the conflict of the flood dating with ancient Chinese history only intensified the ongoing debates. The interest in the origin of China continued for a century or so among European intellectuals. They were deeply involved in the debates on the existence of a "pre-Adam" humanity in the Chinese who had even survived the flood. The debates eventually centered on the textual authority of the Hebrew Bible and the Greek Septuagint, as the two biblical versions presented two different sets of dates for the creation and the flood. Since this issue will occupy a vast area of study in the history of the role and reception of the Bible in the cultural exchanges between China and Europe, more extensive study than what this short paper can accommodate will be needed. This summary serves only to highlight the encounter of the two texts in the history of East–West exchanges. In what follows, we will turn to the Chinese flood traditions in the Han Chinese Classics[4] before engaging with the rich and colorful flood narratives of the fifty-six ethnic minorities in China.

Ordering of Chaos and the Chinese Flood Story of Yu

What Chinese people regard as most fearsome and terrifying is, according to the Chinese Classics, "fierce floods and savage beasts" (洪水猛獸). In

---

4. The Han people are the majority of the Chinese and constitute the single dominant group in the long history of China.

their memory of the flood tradition, it is Yu, the cultural hero, who has been remembered with the greatest honor:

> The world has existed for a long time, now in peace, now in disorder. In the time of Yao,[5] the water reversed its natural course, flooding the central regions, and the reptiles made their homes there, depriving the people of a settled life. . . . Yu was entrusted with the task of controlling it. He led the flood water into the seas by cutting channels for it in the ground, and drove the reptiles into grassy marshes. . . . Only then were the people able to level the ground and live. (Lau 1970: 113)

This flood narrative is one of the earliest and the most popular of all the mythological themes in the ancient texts of China. The story itself is, however, not homogeneous. Traces of it appear in the Zhou literature[6] of *Shijing* (《詩經》, *The Book of Songs*) and *Shujing* (《書經》, *The Book of History*) and occur extensively in a lot of later writings.[7] The hero who conquered the great flood was Yu the Great (大禹), believed to be the founder and so the first emperor of the Xia Dynasty (2783–1751 BCE).

There are tales that attribute the success of Yu's saving of China from the great terrible deluge, which had ravaged the land for nine or ten years, to his intensive labor and hard work. The story has it that he even passed the door of his house several times without sparing a moment to visit his family.[8] Yu was assisted by a winged dragon, which used its tail to mark places on the ground where channels could be dug to drain the disastrous floodwaters. The chapter titled "Tian Wen" (〈天問〉) in *Songs of the South* (《楚辭》) presents the traditions of Yu and his father Kun in the form of a series of questions:

> How did he fill the flood waters up where they were most deep?
> How did he set bounds to the nine territories of the earth?
> What did the winged dragon trace on the ground?

---

5. Yao is one of the sage-kings and Confucian legendary cultural heroes who is believed to have lived in 2358–2258 BCE.

6. Zhou is said to be the most important of the earliest dynasties, to which later Confucian scholars ascribed the cultural achievement of setting a model of excellent government for future generations.

7. For a brief account of the story's outline, see Bodde 1961.

8. On praising the Yu's hard work, see Liao 1959: 275–76; and Confucius 1983: 75. Cf. Fung 1952: 1:329. Kun is believed to be the father of Yu.

Where did the seas and rivers flow?

What did Kun labor on, and what did Yu accomplish? (Qu Yuan 1959: 48).[9]

Yu's task was twofold: conquering the floodwaters (洪水) and expelling wild beasts (猛獸). His success resulted in an orderly society and a settled agricultural life for the people. As was the case for the flood hero in the ancient Near East, Yu was also awarded kingship to rule the land. What Yu achieves is creation in the biblical sense of reducing chaos to order, as well as founding and managing the sociopolitical and economic order of the Xia Dynasty. Scholars have argued convincingly that Yu was a divine being under the commission of the Shangdi (Lord on High) to conquer the floodwaters (Ku and T'ung 1982). Historical events were later "created" and piled up on him, making him the sage-king after the great Yao (堯) and Shun (舜). Yu was praised, together with other cultural heroes of Tang (湯), Wen (文), and Wu, (武), as the Sons of Heaven who were obedient to the Will of Heaven. All of them were awarded the heritage of the empire (Watson 1963: 78–83; Fung 1952: 1:96–97). Derk Bodde (1961: 403) concludes from his studies that "the intense historical-mindedness of the Chinese" and "their tendency to reject supernatural explanations for the universe—caused them to 'humanize' or 'euhemerize' much of what had originally been myth into what came to be accepted as authentic history."

The flood story of Yu, having "the greatest hold on the Chinese consciousness" (Bodde 1961: 404), can contribute to the formulation of a Chinese theology of creation in terms of ordering and managing the human world. Many ancient philosophers and teachers have made reference to it in their writings. In most of the allusions to Yu, his combat of chaos and establishment of order constitute a powerful symbol for the Chinese people in their participation in creating the future. The symbol of Yu also invites readers to identify with Yu, as remarked by someone at the time of Xunzi: "Every human being in the street can become a Yu (涂之人可以為禹')"

---

9. Though it is quite doubtful, I adopt the tradition of attributing the authorship of "Tian Wen" to Qu Yuan, as it is beyond the scope of this paper to go into that discussion. Kun, from whose belly Yu was born, was punished and executed by Shangdi (Lord on High) for his theft of the "swelling mold," "a magical kind of soil which had the property of ever swelling in size." He used the soil to build dams to hold back the floodwaters. Bodde 1961: 399.

(Dubs 1966: 312).[10] According to Chinese myths, flooding is both a natural human experience and symbolic of chaos in political order and disorder in social morality. Derk Bodde, a well-known sinologist in the field of Chinese mythology, makes the following observation when commenting on flood myths of China:

> Between the Chinese and the biblical or other Near Eastern flood stories there is the basic difference: in the Chinese version the flood is not inflicted as divine retribution for human sin, but simply epitomizes the condition of the world before there yet existed an organized human society. What is emphasized, therefore, is not the flood, as such. Rather it is the task of draining the land and rendering it fit for settled human life. In essence, therefore, the Chinese myth is one about the origins of civilization, in which a divine being, Yu, descends from on high, creates a habitable world for mankind, and founds the first civilized state, the perpetuation of which he ensures by marrying a human mortal. (1961: 402–403)

This statement is largely correct only if one confines China to what is inscribed in the ancient classical text and to the majority Han Chinese without any consideration for the literary tradition and oral transmission of the fifty-six ethnic minority groups. Obviously, the vast and diverse China with a long history and wide geographical extent defies any generalization as such. It is true that most of the Chinese Classics, with the intensive philosophical and political baptism of Confucianism, have truncated myths into fragments and historicized them through the process of euhemerization, adding an intensive didactic tone and moral teaching. This is also the case in the demythologizing and theologizing concern expressed in the so-called primeval history in Genesis 1–11. The themes of a destructive natural flood covering the land of China, and the emphasis on the flood control hero and his good work in providing a habitable place for humankind to live in, have contributed to an ideal Confucian governance model for builders of civilization. Flood control and management are acts of creation in terms of putting an order into chaos. Outside the Han Confucian circle, there have been many versions of flood stories with a great variety of colors and shades.

---

10. Cf. Fung 1952: 287.

Reading the BFN and Naxi Flood Myth Cross-Textually: Mythic Structure of Flood Stories and the Divine–Human Continuum

Flood stories are widespread in China beyond their literary representations in the Chinese Classics. In addition to the story of Yu, there is also the Nüwa flood myth, which narrates the collapse of the cosmos, when the whole earth relapses into primordial chaos as the celestial pillars that support the sky and separate heaven and earth topple. The result is a catastrophic destruction of creation with a huge deluge covering the earth.

Furthermore, in recent years, many more versions of flood myths have been identified by scholars in the fields of anthropology, religious studies, and folklore studies. A great flood is a common motif in quite a number of the ancient myths of the minority people in Yunnan (L. Miller 1994: 44). To date, according to Chen Jianxian (2005), 568 versions of flood myths among the fifty-six ethnic minority groups in China have been recorded in literary representations.[11] Most of these were orally transmitted from generation to generation before they were committed to writing in their present literary form. In many of China's minority racial groups, the first creation of humans is not perfect. The defects (e.g., having only one eye or vertical eyes) are to be made complete or made right in the course of time across a few generations. In some cases, the extraordinary features are gradually turned into normal ones, according to what is commonly seen in the present human beings. The genuine ancestor/ancestress of humanity is mostly sought in the survivor(s) of the flood.

The narratives in the flood myths of these minority nationalities employ eight different motifs. They are usually arranged in the following order:

1. Cause of the flood: divine anger or revenge.
2. Announcement of the flood.
3. Instruction to prepare means of escape. Hiding in a gourd or escaping into a leather/wooden drum is the most common.

---

11. In 2005, Chen, a scholar of Chinese flood myths, completed his doctoral dissertation, in which he claimed to have documented 568 versions of flood myths from all over China. However, just a decade before completing his dissertation, he had declared in one of his articles the existence of only 400 versions (J. X. Chen 1996). This increase in the number shows the rapid growth and progress in research on the minority ethnic communities in China in general and on flood myths in particular.

4. Sole survivor or a pair of survivors, male and female.
5. Taboo on incest in the case of brother–sister marriage or divine–human intermarriage when there is only one survivor.
6. Means to ensure divine approval.
7. Abnormality in the first birth and its disposal. This is especially elaborated in Miao traditions, in which the mother gives birth to a piece of flesh or a gourd. The flesh is then cut into smaller pieces that turn into human beings. In the case of the gourd, when it is cut open, out come the ancestors of various ethnic groups.
8. The origin of humanity—the birth of different races/tribes (Shi 1995).

From the structure of Chinese flood narratives, circulated mostly in the ethnic minority groups in the southwestern regions of Yunnan and especially among the Miao and Yao communities, marriage and birth of a new generation of humanity are the two constitutive motifs that concern the postdiluvian account. Most of these stories end with the issue of humanity's continuation through a sexual union of the twin survivors, usually a brother and sister, or intermarriage between the sole survivor and a divine being. There are various combinations of these two major motifs—human incest in reproduction of humanity, and divine–human intermarriage—in the new breed of the human race. In the case of divine–human marriage, the divine being is exclusively female, as the sole survivor is, without exception, a male. This point is significant and coincides with all cases of divine–human sexual intercourse in Chinese mythology and literary writings. The descent of a divine lady to the human world is much anticipated by the common folks.

Of the 568 myths collected, a total of 388 versions include the motif of incestuous marriage. The difficult decision for the incestuous union could only be made after clear signs, portents, and miracles from heaven. There are different means of obtaining the anticipated divine approval. Three of them are quite typical. First, the brother and sister each rolls down one of the two parts of a millstone from two opposite mountaintops respectively, and the two pieces should join together. The second common way is for the two persons to set up a fire on two opposite hills; the smoke from the two fires should cross and intermingle. The third interesting means is for the brother to throw a thread and the sister to cast a needle in the air from two different hilltops. The thread is expected to go through the eye of the needle. In all of the flood myths with sibling marriage, the requested divine signs are fulfilled, and humanity is reproduced from the brother–sister marriage.

The quest for the divine or miraculous approval adds interest to the story. The Chinese narrators do face up to the hard reality of admitting the inevitable consequence of marriage between the survivors in order to have the rebirth of the new human race. Incest is then forbidden beyond the first generation. The notion of all humanity coming out of the same family and the notion of a close kinship relationship are definitely affirmed.

In the flood stories of the majority Han people, there are 108 versions of marriage of a brother–sister pair, usually identified as Nüwa and Fuxi, the cosmic couple of fertility and the ancestral parents of humankind in Han China. They are not strangers to readers of Chinese Classics and Chinese art. The two names were first put together in the West Han Dynasty text known as *Huinanzi* (《淮南子》; Major 1993). In the archaeological excavations of Han tombs, there are graphic representations and drawings of the couple in copulation.

The second motif for the continuation of the human race after the flood is divine–human intermarriage. Thirty-six versions of such a marriage between the male survivor and the female heavenly daughter have circulated in areas at the border of Yunnan and Xichuan, in the southwest of China (J. X. Chen 2005: 75). They originate from the tribes of Naxi, Yi, and Pumi. The most fascinating and richly elaborated myth of origin in Naxi tradition is in the Dongba Classics, a literary work entitled *Genesis Account,* whose original Naxi name is *Chongbantu,* translated as "The Origin of the Generation (or Migration) of Humanity." It contains two major sections: creation and the great flood. The book represents the most outstanding literary creation of the Dongba literature and religious texts.[12] It has an account of the flood story protagonist's postdiluvian search for a wife in the realm of the divine, after failing attempts to reproduce human beings by other means. He goes to heaven to acquire a female nymph/immortal or a daughter of the Heavenly God in order to regenerate and repopulate the earth with human beings.

In China today, there are 250,000 Naxis. Most of them live in the southwestern region of Yunnan and Sichuan. They are believed to have migrated south from Tibet. The majority are located in the scenic mountainous area of

---

12. The full text, with pictographic representations, is found in Li Lin-ts'an 1957.

Lijiang Prefecture. They possess a written script with a combination of pictographic and syllabic systems, commonly referred to as the Dongba script ("Dongba" is the Naxi name for priests and ritual specialists who are able to read and write) (L. Miller 1994: 284–85). A sample of the script on the flood is reproduced in Figure 7.2.

Figure 7.2. Sample of the Dongba Script on the Flood

Source: Lincan et al. 1957: 29.

It is appropriate to present an outline of the Naxi Genesis for those who are not familiar with it:

In ancient times, heaven and earth were in chaos and the Yin (female) and Yang (male) were commingling; trees walked, stones talked—everything was jerking and moving. In the beginning there were three shadows of heaven and earth, and sun and moon. From the sunlight a white egg was formed and Gods[13] and humans were hatched. From the moonlight a black egg was formed and from it emerged various kinds of monsters. The nine brothers of the Heavenly Gods created heaven and the seven sisters of the earthly Gods created the earth . . . . All people came to build the holy mountain, to support firmly the sky above. When it came to the time of Congren Liwei, the tenth generation ancestor of humanity, brothers began to mate with sisters and as a result heaven and earth were contaminated. The Heavenly Gods sent a boar to flatten the cultivated land. Liwei's brothers caught the boar and also wounded the Heavenly Gods. Only Liwei helped

---

13. The author finds it appropriate to capitalize the word *God* or *Gods*, as it does not make enough sense only to honor the Judeo-Christian God and to reserve the word in capital letter for the monotheistic formulation only.

treat the wounds of the Female God and the Male God. So the Yang God taught him how to escape from the coming flood disaster by making a leather drum which would float on water. The flood subsequently covered the earth and only Liwei survived. Liwei could not find a companion. The Yang God asked him to marry the heavenly maid with horizontal eyes but Liwei married the pretty vertical-eye celestial nymph instead. They could only give birth to animals. Liwei again traversed over the land to search for a wife to reproduce humanity and he arrived at the intersection of white and black[14] and luckily met the daughter of the Heavenly God, Qinghui Pupu. Qinghui refused her father's arranged marriage to marry to Kele Kexing, the God of Rain and Hail. That is why she transformed herself into a crane and descended to earth. Liwei fell in love with her and rode on her wing to ascend to heaven in order to seek the consent of their marriage from Apu, the Heavenly God and the father of Qinghui. Apu tested Liwei with many difficult tasks, including cultivating, farming, and harvesting. With the assistance of Qinghui, Liwei met all the challenges in the allotted time. Apu still refused to give Liwei his daughter for marriage. Further he requested Liwei to hunt goats on rocky hills, catch fish, milk the tiger, and perform other dangerous tasks. Liwei succeeded in all of these and Apu was forced to allow his daughter to marry Liwei.

After their marriage, Liwei and Qinghui returned to the earth together with a heavenly dowry from Apu. On the way they experienced dangers one after another. Qinghui later gave birth to three sons who could not speak. After Liwei and Qinghui made a sacrifice to Apu the three sons then uttered in three different languages, respectively. They were the ancestors of the Tibetans, the Naxi, and Bai peoples. The sacrificial ceremony becomes the annual grand offering to heaven in January and the minor offering in July to the God of Rain and Hail. (Summarized from He and Yang 1992: 130–31)

From reading this outline, one immediately notices some similar motifs in the Naxi flood story and the BFN:[15] the flood in both stories was sent by

---

14. This literary work uses different color symbolisms, which cannot be adequately addressed within the scope of this paper.

15. The Bible story differs from its counterpart in giving details on testing whether the flood is indeed over (by sending out birds), and the promise of there never again being another great flood destroying all humankind. The rainbow stands as a sign of God's promise.

God and destroyed all creation; there was a means of escape (the ark and the leather drum); and sacrifice was instituted at the end of the flood as a thanksgiving ceremony. It is at the end of the Naxi Genesis book that the annual rite (in January) of sacrifice and offering to Heaven is instituted as an act of thanksgiving to Apu-Azhu, the Heavenly God and Goddess, who are the foremost Ancestor-Ancestress of the Naxi people. The names Apu and Azhu refer to the "Grandfather" and "Grandmother," respectively, in the Naxi language. They are the heavenly parents of Qinghui Pupu, the daughter of God who descended to the earth to marry Congren Liwei, the sole survivor of the flood, who is the ancestor, giving birth to the present generation of humankind. As divine grandparents, Apu and Azhu are to be worshipped and propitiated. Every year in July, there is another ceremony in reverence to a third heavenly deity, Xu, the Heavenly Uncle and God of Rain and Hail, who was originally engaged to Qinghui Pupu and should be pacified because the latter refused to marry him.

The contrast between the monotheistic orientation of BFN and the polytheistic background of the Naxi story is readily noted.

The Naxis are commonly known not only for their fascinating cultural traits, but also for their practice of matriarchy, especially the Mosuo branch of this ethnic group. Because human beings are descendants of the daughter of the Heavenly Parents, it is not surprising that the matriarchal and matrilineal connection of the Naxi people is highly respected and honored to this day (S. He 2007: 31).

In both stories, the flood stands as the dividing line between the first creation before the flood and the second creation from which we all are descended. In the BFN, Gen. 9:7 is taken as echoing Gen. 1:28, both using the same terminology "be fruitful and multiply." When one reads the BFN and the Naxi flood myth in parallel, a few motifs in the Bible stand out clearly against the contours of the latter story. Genesis 1–11 provides a totally uncompromising biblical conception of the strict boundary that divides the divine and the human. Claus Westermann (1984: 367) even attributes the sinfulness of humankind to an "overstepping [of] the bounds" between God and human." In commenting on Gen. 6:1-4, he takes the whole story as a punishment of the offense of bursting the bounds, which requires divine intervention: "There was once in place of v. 3 a direct intervention of God which punished the transgressors" (368).

It is precisely this biblical understanding of the unbridgeable gulf between God and human beings that constitutes the core of what sinfulness is all about when the desire to become divine is suppressed. In the religious world of the Chinese, on the contrary, both to the majority Han people of the plain and the ethnic minorities of mountains and valleys, the aspiration to become divine is not only endorsed, but also promoted. In the Naxi flood myth, the postdiluvian generation is precisely one that advocates the intermarriage between "the son of humankind" and "the daughter of the God." This will no doubt draw the attention of Chinese readers to the story in Gen. 6:1-4. Perhaps there is room to rethink whether the theme of punishment is intended for the original myth in Gen. 6:1-4, now truncated in its fragmented form[16] and presented theologically as punishment for humanity, with the denial of the permanent residing of the spirit of God in humanity, shortening human life to not exceeding 120 years of age. According to B. S. Childs (1960: 58), the divine–human intermarriage in Gen. 6:1-4 may be providing an explanation for the cause of the flood: "It serves as a plastic illustration of the increasing sinfulness of man before God."

As myth, the intermarriage between the "sons of God" and "the daughters of humankind" (Gen. 6:4) should function etiologically to provide an explanation for the birth of a special breed of human beings.[17] The existence of a sense of punishment for crossing the boundary of the divine and human realms will be very remote in the context of mythology. Furthermore, as noted by scholars, the problem of the punishment of humanity for an initiative taken by the sons of God(s) is extremely hard to justify. The present form of the myths in Genesis 1–11 has definitely been rewritten theologically, and Gen. 6:1-4 is now seen as functioning in giving reason for the flood in terms of the sin of crossing the divine–human boundary.

Contrary to some eminent scholars, I do not see from the text of Gen. 6:1-4 anything resembling punishment of sin of some sort. I would further suspect that the episode is not there to present the cause of the flood in the sin of divine–human union. Chinese readers with a parallel text from the Naxi's flood story may, most probably, read Gen. 6:1-4 as part of the flood

---

16. See Gerhard von Rad's discussion of the truncation (1972: 115).

17. The word for *nephilim* occurs only once elsewhere, in Num. 13:33. For the existence of giants, see also Deut. 2:20-21; Ezek. 32:21, 27; Amos 2:9.

tradition, explaining the regeneration of humanity through divine–human intermarriage.[18]

In reading the intermarriage as the conclusion to the Naxi flood myth, one may also be led to entertain the possibility of transposing Gen. 6:1-4 as a concluding motif of the flood narrative, placing it after 9:28-29: "After the flood Noah lived three hundred fifty years. All the days of Noah were nine hundred fifty years; and he died." At the present placement of 6:1-4, the delimitation of human life to 120 years (v. 3) will have difficulty in accounting for the long life span of Noah and his sons. Furthermore, the theme "When people began to multiply on the face of the ground, and daughters were born to them" (6:1) may also be an appropriate theme for the postdiluvian generation. This theme of multiplying and spreading over the earth is expressed further in Genesis 10 and 11.

As a matter of fact, the motifs of divine–human intermarriage (or incestuous union),[19] birth of descendants, language differentiation, migration to different regions, and the beginning of farming are concerns of the generations after the flood in the Naxi myth. Similar motifs are found in Genesis 9, 10, and 11. Genesis 9:18-27 is concerned with Noah, his three sons, and grandson Canaan, the son of Ham. The role and function of the passage have been cast in doubt by scholars: "strangely murky as to plot and character motivation, and ambiguous as to the very identity of the personae" (Brichto 1998: 167). The unnecessary and unanticipated phrase after the promise of the sign of the rainbow, "the sons of Noah who went out of the ark" (9:18), reveals the intended link between this story of Noah as a first-generation farmer of the soil after the flood (9:20: "Noah, the man of the soil was the first to plant a vineyard") and Noah as the hero of the flood. The three sons of Noah become important in the spread of humanity: "These three were the sons of Noah; and from these the whole world was peopled" (9:19). In Gen. 10:1, connections are also made with the flood: "These are the descendants of Noah's sons, Shem, Ham, and Japheth: children were born to them after the flood." In Gen. 10:8-9, the reference to the mighty and great men (though

---

18. Surely the present form of the BFN does not need to introduce intermarriage, as Noah's whole family survived the flood.

19. The nature of Ham's offense against Noah has been understood in terms of incest, sodomy, or castration. In any case, it is clear that "nakedness" is often taken metaphorically to refer to sexuality in Gen. 2–3 (Brichto 1998: 175).

the Hebrew words used are different) after the flood will also be explained better with 6:1-4 seen in the postflood context.

With the light shed by the mythic structure and perspective of the Naxi flood myth, the attention to the spreading of Noah's family on earth in the "Table of Nations" in Gen. 10:5, 20, 30-31 and the migration of the people in the Tower of Babel story in Genesis 11 should be treated as part of the flood tradition, as they are common themes expressed in flood myths,[20] although it is not possible to reconstruct the original context of the different mythical fragments in Genesis.

In sum, Gen. 6:1-4 will certainly be understood more appropriately as a postdiluvium mythic motif by Chinese audiences who read cross-textually with the Naxi Genesis. The challenge of the divine–human continuum to the reading of the Bible should also be taken up with some degree of seriousness.

Concluding Remarks

The intermarriage between the divine and the human has never been condemned in Chinese literature and mythology. On the contrary, it is the aspiration of humans to be united with the divine. The major difference in comparison with Gen. 6:1-4 is that the divine figure descending to earth is predominately female, whereas the human partner is male. In Chinese popular conceptions and philosophical thought, divine–human sexual union and intermarriage are taken as a special religious experience and a vision of union between heaven and humanity. This lends support to the quest for harmony and peace between heaven and earth.

Nüwa and Fuxi, the ancestral parents of humankind in the Han Chinese tradition, were both glorified and honored by their ascent to heaven. This provides an example of human beings being accredited divinity because of their outstanding achievement. According to the Chinese perception of

---

20. Contrasting with the Naxi narrative, the major differences in the Genesis account in Gen. 6:1-4 are firstly, the plural form in "the sons of God" and "the daughters of humans" and secondly, the gender of the divine agents being male in the Bible instead of female as in the Chinese tradition. Perhaps the third difference is the birth of a generation of giants, not the new normal human race. This very aspect of an extraordinary humanity also characterizes some of the other Chinese stories of postdiluvian divine–human intermarriage and brother–sister coupling.

human beings and divine beings, there is no sharp distinction between them. Popular beliefs have it that there are divine beings being sent by the heavenly court to earth to carry out tasks assigned by the heavenly court. These divine figures were incarnated in human forms and took up various human roles in ancient society. They participated in human affairs and intervened in historical processes. For example, according to Taoist traditions, Laozi was conceived of as being preexistent and descending into the world to assume different historical roles, to communicate the Taoist teachings orally, to deliver Taoist books to individuals, and to act as political adviser to ancient emperors (Lee 2005).

The other side of incarnation is the ascension of historical figures of great accomplishment to heaven, and the reward of immortality to significant sages or cultural heroes. Numerous books in the Taoist canon illustrate this point well.[21] Humans are canonized to become Gods and celestial beings. This characteristic of the Chinese religious world of a divine–human continuum presents a serious problem to Christian theological assertions in Judeo-Christian tradition regarding a monotheistic conception of the divine, in which God is perceived as the radically other and in sharp distinction from human beings. In this connection, the Adapa Story and Gilgamesh Epic of Mesopotamia, and the Genesis narratives of the Bible, maintain the same understanding of immortality being reserved for the Gods only (Jacobsen 1946: 210–11).

Traces of the interaction between the divine and human are, however, not entirely eliminated from the Bible. The descriptions of the coming down of the "sons of God" to earth to have mixed marriages with the "daughters of humanity" (Gen. 6:1-4), and the aspiration of human beings to ascend to the divine realm in the story of the Tower of Babel (11:1-9) are residues of the ancient beliefs, remaining after they were incorporated into a theological reshaping of the Genesis materials.

This insight about a divine–human continuum in Chinese religious belief and mythological representation will present a challenge to the Chinese reading of the Bible. Humanity's aspiration for immortality or divinity will help to detect the same human yearnings recorded in the tradition of

---

21. Ge Hong (葛洪)'s *Baopuzi* (《抱朴子》): The Book of the Master Who Embraces Simplicity) and *Fengshen Yanyi* (《封神演義》); The Creation of the Gods) are just two examples. *Feng Shen Yen I* has been translated into English by Gu Zhizhong (1992) (Li Fengmao 2004). For discussion of religious influences on Chinese folk stories, see Liu 1962.

the Genesis story. When the biblical materials are read cross-textually with Chinese resources, it is hoped that new light can be shed on the different layers of the biblical text, and that often-neglected features will be seen clearly against the contours created by the nonbiblical text being brought into the reading process.

CHAPTER 8

Unity and Scattering
Toward a Holistic Reading of Genesis 11:1-9 in the South African Context

Mark Rathbone

A Neocolonial Reading of Genesis 11:1-9: Colonization of the Afrikaner's Soul

Genesis 11:1-9 has a very important place in the history of South Africa. During the twentieth century, neocolonial readings of this text justified apartheid by giving priority to the scattering of the people gathered at Shinar.[1] This was formalized in the document *Human Relations and the South African Scene in the Light of Scripture,* compiled by the Dutch Reformed Church to biblically justify apartheid (Dutch Reformed Church [DRC] 1976: 16–18).[2]

In the document, Gen. 11:1-9 is read in the context of God's command that people must procreate, fill, and subdue the earth (Gen. 1:28; DRC 1976: 16). The building project at Shinar was in clear violation of God's command and resulted in the confusion of the people's language and their scattering. In this way, the scattering of the people secured the implementation of God's command. Therefore, the scattering has a double meaning as a "curse" and "blessing": "The progressive differentiation of humanity into

---

1. "Neocolonial" implies that these readings are rooted in the colonial history of South Africa. In this regard, racism and segregation can be traced back to Dutch colonialism of the seventeenth and eighteenth centuries. See Loubser 1987: 5.
2. The document served as a report at the Dutch Reformed Synod of 1975. It was accepted during the synod meeting and published a year later in 1976. In the document, the interpretation of Gen. 11:1-9 was the key biblical reference used to justify apartheid.

peoples and races involved not only a curse, but also a blessing, not only judgement on the sinful arrogance of the tower builders of Babel, but also an act of mercy whereby mankind is not only protected from destruction, but God's purpose with the creation of man is achieved" (DRC 1976: 18). The document regards the scattering of the people as a strategy of God to sustain God's creation ordinance through the continued segregation and dispersion of the people (17). This interpretation, in the context of the colonial history of South Africa in which segregation and racism were interwoven, provides a pretext for racial categorization and differentiation: "The diversity of races and peoples to which the confusion of tongues contributed, is an aspect of reality which God obviously intended for this dispensation. To deny this fact is to side with the tower builders" (18).

The implication of this reading was the moral justification of apartheid, resulting in the fact that the Afrikaner exploited the mineral resources of South Africa and controlled the land as a gift from God [sic]. However, this is where the irony starts, because the benefits of apartheid were at a price. The biblical justification of apartheid resulted in moral schizophrenia in the soul of the Afrikaner. It is here that my story starts.

The neocolonial reading of Gen. 11:1-9 by the Dutch Reformed Church filtered through the Afrikaner population, using the pulpits of the church and structures of the government. One of the most powerful structures was the education system. During those days, the intertwining of the Bible and education resulted in the Christian National education system. The problem is that reading the Bible through ideological lenses made it a mixed blessing. I still remember the day more than twenty-five years ago when my faith was shattered during a Bible class on Gen. 11:1-9. The teacher carefully explained that God scattered the people of Shinar because they disobeyed God's command to fill the earth. Then suddenly, implying a leap of faith, the teacher solemnly stated that because of the scattering of people at Shinar, God blessed the Afrikaner with this beautiful land (referring to South Africa). I raised my hand in naïveté to inquire about the logic of the teacher's argument. Without blinking an eye and in a stern tone of voice, she reminded me that God punishes those who question God's wisdom. That was the last time anyone dared to ask a question. Years later, I discovered Desmond Tutu's reading of Gen. 11:1-9, confirming my suspicions that the teacher's response to my question was informed by fear and ideological reasons.

An Anticolonial Reading of Genesis 11:1-9

Desmond Tutu (1983) responds to the interpretation of Gen. 11:1-9 in the *Human Relations* document by following an anticolonial reading.[3] Tutu reads the text in the context of the creation narrative by taking his point of departure from Gen. 1:26: "In view of the biblical storyteller in the first creation narrative, the climax is reached when God creates human beings, and the most important feature of that part of the story is that they are created in the image of God (Gen. 1:26). This is man's most important attribute. The Bible at this point makes no reference to racial, ethnic or biological characteristics" (Tutu 1983: 39–40). The rest of creation also reflects the same peace and unity that is present between people: "There is order and harmony. . . . Here we find God's *shalom*" (40). Sin disrupts this harmonious state of affairs. The rebellion of the people of Shinar against God (hubris), at the end of the prehistory of Israel, is a clear example of the devastating impact of sin (40). Therefore, "God confuses men's (*sic*) tongues so that they are unable to communicate (Gen. 11:7)" (40).

Desmond Tutu argues that this state of chaos is not the end of the biblical story. The story continues and finds its climax in act 2 through the Holy Spirit that unites "God's children of all races, colours, cultures, sexes and nationalities in one fellowship, thereby transcending all those barriers and distinctions humans often regard as overriding. This work is continued in the person of the Holy Spirit that brings diverse peoples into one fellowship" (43). In this regard, there are theological and moral flaws in the *Human Relations* document's justification of apartheid: "Apartheid contradicts the testimony of the Bible categorically. Whereas the Bible says God's intention for humankind and for His entire universe is harmony, peace, justice, wholeness, fellowship, apartheid says that human beings fundamentally are created for separation, disunity and alienation" (Tutu 1983: 40–41).

The Scattering/Unity Dichotomy

The readings of the *Human Relations* document and Desmond Tutu's commentary on Genesis 11:1-9 reveal a dichotomy between scattering and unity.

---

3. "Anticolonial" refers to a reading strategy that reverses the colonizer/colonized dichotomy, hence reading in solidarity with the colonized.

In the case of the former reading, Gen. 1:28 is the point of departure regarding the scattering as the fulfillment of God's command to scatter people over the earth. Contemporary scholarly readings of Gen. 11:1-9 (Van Wolde 2000; Wenham 1987: 245–46; and Brett 2000: 5–46) follow a similar argument that affirms the importance of cultural diversity and identity. The danger of these readings, as the history of South Africa clearly demonstrates, is that the incorporation of an ideological pretext can result in unjust forms of ethnocentrism.

The latter reading leans on Gen. 1:28, arguing that the scattering is the result of sin (hubris), but unity is restored through the work of the Holy Spirit. Claus Westermann (1984: 546–47) reaches the same conclusion as Tutu. The danger of these readings is that they may lead to cultural relativism. The legacy of British imperialism and its civilizing mission [sic] in South Africa requires vigilance to the dangers of unity at the expense of cultural identity. The problem with the previously mentioned readings is that they attempt to resolve the unity/scattering dichotomy by favoring a particular side of the dichotomy that may end in racism (in terms of the former reading) or cultural relativism (in terms of the latter).

Nonscholarly Readings of Genesis 11:1-9: Toward a Holistic Reading

During a study of nonscholarly readings of Gen. 11:1-9,[4] I stumbled upon an alternative interpretation that did not attempt to resolve the dichotomy but kept it in a critical tension (Rathbone 2006). The study focused on the readings of Bible study groups, African mythology, and a linocut by the artist Azaria Mbatha. Most of the Bible study groups consisted of white and black participants.

The majority of the participants in the Bible studies stated that the sin of the people at Shinar is their rebellion against God. African readers gave high priority to the unity of the people at Shinar. Unity is the primary

---

4. "Nonscholarly readings" refers to interpretations of text by readers who have not received formal education of the theories and methods of text interpretation. This is a theoretical term accenting the power imbalance between scholarly readings, informed by theory and methods, and nonscholarly readings, usually regarded as inferior or naive.

characteristic of humanity. One of the participants used the metaphor of a tree to explain his argument: "A tree has many branches but when a couple of branches are cut off, a day or two later, you will see that the tree is dying." On the surface it seems that these readings that focus on unity follow a similar argument to the reading by Desmond Tutu. But as the participants became more comfortable, deeper cultural aspects rose to the surface.

Many African participants highlighted the fact that the inhabitants of Shinar wanted to make names for themselves. A participant said, "People were made to be one, unified, but people want power to show how great they are. The people wanted to make a name for themselves. This destroys the unity among people." This reading reflects the important role that names play in African culture. During naming rituals, the ancestors are invoked to bless the child. At birth, the rite of *imbeleko/thari* introduces the baby to the living spirits of the ancestors that guide and protect the child. Thus, the African child grows up in an atmosphere of sharing, caring, and together-ness, rather than in the typically Western atmosphere of individualism and isolation (Ngada and Mofokeng 2001: 24). The attempt of people to make a name for themselves is a blatant disregard of their ancestors.

In Solomon Avorti's (1999) comparative reading of Gen. 11:1-9 and the "African Blue Bird Song," he argues that the people of Shinar's quest to make a name for themselves was an arrogant attempt to disregard their ances-tors and assert their independence. The ancestor cult is the most prominent aspect of African traditional religion—the heart of the African spirit world. The ancestors constitute the individual's connection to the community and the land. The main function of ancestors is that of protection, but when neglected, they unleash destructive powers (Anderson 1991: 79). This was confirmed by the following response of a participant: "The people became self-centred and wanted to control the land and resources. We just want to take. We do not think of others. We lack love." The land is not an entity to be controlled or owned. It belongs to the community and the ancestors; the land is sacred.

In the art of Azaria Mbatha, it is clear that the sin of the people is more than arrogance; it is also a disconnection from the ancestors themselves. In his 1979 depiction of the Tower of Babel (Figure 8.1), the mood is somber. The tower is constructed of two pillars moving vertically into the sky. At the crest, the pillars are splitting, representing the suspension of the building project. The homes of the people are dark and empty. The people are naked, scattered all over, and huddled in small groups. Parallel columns penetrate the top of the tower. The columns symbolize the disruption caused by the scattering and the separation of people. In the fields that surround the tower, a lonely, fully clothed man approaches an ancestor, who is witnessing the destruction of the tower.

Figure 8.1. Azaria Mbatha, *The Tower of Babel* **(1979)**

Reflecting on his depiction of *The Tower of Babel*, Mbatha states, "The African approaches his ancestors by working for them, carrying wood to prepare a festival for the ancestors. When Man began to aspire to higher things, his simple life no longer satisfied him. He left his simple mud huts behind, gave up his tradition and together with others he built a mighty tower many storeys high. But the tower cracked and broke in two. . . . The tower is destroyed. The huts are empty and dead. Humanity is naked and vulnerable, without shelter" (Eichel 1986: 15). Working the land is intertwined with the worship of ancestors, but technological advancement, or the vertical violence of humanity, disconnects people from the land, resulting in chaos. According to the African worldview, all "things are saturated with religious meaning. Because there is no distinction between sacred and secular, physical and spiritual—everything is at the same time 'sacred' and 'spiritual'. This 'everything' is all embracing, including people, events, nature, work—in fact, all facets of the African's life" (Anderson 1991: 75).

The sin of the people is their loss of connection with their tradition, primary identity, or the culture that connected them to the ancestors, the land, and each other. This is in direct contrast to Western metaphysics, which generally focuses on a static concept of being, whereas African philosophical thought is dynamic (Onyewuenyi 1991: 40). "Existence-in-relation sums up the African conception of life and reality. The African does not separate being from force as its attribute. Rather Africans speak, act and live as if for them beings were forces. . . . There is the divine force, terrestrial or celestial forces, human forces, and vegetable and other mineral forces" (40). The essentialist concept of separate beings that function in a disconnected cosmos is foreign to African thought: "The African thought holds that created beings preserve a bond one with another, an intimate ontological relationship" (41).

The African nonscholarly readings, informed by a holistic cultural matrix, maintain the scattering/unity dichotomy by affirming the importance of cultural identity and, at the same time, subscribing to unity. The scattering of people is the result of the disconnection between people, land, and God due to the loss of cultural identity. Unjust systems like apartheid consume the fabric of cosmological equilibrium, resulting in the universal yearning for balance to be established. According to a bishop of the African Initiated Church,[5] the delicate balance that permeated the cosmos is a function of the Holy Spirit or *moya* (a Sotho word that refers to the Spirit): "In everything our guide and our teacher is the Holy Spirit" (Ngada and Mofo-

---

5. One of the reasons for the establishment of the AIC is discontent of African people with Western culture and its essentialist worldview.

keng 2001: 23). *Moya* is the universal spirit of life that connects people, the land, and God. It is not only a function but also a methodological key to the interpretation of the Bible (Dube 1996).

Conclusion: Implications of a Holistic Reading for the Global Context

The holistic cultural matrix has three important methodological implications for reading of Genesis 11:1-9 in the global context:

1. The holistic worldview moves beyond classical Western essentialism that fragments and divides reality. Modern biblical interpretation incorporated this essentialist and rational worldview, resulting in the fragmentation and desacralization of the biblical text. A holistic reading places high priority on the unity and spiritual meaning of the text.

2. Classical colonialism resulted in the subjugation of non-Western peoples and exploitation of the land. Neocolonial ideologies like apartheid continued this trend. Currently, the effects of globalization, coupled with the influx of multinational companies and advances in scientific discoveries, are disconnecting people from the land, with disastrous consequences. Although science and technology advanced humanity, the price of disturbing the balance between people and nature is clear from ecological and meteorological disasters of recent times.

3. Unity in terms of a holistic worldview is a nonhierarchical concept, kept in balance by an awareness of cultural identity—an ethic of equality and justice. In other words, because people are connected, the exploitation of a single part results in the dislocation of the equilibrium of the whole. Congruently, this process is also an ethic of healing because disturbance of balance results in a yearning for the return of equilibrium.

CHAPTER 9

Vegetarian Ideology in Talmudic Literature and Traditional Biblical Exegesis

Yael Shemesh

Preface

Childhood memory no. 1: I'm five years old, and my father takes me to the supermarket in the big city. It's a big event for someone who grew up in a rural village. What a nice surprise awaits me there! Lots of silvery fish swimming in a big tub. I watch them, enthralled. Suddenly the vendor pulls out one of the fish I had just been smiling at and gives it a sharp blow on the head. My smile is replaced by bitter tears and cries of "Murderer, murderer!" much to my father's embarrassment. And that was how I first became aware of the connection between the animals I love so much and their bodies (their meat), which I had always enjoyed eating until then. The trauma turned me into a vegetarian overnight.

During my first seven years as a vegetarian, I stayed "in the closet" to the extent possible. Although my dear mother assured me that there were other vegetarians in the world ("Yes, yes, even here in Israel!"), I never met one, and I was embarrassed and even ashamed by the difference between myself and others. At age twelve, I met "my first vegetarian," as I gratefully called her to myself (she will never know the role she played in my life!)—a total stranger who unabashedly proclaimed herself a vegetarian. Only then did I start shedding my shame and embarrassment about my vegetarianism, come out of the closet, and speak (and, later, write) in favor of vegetarianism and, later on, of veganism.

Childhood memory no. 2: I'm in second grade (if I'm not mistaken), fascinated by the stories from Genesis we have just started studying. The teacher tells us the story of the binding of Isaac (Genesis 22).[1] Isaac has been saved in the nick of time and will not be sacrificed. Abraham looks up and sees a ram caught in the thicket. "And what do you think that Abraham is going to do now, children?" asks the teacher. Most of us are silent. A few clever pupils shout excitedly, "He'll sacrifice him!" I shout, just as excitedly, "He'll let him go!" You can imagine my humiliation—and, even worse, deep disappointment—when I learn that God, Abraham, and the biblical story do not adhere to my moral code. Along with the embarrassment, perhaps even then I was starting to be aware that how we read Scripture is affected by who we are, by our life stories and psyches, which accompany every act of exegesis.

Despite my disappointment at my first encounter with the story of the binding of Isaac and its protagonists, when I fight for animal rights today, I prefer to emphasize the positive side of the traditional Jewish attitude toward animals. I do not claim that this is the only correct strategy, but I am convinced that in my case, as a religious person, it is more appropriate for me and also more effective in my contacts with influential figures from the religious world. When I am lobbying rabbis or religious members of the Knesset (the Israeli parliament) on various issues connected with animal rights or welfare, I find this approach to be of greater use.

I was moved to write "Vegetarian Ideology in Talmudic Literature and Traditional Biblical Exegesis" because this is such a large part of who I am. The article originally appeared in fuller form, but without this preface, in the *Review of Rabbinic Judaism* 9 (2006): 141–66.

---

1. Biblical passages are rendered on the basis of the RSV and/or the New JPS, modified as best seems to suit the sense. Talmudic passages are rendered on the basis of the Soncino translation, again modified where necessary. In the interest of consistency, biblical and talmudic quotations embedded in passages from previously published translations of commentators quoted here have been rendered as they appear in the present chapter, rather than as they appear in the translation cited. I would like to thank Prof. Athalya Brenner for her helpful comments and suggestions.

It is quite impossible to imagine that the Lord of all works, Who has compassion for all His creatures, Blessed be He, would enact an eternal law in his "very good" creation so that the human race can survive only by transgressing its moral sensibilities and shedding blood, even if only the blood of animals. (Kook 1983: 8)

Let me make it plain at the outset that Judaism is not a vegetarian religion (A. Cohen 1981; Sliw 1993).[2] Many rabbinic texts display a favorable attitude toward the consumption of meat, which they consider to be a satisfying and wholesome food. In addition, eating fish and meat on the Sabbath and festivals is deemed to be an appropriate way to honor those sacred days (A. Cohen 1981: 40–43; Schochet 1984: 168–75). Nevertheless, in recent years, many works have been published that try to demonstrate that, in the modern world, meat eating is incompatible with Jewish values. Various justifications of this view are advanced, of which the most important are the pain caused to animals by the modern food industry, the ecological damage caused by the meat-packing industry, and the health hazards associated with the consumption of meat—hazards we are aware of today but that were unknown in the past (for example, Kalechofsky 1995; 1998; Schwartz 1988). Even though I accept these arguments—especially that about causing pain to animals—my aim in the present article is not to offer halakhic or metahalakhic arguments in favor of vegetarianism, but to extract from the talmudic literature and the traditional commentators those voices that provide support for vegetarian ideology.

Before I begin, however, it is important to note the widespread contemporary consensus that there is no such thing as objective, neutral, and totally unbiased exegesis (for example, Eagleton 1996).[3] As Danna Nolan Fewell (1987: 77) asserts, the very choice of a research topic is the result of subjective factors. The present article, too, was not written from an "objective" or "neutral" standpoint, but out of emotional engagement with its theme. As a vegetarian since childhood and a vegan since December 1993, on the one hand, and as a believing and observant Jew, who teaches Bible at the religiously affiliated Bar-Ilan University, on the other hand, I want to see

---

2. Sliw (1993: 27) notes, inter alia, that as long as the temple stood, it was impossible to be a vegetarian, because of the obligation to eat of the Paschal lamb.

3. For the application of this realization to biblical criticism, see, for example, Fewell 1987: 80–81; Exum 1993: 12; Greenstein 1999: 211–12.

whether it is possible to build a bridge, however flimsy, between these two essential elements in my life. You might say that I am trying to do for the vegetarian party what religious feminist scholars like Phyllis Trible have done for feminist ideology, trying to bring distant realms—their religious faith and their feminism—closer together.[4]

My ideology clearly influenced my choice of topic and decision to present one side of the coin, the more subversive and lesser-known one—the support for vegetarianism in the talmudic literature and traditional commentaries. Still, I have endeavored—I hope, successfully—not to distort the texts and not to allow my ideological fervor to win out over intellectual honesty.

Biblical scholarship related to ecology has flourished in recent years, as attested by the *Earth Bible* series, edited by Norman C. Habel (2000),[5] and many other studies. But this literature focuses on Mother Earth or nature and on balanced ecology in general. The suffering of individual animals, animal rights, and a fortiori the issue of vegetarianism are hardly mentioned by scholars of the Bible, the Talmud, and Jewish philosophy, nor by their Christian counterparts.[6] Such issues seem to be expressed almost exclusively in the publications of animal rights organizations (see Kalechofsky 1995; 1998; Schwartz 1988). As John Olley (2000: 131) notes, "Animals can rightly feel slighted by the lack of attention they receive from commentators." Even scholars who do raise questions related to animal welfare generally do not favor vegetarianism. For example, W. Sibley Towner (1996), one of the few who see the idyllic picture in Isaiah 11 as an ethical demand about how we treat the environment, maintains, "Whatever the Bible may say about the future of the natural order of which we are a part, we have to accept the biological fact that until life on earth ceases altogether, nature will prey upon itself. *People will participate, too, because we have to eat*" (30–31; italics added).

In the present article, I would like to fill in the lacuna concerning the vegetarian idea in classical Jewish texts. I will show that vegetarian ideology was not alien to the Sages and the traditional commentators, and that voices

---

4. See, for example, Trible's pioneering and trailblazing article (Trible 1973).
5. Five volumes are available: an introductory volume and volumes on Genesis, Wisdom traditions, Psalms and the prophets, and the New Testament. For further details on the Earth Bible Project, see http://www.webofcreation.org/Earthbible/earthbible.html.
6. See Webb's (1996: 239) argument, directed at Christian theologians, about their disregard for the suffering of individual animals.

in these texts can be invoked to support it. Let me make clear that I do not deal here with the more general and important idea of not causing pain to animals or of animal welfare, which is dealt with at length in talmudic literature and by the traditional commentators—some of their statements are astonishingly forceful and even radical[7]—but only with direct references to vegetarianism, as it existed in the past, at the dawn of humankind, its feasibility in the present (of the commentator), and its restoration in the future—at the End of Days.

The Past: Belief in a Primeval Vegetarian Age

"Adam Was Not Permitted to Eat Meat"

The prevalent opinion among talmudic sages and the traditional commentators is that the ten antediluvian generations, from Adam to Noah, were vegetarians. Only after the flood did the Lord permit human beings to eat meat:

> Rav Judah said in Rav's name: Adam was not permitted to eat meat, for it is written, "[See, I give you every seed-bearing plant . . . ;] they shall be yours for food, and to all the animals on land" (Gen. 1:29–30), implying, but the beasts of the earth shall not be for you. But with the advent of the sons of Noah, it was permitted, for it is said, "[Every moving thing that lives shall be food for you;] and as I gave you the green plants, I give you everything" (Gen. 9:3). (*Babylonian Talmud*, Sanhedrin 59b)

Something similar is stated in *Genesis Rabbah:*

> "Every moving thing that lives shall be food for you. . . . Only you shall not eat flesh with its life, that is, its blood" (Gen. 9:3-4). R. Jose b. R. Avin said in R. Johanan's name: Adam, to whom flesh to satisfy his appetite was not permitted, was not admonished against a limb torn from the living animal. But the children of Noah, to whom flesh to satisfy their appetite was permitted, were admonished against eating a limb torn from the living animal. (*Genesis Rabbah* 34:13 [Freedman and Simon 1939: 1:278])

---

7. I have dealt with this in Shemesh 2008.

Most classical commentators followed in this vein.[8] The Babylonian Talmud (Sanhedrin 59b) explains the injunction "Have dominion over the fish of the sea and over the birds of the air and over every living thing that moves upon the earth" (Gen. 1:28), which seems to be incompatible with primeval vegetarianism, as license to use animals to perform work, not to eat them. The text there even offers rather far-fetched examples of useful labor done by fish and birds.

Nachmanides, in his commentary on Gen. 1:29, invokes the traits shared by human beings and animals to explain the antediluvian ban on the consumption of meat:

> However, meat was not permitted to them until the time of "sons of Noah," as is the opinion of our Rabbis. And this is the plain meaning of the verse. The reason for this [prohibition of eating meat] was that creatures possessing a moving soul have a certain superiority as regards their soul, resembling in a way those who possess the rational soul: they have the power of choice affecting their welfare and their food, and they flee from pain and death. And Scripture says: "Who knows whether the spirit of man goes upward and the spirit of the beast goes down to the earth?" (Eccles. 3:21) (Chavel 1971: 1:57)

The question of antediluvian vegetarianism is bound up with the question of why the animals were created. The dominant Jewish view is that they were created to serve human beings, as stated by R. Simeon ben Eleazar: "Were they not created for naught else but to serve me?" (*Mishnah*, Qiddushin 4:14 [trans. Danby] et passim). Nevertheless, some other passages hold that the animals were not created to be eaten by human beings. For example:

> "God said, 'See, I give you every seed-bearing plant that is upon all the earth'" (Gen. 1:29). From this you learn that Adam was not permitted to eat meat, because the Holy One Blessed be He did not create His creatures to die—for had Adam not sinned no being would die. Should you ask why Adam was not permitted to eat meat after he had

---

8. See the commentaries by Rashi (Rosenbaum and Silbermann 1973: 1:37), Rashbam (Cohen M. 1997: 30), Abraham Ibn Ezra (Strickman and Silver 1988: 47), David Kimhi (Cohen M. 1997), and Nachmanides (Chavel 1971: 1:56–57) on Gen. 1:29–30; Midrash *Lekah Tov* (Buber 1960 1:24) on Gen. 9:3, and Sforno (Gottlieb 1980: 232) on Lev. 17:4. However, Gersonides (Braner and Freiman 1993: 1:72–73) and S. D. Luzzatto (Klein 1998: 27) reject the idea that Adam was a vegetarian.

transgressed—[the answer is that] this would be a case of a transgressor emerging rewarded. (*Midrash Aggadah* [ed. Buber] for Gen. 1:29, s.v. "God said")

This is also the view of Rabbi Löw, who goes further than the midrash and holds that the animals were created for their own sake:

> Everything, like grasses and fruits, were created for the sake of animals, which are flesh, for He gave them everything to eat, as the verse states, "I give you" etc. From this you see that everything else was created for the animals, while the animals were created in the world for their own sake. Even though animals serve as food for human beings, this was not the case when the world was created, for human beings were not permitted to kill an animal and eat it until the time of Noah. (Löw 1972: 23)

Why Were Human Beings Permitted to Eat Meat after the Flood?

Various opinions are offered as to why human beings were permitted to eat meat after the flood—some of them complementary, others mutually contradictory. R. Joseph Bechor-Shor (M. Cohen 1997: 99), in his commentary on Gen. 9:3 (under "as I gave you the green plants, I give you everything"), explains, "Because they were saved in the ark that you made and their salvation came through you, now they are yours to do with as you like."[9] This explanation is also advanced by Meir Malbim (1809–1879), in his commentary on Gen. 9:3, along with two other explanations. The first is that human physiology and the nature of vegetable foods changed after the flood: "In Adam's time human bodies were strong and fruits had not yet been corrupted and could nourish human beings like meat does. But after the flood foodstuffs deteriorated and human beings were made ready to spread to the corners of the earth and far islands, which from that time became cold and hot, so meat was needed to keep them healthy"[10] (Malbim 2008: 146). According to the second explanation, as long as human beings were only of the animate degree, they were not permitted to consume animals, which are of the same degree. Only after the flood, when they ascended to the degree of rational being (*medabber*), were they permitted to eat the flesh of animals—a

---

9. See also David Kimhi (M. Cohen 1997: 1) on Gen. 9:4 and Nachmanides (Chavel 1971: 1:57; 3:239) on Gen. 1:29 and Lev. 17:11.
10. So also Samson Raphael Hirsch (1971: 1:37) on Gen. 1:29-30.

license that benefits the animals consumed as well: "Just as there is no injustice if animals eat plants, for the latter are thus elevated by being converted into animal bodies, so there is no injustice if rational beings eat animals, by which the latter are elevated and converted into the body of a rational creature, as the verse states, 'as I gave you the green plants, I give you everything (Gen. 9:3)'" (ibid). Rabbi Shlomo Ephraim Luntshitz (1545/50–1619) offers a similar explanation in his *Keli yaqar* on Gen. 9:2: "The reason that Adam was not permitted to eat meat is that all uneducated persons ('*ammei ha-'aretz*) are forbidden to eat meat; but Noah, who studied the Torah, was permitted to do so" (Rabinovitch 2001: 1:59).[11] On a different track, S. D. Luzzatto (one of the few who do not believe in an antediluvian vegetarian age) holds that it was actually the sins of the flood generation that resulted in the explicit license to eat meat, which, he asserts, had been implicit before then (his commentary on Gen. 1:30 [Klein 1998:28]). Like Luzzatto, Rabbi A. I. Kook (1865–1935) thought the decline of the generations and moral weakness of the human race were the sources of the permission granted it to consume meat; unlike Luzzatto, however, Kook did believe in antediluvian vegetarianism.[12]

Saadia Gaon, in his commentary on Gen. 1:29, ignores the moral dimension but offers a pragmatic rationale for the ban on meat eating before the flood. According to him, this prohibition, which applied to both human beings and animals, was only temporary, because in that age, the population of each species was very small, and "had they eaten one another all of them would have become extinct. Consequently He [God] deferred [the permission to eat meat] until they had multiplied, and allowed them to do so only then" (Zucker 1984: 260).[13] (Saadia ignores the fact that the population number of each animal species in the generations before the flood had certainly far exceeded the number that left the ark with Noah and his family.)

---

11. So, too, Isaac b. Arama (1961: §41) (commentary on the weekly portion of *Beshalah*). He explains that the sect that was given permission to eat meat in Noah's time was on a higher spiritual level than the animals.

12. For the decline of the generations as the reason for meat eating, see Kook 1983: 13.

13. David Kimhi (M. Cohen 1996: 92) offers a similar view in his commentary on Isa. 11:6, although he advances a different opinion in his commentary on Gen. 1:29 (M. Cohen 1997: 31): meat eating was not allowed because the Lord knew that Noah would later save the animals from the flood and wanted a way to reward him for his exertions—since God does not detract from the reward of any creature.

Approaching the matter from a different angle, Isaac Abravanel on Gen. 9:3 advances a pragmatic reason for the new permission to eat meat, replacing the earlier ban: the original divine intention was that human beings be vegetarians. But the flood devastated the flora, so Noah and his sons could not survive on plants alone: "Had they waited to eat until they sowed fields and planted vineyards they would have died of hunger. So He permitted them to eat meat" (Abravanel 1964: 1:163).

Manna: A Divine Attempt to Reinstitute a Vegetarian Diet for the Israelites

An inference that can be drawn from Abravanel's commentary is that the Lord wanted to reinstitute vegetarianism for the Israelites only, after delivering them from Egypt. In his commentary on Exod. 16:4, he asks why the Lord provided the Israelites with "bread from the sky" (that is, manna) rather than meat, and replies:

> The Holy One Blessed be He told Moses: Meat is not an essential food, but is rather a matter of gluttony, filling the belly, and an overwhelming craving. In addition, meat generates maleficent and cruel blood in human beings. This is why you find that the predatory carnivorous beasts and birds are cruel and bad. But sheep and cattle, chickens, turtledoves, and doves, which live on the grass of the field, have no cruelty or wickedness. This is why the prophet foresaw that at the time of the future redemption, "the lion, like the ox, shall eat straw" (Isa. 11:7; also 65:25). He explained the reason when he said that "they shall not hurt or destroy . . ." (Isa. 11:9; also 65:25). This is why the Holy One Blessed be He did not tell Moses to give meat to the Israelites, but only bread, which is a fitting and essential food for the human constitution. This is what is meant by "I will rain down bread for you from the sky" (Exod. 16:4).[14] (Abravanel 1964: 2: 133–34)

---

14. See also his commentary on Isaiah 11:6-7, concerning meat's baneful influence on the soul. Before Abravanel this argument had been advanced by the philosopher Joseph Albo (ca. 1380–1444). His explanation for the belated permission to eat meat is that "the Torah spoke only to ward off the evil inclination, just as it permitted them the beautiful captive in the same fashion." As for the spiritual impact of meat eating on the human soul, he cautions, "in addition to the fact that killing animals partakes of cruelty, wrath, anger, and teaching human beings the bad trait of shedding blood for nothing, eating the flesh of some animals makes the soul dense, foul, and dull" (*Sefer ha-Iqqarim* 3.15).

Abravanel's interpretation seems to have been influenced by that of Isaac Arama (ca. 1420–1494), in his *'Aqedat Yitzhak* on the weekly portion of *Beshalah.* Arama argues that the divine plan was for the Israelites to be satisfied with the manna, which is the food best suited to the human body and intellect. The people, however, longed for the fleshpots of Egypt, where they could sate themselves on bread (Exod. 16:3). The Lord initially responded with bread only, and not meat, as we read: "I will rain down bread for you from the sky" (Exod. 16:4). This was because God wanted them to rise to the loftiest spiritual level, that of those who opt for an ascetic life and refrain from eating meat (Arama 1961: §41).[15]

With regard to the fact that meat was not essential for the nourishment of the Israelites in the wilderness, Samson Raphael Hirsch, in his commentary on Num. 11:13, asserts that Moses was angered by the people's demand for meat, not only because they were asking for something he clearly could not provide, but also because "what they are asking for is something dispensable and superfluous." And, he adds, "just because the demand was for something quite dispensable and superfluous, neither Moses nor the people could expect that God would grant it in some miraculous manner" (Hirsch 1971: 4:176).

The Mekhilta (the halakhic midrash to the Book of Exodus) draws a distinction between the manna and quail given to the Israelites:

> "And in the morning . . . you shall know": From this you learn that the manna was given to Israel with bright countenance. The quail, because they asked for it out of full stomach, was given to them with a frowning countenance. But the manna which they were justified in asking, was given to them with a bright countenance. (Lauterbach 1933: 2:105 [tractate *vayassa'*, chap. 3])[16]

The sages used the reference to the time of day—morning versus evening—to support a symbolic statement about the Lord's positive attitude toward eating manna and negative attitude toward eating meat.

---

15. For an abridged English version, see Munk 2001: 1:386.

16. See also Rashi (Rosenbaum and Silbermann 1973: 2:82), Nachmanides (Chavel 1971: 2:223–24), and Midrash *Sekhel Tov* (Buber 1900: 212) on Exod. 16:7. The assertion that meat was given to the Israelites with a "frowning countenance" is based on the verse "And Moses said, 'When the Lord gives you in the evening flesh to eat and in the morning bread to the full'" (Exod. 16:8).

The Present: Rabbis' and Commentators' Reservations about Meat Eating

In general, the talmudic sages and traditional commentators took meat eating for granted. None of them preaches or recommends that their flock or readers switch to a vegetarian regimen.

Nevertheless, talmudic literature and the traditional commentators do present the idea of limiting the consumption of meat and even include statements that encourage vegetarianism or indicate reservations about killing animals. Both the talmudic sages and the traditional commentators were familiar with the phenomenon of vegetarianism; one commentator—Joseph Ibn Kaspi—reports that he himself adopted such a diet (see page 119 below).

Hunting

The midrash views Nimrod, of whom the Bible reports that "he was the first on earth to be a mighty man. He was a mighty hunter before the Lord" (Gen. 10:8-9), with extreme disfavor.[17] According to *Midrash Aggadah* (ed. Buber) on Gen. 10:8, Nimrod was the first person to eat meat: "Before Nimrod human beings did not eat meat, until Nimrod came and hunted and ate them. This is why it says that 'he began to be a [that is, was the first] mighty hunter.'" The midrash's disapproval of the first hunter is evident from what comes next: "'He was a mighty hunter': This means that he hunted men [*beriyot*] and killed them. 'Before the Lord': This means that he knew his Master and intended to rebel against him: 'He was a mighty hunter before the Lord': This refers to Esau, who is called 'a skilful hunter' (Gen. 25:27)." The midrash evidently draws a link between harming animals and harming human beings: someone who overcame the basic human revulsion at shedding the blood of animals is a villain who also hunts and kills human beings. As for "before the Lord," which might be interpreted as favorable, the midrash reads it negatively: even though he knows the Lord, Nimrod intends to rebel against Him.

Slaughtering Animals for Food

Even ritual slaughterers, who do their job not for pleasure but to satisfy the community's need for kosher meat, receive the back of the hand in the

---

17. See, for example, *Genesis Rabbah* 37:2.

dictum reported by Rabbi Judah in the name of Abba Guria: "The worthiest of butchers [that is, ritual slaughterers] is Amaleq's partner."[18] The underlying assumption seems to be that a person who can engage in this profession, which involves killing, is contaminated by cruelty, the hallmark trait of Amaleq.

This, at least, is how this passage is understood by Nachmanides, who quotes it approvingly in his commentary on the precept of sending away the mother bird. He refers to the educational rationale of all the precepts associated with animals, notably the ban on slaughtering an animal and its offspring on the same day (Lev. 22:28) and that of taking both the mother bird and her fledglings (Deut. 22:6):

> But the reason for the prohibition is to teach us the trait of compassion and that we should not be cruel, for cruelty proliferates in man's soul as it is known that butchers, those who slaughter large oxen and asses, are men of blood; they that slaughter men, are extremely cruel. It is on account of this [cruelty] that the Rabbis have said: "The worthiest of butchers is Amaleq's partner" (*Babylonian Talmud*, Qiddushin 82a). Chavel 1971: 5:271)

Eating Meat

Disapproval of those who gorge themselves on meat and praise for those who derive the bulk of their nourishment from the plant kingdom may underlie the talmudic explanation of the verse "The curse of the Lord is on the house of the wicked, but He blesses the abode of the righteous" (Prov. 3:33):

> R. Johanan said: What is meant by, "The curse of the Lord is on the house of the wicked: but He blesses the abode of the righteous"? "The curse of the Lord is on the house of the wicked" refers to Pekah the son of Ramaliah, who ate forty se'ahs of young birds as a [mere] dessert; "but He blesses the abode of the righteous" applies to Hezekiah, king of Judah, who ate [but] a litra of vegetables for his [entire] meal. (*Babylonian Talmud*, Sanhedrin 94b)

---

18. *Mishnah*, Qiddushin 4:14 (*Babylonian Talmud*, Qiddushin 82a); *Jerusalem Talmud*, Qiddushin 4:11 (65b); *Soferim* 15:7. Simoons (1994: 313) mentions various societies in which butchers were relegated to an inferior caste and sometimes even deemed untouchables.

The talmudic sages believed that one should limit the consumption of meat, although they seem to have been driven by economic rather than ethical motives (Hammer 1986: 128). This idea is expanded in tractate *Hullin* 84a. According to the latter source, there are two conditions for eating meat: the economic wherewithal and a genuine appetite for it. But even when these conditions exist, one should not be a glutton.

Joseph Ibn Kaspi viewed animals as our "nearest genus" and "brothers" (Last 1905: 35), because human beings and animals both belong to the animal kingdom. His reservations about meat eating are evident in what he writes about the precept of sending away the mother bird (Deut. 22:6) and reference to the original divine intention that human beings adhere to a vegetarian diet:

> "Should your soul yearn to eat meat": that we not kill them without need, but only for food, because it is human nature to have an appetite for meat. *But the authentic intention is that we eat no meat and make do with plants.* Accordingly after Creation we were permitted only the grasses of the field. Only after the Flood did the consumption of animals spread, *which is as if we were to eat our parents, because they are our nearest genus.* This is why the Torah commanded us to have compassion for them, as we remember the precept "it and its offspring" (Lev. 22:28) and "do not seethe a kid in its mother's milk" (Exod. 23:19 et passim), and "should you encounter a bird's nest" (Deut. 22:6). *If the Torah could restrict us more it would do so.* But because our proximity to the animal type is less than our proximity to the rational type, He diminished and minimized the precepts out of his His love and His compassion. (Last 1906: 294; italics added)

The practical nutritional implications of Ibn Kaspi's notion of the closeness between man, the rational being, and the lower animals are slight, given that he also viewed plants as brothers and companions, because animals, too, belong to the vegetative kind (Last 1905: 35).[19] In fact, Ibn Kaspi alleges an economic rather than an ethical rationale for his own decision to stop eating meat. In a rather amusing account (32–33), he describes how his diet was influenced by the biblical story of Elijah. After stating his view that a scholar

---

19. At the same time, as he explains, the proximity between human beings and plants is less than that between human beings and animals. Consequently, human beings have less of a duty to plants than to animals.

must support himself financially and not depend on charity, he tells what happened to him. Formerly, he had believed that it was appropriate for those pursuing health to eat bread and meat every morning and evening, this being the regime on which Elijah was maintained by the ravens when he hid in Wadi Kerith (1 Kings 17:6). But two years later, when his economic situation had deteriorated, he reviewed his expenses, including those on food. When he went back to the story of Elijah, he was delighted to discover that after the prophet left Wadi Kerith, where he had lived on bread and meat, he resided, at God's command, in the house of the widow of Zarefath, where he ate only bread cooked in oil (1 Kings 17:11).

The talmudic sages saw moderation in the consumption of meat as a virtue in which one should educate one's children: "The Torah teaches a rule of conduct that a parent should not accustom his son to flesh and wine" (*Babylonian Talmud*, Hullin 84a). It is no accident that one of the traits of the wayward and rebellious son, according to the sages, is that he consumes meat and wine gluttonously (*Mishnah*, Sanhedrin 8.2; *Babylonian Talmud*, Sanhedrin 70a; see Rashi (Rosenbaum and Silbermann 1973: 5:107) on Deut. 21:18).

Nachmanides, in his commentary on Lev. 19:2, referring to the injunction "you shall be holy," notes that one may be "a sordid person within the permissible realm of the Torah" *(naval bi-rshut ha-Torah)* and do unseemly things, indulging to excess in sexual intercourse, drinking wine, and eating meat, and excusing himself by saying that these acts are not forbidden by the Torah. But the appropriate and seemly path, according to Nachmanides, is to be abstemious in all these matters (Chavel 1971: 3:282–83).

The Tanhuma reads "and you say, 'I will eat flesh'" as a directive to limit one's consumption of meat: "R. Eliezer b. R. Joshua said, 'hence you learn that a person should not buy a pound of meat until he consults with his household" (*Midrash Tanhuma* [Warsaw], Re'eh, §6). In Rabbi Ishmael's opinion, the Israelites in the wilderness were forbidden to eat meat at will, unless they first offered the animal as a sacrifice in the sanctuary (*Babylonian Talmud*, Hullin 16b). A restriction of another sort, which does not relate to the quantity eaten or the period during which the consumption of the flesh of nonsacrificial animals was permitted or forbidden, but seeks rather to exclude an entire class from eating meat, is the opinion that "an *'am ha-'aretz* [uneducated person] may not eat the flesh of cattle, for it is said, 'This is the law [Torah] of the beast and of the fowl' (Lev. 11:46): whoever engages in [the study of] the Torah may eat the flesh of beast and fowl, but he who does not engage in [the study of] the Torah may not eat the flesh of beast and fowl" (*Babylonian Talmud*, Pesachim 49b). The conventional explanation is that an uneducated person is not proficient in the regulations that govern ritual slaughter; the ban on eating meat is intended to prevent the person from sinning. But Abravanel (1964: 1:70), in his commentary on Gen. 1:26, suggests another reason: "The sages held that an uneducated person is forbidden to eat meat, and this is not astonishing, since he is in no way superior to the animals and it is not appropriate that someone who is like them rule over them."

As already noted, Abravanel (1964: 2:133) believes, "Meat is not an essential food, but is rather a matter of gluttony, filling the belly, and an overwhelming craving. In addition, meat generates maleficent and cruel blood in human beings" (on Exod. 16:4). Moreover, in his commentary on Isa. 11:6–7, describing the Lord's apprehension when he permitted human beings to eat meat, Abravanel (1979: 92) establishes a cause-and-effect relationship between eating the flesh of animals and murdering human beings: "When the Holy One Blessed be He gave Noah and his sons permission to eat meat He said, 'for your lifeblood I will surely require a reckoning' (Gen. 9:5), because of His apprehension that the cruelty and malevolence that meat eating would generate in them would lead them to start killing one another."

Abraham Ibn Ezra (1089–1164) saw abstinence from meat as a virtue— not for moral reasons, but as part of his view of the virtue of ascetic separation from material comforts.[20] In his philosophical work, *Sefer Yesod mora' ve-sod ha-Torah* (2.12), he wrote: "There is no doubt that one who fasts and keeps himself from eating meat, as Daniel did, will receive a greater reward from God" (Cohen and Simon 2007: 107–8).[21]

Rabbi Isaac Arama, too, saw avoiding meat as a virtue and a lofty ideal, although he believed that such a diet was appropriate only for the elite few. In Arama's view, the human race is divided into three degrees. The lowest degree consists of the uneducated and ignorant, whose rational faculty

20. On this, see Cohen and Simon 2007: index, s.v. "Nazaritism and Asceticism."
21. See Strickman 1995: 54.

is weak. Of them, the talmudic sages said, "An uneducated person ('am ha-'aretz) may not eat meat" (Babylonian Talmud, Pesachim 49b). Arama explains that this is because the rank of the eater and eaten would be the same: because every creature is nourished by creatures of an inferior rank, the unlearned are not permitted to feed on what is essentially of their same degree. The intermediate degree consists of persons whose rational faculty does not rise above the mundane. Because they are on a higher level than the animals, they received permission to eat meat, as in the time of Noah. The highest degree consists of the elite few who do not need to eat meat because their intellect is so developed that it no longer requires the vital force provided by meat. These people live an ascetic life in the mountains or forests, far away from other human beings and meat foods (Arama 1961: 70 [Eng., 385]).

As for whether a vegetarian diet is adequate to keep human beings healthy, we have already noted that the dominant thread among the talmudic sages and the commentators is that meat is beneficial if not indeed essential for health. There are dissenting views, though. The various interpretations of the story of Daniel and his comrades who, for reasons of kashruth, sustained themselves on a vegetarian diet in a foreign land (Daniel 1), reveals the commentators' positions on this issue. For some of them, the fact that at the expiration of the ten-day trial Daniel and his comrades looked healthier and plumper than the children who had eaten the royal food is evidence of a miracle.[22] But Abraham Ibn Ezra, in his commentary on Dan. 1:15, rejects this notion.[23] He explains that Daniel and his comrades lived on rice—the food of the people of India—which is a nourishing food, even more so than wheat, and endowed with the property of cleansing the blood. He also believes that they ate various types of pulses, which grow in hot countries like Spain and Egypt, and which "make the face glow more than wine does," and purge the liver. He considers rice and beans to be nourishing and healthful foods, especially because "any food that is attractive to the soul is more beneficial than food the soul does not like, even though it be warm and moist, like the

---

22. See, for example, Moshe Alshekh's commentary on Dan. 1:13 and 17 (Alshekh 1876: 11, 12).

23. "The Gaon said that this was a great miracle, but this reading is unnecessary" (Ibn Ezra 1992: 8). "The Gaon" is how Ibn Ezra refers to Saadia, but I have not been able to find any suggestion in Saadia's commentary on Daniel that Daniel and his comrades were the beneficiaries of a miracle.

generation of life. For these [children] ate what their soul desired and it was good for them" (Ibn Ezra 1992: 8–10).[24]

Abravanel, too, speaks of the health benefits of a vegetarian diet in general and of that followed by Daniel and his comrades in particular—though he does not overlook the element of divine providence. After explaining that Daniel deliberately asked the steward for a ten-day trial (Dan. 1:12) because, according to physicians, it takes up to ten days for the pernicious effects of eating bad foods to be evident, he continues as follows:

> God, who saw their meritorious intention, consented to their plan. So after the trial they looked well and full, that is, they were healthy—even healthier than the other children—because there is no doubt that a diet of meat and wine, for all that it is full of nutrition and energy, causes many ailments when a person is saturated with them; whereas a diet of pulses, being simpler, is healthier. This is why at the beginning of creation, when human beings ate only plants and drank water, their lives were longer. But when Noah came and was permitted to eat meat, and he added the drinking of wine, their life spans diminished to the range we have today. (Abravanel 1960: 302)[25]

Both the talmudic sages and traditional commentators were familiar with the phenomenon of individuals who voluntarily eschewed the consumption of meat. But the motive cited in the Talmud is quite different from modern ideological vegetarianism. The classical texts never suggest an ethical rationale (or even a health rationale) for vegetarianism. Rather, abstaining from meat (and wine) is an expression of mourning for the

---

24. With regard to the nutritional value of the foods eaten by Daniel and his comrades, see Gersonides (2001: 9–11) on Dan. 1:11. He, too, writes that they ate various pulses that are good for one's health and some of which purge the liver. As for the general statement, accepted today, that food that people enjoy is better for the body than food that repels them, see R. Tanhum's comment on Dan. 1:15: "'Fatter in flesh': plump and round, which is not astonishing under Divine providence, because food that has slight nutritional value, with which they are happy and comfortable, is more nourishing and beneficial for the body than fat foods that are full of nutrients, if it disgusts those who are forced to eat it" (in Kappah 1981: 24).

25. With regard to the damage caused by excessive consumption of meat, see Sforno (Gottlieb 1980: 273–4) on Num. 11:20, s.v., "and it becomes loathsome to you." See also Malbim (1992: 9) on Dan. 1:12. Cf. his commentary on Gen. 1:29, where he asserts that human anatomy and physiology are not suited to meat eating and praises the tranquil nature of people who abstain from meat (Malbim 2008: 42).

destroyed temple: "When the Temple was destroyed for the second time, large numbers in Israel became ascetics, binding themselves neither to eat meat nor to drink wine" (*Babylonian Talmud*, Baba Batra 60b). The sages were not pleased by their behavior, as is evident from Rabbi Joshua's rebuke of this group (ibid).[26]

When we reach the medieval commentators, though, we find that Abraham Ibn Ezra does refer to ethical veganism. In various places in his commentaries, he mentions that the people of India avoid all animal-derived foods. For example, in his long commentary on Exod. 8:22 [RSV 8:26], dealing with Moses' reply to Pharaoh that "it would not be right to do this, for what we sacrifice to the Lord our God is untouchable to the Egyptians," Ibn Ezra suggests that the Egyptians of that era followed the same diet he attributes to the Hindus of his own day, one that excludes all foods of animal origin.[27] He even describes the Indians' moral indignation when they find themselves in the company of meat eaters (Strickman and Silver 1996: 165–66).[28]

It is worth noting that Ibn Ezra had a very positive view of the Indians in general. He believed that they excelled in rational morality, as reflected in his short commentary on Exod. 23:20. There he asserts that the laws of torts were given to remedy injustices. But "if we lived in a place where there are no oxen we would have no need for laws about an ox that gores. If we lived in tents, like the Kedarites, we would not need [the precepts of] the parapet or the mezuzah. And if in India, there would be no need for laws about theft and murder and fraud and false witness" (Weiser 1976: 305). In other words, Ibn Ezra believed that none of these moral failings was found in India, so the Indians did not need laws against them.[29]

---

26. On vegetarian sects during the Second Temple period and the reasons for their diet, see Berman 1982: 29; Beckwith 1988.

27. We must not forget that Ibn Ezra never visited India. His knowledge of the country was based on books and hearsay. So he is clearly exaggerating in his description of the Indians as vegans.

28. See also Ibn Ezra's long commentary on Exod. 19:9 (Strickman and Silver 1996: 377–78) and his commentary on Gen. 46:34: "The people of India until this very day do not eat or drink anything derived from a living creature" (Strickman and Silver 1988: 406).

29. The belief that the Indians are a just people is also found in the *Kuzari* (1.19). I would like to thank Professor Uriel Simon for calling my attention to Ibn Ezra's and Judah Halevi's idealization of the Indians.

The Future: The Return of Vegetarianism in the Messianic Era

Isaiah's vision of the end of days describes an era of concord among the animals and between animals and human beings:

> The wolf shall dwell with the lamb,
> and the leopard shall lie down with the kid,
> and the calf and the lion and the fatling together,
> and a little child shall lead them.
> The cow and the bear shall feed;
> their young shall lie down together;
> and the lion shall eat straw like the ox.
> The sucking child shall play over the hole of the asp,
> and the weaned child shall put his hand on the adder's den.
> They shall not hurt or destroy in all my holy mountain;
> for the earth shall be full of the knowledge of the Lord
> as the waters cover the sea. (Isa. 11:6-9; cf. 65:25)

Some have interpreted these verses as figurative. But Abravanel, in his commentary on Isa. 11:6-7, rejects the idea that the passage is metaphorical and understands the prophecy literally, although he limits its scope to the Holy Land. In his reading, in the messianic era, Israel will return to the harmony that prevailed among all creatures in the Garden of Eden: "In other words, in the messianic age things will return to their original state, predatory beasts will not hunt and domestic animals will not be eaten" (1979: 91). He repeats the explanation he advanced in his commentary on Exod. 16:4, that meat eating leads to cruelty, and adds, "This is why the prophet stated that in the messianic age the lion will eat straw like the ox, meaning that this will be its sustenance, rather than meat, and consequently it will not be cruel, angry, or wrathful, and, what is more, 'they shall not hurt or destroy'" (Abravanel 1964: 2:134).[30] It is true that Abravanel does not refer explicitly to human dietary habits in this context, but from his commentary on Exod.

---

30. Saadia Gaon (*Beliefs and Opinions* 8:8 [Rosenblatt 1948: 315]) and Nachmanides (Chavel 1971: 3:456–57, on Lev. 26:6) understand the prophecy literally: peace between human beings and animals and among the animals themselves. But they say nothing about the diet of human beings in that era and do not explicitly state that humans, too, will no longer dine on animals.

16:4 (Abravanel 1964: 2:133–34; see above), we see clearly his belief that in the messianic age, human beings will no longer eat meat.

Rabbi Samuel Laniado, in his commentary on Isa. 11:6, mentions Abravanel's remarks approvingly and offers a similar interpretation. Even though he does not reject the possibility that Isaiah's prophecy is a metaphor for the fraternity that will prevail among human beings, he asserts that it should also be understood literally: fraternity among all living creatures, the human race, and all other species. In his reading, in the messianic age

> the world will return to its youthful days, as at the time of the Creation, with everyone inclined toward the good, because God made man upright. . . .[31] So too the lion, like the ox that eats straw contentedly, so the lion, too, will be glad of heart when it eats, and this is why it is compared to the ox. . . . For no one thought of eating through violence before the Tree of Knowledge of Good and Evil, and when this evil is amended all will be amended. (Laniado 1996: 404)

Even though Laniado, like Abravanel before him, does not refer explicitly to what human beings will eat in the messianic era, it is clear, both from the quotation from Qoheleth, which deals with human morality, and his mention of the sin of eating from the tree of knowledge as the cause of violence in the world, that he believed a carnivorous diet will be inappropriate for human beings, too, in the reformed world of the future.

Conclusion

The belief in a vegetarian epoch in the youth of the human race, which lasted until after the flood, is dominant and widespread among talmudic sages and medieval commentators. Isaac Arama and Isaac Abravanel even suggest that God planned to provide the Israelites with a strictly vegetarian diet after they had left Egypt and accordingly first gave them "bread from the sky" (that is, manna), not meat.

None of the sages or commentators calls for their contemporaries to switch to a vegetarian diet. Nevertheless, one can certainly find suggestions to limit the consumption of meat for educational, economic, and health

---

31. An allusion to Eccl. 7:29: "God made man upright, but they have sought out many devices."

reasons, as well as passages that may reflect reservations about killing animals, or encouragement for vegetarianism.

Talmudic sages as well as the medieval commentators were familiar with the phenomenon of vegetarianism. One commentator, Joseph Ibn Kaspi, reports that he himself gave up meat for a time, though for economic rather than ethical reasons. Abraham Ibn Ezra and Isaac Arama promote vegetarianism as a lofty ideal. Other commentators refer to the hygienic or spiritual advantages of a vegetarian diet.

The sages and commentators almost never refer to vegetarianism as the norm in the Messianic Era. Still, Abravanel and R. Samuel Laniado do suggest that, in the Messianic Era, the world will return to its ancient equilibrium, and the human race, like all other carnivorous species, will adopt the vegetarian diet that satisfied it at the beginning of time.

Part Two

———

Redreaming with Joseph and Others

CHAPTER 10

"Here Comes This Dreamer"

Reading Joseph the Slave in Multicultural and Interfaith Contexts

Carole R. Fontaine

My hermeneutical method in approaching Genesis takes up a modern reading of Genesis for the multicultural venue of human rights discourse, drawing upon many of the insights of our guild about the ethics of reading the Bible. Much of this approach draws upon Daniel Patte and others' seminal work on this topic in the *Global Bible Commenary* (2005) volume and elsewhere. I do not come with the latest news on the Joseph story nor historical questions concerning the caravan trade conducted by Semites in the Nile Delta during the fifteenth Egyptian dynasty (those pesky Hyksos, notable for their place in older attempts at historical readings of the Joseph novella) (Bietak 1995). Rather, my reading inquires into the fates of the Josephs (and Hagars) of today, in a world that has not changed much in its willingness to abuse the unprotected and marginalized. My husband first named my method "lunching around with strange scholars"—from a husband's point of view, a much better thing than "sleeping around"—but I like to name it "Reading in Company" (Fontaine 2008: 148–49), and I choose my company very carefully these days, for reasons I shall name. Simply put, my most potent experiences of the Bible have come since I moved into the area of "contextual interpretations," seeking modern contexts where the Bible might actually make some practical difference for the good.

Since 1999, I have worked on human rights (HR) issues, mainly on the problems of violence against women in Muslim communities of the Middle

East and South Asia. I serve as a . . . shill? pimp? networker? for a nongovernmental organization (NGO) entitled the Women's United Nations Report
Network (WUNRN 2008b), for which I manage the New England region
and all matters feminist and religious. We used to report directly through our
own Special Rapporteur to the UN High Commission on Human Rights.
However, most women and NGOs were excluded from having any input
to the newly reconstituted Human Rights Council in Geneva, so almost
all of the UN groups, bodies, and entities focused on women and children
have migrated over to the policy-making side of the United Nations—in our
case, the Commission on the Status of Women (UNCSW 2008). I started
in Muslim honor killings, and worked my way up to serving on the CSW's
Working Commission on Female Infanticide. I also serve as a consultant
to the occasional group of Congressional functionaries attempting to "show
empathy" while simultaneously doing little. Along the way, I have become an
active board member for an international charity aimed at Muslim women,
founded in the United Kingdom, which has also brought me an investigation
by the British Ministry of Intelligence (when we applied for charity status), a
secret audit by the U.S. Internal Revenue Service, a denunciation by a set of
hard-line mullahs on talk radio in the United States, and listing as an enemy
of the Islamic Republic of Iran.

All this for reading the Hebrew Bible, the New Testament, and Qur'an
in a principled, self-reflective way that tries to be honest and compassionate,
reading for the best instead of the worst.

My basic hermeneutic principle is that one does no violence to text or
audience, but as long as there are true forces of evil out there reading for
the worst, cynically manipulating scriptures for political opportunistic goals,
there is no shame in trying to call attention to a counter-reading, if it be true
to the text in whatever way truth and text are conceived of in the eye of the
interpreter (Fontaine 2008: 118–49). Indeed, I am under direct orders from
our Special Rapporteur to use every form of moral persuasion and expertise at my disposal as an expert to challenge oppressive, intolerant, exclusive,
restrictive readings (Ertürk 2003). I try to do my best, but sometimes I find
that puts me in direct violation of some of our guild's most cherished rules
for reading, even in such generous company as contextual critics!

In particular, as I call out the groups I "read around" with—HR orga-
nizers, government and agency policy makers and aid workers, and Muslim

women's groups—I breach Patte's most basic principle in the *Global Bible Commentary* (Patte and Okure 2005: xxi–xxxiii), and not just because I am standing with brown people *inside* the ring of police dogs, men in black, security operatives, and what-not (not usually the social location of the biblical liberation traditions of interpretation). But because I am a woman, I have come to understand that, in much of the world, I am considered less than a person, less than rational, less than able, and that sadly, in human rights work, physical protection must wrap any woman around like a chador should she dare to speak truth as she knows it! Yet I have learned much: the dogs are friendly and no threat to those they protect; the security people not only check the bathroom stall for bombs, they will also hold your purse and hand you toilet paper, if need be. And from time to time, what I do seems to make a difference.

Aside from the discord of being part of a trophy "minority"—religious scholars who will speak up—my sense of discontinuity is not simply at the discovery that being a biblical theologian is enough to get you many death threats, if you do it properly. Rather, I read with groups who, unlike my Christian seminarians, really don't have much stake in the outcome. Quite frankly, they *want* me to read "for" them, or "to" them, not read "with them" (Patte and Okure 2005: xxix), as my groups are hard beset in myriad ways—a bit like Joseph. Theologically, I am their foreign dream master: the secular HR movement is largely disgusted by religion and suspicious of it—and who is to blame them? Yet I dream that one day aid and rescue workers with supplies could partner with in-country religious groups that know how and to whom to distribute the aid. A simple dream, one would think, but as hard to achieve as family harmony in the tents of Jacob! Add in the mixture of the secular European context (where many of my Muslim women wind up), and I am often astonished that they even listen to me at all! The HR side of my reading community is gratified and shocked if I can give them anything useful whatsoever, so low is their expectation of members of the religious guilds of scholars or believers. When I read for them and return my results, they are relieved and (so they say) edified by what I have given them, without their having to wade through the things that are anathema to them and constant irritants as they try to get their work done in the world. Every now and again, I see movement toward an appeal to Scripture as warrant for a human rights–based issue, and I am glad to be some small part of that reconciliation between the secular and the symbolic world from which our texts take some of their power.

On the Muslim side of the equation, things are quite different—but no less weird—for the biblical scholar. Here, we have not a clash of civilizations but a clash of ignorances, as Harvard University scholar Ali Asani likes to put it. Muslims not only don't know Christian or Jewish scriptures, they do not know their own (though they think very highly of it, by nature of their socialization). Any readings I bring them of anything are welcomed like manna from heaven. The Queen of Sheba (Fontaine 2002: 206–40)? Sure! David and music (Fontaine forthcoming)? Why not? Leviticus (Fontaine 2008: 1–30)? Bring it on! Jesus (Fontaine 2008: 262–79)? Well, of course! Qur'an—well, I think they are taking it very well, frankly, as I only do what a person with first-year Arabic, a specialization in Qur'an during Ph.D. work in a Western department of religion, and a whole lot of thinking about interpretation and method in Hebrew Bible would do. As you are doubtless aware, Muslim feminists have been excluded historically from the study of sacred texts, not only by social design but also by the nature of the difficulties of the Qur'an's original language. A helpful feminist sister from the other side of the aisle saying, "You know, we tried that argument, and here's how it turned out," is, they tell me, "help from afar," which Allah sends just when things look the worst.

So here I am presenting the result of reading "Joseph the Trafficked Slave" for my three distinct groups: first, vulnerable Iranian refugees sitting in horrific danger in a refugee camp for protected persons in Iraq (see ICSPPAI 2008); second, the students I mentor in Muslim countries; and finally, the friends—Shia and Sunni—whose daily lives and traditions are shared with me in so many generous ways. Likewise, I read "Joseph the Food Aid Worker" for my secular HR defenders and policy makers: the baronesses (three of them), first ladies (two), presidents of exile communities (one), lawyers (too many to count), filmmakers, writers, prisoners, and others, all bonded together by their dedication and determination to leave a better world for their daughters and sons. I am not reading for Hyksos scholars, biblicists, bishops, or believers of the normal sort, but rather for those who stand outside the kinds of communities doing the reading in the *Global Bible Commentary*. Like Joseph, I recognize that my own origins are in the ever-present slaveries imposed by imperialism, racism, and sexism: I grew up next to trafficked Haitian girls working in the sex trade, regularly ignored (except for denunciations of the girls) by all the believing communities of my home region. That experience in childhood and my work now have shaped how I stand in these multicultural "foreign courts," sharing my texts and daring to dream of them that they might lead to a world that is better fed and less violent than the one we have now.

The Dreaming of Joseph: From Survivor to Slave to Savior (*Whose?*)

After all these disclaimers, my actual contextual interpretation is pretty cut-and-dried, and not all that far removed from what one might get from any alert biblicist: in one young person, Joseph, we have at least two tales (and probably plenty more). Our hero is a survivor of human trafficking who becomes a successful state food aid distributor. He then colludes to enslave people in their own lands in return for the bread he has stored up with God's help. Can the modern trade of trafficking shed any light on the shadows lying beneath the cloaks of many colors that interest scholars in Joseph? Joseph's story is often called out as an example of slave trade or human trafficking in the Bible, along with Judg. 5:30, 2 Kings 4:1, and Rev. 18:11-13 (Crawford and Crawford 2005: 18).

Our hero is a younger son, disadvantaged by that *and* by his father's special recognition of him as a son of the favorite dead wife so long barren. It is the younger Joseph who checks up on his brothers and tattles to the father when necessary, a reversal of expected order in the patriarchal family. According to some scholars, Joseph can be conceived of as a cipher for the standard dying-and-rising gods celebrated in the Akitu New Year festival (Isaac 2006: 240, 242–46). Joseph loses his clothes, descends, and is resurrected in a new status—repeatedly.

But there is more from the underlying ancient cultural context of the Joseph story than that. We have a bundle of mythic or folktale elements in the Joseph story, sprinkled throughout the work: the portents and the dreams that come true, the mistaken identities, the magic cup hidden in the sack, reversals of fortune, difficult tasks and solutions, and of course, a personal favorite, the folklore motif K2111 in the Folktale Motif Index (Fontaine 2008: 224–25; Thompson 1993). This is the so-called Spurned Seductress

Motif, who, in her multicultural stories, tries to set up the poor, innocent, comely, and moral male youth who refuses her advances. The occasion of all these traditional elements in the telling of Joseph's story should tell us that this narrative is not quite the historical document scholars once made of it. If anything, it sounds like a propaganda tool or docudrama that whitewashes the experience of captivity for a much later audience with a simple message: don't ask about the mechanisms of your oppression (you may one day engage in them!); just keep being a good believer, and things will be fine. Sometime. Somehow. Strange messages get transmitted with myth and tales when they are elevated to the level of history or "court wisdom" (Von Rad 1966: 292–300). Notice how the individual hero is allowed to succeed (with attendant notice of how well it went for the population in general with him in charge), but the mechanisms of his low estate are not challenged or changed; indeed, by the end of his story, *he* has become the slaver, and all this is somehow part of God's plan! We are, of course, glad that all involved survived the famine, due to Joseph's ability to interpret and act; but wouldn't we be happier and better served if the text proposed some strategy other than "wait for God to fix it"? Perhaps a bit of that may be supplied by reading Joseph through contemporary categories we might assign to his circumstances: Joseph is a story of human trafficking, and it is *not* irrelevant to the modern world, no matter how the narrator tried to pretty up the story by assigning the actual trafficking to foreigners and providing us with a happy ending! The narrative of Joseph the successful food aid worker also has a point to make for people in similar settings in the here and now.

Human Trafficking Then and Now

If you follow such statistics, you will know already that international organizations and monitoring bodies tell us that, currently, there are more slaves on planet Earth than there ever were during antiquity (Rome) or the slave-owning era in Russia or the United States. The UN Office of Drugs and Crime concludes that 2.5 million persons every year are trafficked.[1] Modern groups find a key methodological issue in determining the differences

---

1. This refers to those who are "recruited, entrapped, transported and exploited" each year but does not include those already trapped within the trade (UNODC 2008). See also UNESCO 2008.

between "smuggling" and "human trafficking," and you will find this amply covered in documents from the Human Smuggling and Trafficking Center, formed by section 7202 of the U.S. Intelligence and Reform and Terrorism Prevention Act of 2004 (HSTC 2005). For our purposes, the elements of smuggling and transnational terrorism will not be discussed here, due to space limits. Just for reference, one can, of course, be a smuggled person who is trafficked, but one can also be trafficked in one's own society without having to cross any borders. Interesting as well is the fact that terrorism has now made this a national problem (whereas before it may have been one of personal morality or border enforcement), but no government department calculates in its measures the terror experienced by the person who has been trafficked.

The Egypt of the Hyksos and later periods certainly worried about its borders and controlled them zealously, but in order to control profits from trade and collect "protection" money from caravans, merchants, and travelers, not because of some feared terrorist threat. Generally, we see grain, wine, and oil moving into the delta from the southern Levant, and grain and incense moving from Arabia and Egypt north up into the Delta, but no clear estimation can be found of the amount of slave traffic that might have been taking place.[2] We must assume that armies bring the prisoners of war back to their home base, while target populations are recruited in some less violent way. In fact, archaeology is clear in painting a portrait of increased southern Levantine population migration into the Eastern Delta of the Nile starting in the twelfth and thirteenth dynasties, some probably brought as war captives and others recruited as mercenaries, seamen, shipbuilders, craftsmen, as well as transhumant nomads following their yearly range (Oren 1997b: xx–xxii).

The trafficking story almost always includes the key components of fraud and deception, coercion, threats, force, and greed. It is bound up with identifiable human rights abuses such as debt bondage, deprivation of liberty, lack of control over personal freedom and labor, sexual torture, and so on (Oren 1997b: 1). Do we see these in Genesis? We do.

---

2. There may be a significant difference in the materiel required to transport human captives to market, compared with, for example, the small but fabulously lucrative cargo of frankincense. Likewise, changes in both market and caravan methods (from donkeys in the Middle Bronze Age to camels in the Early Iron Age), along with the phases of trade development made possible by improvements in saddle technology, must have produced changes in the configuration of human trafficking in the ancient Near East (Finkelstein 1988).

The origins of trafficking are directly linked in many societies to poverty, birth rate, and cultural preference for boy children (WUNRN 2008a), but one must identify which aspect correlates to which group engaged in the trafficking: the traffickee, the family of the traffickee, the traffickers, the buyers, and the eventual society in which the trafficked person will be held captive. There is usually plenty of guilt to go around, and not much salvation. Poverty is usually the reason given for a family's decision to sell off an "extra" female child who, due to preference for boys, is considered only a burden to her family, a financial investment from which some other family will benefit when she eventually becomes their sexual property. However, boys are trafficked, too, as manual laborers, sex workers, beggars, and—in the modern Middle Eastern scenario—as camel jockeys (Iran Focus 2006). Many families in the developing world, but even in Europe and elsewhere after the breakup of the Soviet Union, do not know that they are selling or giving their children to traffickers. They often believe they are sending the child off to school, in some fashion, or to a decently paying, honest job. And if these were the true destinations for the unwanted child who burdens the family's budget, who could blame the family for trying to do its best by everyone with only limited means at their disposal? Tragically, however, these are *not* the real destinations of trafficked children, and indeed, it is terrible to report that sexual or physical enslavement are not even the worst things that happen to trafficked children, especially females. Fraud, practiced by the traffickers on the family or by the family on the traffickee, is one of the hallmarks of the trafficking operation, and we see it in spades in the text in Genesis.

When we look at the family context of Joseph, we see that the story is inverted from the modern reality in a number of ways, whether fraudulently or not. Jealousies among the siblings and the favoritism of the father pave the way for the brothers' fraud perpetrated upon their father and the traffickers, who believe the brothers must have a right to sell their sibling—but these brothers are so venomous, they even try to defraud each other! Reuben attempts a good trick within a bad trick: instead of killing him outright, he proposes that Joseph be thrown into a pit, thinking that he will rescue him later (Gen. 37:22). However, Judah sees a prime opening: why just kill the troublesome youth, when one could sell him for a profit and defraud the father with the bloodied gift that inspired the jealousy (37:26-27)! Luckily for everyone but Joseph and Jacob, a caravan apparently operating in the slave trade appears at the very moment it is needed, though there is considerable confusion over exactly *which* group of foreign evildoers is to be blamed for the actual acts. In these early episodes, greed or poverty may be at work, but we certainly see fraud in the brothers' dealings all around, and the use of force to deprive Joseph of clothing and freedom of movement. I'm sure there is theft in there, too, as Joseph did not belong to his brothers' households, such that they might legitimately sell him; that would have been Jacob's prerogative.

Yet notice that, unlike a modern trafficking story, this one offers no *overt* hint that this family had any financial motives that might explain the sale of a child, unless we take it from the peculiar interruption of Joseph's story by the one of Judah and Tamar in Genesis 38. Joseph's plight results from nothing but malice, plain and simple, our story suggests—but one wonders how accurate that may be, given the overwhelming evidence of the role of poverty in the sales of children for exploitation. We will learn later that Joseph is quite a pretty boy (39:6); everyone in Egypt thinks so, and it is no little part of his servile charm, apparently! I cannot help thinking that Joseph's splendid appearance as a youth makes him a very attractive purchase, sure to turn a good price for that special kind of master who enjoys male beauty. Perhaps Judah's fiscal plans are a foreshadowing of the new family financial pressures that will be caused by the taking of a new wife and the arrival of Tamar's twins in Genesis 38.[3] We never hear *who* receives the payment for the sale of Joseph or how it was shared out—if it was—among the perpetrators. Someone has made out on this deal, and it's certainly not Joseph or Jacob! The text's secrecy on this issue fits the modern profile: traffickers are careful to guard their secrets, and too often families join in the game, as we see in Genesis.

The Bible seems to reference the shameful underbelly of shared guilt in the trafficking story in its confusion about exactly who bought and traded Joseph. Sometimes it is the wicked Ishmaelites (Knauf 1983; Dumbrell 1975) who see their chance to make a quick and easy "buy" (39:1); elsewhere it is

---

3. Mieke Bal has argued that the so-called intrusion of the Judah–Tamar story into Joseph's narrative is designed to reassure us that no matter what sexual charges are made, the chosen, righteous one—Tamar or Joseph—will be just fine in God's hands, and that we, the audience, should not worry over their ultimate fates (Bal 1987: 91–103).

the Midianites who are responsible, or perhaps both. As far as my research went into this, we cannot say if we have here a doublet, a confusion of an earlier entity with a later one, or some other dislocation of the text with respect to the identity of the traffickers. We may simply say that it is always more convenient to ascribe the evil deeds to foreigners just passing through—they are not there to defend themselves against such accusations. Is it not a little fishy that Jacob's good ol' boys just happen to look up and see a caravan of slavers right when they need them—or did someone know that such caravans usually passed that way, all the better to make a quick shekel on a sale?

Whether Midianites or Ishmaelites are the perpetrators, it is natural enough to suspect that all caravans in import–export trade might also include children and adult slaves on their way to market or sent in tribute—another form of trafficking coercion (accept it for the good of the state or your family's lineage!). Certainly, we see such possibilities in the tomb paintings from Beni Hassan, showing us a donkey caravan arriving with tribute for Egypt, including donkeys, musicians, small children, and perhaps others (Bietak 1997). However, I was shocked to see how little the particulars of the slave trade in biblical times figure in the standard discussion of Joseph's plight, or in slavery in general in the Bible. You will find more scholarly interests in the equid burials in Canaanite-influenced Hyksos' levels at Avaris than any outrage on behalf of the murdered servant girls, ages twelve to seventeen, also placed in the ground as tribute to their masters in death and a sign that their servitude will never end (Bietak 1997: 109). I take it as heartening that the Hebrew Bible is the only text I know of from the ancient Near East that actually prescribes compensation and freedom to slaves who have been permanently injured by violence by masters or others, and that slaves in one's own ethnic group, at least, are not to be returned to their foreign masters (Exod. 21:26-27; Deut. 23:15-16). But the Bible does not touch slavery as a concept, and I always marvel at conservative white believers who yearn to be God's slave and keep murmuring "Master, master!" as they go about their business as free persons. Let them query the great-grandchildren of slaves or visit an ICE[4] detention facility for rescued traffickees before they unleash such piety on the rest of us.

---

4. Immigration Control and Enforcement, now a part of the Department of Homeland Security in the United States.

In fact, the Bible simply doesn't have much to offer those enslaved ones who have little reason to conclude that "the Lord is with them." It's nice, of course, that one can be just as good and worthy a Christian as one's master, according to the New Testament, but nicer still would be a clear and effective statement on this abiding evil of societies that treat the poor as disposable, and children as property and prey. When I talk to survivors, I make much of the Decalogue's law "You shall not steal" in its relationship to a parallel verse in the Covenant Code as Exod. 21:16: "Whoever steals a person, whether sold or found with him, shall be put to death," but it isn't exactly the same as being the outright command, coded right into our dearly held religious morality.

Joseph in Egypt

The trouble that Joseph encounters in Potiphar's house (Gen. 39) tells us textually, however, that the modern story of the sexual exploitation of the trafficked teenager may not be absent from Joseph's real experience as a trafficked slave of unusual beauty. First of all, as a trafficked resident of Egypt, Joseph has before him in every public building or elite household decoration a blatant portrait of how Egypt feels about the Other: the smiting of the foreign enemy (often labeled as the "wretched Asiatic enemy"—another translation for the Egyptian for "Hyksos") figures from the Early Dynastic Period down to the end of the days of late antiquity.[5] He knows his status as an "Other": any dispute or failure to please will leave him bound for the pit, just as his trafficking journey began. Next, one might be forgiven for suspecting that the brothers had a little more degradation in mind for Joseph than just an afternoon in a pit followed by simple slavery. The public stripping away of his special clothes signifies what his eager masters may do in private: make him into a female. What excellent revenge for being Daddy's pet! What *is* unusual is that Joseph is male, not female, but we are put in mind of Esther, coerced one way or another into a foreign harem, where only her beauty (Esth. 2:7) qualifies her for any kind of life at all in a world where her

---

5. See Fontaine 2008: 31–89; and "Combat Art in the Ancient Near East," a video of Egyptian and Assyrian iconography denigrating the Male Other (Greenheart Studio 2008, at www.YouTube.com/greenheartstudio).

ethnicity puts her at risk. Everyone likes a pretty slave, and modest, docile ones—well, the God of the Masters is certainly with *them!*

From modern documentation, we know how heart-rending is the futile hope of trafficked slaves: that some master, user, customer, pimp, or government agent will end their spiral into despair by finding them especially attractive or useful and making them into an "exclusive" property to be guarded from abuse by others. A ring on the finger in the form of a legitimate marriage into a single household is the ultimate prize for the earnest female sex worker, or sometimes the escape is made through rising through the ranks of the exploited to serve as an overseer and manager of other newly trafficked victims. Both happen in Genesis: Joseph gains a high-ranking protector, who gives him a ring when he is "adopted" into Pharaoh's household as an honored member; and his later career as food aid worker gives him power over others, who then become slaves in return for food aid.

We know how the trafficking story ends in modern times. Given the prevalence of STDs in the populations of sex workers, most of whom are trafficked, the tale is a brief one: most children and adults live only about four years once taken into the trafficking trade (EDWON 2006). In Dubai, it is customary to simply dump the dead bodies of used-up child sex workers from Iran into any cargo hold of a flight into Tehran—no muss, no fuss, no papers needed. Joseph's personal commitment to the smooth running of Potiphar's affairs, along with his proud statement of his master's trust and favor, suggests that a bit of the master-savior, Stockholm syndrome mentality is at work in the teen's desire to please his master (Joseph will show similar fidelity to his masters in prison and to Pharaoh at court).

Conditions are relatively decent for the young slave in Potiphar's house, at least at first. Like so many persons trapped in the trafficking world, Joseph becomes the object of sexual coercion, and later fraudulent testimony by the lady of the house—who some have suggested may have envied Potiphar's preference for Joseph over his own wife. Similar to modern stories, such threats as acted upon by Mrs. Potiphar show how precarious is the position of the trafficked slave: in any legal dispute, it is unlikely that the slave will be the winner.[6] Joseph is again consigned to a pit, only to be delivered yet again by his

---

6. In the modern story, coercive threats to turn the trafficked person over to "authorities" for being undocumented or participating in criminal activities are quite common, and highly effective.

dream expertise. However, Joseph's story varies from the other ancient Near Eastern examples of K2111: only in Genesis does the issue of ethnicity come into play; only here does the wife escape punishment (as far as we know) and the accused youngster come out relatively unscathed. This may be attributed to the fact that the K2111 motif is only a plot entanglement designed to move our hero along to his final destination at court; in other myths, it is much more of a complete episode whose end is itself, although the Egyptian version does use the complication to move the hero into the forests of the Levant to await yet more female treachery (Fontaine 2008: 222–46).

It is a point of honor to read this story all the way through, I think. I would love to tell it the Bible's way, with a big emphasis on God's care for the trafficked child, the starving people, and even the miserable brothers when they repent. "Hooray for the Egyptians!" we might say, because eventually they see and acknowledge Joseph's excellent abilities and make him highest in the land, except for Pharaoh. Or we might note that it is always useful to have an expendable foreigner do the dirty work: like medieval Christians employing Jews to collect taxes so the employers could stay pure in their own eyes, Pharaoh gives Joseph the tough job of overseeing the collection of grain and its later disposition during the famine. (Were we aware that food would be returned at a price to those who grew it?) If things go well, Pharaoh can take credit for his wise choice of a factotum; if they go badly, well, it was only a Hebrew slave after all, and if an angry mob destroys him, it is no great loss, and Pharaoh can remain beneficent in the eyes of his people.

Maybe Joseph's later behavior in his successful food aid project betrays a knowledge on his part that he is being used as a front man for the unpleasant choices the Egyptian leaders do not want to be seen as making themselves. Or perhaps, as suggested in the names of his children, he accepts that he is socially dead to his father's house and is eager to serve his new lineage in Pharaoh's court in the land that has treated him well (Steiner 1954). Joseph enriches himself and the Pharaoh of Egypt, or at least claims some sort of fitting reversal to his story of servitude—so the text implies—in enslaving the people in their own land. We did not hear in the beginning that the grain stored up from surplus was to be *sold* to the very people from whom it was taken, once the famine took hold. When their money is gone, they offer themselves as slaves for the grain rations that were taken from them in the first place, while Jacob's household, under Joseph's protection, is living large in the eastern delta! In the end, all Joseph's dreams come true: all those who betrayed him now bow down before him, the Big Sheaf. At the same time, the House of Israel's dreams of survival of the famine become a nightmare: generations later, they will find themselves enslaved in the same system of servitude that Joseph devised. I say to my governmental friends and aid agency workers, based on this text: Beware of unintended consequences! The final exegesis of your wonderful development plans, drawn up for the good, may someday have evil outcomes, despite your best efforts! This is no reason to refrain from doing good, but it *is* a good reason to remember to pay attention to the details and the future, and to place means of oversight and reform into every scheme of food aid. One must always follow the money.

Does a contemporary reading for my non-Christian communities, then, get us anywhere? From modern stories of trafficking, I am suspicious of the Genesis happy ending, even though it has a downside that will become evident in another epoch. My reasons are all too personal for looking askance at the happy reunion: I personally do not want to believe that Joseph's experience of slavery left him so willing to engage in the trade himself as a successful adult. I would prefer to think that much of Joseph's experience of being trafficked has been hidden from us for reasons of theology, ideology, or embarrassment, but that its deep wounds—along with those received at the hands of his brothers—account for his later descent into administrative slaveholding.

We have seen that the trafficking story is a complex one, a guilty and shameful one, and found many coherences and suggestive interpretations by reading the modern and ancient stories together. The modern story attends more closely to the ambivalent outcomes for the trafficked persons, enlarging the narrative to include "prevention, protection, recovery, rehabilitation, reintegration, return, repatriation, and prosecution of traffickers" (UN ESCAP 2003); and with more time, we could delineate these elements within Genesis as well. I would place Joseph's complex machinations with his brothers over Benjamin as a set of tests that are designed to reveal the brothers' rehabilitation. And it would be good to keep reading these ugly stories with the world's children in mind. Others in the world outside biblical scholarship or believing communities are watching as we read, and wonder what we will do. Writes one couple interacting with church networks and government agencies working on trafficking in Asia:

Churches are the single largest untapped resource in the fight against child exploitation. They are present in every country of the world and have a mandate to protect and advocate for the abused. Even governmental and secular agencies are crying out for the Church to help. (Asha Forum 2008)

My dream is less abstruse and personal than Joseph's, although I, too, have forgotten all the misery of my father's house in my new territory. I dream that one day, the church and all other religious bodies might become part of the solution instead of part of the problem, and that many might be freed and fed without a concomitant enslavement as the price of their deliverance.

CHAPTER 11

Joseph's Journey
From Trauma to Resolution

Meira Polliack

A Personal Note: Scholarly Interest and Context

I first began delving into what may loosely be described as traumatic aspects of the Joseph narrative in Cambridge, during the autumn of 1993.[1] It was a time of great personal hardship and emotional difficulty that, perhaps unsurprisingly, coincided with the final stages of the writing and completion of my Ph.D. thesis. What was supposed to be a happy time—a satisfactory crowning of years of hard work—had become a time of sadness. In retrospect, I realize that the hollowness that naturally follows the completion of any long intellectual and writing effort was enhanced by the emptiness that follows the breakup of personal relationships. I am sure it is quite a common experience in student life, though at the time it felt devastating. I became engrossed in the Joseph narrative as a kind of intellectual and emotional solace, finding myself especially drawn to its emotive and psychological aspects and to its subtle interplay between denial and recognition, rejection and acknowledgment in the scenes of Joseph's reencounter with his brothers. I had come to perceive a certain pendulum behind the narrative that swings between these

---

1. A longer and slightly different version of this article, under the title "Joseph's Trauma: Memory and Resolution," is also published in A. Brenner and F. H. Polak, eds., *Performing Memory in Biblical Narrative and Beyond* (Sheffield: Sheffield Phoenix, 2009), 72–105. Reprinted by permission.

psychological spheres, and to see in the question of recognition—namely, what is recognition and how does one recognize the love and the pain of the other, as well as those within the self?—as central to the meaning of the story. I had not thought then at all of the distinctively traumatic aspects of the story, as evident from the notes I made at the time. Among them there is a quotation from T. S. Eliot ("Four Quartets"): "And the end of all our exploring will be to arrive where we started and know the place for the first time." I had then felt (and to some extent still do) that these words capture the essential process undergone by the character of Joseph in the story.

After several months of intensive writing, during which I had begun to address, inter alia, aspects of family relationships, love, and denial, within the Joseph narrative and in Genesis as a whole, I abandoned the project. It was in the autumn of 2007, some fourteen years later, that I found myself clearing the dust off my materials and sat down to write on this topic again, this time in Tel Aviv. What made me return to the story after so long was clearly connected, also in my own consciousness, to a traumatic experience undergone that summer. Unlike the heartbreaking moments of one's student life, this more recent experience was of a much more sinister and threatening character, I felt threatened by a sense of mental and emotional disintegration the likes of which I had only experienced in early childhood. Knowingly, I began immersing myself, yet again and for the second time, in this deeply emotive "most beautiful" of tales, that of Joseph and his brothers, as many, I dare say, have done before me and do now.

This time, however, what drew me was not the pendulum but something more sinisterly captivating that I came to consider as the story's central theme—namely, that it is not so much a rectifying tale of family love, denial of love, and the recovery of recognition as it is a troubling tale about the much murkier parts of the self and the other, and of the family, a story of victimization and even abuse. It was only when Athalya Brenner offered me the key to unlocking my interpretation of the story, through suggesting I write about it for a volume on memory, that I myself came to realize that memory is the dimension chosen by the biblical authors through which to convey the characters' despair—and that these desperate characters are a threesome: Joseph, his brothers, and Jacob, all locked in a posttraumatic triangle, out of which only Joseph is strong enough to fully emerge. The resolution of Joseph's trauma in the story is through memory, dreams, and the mechanism of acting out. I came to understand and reflect upon Joseph's ability to release himself and climb out (almost literally) of his traumatic experience as a major theme of the story.

In contemplating this theme, I felt for a time I was sublimating my own sense of personal trauma: inasmuch as engaging in biblical literature is a form of sublimation, the process was partially therapeutic. The sublime nature of this particular biblical story (which undoubtedly nurtures its religious meanings) is connected, I believe, with its telling and showing of a traumatic and therapeutic process. The previously quoted words of T. S. Eliot still reverberate in my mind when I think of it. But of late, I have come to think of a verse from scripture that no less captures its more sinister essence: "whatsoever thing from without entereth into the man, it cannot defile him; beacause it entereth not into his heart" (Mark 7:18-19; King James Version).

Joseph's Dreams and Traumatic Memory

Joseph "remembered the dreams," not just any dreams but, as the narrative stresses, those "which he had dreamt about them," about his brothers (Gen. 42:9).[2] This moment of recollection is described in the sequence of Joseph's estranged encounter with his brothers as a flicker of his consciousness. The content of the dreams, which he had dreamed a long time before, is not conveyed or retold by the narrator, for in identifying with the stirring of Joseph's memory, the reader is also to awaken in himself or herself some recollection of these dreams, however flimsy, registering them, for a passing moment: the first dream, about the brothers' sheaves; gathering round in the field and bowing down before Joseph's upright sheaf, and the second dream, about the sun and the moon and the eleven stars bowing down to him (37:5-11).

Joseph's indistinct reminiscence of the dreams is in tune with the terseness of biblical narrative art and with the ellusiveness of memory as a psychic phenomenon. However, "other" dreams, namely nightmares of remembered or unremembered horrors Joseph may have dreamed "about them," his brothers, in the twenty years that have lapsed since their last fatal encounter, also are evoked by the particular wording and the immediate and wider narrative context of the phrase "And Joseph remembered the dreams he dreamt for them" (a verbatim translation of 42:9). As if behind the memory of the

---

2. All English translations are from the NEB, unless otherwise stated.

symbolic dreams, there lurks another memory, unstated, that of a traumatic event, which tends to surface in dreams, of what occurred to Joseph when his brothers had come close to his attempted murder by throwing him, after stripping him of his exceptional garment, presumably close to naked, into a pit, later selling him off to merchant travelers who happened to pass by, brutally severing him from his protective father and destining him to what in all likelihood can be imagined as a life of slavery and exile (37:23-30). Surely, in paraphrasing Shakespeare's *Tempest*, "such stuff" are nightmares made of.[3] The ambiguity of Joseph's act of memory has intrigued commentators through the ages. In premodern exegesis, it was usually solved by relying on the main biblical (and premodern) conception of dreams as prognostications, encodings of future events.[4] The medieval Jewish commentator Nachmanides suggests, for instance, that Joseph most accurately "remembered," when meeting his brothers, the detailed images of both his symbolic dreams as a complementary pair. Having realized the first dream had come true in their present bowing before him as ruler of Egypt (42:6), Joseph sought the complete fulfillment, in detail, of his second dream, wherein Benjamin and Jacob were also to come under his authority. Joseph's subsequent actions, according to Nachmanides and other commentators, are not so much motivated by his revenge upon his brothers (though this psychological level is acknowledged by some); rather, they anticipate and are even meant to create the necessary conditions for the enactment in reality of the second dream (see Shavel 1996: 232–33).[5]

---

3. The connection of dreams to traumatic symptoms and to repression in general is essentially based on Sigmund Freud's *The Interpretation of Dreams* (first published in 1900), most notably the first full account of his dynamic view of mental processes and of the unconscious. For a recent appraisal, see Frieden 1990. Since then, the subject of dreams and traumatic memory has been researched in depth; see further bibliographical background in the postscript below.

4. On dreams in the Bible and the ancient world, see "Postscript."

5. For Nachmanides's commentary, see the Rabbinic Bible (*Mikra'ot Gedolot Haketer*) edited by M. Cohen 1999: 130–33. Other medieval Jewish commentators (e.g., Rashi and Radak) emphasize Joseph's realization that his dreams are coming true. This approach is also found in modern commentaries on this verse (see those mentioned in "Postscript"). The biblical plot underlines the eventual physical hierarchy between Joseph and his siblings, less so with regard to his father (Gen. 42:6; 43:26; 45:28; 46:29). Radak's psychological reasoning stands out in his comments on the wider implications of Joseph's "memory" (42:9): "and when he remembered all that they did to him he did not repay them badly, but caused them sorrow and annoyed them" (*Mikra'ot Gedolot Haketer*, Cohen 1999: 133).

Modern literary analysis of the Joseph narrative highlights the complex role of the memory flashbacks by the various characters as contributing to the portrayal of their consciousness, as well as to the structuring and buildup of the plot. Thus, Joseph's "remembering" of his dreams characterizes his wider state of mind upon encountering his brothers—not only for their symbolic content, now about to be realized, but also for the memory of his ordeal at his brothers' hands, one that came about as the result of his symbolic dreams.[6] The interpretive history of 42:9 illuminates the deep structure of memory, dreams, and the connection between them in the Joseph narrative, as well as other aspects of its prophetic and religious-historical significance. Within a traumatic-centered psychological reading of the story, as I would like to suggest here, Joseph's unspecified reminiscence of his dreams, at this charged moment of his reencounter with his brothers, hints at a wider traumatized facet in his character. This facet is further revealed in the narrative span of chapters 42–45, wherein Joseph's behavior can be analyzed as reflecting the distress symptoms and behavioral patterns typical of traumatized people. This approach has wider implications for the story of Joseph and his brothers as a whole, suggesting that the theme of trauma and its resolution is central to the understanding of its plot.

---

6. See especially Polak 1994: 173–74, who illuminates the contrastive structuring of the scene of Joseph's memory of his dreams, and the scene of the ordeal in which the brothers remember them (37:18-19). Alter (1981: 163) comments on 42:9 as triggering "a whole train of memories in Joseph" and as a rare instance in which the biblical narrator reports "the character's consciousness of his past . . . which unlike knowledge of the future, is not a guide to policy but a way of coming to terms with one's moral history, a way of working towards psychological integration." Sternberg (1987: 288) considers the act of memory as a trigger in the tit-for-tat process of Joseph's revenge upon his brothers that is about to unfold: "The hypothesis that Joseph is bent on revenge gains further psychological support from the object of remembrance—the dreams, whose narration led to the crime and whose fulfillment enables the punishment—and more subtly from the playacting that follows. . . . In ethical terms, moreover, such vengeance has a rough justice about it that might appeal even to one who has not gone through, and just relived, a series of traumatic experiences: attempted murder, enslavement, seduction followed by the charge of attempted rape and three years in jail." In the detailed traumatic contextualization of the narrative, I will suggest that revenge (and fantasies relating to it) is recognized as a minor motivation in the story, as one stage, in fact, of Joseph's reckoning with the past, whereas the process of psychological integration of the initial trauma of domestic abuse into Joseph's life story becomes central to the unraveling of Joseph's subsequent actions in the buildup of the plot.

In her classical study on *Trauma and Recovery,* the psychiatrist Judith Lewis Herman defines the common core of the varied traumatic experiences of victims of captivity and domestic abuse:

> Psychological trauma is an affliction of the powerless. . . . Traumatic events overwhelm the ordinary systems of care that give people a sense of control, connection, and meaning. . . . Traumatic events are extraordinary, not because they occur rarely, but rather because they overwhelm the ordinary human adaptations to life. Unlike commonplace misfortunes, traumatic events generally involve threats to life or bodily integrity, or a close personal encounter with violence and death. . . . Certain identifiable experiences increase the likelihood of harm. These include being taken by surprise, trapped, or exposed to the point of exhaustion. . . . In each instance, the salient characteristic of the traumatic event is its power to inspire helplessness and terror. (Lewis Herman 1992: 33–34)[7]

Joseph's ordeal at the hands of his brothers, as described in Gen. 37:23-30, can be identified within this definition as a traumatic experience. For in being stripped and then thrown, partially or completely naked, into the pit, as into a live grave, he is not only rendered completely helpless by the overwhelming force of his gang of brothers, the threat to his life and bodily integrity evident, but he is also taken by surprise, completely unaware of the extent and fervor of their hatred toward him.[8] The silent reaction afforded to him by the narrator, in the primary record of the event, can also be interpreted, when contrasted with the talkative conniving of the brothers, as a sign of complete shock, reflecting the alteration of the victim's consciousness (as a means of self-defense). Such alteration has been identified behind the known symptom of "constriction and numbing," typical of posttraumatic stress disorder.[9] Joseph's subsequent actions also reflect the "dialectic of psychological trauma," defined as "the conflict between the will to deny horrible events and the will to proclaim them aloud. . . . When the truth is finally recognized, survivors can begin their recovery. But far too often when secrecy

---

7. For more on this work, see "Postscript."

8. Joseph's unawareness is underlined in the narrative by his father's ignorance in sending him after his brothers (37:12-14), and further echoed by Jacob's shock when learning of Joseph's "disappearance" (37:32-33).

9. Lewis Herman 1992: 42–47.

prevails, the story of the traumatic event surfaces not as a verbal narrative but as a symptom."[10]

Trauma-related behavioral patterns can also be uncovered in the narrative portrayal of the brothers and Jacob. As will be shown more briefly at the end of this paper, these characters are contrastively juxtaposed with that of Joseph inasmuch as their ability to cope with trauma is concerned. Joseph's place in this triangle of traumatized behavior is the most developed and pronounced in the story, not only because he is the main character, but also since, after all, he is the direct recipient of his brothers' victimization.[11] In this light, Joseph's "remembrance" of his dreams at the start of the story, beyond their known interpretations, is also an expression of his "dialectic of trauma," reflecting the tension between "the twin imperatives of truth-telling and secrecy," namely, between hiding his victimized sense of self (as one would hide a secret) and proclaiming his victimization, and bringing it out into the open. This tension builds up in his psyche from the moment he sets eyes upon his brothers, his behavior from that point reflecting his fluctuation between these two pulls until they implode. The memory of "the dreams," when followed by the unspecified relative phrase "which he had dreamt about them," can thus also be alluding to other, unspoken dreams he may have had about them, in which the traumatic experience finds its primary unconscious outlet.[12]

The immediate context of Gen. 42:7-9 supports this analysis from several angles. On the one hand, the occurrence of reminiscence, as it is described in this narrative sequence, is manifestly associative. It is a moment all of us recognize in the workings of our own memories, for it is triggered by an associative image: in seeing his brothers bowing to the ground before him (42:6). Joseph is thrown back in time upon the bending movement of the sheaves and

---

10. Lewis Herman 1992: 1.

11. Moral and psychological aspects of offensive forms of familial and domestic relations have been widely addressed in relation to biblical narrative in general and the patriarchal and Joseph narratives in particular in biblical study. See, for instance, the works and commentaries embedded in n. 21 and Lewis Herman 1992: 41–42, as well as in works of rabbinic teaching (e.g., N. J. Cohen 1995). Nonetheless, as far as I am aware, the specific expression of trauma-related behavior has not been discussed with regard to Joseph's character and this narrative at large.

12. The peculiar usage of the pronoun ל after חלם ("dreamt about/of/on/for"), not attested in other biblical instances of this verbal form, may also accentuate the ambiguity of Joseph's unspecified memory of his dreams.

heavenly elements, the common core of his dream pair. Hence, he is provided with a hint to their symbolic "unlocking"; this would suggest that what he primarily remembers are his adolescent dreams, which have now passed from unconscious to conscious memory. On the other hand, the intervening verses between the physical encounter (42:6) and the registered birth of memory (42:9) reflect Joseph's volatile state of mind, strained between his awakening mental perception and his unkempt emotions, mostly that of anger, on the verge of bursting: "And Joseph saw his brothers and he recognized them but he pretended not to know them. And he spoke harshly to them: 'Where do you come from?'" (42:7). Though Joseph may have expected some memory to have been stirred in his brothers' consciousness as well, especially after hearing his voice upon questioning them, the narrative stresses their failure to identify him just after seconding his recognition of them (v. 8). It is only after his short exchange of sorts with his brothers that Joseph is said to have "remembered" his dreams "about them" (v. 9).[13]

The brothers' unawareness, when juxtaposed with Joseph's act of memory, can also be construed as the trigger that creates a linkage to the trauma. For it is interpreted by Joseph (wrongly, perhaps, as he shall later learn) as a sign of their ongoing indifference, a hurtful reminder of their emotional relationship to him: one of rejection, hate, and victimization. It is his understanding that he does not exist for them that awakens in him the memory and experience of his dreams. This memory is illuminated not only by the association of an image in reality to one stored in the mind, but also by other associations in the inner stirrings of his mind. The downward movement of being thrown into the pit may be one of them. The sequencing of the narra-

---

13. On the opposition between Joseph's knowledge and the brothers' ignorance as emphasized by the narrative structuring, see Polak 1994; and by the usage of the leading root נכר (n-k-r), Alter 1981; and cf., in premodern exegesis, *Gen. Rab.* 91:7: "Said R. Levi: when they fell into his hands, 'And Joseph recognized his brothers'; when he fell into his hands, 'And they did not recognize him'." For a detailed study of the consistent recurrences and special constellation of lexemes of sight, insight, and oral communication in the Joseph narrative, see Sutskover 2007. According to her analysis, "dreaming" is related to the semantic field of "seeing" in this story and is combined with that of oral communication at strategic points in the narrative (i.e., 37:7: "saw, recognized, spoke roughly"). On complementary aspects of the visual and the verbal in the buildup of "perception" as a field of meaning in biblical narrative, see also Polak 1994: 102–106. In light of these studies, it is interesting to consider whether the theme of traumatic memory and its resolution is also underlined by the interplay of the semantic fields in the Joseph narrative—mainly since traumatic memory is distinguished by its silent visual imagery, whereas its therapeutic resolution is distinctly verbal.

tive, therefore, which creates a psychological linkage between Joseph's sense that he has been "forgotten" by his brothers—completely annihilated, as it seems, from their consciousness—and his "remembering" of them, points to the traumatic undertone of his memory. This sequencing also emphasizes Joseph's sense of being completely cut off from his brothers, isolated by his self-awareness and required to contain, as he does, the "dialectic of trauma" imploding inside him.

Lastly, the traumatic air of Joseph's memory is also apparent in its description as an irruption of his stream of consciousness, which is instantaneously subdued, to be immediately followed by the surprising accusation that the brothers are spies (in the space of the same verse 8, to which I shall return later). This immediacy accords with Lewis Herman's description:

> Long after the danger is past, traumatized people relive the event as though it were continually recurring in the present . . . for the trauma repeatedly interrupts. It is as if time stops at the moment of the trauma. The traumatic content becomes encoded in an abnormal form of memory, which breaks spontaneously into consciousness, both as flashbacks during waking states and as traumatic nightmares during sleep. (1992: 37)

Notwithstanding the dominant biblical (and premodern) interpretation of dreams as prognostications, and their alternative view in Freudian wish fulfillment interpretation and in Jungian dream symbolism as encoded expressions of repressed desires and emotions, the folk wisdom of various societies is known to recognize in dreams, and especially in nightmares, windows to real—often traumatic—experiences.[14] In this light, Joseph's memory of his dreams, as it appears in the immediate context, can be taken at face value, primarily (or at least consciously) referring to the symbolic dreams without excluding murkier nightmarish connotations. Their significance lies not in the details of the dreams themselves, but rather in how they were received by the brothers (and to a lesser extent, by the father), and in the horrific acts of violence that ensued some time after their telling and, no less importantly, as a result of the telling. Hence, the dreams become iden-

---

14. This notion growingly came to serve in the analysis of traumatic dreams as a means of recovering a person's memory of the traumatic event; see further in "Postscript." On Freud, see n. 3; for Carl Gustav Jung's *Dreams*, see Jung 2002.

tified with Joseph's trauma (whatever their content) and with his "altered" state of consciousness, which is typical of the dialectic of trauma. The layer beneath layer of the dreams' memory is suggestive of the process known as "doublethink" or "dissociation" in which "the psychological distress symptoms of traumatized people simultaneously call attention to the existence of an unspeakable secret and deflect from it. This is the most apparent in the way traumatized people alternate between feeling numb and reliving the event. The dialectic of trauma gives rise to complicated, sometimes uncanny alterations of consciousness" (Lewis Herman 1992: 1). What lies beneath Joseph's apparent memory is another, deeply disturbing, and yet unprocessed and uncontainable memory. As he is still in complete denial, he has yet to unravel its connection to the dreams—namely, the memory of his abuse.

The linkage between trauma and memory is also perceptible in the extended narrative context, wherein the dreams are thrice mentioned as motivating the brothers' actions:[15] first in their open rebuke of Joseph's sheaf dream and their inner reaction to it, as disclosed by the narrator: "And they hated him still more because of his dreams and what he said" (37:8),[16] and then twice in the frame structure of their murderous plan: "They saw him at a distance, and before he reached them, they plotted to kill him. They said to each other, 'Here comes the dreamer. Now is our chance; let us kill him and throw him into one of these pits and say that a wild beast has devoured him. Then we shall see what will come of his dreams'" (37:18-20). In this manner, Joseph's victimization is directly connected to the dreams he boastfully "told" (37:5-6, 10). That the actual telling of the dream has an effect on reality is a known feature of the ancient conception of dreams.[17] It is almost as if the brothers, in their subsequent actions, are engaged in an inverted performance of Joseph's dreams. The reader is left with the disturbing sense that other things might have happened had Joseph not "told" his dreams, had he not released them from the unspoken visual register (of the unconscious) to the spoken verbal register (of the conscious) and so had begun to make them operable in reality.

---

15. This factor has been recognized in literary analyses of the story; see n. 5.
16. This is echoed in Jacob's taking him to task over the second dream (37:10-11).
17. On dream telling as a form of performance of dreams (and their memory) in late antiquity, see Cox Miller 1994.

From a psychological perspective, moreover, Joseph's distant experience of "telling" his dreams has taught him to be wary of what he can let out into the open, expose of his inner self, despite and even against his natural inclination—once a manifestation of his confident and (untraumatized) egocentric character to "show off," let out, and tell. Against the wider background of the story, Joseph's momentary memory of his dreams (42:8) may be construed as adding to his self-defensiveness by way of inner warning and apprehension; he now must be on double guard, for as the dreams he once told intentionally drew attention to his destined grandeur and proved destructive when released into reality, their actual fulfillment in his present standing above his brothers may do so as well. This time, putting his dreams and, more precisely, the transitory memory of his dreams into words may draw unwarranted attention to the weakest and most fragile moment of his humiliation and despair and may destroy him, in his own eyes and those of the Egyptians. That this process of "telling" might not prove destructive but, on the contrary, become the means of Joseph's inner and outer release is actually a discovery the hero will make in the unfolding of the plot.[18]

Before the resolution of the traumatic state is enabled, however, the description of Joseph's traumatized state intensifies and thickens as the plot progresses, in that his behavior and reactions build up into a realistic psychological portrayal. The most recognizable feature that identifies him in a state of posttraumatic stress disorder is the uncontrolled oscillation of his feelings and reactions, alternating between pacified indifference or inactivity and active anger.[19]

This state of altered consciousness is also captured in Joseph's defensively sardonic accusation, which follows immediately upon the "memory" of his dreams: "So he said to them, 'You are spies; you have come to spy out the nakedness of the land'" (42:9). The connection between the dreams and the seemingly unexpected choice of accusation has perplexed many commentators.[20] However, when interpreted in the context of posttraumatic stress disorder, it reflects Joseph's tormented attempt to secure his denial—his oscillating reaction to the threatening content of his "unspoken" nightmarish dreams and experiences. The accusation of spying may also be construed, in

---

18. See the section below titled "Transforming Traumatic Memory."
19. Cf. the sources mentioned in n. 13.
20. For various solutions, cf. the commentaries mentioned in "Postscript."

this light, as a form of psychological dissociation or projection, self-referential in nature: for it is Joseph, in fact, who is in real danger of being stripped of his defenses, of being confronted with the "nakedness" (עֶרְוָה) of the truth about his anguished relationship with his brothers. The abusive core lies in his having been stripped by them and then deliberately thrown into a dry pit as a dead body (or any other "object") might be cast into a grave (37:24). It is this memory of this most humiliating experience, the helpless sensation of his having been turned into an object, dehumanized, that is on the verge of being "exposed" or "found out."[21] And so Joseph must defer, for now, the pain and shame of recognition, buy time, suppress emerging memories so threatening to his integral sense of self, of reconstructed identity, now ruler over the whole of Egypt. With time, however, this transitory memory is bound to be self-revealing to an expert dream interpreter such as himself.

In the accusation of spying and the reversed victimization that will ensue from it—this time directed by Joseph at his brothers, wherein they will be imprisoned, then released, then imprisoned (Simeon) again, then released, and yet again be threatened with death and imprisonment (Benjamin)— commentators have recognized the structural "measure for measure" principle, prevalent in the Joseph narrative and other biblical narratives.[22] Yet in the context of posttraumatic stress disorder, Joseph's conduct may be analyzed

---

21. The root עֶרְוָה generally denotes "uncovering," also by way of "emptying" or "pouring out" (cf. Gen. 24:20; Lev. 20:18; Isa. 53:12). Cf. Rashi's comment on this verse: "Every עֶרְוָה (nakedness) in the Bible is in the sense of finding out" (Cohen 1999: 132). According to the psychological interpretation offered here, the accusation of spying is a form of projection onto the brothers, which inverts Joseph's inner fear of being stripped (this time metaphorically) of his defenses. On the connection of the lexeme עֶרְוָה to the semantic field of "seeing" in the story, see Sutskover 2007: 44. Alter (1981: 164) connects עֶרְוָה here to the possibility that "Joseph feels a kind of incestuous violence in what the brothers have done to him and through him to his father." In this, he points to a distinctly traumatic dimension in Joseph's accusation, though, in my view, the incestuous contextualization is less convincing here. While a sexual threat may indeed be implied in Joseph's stripping by his brothers, the survivor's deep-seated fear of the truth being found out, common to victims of various forms of abuse (including sexual abuse), offers a more comprehensive psychological explanation for Joseph's accusation and his wider behavioral pattern in the narrative sequence.

22. On the one hand an expression of vindictiveness and revenge, interpreters have recognized this is also a trial inflicted by Joseph upon his brothers, which enables the maturing process of the characters in coming to terms with the past. This understanding is already reflected in *Gen. Rab.* 91:6. For modern literary analyses, see, in particular, Sternberg 1987: 285–308; Alter 1981: 155–77. On this pattern in the structuring of the Jacob cycle as well as the fashioning of Jacob's maturation, see, e.g., Fokkelman 1975: 126–30; Fishbane 1998: 40–62; Pardes 1992: 60–78; Polak 1994: 291–92.

as a symptom, namely, that of the repetitive and uncontrolled "intrusion" of the trauma into the survivor's life, which is often manifested in forms of "reenactment": "Traumatized people relive the moment of trauma not only in their thoughts and dreams but also in their actions. The reenactment of traumatic scenes is most apparent in the repetitive play of children. . . . Adults as well as children feel impelled to re-create the moment of terror, either in literal or in disguised form" (Lewis Herman 1992: 39).[23]

It is plausible, I think, to recognize in Joseph's repeated staging of his brothers' incarceration a form of "repetition compulsion," a reenactment of his moment of terror. For in afflicting it time and again on his brothers, he is actually reexperiencing his own moment of terror, in subtle variations. Remarkably, the reader senses that Joseph is playing a game with his brothers, but one of a threatening compulsive nature, for "there is something uncanny about reenactments. Even when they are consciously chosen, they have a feeling of involuntariness. Even when they are not dangerous, they have a driven, tenacious quality" (Lewis Herman 1992: 41).

Beyond the expression of natural vendetta, Joseph's staging of the repetitive drama can indeed be interpreted as a trial he consciously inflicts upon his brothers, one of measured moral punishment for their crimes (as they themselves guiltily admit at the first instance of their confinement).[24] Yet the psychological functions of reenactment appear to me no less suited to the story. One possibility is that Joseph is reenacting the traumatic moment, as traumatized people often do, with a fantasy of changing the outcome of the dangerous encounter or, at least, toying with this outcome.[25] This sense receives daunting religious expression in his self-reflective statement at the very end of the narrative: "As for you, you meant evil against me; but God meant it for good" (50:20), to which I shall return later. That there was indeed a different outcome to his victimization is made clear in the plot itself. In this manner, Joseph's reenactment of his trauma is a rare case of such a fantasy that, luckily for him and all concerned, has miraculously (and through divine intervention) come true.

---

23. Freud had initially recognized "repetition compulsion" as the recurrent intrusion of traumatic experience (see Lewis Herman 1992: 41).

24. See the section below titled "Transforming Traumatic Memory," and cf. n. 21.

25. "A fantasy of magical resolution through revenge, forgiveness, and compensation" is typical of trauma victims at the stage in which they resist the mourning of the traumatic loss. See Lewis Herman 1992: 189.

The more persuasive view of reenactments, developed by recent theorists, is as "spontaneous attempts to integrate the traumatic event" or "an attempt to relive and master the overwhelming feelings of the traumatic moment" (Lewis Herman 1992: 41–42). This motivation is adroitly depicted in the development of the story line, wherein the more Joseph reenacts the memory of his trauma, the more he becomes emotional and vulnerable, yet the more he is able to confront the traumatic experience and come to terms with it. This process is sketched out primarily in his position as observer of his brothers' affliction (of which he is self-aware as perpetrator), through which he relives his own trauma. The recurring outbursts of crying may also reflect, according to this interpretation, his anger and pain at experiencing anew what had originally happened to him.

In the subsequent traps Joseph lays for his brothers, in varying mirror reversals of fortune and outcome whence they are always "found out" over things they have not done, there is an obvious element of disguise—one underlined by Joseph's own self-revealing (but possibly self-deprecating, in hindsight) statement: "Did you not know that a man like me is bound to find out?" (44:15). The literary and theological aspects of this disguise, and the interplay of apparent and hidden motivations in the human and divine spheres, have been discussed in various studies of the Joseph narrative (see, for example, Gunkel 1922; Redford 1970; Speiser 1986; Westermann 1987; Wenham 1994). But here it is considered as a symptom: "Traumatized people find themselves reenacting some aspect of the trauma scene in disguised form, without realizing what they are doing" (Lewis Herman 1992: 40). In a similar fashion, Joseph's behavior is portrayed as uncanny: there is a tension between his revengeful, as it were, choice to inflict measured pain on his brothers and "watch" this pain, on the one hand, and his lack of control over his actions and reactions, on the other hand. These too are compulsive in nature, chosen at a whim.

Reliving the traumatic moment is usually dreaded by trauma survivors, who do not consciously seek or welcome this process, since the emotions of terror and rage aroused by it "are outside the range of ordinary emotional experience, and they overwhelm the ordinary capacity to bear feelings" (Lewis Herman 1992: 42). When viewed in this light, Joseph's "reliving" of his trauma, through its reenactment, is an effort at mastering it. The fact that he takes this opportunity is a sign of his emotional resilience and vitality, which will enable him eventually to reach resolution. The game of hide-and-seek he plays with his brothers becomes a way of restoring his sense of efficacy, a form of empowerment. Since trauma is known to shatter the inner schemata of the self and the world, Joseph's choice to confront the past, however draining or threatening this may be to his damaged self, is part of his characterization as a person of great mental courage, and as such can also be seen as the internal, spiritual fulfillment of the content of his symbolic dreams.

Transforming Traumatic Memory

The first part of this study focused on the oscillating patterns of Joseph's conduct toward his brothers, including the recurring motif of uncovering and concealment, as a reversal of his repressed traumatic experience. The compulsive reenactment was interpreted as a means for mastering the trauma. In clinical studies, reenactment is said to follow upon remembrance. In our story line, it also follows Joseph's "remembering" of his dreams.

Recovery from trauma has been compared to a marathon run, a prolonged and painful process that consists of several cardinal stages, including the creation of a safe environment, remembrance, mourning, reconnection, and telling. Joseph appears to undergo some of the stages described within the scene of his breaking down and confession to his brothers (Gen. 45:1-16), to which most of the following discussion is devoted. Other stages are reflected in earlier parts of the narrative leading up to his disclosure, as well as in later sections, not all of which can be addressed within the limitations of this chapter.

Two of the scenes preceding Joseph's confession cannot go unmentioned in this context, since they constitute preliminary conditions for the resolution of Joseph's traumas as well as instances of memory. The first of these scenes concerns Joseph's eavesdropping on the story of his brothers' memory of the traumatic event (42:21-24). The discovery that the brothers have neither forgotten him nor have been oblivious to their deeds all along comes as something of a shock to Joseph and to the reader as well. Moreover, the unlocking of the brothers' memory occurs quite immediately at the beginning of what will become their traumatic ordeal, just after being accused of spying on the third day of their imposed captivity, having been taken completely by surprise. The surfacing of their repressed memory of their brother's suffering is triggered by the special conditions of confinement that not only re-create and so enable them to identify with Joseph's situation in the pit, but also force upon them an opportunity for the self-reflection to which they appear to rise in verses 21-22: "They said to one another, 'No doubt we deserve to be punished because of our brother, whose suffering we saw; for when he pleaded with us we refused to listen. That is why these sufferings have come upon us.' But Reuben said: 'Did I not tell you not to do the boy wrong? But you would not listen and his blood is on our heads, and we must pay.'"

In viewing the brothers' confession against the background of traumatic experience, the return of the repressed memory is apparent in their retelling of the event, for it contains at least one "reconstructed" detail that is not recorded in the third-person narrative of the event (37:18-28), namely, Joseph's begging for help. There are other aspects in which their memory differs from what "really" happened, but in a way that is typical of the terseness of biblical narrative and of the selectiveness of memory: their silent and indifferent "sitting down to eat" immediately after throwing Joseph into the pit might have been the time when they heard him cry out. The shamefulness of this behavior is left in denial, and Joseph is now "our brother," "the lad," not the depersonalized "dreamer" of the crime scene; yet Reuben's genuine intention and failed attempt at saving Joseph is more or less correctly reconstructed, and this serves to authenticate the confession as a whole. This authentication is not only employed by the narrator in order to restore the brothers' credibility (for the question of their truthfulness is constantly raised, given that they ruthlessly cheated their brother and father). It is also crucial to the victim, Joseph, who is now the silent bystander in his brothers' ordeal, taking on the precise role of instigator and witness that they had filled in his traumatic experience. Yet, whereas he was aware of their cruelty—all the more so since they did not heed his pleas (as the readers retrospectively learn), they are saved by this awareness. That Joseph's first outburst of crying when turning away from them immediately follows their confession is revealing of its immense psychological importance (37:24). In effect, the brothers tell the story of his trauma; they speak what for him is yet unspeakable.[26]

The brothers' ability to verbalize this reconstructed memory is indispensable to Joseph's recovery. Lewis Herman refers to Pierre Janet's stress on

---

26. And it will remain, in part, unspeakable even when Joseph himself confesses.

the nonverbal nature of traumatic memory as "frozen" and "wordless" when compared with "normal" memory, which he defined essentially as "the action of telling a story." Adds Lewis Herman:

> Traumatic memories lack verbal narrative and context; rather, they are encoded in the form of vivid sensations and images. . . . Just as traumatic memories are unlike ordinary memories, traumatic dreams are unlike ordinary dreams. In form, these dreams share many of the unusual features of the traumatic memories that occur in waking states. They often include fragments of the traumatic event in exact form, with little or no imaginative elaboration.[27]

Joseph's memory of the event is traumatic, rendering it—like his dreams—unspeakable. This explains the ambiguous content of his first memory of "the dreams" and the silent imagery of his confession, which is to come later. The brothers' memory, however, is "normal," as their dreams might be; hence, they are capable of reflecting on what happened not through fragmentary images but within a narrative context. The transformation of frozen imagery into verbal narrative is beautifully captured in their description of having seen "the plight of his soul" (as in a visual image of sorts) when he "pleaded with them" (now a verbal context) and they "did not hear" (his words). The verbalization of the memory is intensified in the citation of Reuben's "saying" at the scene of the crime, and the repetition of "yet you did not hear."

Through hearing his brothers' verbal construction of his own memory, Joseph will be affected in due course to develop a "narrative language" in which he can "tell" his trauma, albeit by transforming it. As the true survivor of the events, Joseph "is continually buffeted by terror and rage, emotions qualitatively different from ordinary fear and anger" (Lewis Herman 1992: 42). That he is still far from the point of conscious remembrance is made clear not only by his crying spurt and its concealment, but also by his subsequent action: "And he came back to them and spoke to them and took Simeon from them and shackled him in front of their eyes" (42:24).

Joseph's awakened consciousness of the past is like a window that gradually opens: He first remembers his dreams, then hears his brothers' verbal

---

27. "Strictly speaking, then, one who retains a fixed idea of a happening cannot be said to have a 'memory' . . . it is only for convenience that we speak of it as a 'traumatic memory'" (Lewis Herman 1992: 37–39).

affirmation of his ordeal and of their guilt, and now has to confront memory on his own. Before he himself can recall, give words to what happened, he must reenact the trauma as a means of mastering it and integrating it into his life. On the one hand, Joseph's intended overhearing of his brothers' testimony moves the process of self-discovery forward. There is also reinforcement in the fact that the brothers were part witnesses, part instigators of the traumatic event itself. The affirmation of a survivor's reconstructed story by a live witness to the traumatic event is known to be beneficial to the recovery process (see Lewis Herman 1992: 194, 200–202). On the other hand, Joseph's reaction to the testimony also reflects, quite realistically at this stage, his complete lack of readiness to contain the traumatic experience. The reenactment stage is thus set in motion, for it cannot be "skipped" in the psychological resolution of the trauma.

The second scene that stands out as a precondition to Joseph's recovery, pointedly preceding his disclosure to his brothers, is Judah's speech (44:18-34). In the limits of this study, I will only point out one aspect of the speech that is the most relevant to traumatic resolution—namely, its restoration of Joseph's sense of communality. The speech has a reassuring effect on Joseph in revealing himself to his once victimizers, because it stresses a lasting emotional bond, cross-generational, in Jacob's dysfunctional family. In doing so, it induces a humane reconnection between Joseph and his father and brothers:

> Traumatic events destroy the sustaining bonds between individual and community. Those who have survived learn that their sense of self, worth and humanity depends upon their feeling of connection with others. Group solidarity provides the strongest protection against terror and despair; and the strongest antidote to traumatic experience. . . . Repeatedly in the testimony of survivors there comes a moment when a sense of connection is restored by another person's unaffected display of generosity. (Lewis Herman 1992: 215)

Judah's emotional speech undoubtedly functions as such a display of generosity, not only by endearingly acknowledging Jacob's deep bond with Joseph and Benjamin (44:20), but also by verbalizing yet again the traumatic event, this time through the father's eyes (vv. 27-29), and by its expression of binding commitment to Jacob and Benjamin, even at the price of self-sacrifice (vv. 30-34). The augmenting psychological and rhetorical force of this display enables Joseph to form a "reconnection." In hearing this speech, therefore, Joseph is not only witnessing how his brothers have changed due to their experience, but in Judah's words, he also recognizes and hence reclaims a lost part of himself, through which he may rejoin his brothers in human communality.

The turning point that allows for the therapeutic process to take place is captured in a condensed fashion in the scene of Joseph's emotional break-down, in which Joseph "gives voice" or "tells" in some way the story of his trauma. The cathartic aspects of this scene have been widely noted in studies of the Joseph narrative.[28] Here I would like to point out the scene's psychological credibility as a compressed manifestation of the stages necessary for recovery from trauma—namely, the creation of a safe environment, remembrance, mourning and reconnection, and telling (which were mentioned before), as well as three subsequent stages unmentioned earlier: reviewing the meaning, reconstructing a system of belief, and decision upon action (Lewis Herman 1992: 155). Behaviorally, traumatized people tend to follow this clinically documented sequence, though the main axis of recovery lies in the survivor's ability to verbally reconstruct the story of the trauma and "put the story, including the imagery, into words" (177). In the biblical narrative, however, Joseph appears to undergo several of the main stages here described concurrently within the scene of his breaking down and confessing to his brothers. In this, as in other aspects, a work of art and poetic genius differs from a live study; the elements are dexterously woven into the narrative plot, not altogether gradual or as timely as would be the case in a clinical observation. Nevertheless, the strength of the psychological portrayal, in what is so aptly described by the Qur'an (Sura 12:3) as "the most beautiful of stories,"[29] derives among other aspects from the authentic exposé of Joseph as a traumatized person, and the realistic fashioning of his resolution of the trauma or (in therapeutic terms) recovery from it.

It is admittedly only through undergoing the earlier stages of traumatic disorder and reaction that Joseph can reach the cardinal stage of confronting the past by "retelling" the traumatic event. This ability is linked in the story to Joseph's "memory" of his dreams and to his wider, famous acumen

---

28. See, for instance, the studies mentioned in nn. 6 and 22.
29. According to some commentators, however, this verse describes the Qur'an as a whole. See Yusuf Ali, 1934: 550.

as a dream interpreter—aspects of his personality that contribute, in some mysterious way, to his reaching this point. As the psychological study of testimonies has shown, the telling of a traumatic event—namely, that of its memory—is never an accurate reportage but always entails a transformation of sorts of the event itself on the part of the survivor. This, in effect, is what happens in the scene of Joseph's disclosure to his brothers:

> Then Joseph *could not control himself* before all those who stood by him; and he cried: "Make every one go out from me". *So no one stayed with him when Joseph made himself known to his brothers. And he wept aloud,* so that the Egyptians heard it and the house of Pharaoh heard it. And Joseph said to his brothers. *"I am Joseph; is my father still alive? . . .* I am your brother, Joseph, *whom you sold into Egypt. And now do not be distressed, or angry with yourselves, because you sold me here;* for God sent me before you to preserve life. For famine has been in the land for two years; and there are yet five years in which there will be neither plowing nor harvest. And God sent me before you to preserve for you a remnant on the earth, and to keep alive for you many survivors. *So it was not you who sent me here, but God*; and he has made me a father to Pharaoh, and lord over all his house and ruler over all the land of Egypt. *Make haste and go up to my father.* (45:1-8; italics added)

Whereas some of the previous scenes leading up to Joseph's momentous testimony can also be analyzed as *reflecting* the previously mentioned stages in the psychological process of recovery from trauma, this scene *contains* most of them in condensed intensity. The creation of a safe environment is mirrored in Joseph's request to remain utterly alone with his brothers. The stages of remembrance and mourning of the traumatic event find pulsating expression in the outburst of weeping that, despite Joseph's attempts to control it and keep it confined, is uncontrollable, magnified as in measurement of his pain to the extent that it reaches "the outsiders" (those he strived so hard to keep out of its sphere), namely, Egypt and the House of Pharaoh. Their "hearing" of his crying serves as an extended metaphor of Joseph's outing of his pain, which has no bounds, as well as a form of outside affirmation of his testimony. Lewis Herman describes this stage in the trauma victim's ordeal in very close terms: "The reconstruction of the trauma requires immersion in a past experience of frozen time; the descent into mourning feels like a surrender to tears that are endless" (1992: 195).

Consistent and repetitive crying is widely documented in studies of trau-matic recovery as an essential accompanying emotion of the recitation of the facts. If the recitation occurs without the accompanying emotions, it is considered "a sterile exercise, without therapeutic effect" (Lewis Herman 1992: 177). In this respect, Joseph's weeping is also an expression of his long-deferred mourning over what had taken place. In clinical records, this stage usually follows the recitation, but in our story it is compressed into the crying that precedes the confession. According to Lewis Herman (1992), mourn-ing is only enabled when the survivor recognizes there is no compensation for the suffering undergone.[30] Such recognition, which appears to have been gained through Joseph's fantasy of reenactment, gives way in this scene to a thickened expression of mourning, and is generally intimated by the scene as a whole. Joseph's repetitive crying, which is widely recognized as a leitmotif throughout the narrative, also accentuates the theme of trauma and recov-ery, for in it lies the traumatic experience itself: its *unspeakable* nature. The unbearable emotions it arouses are "qualitatively different from ordinary fear and anger" and hence cannot be expressed in words (Lewis Herman 1992: 42).[31] After this preparation, the cardinal stage takes place: that in which the survivor puts the trauma into words and tells the transformed memory of the traumatic event in a manner that turns the story into a live testimony, one with a private as well as a spiritual and public dimension. This stage is already foreshadowed in the narrative span by the Hebrew idiom ויתן קולו בבכי, literally "and he gave his voice in crying," signaling the beginning of a "giv-ing of voice," not necessarily words as yet, to what had happened. The words themselves are relatively sparse, but all the more so evocative: first the actual disclosure of Joseph's identity, his name, which has been hidden till now,

---

30. "During the process of mourning the survivor must come to terms with the impos-sibility of getting even. . . . The fantasy of compensation, like the fantasies of revenge and forgiveness, often becomes a formidable impediment to mourning. . . . The quest for fair compensation is often an important part of recovery. However, it also represents a potential transition. Prolonged, fruitless struggles to wrest compensation from the perpetrator or from others may represent a defense against facing the full reality of what was lost. Mourning is the only way to give due honor to loss; there is no adequate compensation" (189–90).

31. The crying in 45:2 is represented as a culmination of previous outbursts (cf. 42:24 upon hearing the brothers' confession; 43:20 upon seeing Benjamin) and will also recur after Joseph's disclosure; yet then it appears more as an expression of release of tension, relief, and even happiness than one of pain, anger, and perplexity (45:14-16 just after his confession; 46:29 upon encountering Jacob; 50:17 upon the brothers' request for forgiveness).

and then immediately the inquiry regarding his father. In this psychological context, the mention of the father is part of the traumatic experience, in that it reflects Joseph's mental and emotional suffering at being cut off from his protective home. After the record of the brothers' perplexed astonishment and Joseph's second affirmation of his identity in relation to them ("I am Joseph, your brother"), reference is made to the traumatic event itself, wherein Joseph's "selling" is mentioned twice: "I am your brother, Joseph, whom you *sold* into Egypt. And now do not be distressed, or angry with yourselves, because you *sold* me here; for God sent me before you to preserve life" (45:4-5; italics added).

As Lewis Herman points out, the transformed trauma story becomes a "new story . . . no longer about pain and humiliation" but rather "about dignity and virtue" (1992: 181). Accordingly, the stripping and throwing into the pit, the most humiliating aspects of Joseph's victimization as recorded in the third-person narrative of the event (37:23-24), are never uttered by Joseph. Rather, they are consigned to silence. As mentioned earlier, in the telling of Joseph's memory, there is a static nonverbal element: what we see in his confession is the silent movie of his sale, no more. The description of the sale is the closest he comes to touching what "really" happened, but it is enough; the unspeakable remains locked as it were in the space of visual memory, of dreams.

Jessica Wolfe describes her approach to trauma narrative with combat veterans as follows: "We have them reel it off in great detail, as though they were watching a movie and with all the scenes included. . . . The completed narrative must include a full and vivid description of the traumatic imagery" (quoted in Lewis Herman 1992: 177). The Joseph narrative conveys an artistic expression of this "fullness" by splitting up the reconstructions of memory. In this case, we have heard the pit scene from the brothers (somewhat reverberated in Judah's speech); now we hear the sale scene from Joseph.[32] This sequencing of reconstructed memories suggests, in my view, that the memory of the casting into the pit is not omitted from Joseph's confession by way of its continuing denial on his part, as if it never happened to

---

32. As mentioned earlier, Joseph's telling is visual, whereas the brothers' telling is intensely verbal. In this, Joseph's traumatized state is highlighted as one still imprinted with the traumatic imagery of the crime even when reconstructing the scene of his sale into slavery.

him. Rather, the omission serves the complex and masterful portrayal of his coming to terms with this memory as well, not through his own putting it into words, but through his reciprocation of the brothers' testimony and his own emphasis on the sale as a substituting, "transformative" account of his trauma. "This work of reconstruction actually transforms the traumatic memory, so that it can be integrated into the survivor's life story" (Lewis Herman 1992: 175). Accordingly, in Joseph's "new" story, the selling into slavery, initially described by the narrator in the record of the events themselves as a mellowing of the brothers' original plan (37:25-28), takes on a "transformed" meaning: "For God *sent* me before you to preserve life. . . . And God sent me before you to preserve for you a remnant on earth, and to *keep alive* for you many survivors. So it was not you who *sent* me here, but God" (45:5, 7-8a; italics added).

This religious explanation is in tune with the stages in which victims of trauma, in the process of recovery, are said to be engaged in "reviewing of meaning" and "reconstructing a system of belief." After admitting a form of what happened, Joseph is engaged in finding meaning and virtue in what happened. The brothers' deprecating "selling" of him, for money, becomes a form of "sending" (thrice repeated), intended by God. The murderous plan that preceded the selling is hinted at by its reversal, due to divine intervention, into a life-preserving mission:

> The traumatic event challenges the ordinary person to become a theologian, a philosopher, and a jurist. The survivor is called upon to articulate the values and beliefs that she once held and that the trauma destroyed. . . . The arbitrary, random quality of her fate defies the basic human faith in a just or even predictable world order. In order to develop a full understanding of the trauma story, the survivor must examine the moral questions of guilt and responsibility and reconstruct a system of belief that makes sense of her undeserved suffering. (Lewis Herman 1992: 178)

In his emphasis on God's ultimate plan, Joseph is effectively engaged in giving meaning to his trauma. He is reframing his personal trauma of survival from near death and exile within a life-affirming collective narrative that rearticulates a system of values and beliefs common to him and to his brothers. The horrific act of individual memory is thus encompassed by collective memory. It cannot be left as a sign of human brutality, of all that is unexplained, irrational, and out of our control. For this reason, among others, Joseph's moral reckoning will be further reechoed, after his father's death, in the final dialogue with his brothers. It becomes part of his ongoing legacy to them, in the closure of his story and the book of Genesis as a whole: "As for you, you meant evil against me; but God meant it for good, to bring it about that many people should be kept alive" (50:20). It is as if only after personal ordeal has been reviewed and given meaning within the wider memory of the group that the collective history of the sons of Israel can begin.

The very last stage of Joseph's "recovery" occurs at the end of his speech (45:9-13), when he ushers the brothers (twice using the verb *hurry*) to bring his father to Egypt, and provides them with the right words to convince Jacob and move this old and suspicious man into action. Joseph's resort to action is related to the resolution of his trauma, for as Lewis Herman points out, "Finally, the survivor cannot reconstruct a sense of meaning by the exercise of thought alone. The remedy for injustice also requires action. The survivor must decide what is to be done" (Lewis Herman 1992: 178).[33] Joseph's decision is not only the active expression of his existential life-affirming reasoning, but also a form of "letting go" of the past and looking forward to the future. The frame structure of Joseph's confession, beginning with "Is my father still alive?" and ending with "Hurry! Go up to my father!" reflects the process of Joseph's coming full circle: what was conceived for years as an insurmountable journey back to his father (at least mentally, even if physically it could have been undertaken) is now a matter for swift action, wherein the closing of distance is easily manageable, at least with respect to his father, and some measure of immediate consolation and repair is at hand in the here and now. Decisive action after a drawn-out process of indecisive games, in which he reenacted the trauma time and again in different variations, signals

---

33. Furthermore, "after many repetitions, the moment comes when the telling of the trauma story no longer arouses quite such intense feelings. It has become a part of the survivor's experience, but only part of it. . . . It occurs to the survivor that perhaps the trauma is not the most important, or even the most interesting, part of her life story. . . . When the 'action of telling a story' has come to its conclusion, the traumatic experience truly belongs to the past. At this point, the survivor faces the tasks of rebuilding her life in the present and pursuing her aspirations for the future" (Lewis Herman 1992: 195).

Joseph's resolution of his trauma and is a psychological manifestation of his recovery.[34]

Postscript

The word *trauma* has various definitions. In psychoanalysis, it is "any totally unexpected experience which the subject is unable to assimilate" and, by extension, "any experience which is mastered by the use of defenses."[35]

The study of psychological trauma began in the late nineteenth century, led by the pioneers of modern psychology and psychiatry, especially Charco, Janet, and Freud, who first recognized "hysteria" as a condition caused by psychological trauma. However, only in the late 1960s, when the systematic, large-scale investigation of the long-term psychological effects of combat veterans of the Vietnam War converged with the feminist movement's demand that society take seriously the domestic and sexual abuse of women and children, did modern systematic study of psychological trauma begin. Judith Lewis Herman was among the first psychiatrists to conduct a detailed and comparative group study of traumatic disorders and stages of recovery in victims of captivity (war veterans, prisoners, and Holocaust survivors) and abuse (children, battered women, victims of incest and rape). The results of her clinical work, which was conducted throughout the 1970s, were published in her book *Trauma and Recovery* (1992). The first study to bridge the gap between the worlds of domestic abuse and political terror, it has since become the classic point of reference on the subject. I have found this illuminating work most helpful in providing a framework from which to consider traumatic aspects in the Joseph narrative, even though from a nonprofessional perspective.

---

34. It is fruitful to consider the brothers' silent listening to Joseph's confession as functioning similarly to that of the therapist, who "plays the role of a witness and ally, in whose presence the survivor can speak the unspeakable" (Lewis Herman 1992: 175). The brothers' function as affirming witnesses to the traumatic event has been noted with regard to their confession earlier on in the narrative span. The silence in this scene can also be said to fulfill a similar function. In this manner, Joseph's "telling" is also transforming their status from mainly instigators to mainly witnesses of the crime, affording "new meaning" to their place in Joseph's life and enabling his eventual (full) pardon of them, as portrayed in 50:15-21.

35. See also the continuation of this quote: "Trauma, in this sense, produces anxiety, which is followed either by spontaneous recovery or the development of psychoneurosis" (Rycroft 1972: 170–71).

For a detailed survey of research history on psychological trauma, Lewis Herman's introduction (1992: 7–32) is helpful, with further rich bibliography in the notes. Chapters 2 and 9 are the most relevant to my study. In chapter 2 ("Terror"), Lewis Herman defines and analyzes trauma as "an affliction of the powerless" which, though once believed to result from uncommon events "outside the range of human experience," is now considered common human experience. Domestic abuse, of the kind reflected in the Joseph narrative, is defined as among the most common causes of trauma. Lewis Herman's discussion of the three main categories of the symptoms of posttraumatic stress disorder in this chapter, as encodings of the traumatic experience itself, are particularly relevant to the Joseph narrative, especially the symptom of "intrusion," as one "reflecting the indelible imprint of the traumatic moment." In this context, Lewis Herman also explains, in light of Janet's earlier work, the wordless and passive quality of traumatic memory and traumatic dreams as opposed to the verbal, narrative essence of regular memory. This differentiation was especially helpful to me in distinguishing between Jacob's traumatic memory and that of the brothers.

The connections between traumatic experience and dreams and the patterns of posttraumatic nightmares have been widely researched since the 1980s (see, for instance, the introduction and articles assembled by Barret 1996). There it is claimed that though the folk wisdom of people in centuries past reflects the understanding that dreams can have a special relationship to traumatic events, serving as a unique window to remembered or unremembered horrors, it was, ironically, the influence of Freud and Jung that turned wish fulfillment, metaphor, and symbolic interpretation into the focus of modern dream psychology, diverting interest from dreams as representing repressed memories of trauma, even though both thinkers were well aware that real traumas (such as sexual abuse or the shock of war) could show up quite realistically in dreams (Barret, "Introduction," 1–6).

It was only with the systematic study of posttraumatic stress disorder in the victims of captivity, atrocity, and abuse, given rise and legitimization by twentieth-century social developments and movements, that the connection between trauma and dreams was fully developed as a field of research. Chapter 9 of Lewis Herman's *Trauma and Recovery* (1992) was very helpful in highlighting the role of the interpersonal telling out loud of traumatic memory within a safe environment as an essential stage of healing and recovery, and also as a means of uncovering unconsciously repressed aspects of the traumatic event, thus coming closer to what actually happened.[36]

This type of psychoanalytic approach to Joseph's dreams, their memory, and relation to past traumata departs from the general conception of symbolic dreams in ancient Near Eastern and biblical thought, which usually conceived of dreams as forms of prediction, hinting at the dreamer's future or destiny (cf. the other pairs of symbolic dreams in the Joseph narrative—those of Pharaoh's ministers [40:5-20] and Pharaoh himself [41:1-36]). For detailed comparative studies and surveys of the literature, see Lipton (1999: 9–33). Lipton also emphasizes the distinctiveness of the conception of dreaming in the Joseph narrative in comparison to the dreams of the patriarchal narratives, which form the topic of her book (9). It is also worth consulting the works by Husser (1999), Lanckau (2006), and Ruth Fidler (2005).

Nevertheless, some notions of dreams in antiquity have relevance to the present outlook. I thank Athalya Brenner for drawing my attention in this regard to Patricia Cox Miller's work (1994), which has an illuminating discussion on "Dreams and Therapy" (chapter 4). Here, Cox Miller shows how "in crises of physical disease and mental distress, many people in the Graeco-Roman era turned to dreams for the healing of their ailments. . . . The ill could seek oneiric remedies from religious institutions, in the temples and shrines that had special 'incubation' chambers, where sleepers sought healing dreams" (106). The fascinating cases she studies, some of which suggest "dreams were viewed as vehicles of a very material kind of metamorphosis" (113), do not disclose a pre-Freudian, as it were, understanding of the connection of dreams to repressed memories of traumatic events. Nonetheless, the view that dreams, when processed in some way, can heal emotional as well as mental or physical pain recognizes their therapeutic function. This idea, I think, may also have been shared by the biblical writers, at least when it comes to the specific function of Joseph's memory of his symbolic (or other) dreams. Another Greco-Roman notion discussed by Cox Miller (chapter 3, "Interpretation of Dreams"), which has more relevance to the psychological reading offered here, is the importance attached to giving verbal expression to a dream by way of its interpretation. This idea is also found in later biblical

---

36. Some other general works in this field consulted are Alston et al. 1993; Hunt 1989; and Gollnick Lewiston 1987. See also Rimmon-Kenan 1987 for articles bearing on this study.

literature and postbiblical Jewish sources. More specifically, the aspect that concerns us here is that in order to understand the dream's meaning, one must move from "the visual image to the linguistic register of the textual word" (74). The same can be said of memories in general, since these are also encoded in the register of the visual image. In the recognition that images have to be "transformed" into words in order to enable recovery, there lies a basic tool that anticipates the modern psychoanalytic approach to dreams as vessels of traumatic memory. This tool is also reflected, in a wider sense and as I have tried to show, in the biblical portrayal of Joseph's character.

That having been said, this study is by no means an attempt at a full-scale or in-depth psychoanalytical study of the Joseph narrative, nor does it imply that the story was composed with such consciousness in mind. The point underlined here is that in the literary characterization of the main protagonists—and in the underlying themes and imagery of the story—the notion and process of trauma and recovery (or lack of recovery) is at work, and it is fashioned, in a psychological realism of sorts, through the appeal to the characters' memory. Some of the protagonists undergo a therapeutic process of sorts, wherein they are released in some way from the grip of the past, although not by others.

To the best of my knowledge, such a reading, focused on traumatic memory, has not yet been offered in relation to the Joseph narrative, although since the history of its interpretation and critical study has become so immense, I may have overlooked previous attempts in this direction. Psychological aspects of the story have engaged commentators since ancient times, and various psychoanalytic readings of biblical literature have, of course, served as a focus in modern studies. I cannot exhaust the relevance of those to my discussion, nor of the enormous exegetical and literary analyses of the Joseph narrative. At the advice of the editors, I have only touched upon these selectively in the notes.

CHAPTER 12

"Leadership and Land"
A Very Contextual Interpretation of Genesis 37–50 in KwaZulu-Natal, South Africa

Gerald West and Thulani Ndlazi

Introduction

For more than five years, a nongovernmental organization, a university-based community development and research center, and a range of community-based organizations have worked collaboratively in reading biblical texts. This essay gives an account of our reading of Genesis 37–50.

The initiating partner was the Church Land Programme, a nongovernmental organization (NGO) established to work with the churches around land redistribution issues (in the context of the apartheid legacy). Their ongoing partners are a wide range of community-based organizations (CBOs) in the KwaZulu-Natal province of South Africa. The Ujamaa Centre for Community Development and Research, which is a collaborative project involving socially engaged biblical scholars, organic intellectuals, and local communities of the poor, working-class, and marginalized, was invited to work with them in a project that would generate a series of contextual Bible studies dealing with land issues.

This tripartite alliance has been working together for the past five years. During this time, we have met regularly in day-long workshops to construct a series of contextual Bible studies. We have created a series of four studies under the following themes: "Land Possession and Land Dispossession," "Women and Land," "Food Security and Land," and "Leadership and Land."

The fifth in the series, "HIV and AIDS and Land," is still in process. Each of these themes was the result of an extensive process of focus group discussions and workshops.

Each of these contextual Bible studies is a collaborative act between the Ujamaa Centre, the Church Land Programme, and various church and community-based organizations. In each case, the Bible study has been extensively workshopped, tried out in local communities, reworked, edited for accessibility, and laid out in a format that is usable to facilitators.

The main objective of producing the contextual Bible studies was to create tools that could be used by church leaders, community activists, local churches, and other stakeholders to facilitate action dialogue around critical land issues affecting the marginalized and landless communities in rural areas. These Bible studies were and continue to be produced as community tools for ongoing struggles around land. They do not purport to be the only effective tool for community mobilization. Instead, they emerge from collective processes, involving academics, NGO activist-researchers, and community members, as one among many other local assets (Kretzmann and McKnight 1993). On their own, they cannot bring about transformative change, but when used in conjunction with other community assets in either animating new struggles or supporting ongoing struggles, they have shown signs of being extremely effective and adding value to people's struggles for land.

This essay provides a preliminary analysis of one of these Bible studies, the one that focuses on "Leadership and Land," drawing as it does on the story of Joseph in Genesis 37–50.

The Land Struggle

In 2003, nine years after the historical liberation of South Africa from the yoke of apartheid, the majority of land was still under the ownership of those who benefited from centuries of systematic dispossession. Cases of abuse and violence directed at indigenous South Africans who are farm dwellers, often living as exploited workers on their own ancestral land, continue to hover like a dark cloud over the South African democracy. Children and women have been the most vulnerable to the injustices on land. KwaZulu-Natal in particular, the site of our work in this essay, had the largest number of evictions between 1988 and 2002 and currently accounts for 21 percent of all land evictions in South Africa. An indication of the scale of farm evictions in KwaZulu-Natal is that this province went from having the highest number of farm employees in the country in 1988 (over 2 million) to just more than half that number (1,134,012) in 2002 (Wegerif et al. 2005: 58–59). Children make up half of the farm evictees, and three-quarters of farm evictees are women and children (41–76).

The failure by the South African government to deliver on its own land reform program has exacerbated the land problem. When the new democratically elected government took over from the apartheid regime in 1994, it promised the nation that 30 percent of the commercial agricultural land currently owned by white landowners would be transferred to indigenous (black African) South Africans by 1999. Since that promise was made, the deadline has been shifted several times. Recently, the deadline was set to 2014. To date, only 4.5 percent of land has been returned to the rightful land owners.

The government has cited a shortage of capacity, insufficient funds, and demands by farmers/landowners for unreasonable settlement amounts for their land. In the meantime, farm dwellers are evicted from their homes and are often physically attacked by landowners. Although the government has enacted laws that are supposed to protect landless people's rights, the laws are so ill designed that landowners are able to use the very same laws, laws such as the Prevention from and of Illegal Evictions (PIE) Land Act No. 19 of 1998 and Extension of Security Tenure Act (ESTA) No. 62 of 1997, to evict people. Furthermore, the exorbitant legal costs necessary to defend their rights in the court of law make it impossible for landless people to access the justice system.

A Religious Response to the Land Struggle

By 2003, the failure of the government's land reform programs was so apparent in KwaZulu-Natal that local ecumenical church structures began to mobilize a response. The Church Land Programme was mandated by the KwaZulu-Natal Christian Council and the KwaZulu-Natal Church Leaders Group to roll out a project that would enable the church in the province to respond to land matters. The project was launched in 2003 and named Land Matters in KwaZulu-Natal: An Ecumenical Response, commonly known as the Land Matters project. The project's objectives included, among others, enabling the institutional church in the province to respond to the challenges related to land that were (and still are) facing the landed and the landless (both being part of the church's constituency) in the province. Though the church saw a particular need to intervene on behalf of the landless and marginalized communities with a hope of strengthening their local struggles and amplifying their voices, one of the challenges facing the church was the fact that it is not a homogenous institution but comprises both the landed (landowners) as well as the landless (those without land). The core challenges were (and are) evictions, landlessness, insufficient access to the justice system, violation of basic democratic rights, gender discrimination, poverty, and underdevelopment.

The Church Land Programme entered a terrain in which landless communities were already working for change. The contribution of the Church Land Programme was to add capacity and resources in the struggle for access to land, food security, and sustainable livelihoods. The Bible studies that we will discuss more fully in this report were seen as tools that might assist with creating spaces for critical dialogue within local communities and between churches and communities. The Church Land Programme initiated these Bible studies for its own use, for the use of the church, for the use of local communities, and in response to the request from the Land Matters project. The Land Matters project felt that there was a need to develop materials that could help people respond to the land struggle in the province of KwaZulu-Natal (CLP n.d.).

To respond to these various needs, the Church Land Programme invited the Ujamaa Centre to work with them, together with local church and community leaders and activists within the constituencies and networks of the Church Land Programme, the KwaZulu-Natal Christian Council, and the KwaZulu-Natal Church Leaders' Group. The core of this collaborative project was made up of the Church Land Programme, the Ujamaa Centre, and local communities of the Rural Network. The majority of the participants in the core group came from various local communities that are affiliate members of the Rural Network, a social formation based in KwaZulu-Natal province, South Africa, constituted by about fourteen different rural and farming communities. Communities linked to the Rural Network nominated one or two people to participate in the Bible study focus group on their behalf. This nomination gave participants a mandate to represent their communities and to return to their communities to share the resources they had participated in constructing with their constituencies back in their local domains. The expectation was always that this feedback would contribute to enriching the ongoing local struggles for land rights. The mandate that participants obtained was of utmost importance in the process of producing the Bible study series. It created a sense of ownership among those engaged in each of the local struggles.

The Church Land Programme Bible study series aims to provide the church (both leaders and members) with broad values and commitments from the Bible when it comes to land issues; to provide the church (both leaders and members) with appropriate Bible study materials that would help to formulate effective, strategic, and proactive responses to land issues in South Africa; to help participants in the church and community become more conscious of land issues and, in particular, of how the Bible "speaks" about land issues; and to help participants talk about land issues within their community and within their church, by providing a framework for participants to share their experiences and express their emotions when it comes to their relationship with the land.

There were six phases in the collaborative project. In the first phase, representatives from the Rural Network worked in a focus group workshop to list as many issues affecting their landless and rural communities as possible. The representation from the Rural Network was quite diverse, including ministers of local churches, local community leaders (including traditional leaders), and land activists. So their respective contributions were also quite diverse. In the second phase, the group identified the priority issues from among the list of issues. By a show of hands, the process identified five key issues: land possession and land dispossession, women and land, food security and land, leadership and land, and HIV/AIDS and land. The third phase involved identifying biblical texts that might "speak to" each particular issue. Again, participants debated and then voted on the texts that seemed most relevant. In this phase, the biblical text and issue were brought into sustained critical dialogue, enabling the generative issue and the biblical text to suggest questions that would fit within the contextual Bible study framework of the Ujamaa Centre and that would be useful in the community context. During the fourth phase, the preliminary contextual Bible study was taken into the communities by their representatives, working usually in teams of between two to four, who facilitated contextual Bible studies. The contextual Bible study process and its products were then documented by the facilitators and became the resource for reworking the contextual Bible study in the fifth phase. In the fifth phase, the facilitators from the local constituencies again reconvened with the Church Land Programme and the Ujamaa Centre representatives to revise and rework the contextual Bible study. During this phase, it was reported that the contextual Bible studies were already accomplishing the objectives, enabling critical dialogue around the identified issue and leading to planned community actions, including the formation of a support group for women in one instance and a protest march in another. In the sixth phase, each reworked contextual Bible study was taken back to the community for more widespread use (and at the same time was prepared for publication and dissemination).

As indicated, the process of producing the Bible study series endeavored to be sensitive to issues of power and participation. The norm for projects of this nature is that while the intellectual thinking is treated as the sole responsibility of the elite (academics and NGOs), the involvement of the communities is *participation* in the workshops. In practical terms, this participation usually means that community members attend workshops where they are only expected to respond to prepared questions, so limiting the engagement of people from local struggles who are the very substance of the project. The former gives power to the elite, while the latter keeps the landless poor marginalized, even in spaces where their own liberation from landlessness is discussed. Hence, no overarching frameworks or questions had been prepared before participants engaged in the collaborative workshops.

Central to the contextual Bible study process is the control and ownership of a particular local community. The contextual Bible study is only one resource among the many other resources the community has access to. Among their own resources is their own sense of identity and dignity within their own organized formations. Such formations provide a site within which the articulate and embodied knowledge of the community resides and within which, if the site is safe, this knowledge is shared and becomes the property of a particular group gathering (Scott 1990). The presence of the Bible usually enhances the sense of a site's safety and bestows a sense of the sacred on the group gathering (West 2003).

The contextual Bible study methodology developed by the Ujamaa Centre over the past twenty years was considered a useful vehicle for the aims of the Church Land Programme and its Land Matters project (West 2006; 2009). The methodology combines the critical, structured, and systematic resources of socially engaged biblical scholarship with the experience and interpretive resources already present in local communities. The methodology frames the Bible study with questions that draw on a particular community's ownership of the Bible and the issue being discussed—in this case, issues about land. In between these framing sets of questions is another set of questions that grants the biblical text a voice in the discussion by returning the participants again and again to reread the text (and perhaps to delve behind the text), using questions shaped by the resources of biblical scholarship. Much of this methodology will become clearer as we consider an example of our work.

"Leadership and Land": The Joseph Story

The study entitled "Leadership and Land" was the fourth contextual Bible study that we developed together. So we had already been meeting together for more than a year and had become accustomed to each other and to our various contributions to the workshop process. As usual, we met in the offices of the Church Land Programme in Pietermaritzburg, with local community leadership and activists having traveled from all over the KwaZulu-Natal (KZN) province.

Seated around a large table, with plenty of large sheets of newsprint paper and multicolored felt-tipped pens, we began to brainstorm around this theme, doing social analysis on the issue of leadership and land and also looking for likely biblical texts that might open up this theme for a local community. In terms of social analysis, the primary concern was the slow pace of land reform since liberation in 1994. Under apartheid, white South Africans, who made up no more than 20 percent of the population, had controlled nearly 87 percent of the land. But the liberation government had made only modest progress in redistributing land in its fourteen years of rule, with less than 3 percent of white land being returned to black communities.

While all of the participants would venture biblical texts that might be useful for our task, they tended to look to the Ujamaa Centre for unfamiliar biblical texts. They had been very excited about our use of the story of the daughters of Zelophehad in Numbers 27 for our contextual Bible study on women and land. Unfamiliar biblical texts do not carry the interpretive history and baggage of familiar texts, so they have a potentially greater capacity to generate participatory exchanges in groups. Therefore, participants were eager to see what we might come up with in this case.

Given the emphasis on the failure of political leadership around the restitution and redistribution of land that had emerged from the social analysis, we suggested that the story of Joseph might be a potential resource. We were met with puzzled expressions, for all of the participants in our workshop held Joseph in high regard, as a Nelson Mandela–like figure who had emerged from imprisonment to lead his people to liberation.

So we read Gen. 41:46-57 and then 47:13-26. The workshop was appalled! How could Joseph take the surplus from the people and then sell it back to them? Worse, how could Joseph systematically force the people into servitude by, first, having to pay for their own surplus; second, having to exchange their livestock for food; and third, having to sell their land and themselves into slavery for food? The workshop now began to buzz, and it was not long before we had an outline for the contextual Bible study.

However, those of us collaborating worried that some of the people with whom we would do this Bible study in local churches and communities would not know the Joseph story well enough to be able to locate these extracts within their broader narrative context. We then suggested using the woodcut by South African Azariah Mbatha on the Joseph story as an entry point into the story as a whole. The Ujamaa Centre has used this woodcut in another of its contextual Bible studies (with the permission of the artist), so we were aware of how useful it was as a way into the long narrative of Joseph. We downloaded a picture of the woodcut (Figure 12.1) from our Ujamaa Centre Web site and shared it with the workshop. We all agreed that it would work well as a participatory introduction to the story.

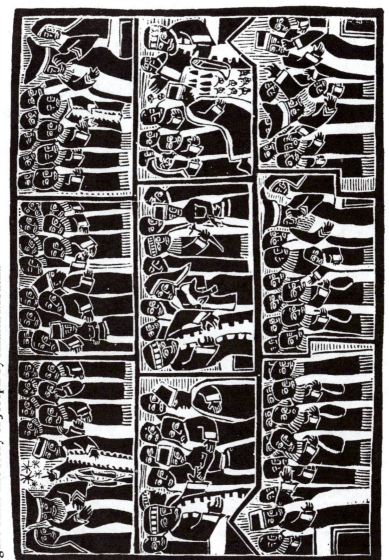

Figure 12.1. The story of Joseph by Azaria Mbatha

By permission of the artist.

Some hours later, we settled on the following as our "Leadership and Land" contextual Bible study (though the actual version used in local communities has been laid out by a communications consultant who has ensured that the Bible study is accessible in English and isiZulu):

1. Using the woodcut by Azaria Mbatha, retell the Joseph story to the person sitting next to you. How would you summarize the Joseph story?

   [The responses from the "buzz-groups" of two are shared with all the participants in plenary and are recorded on newsprint.]

2. Now listen to Genesis 41:46-57. Where and how did Joseph get the grain he stored during the years of plenty? What did he do with this surplus grain?

   [This question is discussed in small groups of about 6 to 8 participants; once they have had time to discuss the question they report back to the plenary, and each group's contribution is recorded on newsprint.]

3. Now listen to Genesis 47:13-26. When the people need food during the years of famine, what does Joseph do with the stored grain?

4. What must the people do in order to get food from Joseph?

   [These questions are discussed in the small groups; once they have had time to discuss the question they report back to the plenary, and each group's contribution is recorded on newsprint.]

5. Do you think Joseph was a good leader?

6. What alternative forms of redistribution could Joseph have used?

7. What should be the role of government in land allocation and relocation?

8. What action will you take around land issues in your community in response to this Bible study?

   [These questions are discussed in the small groups; once they have had time to discuss the question they report back to the plenary, and each group's contribution is recorded on newsprint, with particular attention to each group's "action plan."]

Contours of a Contextual Bible Study

As indicated, the process begins with the participants drawing on their own interpretive resources and experience of the text, prompted by a local African resource, the woodcut by Mbatha. Questions 2 through 4 then slow the process down by asking the participants to pay close attention to particular sections of the biblical text, following the literary detail. While we often focus on character in our "critical" questions in contextual Bible study methodology, in this case, we focus more on plot and setting, though there is some focus on character in the transition Question 5. The report-back session allows participants both to share their contributions and to raise questions about the text. For example, some participants have translations that include the variant readings of 47:21 in a footnote, prompting questions and allowing an opportunity for the socially engaged biblical scholar to share additional resources. However, we do this only when asked.

Question 5 moves the contextual Bible study away from a focus on the text to the participants' context, and questions 6 through 8 enable the participants to spend considerable time discussing the potential lines of connection between text and context. Here, too, the report-back session allows for an exchange of resources among the participants at a plenary level and also provides an opportunity for those with particular expertise in the subject to share their input. Again, however, this is done cautiously and only at the invitation of the participants. The contextual Bible study begins and ends in the hands of the local participants.

In the feedback from the various communities in which this Bible study (and others in the series) was facilitated, it was clear that the contextual Bible studies gave the participants a sense of spiritual affirmation insofar as their aspirations to change their status quo were concerned. The methodology not only provided opportunities for critical discourse, it also animated participants to begin discussions about what could be appropriate action campaigns to organize in order to change their situation. For example, one group that used the "Leadership and Land" study was the Nkosi Vukanathi Land Committee, made up mainly of women from an area called Nkwalini in northern Zululand, where five villages under the Tembeni Traditional Community (under Chief/iNkosi Thandazani Zulu) have been enduring several attempts by a neighboring farmer to evict them from their homes, including the demolishing of their houses and the impounding of their cattle. The group used this Bible study to mobilize other villagers to participate in their local struggle for land. In another area, called Roosboom, more than seven thousand residents were evicted and relocated between 1975 and 1976. There, local land activists (also mainly women) used this Bible study to mobilize other community members to take part in their local struggle for land rights.

The contextual Bible studies also helped local activists overcome traditional beliefs and stereotypes that normally serve as hurdles in making social progress. Although land is a sensitive issue in South Africa, the facilitators were able to use the Bible study series to engage with people at the grassroots level. The Bible was used as a tool to identify needs within the community and engage with what Graham Philpott (1993: 85) calls "progressive criticism" (discernment, judgment, and action that does not destroy but creates power to change reality). Both Nkwalini and Roosboom are traditional and rural areas. Under normal traditional circumstances, women and youth are hardly allowed to discuss land issues. In both areas, it was noticed that the Bible studies assisted local activists-facilitators in overriding gender prejudices. Female facilitators were able to convene people and facilitate discussions with almost none of the resistance that usually comes from men.

In most rural areas of the KZN province, party politics is literally a dangerous game. Speakers in community meetings are generally careful and sensitive about indicating their political preference. The fear and political sensitivity originate from the 1980s, when terrible violence wracked the province as forces of Inkatha (now the Inkatha Freedom Party), often with apartheid state assistance, tried to eradicate the emergence of the United Democratic Front (UDF), a progressive, pro-ANC (African National Congress) formation (Jeffery 1997). Bible studies are usually associated with the church, which is assumed to be nonpartisan, so the "Land and Leadership" Bible study provided a safe space for people to talk about the politics of land and the weaknesses of the political leaders, including government, in addressing issues of land reform, without fear of political repercussions.

The participants' feelings about this Bible study and the encounters within it are reflected in the following quotations, which come from a focus group reflection held on January 24–26, 2006:

- They encourage moral development and revival.
- They are mind openers and they clarify many things that we did not understand before.
- It promotes working together by the community members.

In the rural areas where much pain had been inflicted in the past, especially during the apartheid era, where political affiliation and even village "affiliation" were potentially tendentious, it is never easy to mobilize and organize community members. Many communities remain divided politically and culturally. However, our experience of producing this Bible study and using it in a range of local contexts has demonstrated that it has served as a nonthreatening but effective and empowering tool in drawing participants into a space of critical dialogue. This Bible study enabled people to discuss land issues without the fear of suffering the repercussion of political partisanship.

From the Local to the Public Realm

What emerges in contextual Bible studies such as this, if the group is a sacred and safe space (see Scott 1990), is that the embodied theologies of the participants find forms of articulation.[1] Such emergent articulations are what South African theologian James Cochrane (1999) calls "incipient theology." Incipient theology is a product of the corporate/embodied experience of the group members, who draw on the resources of their own bodies and the biblical text to bring to articulation what is inchoate. In this case, incipient theologies of land find voice and are brought into engagement with the question of the role of government with respect to land.

As South African theologian Albert Nolan (1996) has argued, the socially engaged biblical scholar and theologian are called to serve such communities and their incipient theologies. We are called to collaborate with networks linked to the Church Land Programme, placing ourselves and our resources alongside them and their resources, working together to give theological form to what is already a lived reality. Such collaboration produces forms of local theology that can be articulated and owned by those to whom it is organic.

But the socially engaged theologian's task is not yet done. For a consequent challenge remains: that of in/corporating emerging local theologies

---

1. When we shared some of these ideas with theological students in Chennai, India, they preferred the phrase *embodied theology* for what we had up to that point called "lived" or "working theology." We have taken up their term.

into the public theologies of the institutional church.[2] In/corporation, however, is not uncritical, for implicit in the process of articulation, owning, and in/corporation is, as Cochrane has argued, a communitarian and critical component. First, embodied theologies, as "symbolic structures," arise out of, and are situated in, the strongly communitarian life world of the community, including both the living and the living dead. Second, the discourses of the Bible study, particularly the constructive engagement between local and scholarly reading resources, "bring to the group's attention selected aspects of the taken-for-granted, shared background knowledge of its life world. These aspects move to the foreground, becoming conscious." Third, "this move to the foreground of previously unreflected elements of the life world introduces the possibility of questioning and probing," that is, a critical component. Fourth, the mode of discourse in the Bible studies, including both the facilitation and the interaction between contextual and textual questions, promotes and establishes "a process of communication that allows for open argument and counterargument as the basis for testing claims made." Fifth, this process makes possible "an encounter between traditions (biblically transmitted tradition, local group tradition, and more generally, aspects of African tradition) in the context of a social environment shaped by severe negative imbalances in material resources and access to power." Though the emphasis in the articulation and owning of embodied theologies is corporate, included in this encounter between traditions are also the "personal dimensions in both tradition and everyday life." Sixth, this encounter between the personal and the corporate establishes potential links "between the cultural, social, and personal elements of the life world" as participants in the Bible study endeavor "to understand what a claim made in one sphere, for example, concerning personal responsibility for theft, might imply for another sphere, for example, the struggle against poverty" (128).

Underlying this entire process, then, is what Cochrane refers to as the "communicative rationality" of local knowledge and theologies (28, 132). Embodied theologies that have been articulated and owned are a form of corporate communicative rationality, and as such can be and, we are arguing

---

2. We are grateful to two colleagues, Pat Bruce and Steve de Gruchy, for suggesting this use of "in/corporate," which draws on the root *corpus*, meaning body, and therefore makes a nice connection between embodied theologies and the need to have them in/corporated, that is, brought into, the body of the church.

here, must be communicatively shared: "A public theology that does not take the perspective of local communities of the poor, the oppressed, and the marginalized seriously loses its seminal sources of insight and correction" (124).[3]

Still, the work of the socially engaged biblical scholar is not done. For the final task is to stand in solidarity with the local community when it decides to act in the public realm, as has happened as a result of this particular contextual Bible study on "Leadership and Land." In response to this Bible study and the action plans proposed, some local communities set up meetings with officials in the provincial government to discuss their concerns about land. When their delegation was met by an ill-equipped and dismissive junior delegation from the provincial government office that did not take their concerns seriously, the community's delegation reconvened and decided to embark on a public protest march.

Instead of a Conclusion: The Ongoing Project

Actual implementation of the Bible studies in local contexts revealed other challenges we need to be conscious of as we continue to work on this series of Bible studies. These challenges included continual work at making the Bible studies user-friendly at the grassroots level, recognition of women's vulnerabilities in dialogical spaces, the role of education in sustaining class divisions in communities, where education meant access to resources and so to power, and finally, an awareness that there were often other internal struggles (struggles within struggles) among those struggling together for land.

The issue of literacy was particularly pertinent in the context of textually based resources such as these Bible studies. Like Joseph, who had access to information that could make a difference between life and death and who decided to use that information to enhance state power, so some of those who are literate, at grassroots levels, have power that other illiterate/semiliterate participants do not have. The fact that some participants could read and write while others could not read and write created power differentials among the participants in the Bible study groups. Until the issue was addressed directly, there was an underlying assumption that the literate ones would lead the discussions.

---

3. Cochrane (1999: 132–49) goes on to consider an ecclesiology appropriate to this analysis.

The effects of these power dynamics go beyond Bible study groups; they affect relations within communities on a daily basis. Those who are literate can use that power for the benefit of the whole group, or they can use it to secure for themselves elevated statuses within their community. The literate play a pivotal role in connecting the ones who cannot read with the message contained in written sources, including the Bible. So, for example, for illiterate community members to be able to use these Bible study tools, they needed those who are literate to read for them. Therefore, during the conceptualization and production of the Bible study series, serious consideration was given to participants who cannot read. This is evident in the use of the prompting questions that were designed in such a way that the facilitator would do no more than read them aloud for everyone to hear. The literate facilitator was not and should not be given the role of an expert, though given the status of literacy, the potential for a power differential is difficult to equalize. This is why the use of Azariah Mbatha's woodcut was so important in this Bible study, undermining as it did the normative role of literacy and enhancing as it did the participation of participants who are illiterate and those who are more visual. So this Bible study of "Land and Leadership" challenges us as socially engaged scholars and educated NGO activists to be aware of our power inclinations when we work collaboratively, lest the very process of contextual Bible study become a tool to maintain the status quo.

Finally, this collaborative project is a reminder that socially engaged scholars and NGO activist organizations are called not only to engage with the Bible in word but also in works. In other words, the participation goes beyond the spaces of progressive criticism and extends also into participation in forms of action that might emerge from resources such as these contextual Bible studies. We are called also to accompaniment (Butler et al. 2007).

CHAPTER 13

"Same Bed, Different Dreams"

An Engendered Reading of Families in Migration in Genesis and Hong Kong

Wai Ching (Angela) Wong

Introduction

The Flying Carpet, a famous novel by Xixi, a renowned woman writer of Hong Kong and Taiwan, starts with a literary allusion to one of the most classic Chinese dreams, *Zhuangzhou mengdie* (The Butterfly Dream of Zhuangzi),[1] and narrates the significance of dreaming as an act of resistance to the human sleeping state. This is then followed by the second scene, which compares the movement of the biological clocks in a man, a French Consulate-General, and a woman, his wife, who have just returned home after a special theatrical performance on "The Butterfly Dream of Zhuangzi," attended primarily by the expatriates and foreign dignitaries of Hong Kong.[2] While the man's clock

---

1. It is an analogy taken from Zhuangzi's "Discussion on Making All Things Equal" (Burton Watson's translation of *Qiwulun*), chapter 2. The story is about a dream of Zhuangzi in which he finds himself turning into a butterfly. When he wakes up, he doubts if it is he who dreams a butterfly or that the butterfly dreams of him. It is a philosophical questioning of the distinction between reality and illusion: how would one know for sure which is illusion and which is reality? The analogy posts a fundamental epistemological question to how much we may know through our senses and experiences, or whether everything is illusion. Zhuangzi was one of the most important ancient philosophers associated with the origin of Taoist thought in the fourth century BCE during the Warring State period of China.

2. Xixi is a famous novelist who writes extensively and highly imaginatively on the history of Hong Kong's transition from colonial governance and her search for identity. "Foreigners" not only frequent Xixi's novels but also often play the role of a parable for Hong Kong's intricate ties to her "rich" colonial heritage.

clicks normally and gets the Consul-General fast asleep, soon, at night, the woman's clock clicks "slowly" and leaves her wide awake beyond midnight. Because of that, the Consul-General's wife gets to see a flying carpet drifting through the nightly sky of Hong Kong, by means of which the epic-like novel of a hundred-year-old city unfolds (Xixi 1996: 3–9). In the book's preface, Xixi describes the amazing location of Hong Kong, situated on the southern periphery of China, as likened to a small and insignificant doormat lying at the foot of a big country.[3] Throughout its history, this small city served primarily as a quiet mattress on which the big traders, foreign commercial companies, and political dignitaries would trample and "dust off their shoes" before they moved onto "China proper." Yet in spite of its seemingly fated destiny, the small city thrives by faithfully serving her role, "protecting the many feet that walk over it," and eventually soars and flies high up in the sky to turn into "a flying carpet" (Xixi 1996: v). In short, the story of *The Flying Carpet* for Xixi is the realization of the dream of a city "on the margin" that reinvents itself against all odds and impossibilities. When Xixi received her prize for this work at the Eighth World Chinese Literary Biannual Award in 2005, Wang Anyi, a famous literary critic, named her a "Hong Kong narrator of dreams" (Wen-waipo 2005).[4] Considering that Xixi is an immigrant from China to Hong Kong, what is so precious about her dreams is her esteem for the identity of a city of migrants—the dreams of the people of Hong Kong.

Xixi's interpretation of the dream of Hong Kong in *The Flying Carpet* highlights at least three aspects for a cross-textual reading of the dreams of the patriarchs in the book of Genesis. First, dreams may be read as an act of resistance. Given Sigmund Freud's theory of dream interpretation, it is not difficult to understand the integral relations between dreams and the activities of the human unconscious. In short, dreams are symbolic expressions of repression that slipped through the censorship of the conscious in sleep. Once they explode, they are acts of resistance and subversion of reason and its controlling order. Second, the novel delineates a difference between the dreams

---

3. In a series of her short novels, Xixi tells the story of a city by the name of *Feituzhen* (The City of Fertile Soil) on the margin of a country called *Qulungguo* (The Great Dragon Country), both analogical names for the prosperous Hong Kong city and its mother country, China, known by its auspicious mythical animal, the dragon.

4. Comment made by Wang Anyi during his address to the Eighth *Huachong* World Chinese Literary Prize Award Ceremony in Kuala Lumpur in December 17, 2005. This Literary Prize Award Ceremony is a biannual event hosted by the *Sin Chew Daily* of Malaysia.

of a man and a woman. In *The Flying Carpet*, Xixi does not only begin with the wife's half-dreaming of a flying carpet but also assigns, throughout the novel, the dream of the city—to be prosperous—to be carried largely by two women protagonists—Ye Chongsheng (literally, "Rejuvenation of Leaves") and her daughter, Hua Yanyan (literally, "Flowers Most Beautiful"), with Ye a great dreamer and Hua a sleepwalker. Xixi's recurrent allusion in the novel to a woman's different biological clock sets apart a unique time and space for women, for a different kind of dreams in the city of migrants such as that of Hong Kong. Third, Xixi's "dreams" in her novels of the city-series are, almost the whole time, tied to the growth and fall of the city of Hong Kong. Since her first successful novel, *Wo Cheng* (My City: 1979), she persists in writing the story of Hong Kong from the angle of the common folks, a majority of whom migrated from the mainland beginning in the 1950s, who feel the brunt of living in a city on the margin of a "motherland"—between their "backward" ancestral villages and one of the world's last colonies and the fastest-growing capitalist economies. Migration is part of the story of almost all common folks of Hong Kong, yet their transition from the north of Shenzhen River[5] to the cosmopolitan colony has never been easy. It comes at a cost of disorientation for political identities and social status, and confusion of familial and personal values.

Xixi's "dreams" are echoed by many of the dreams expressed throughout the history of the city. In fact, dreams have been an amazingly dominant theme through some of the most moving stories in literature and films searching a Hong Kong identity during the 1990s, when the city was in transition from British colony to a Special Administrative Region (SAR) of China. Despite the million miles of historical and cultural distance between the dreams of the always migrating population of Hong Kong and the dreams of the patriarchs in the book of Genesis, these three factors—dreaming as an act of resistance, women's dreams, and ties to migration—shall form the basis of my reading between the two different texts and contexts: that of families in Genesis and families of the new immigrants in Hong Kong.[6]

---

5. This border separates Hong Kong from mainland China.
6. According to the Hong Kong Immigration Policy, any resident who lives in Hong Kong consecutively for seven years will be considered a permanent resident, who shall enjoy full citizenship rights and related benefits. Anyone living in Hong Kong for less than seven years will be considered a new immigrant.

Dreams of the Patriarchs in Genesis

In the Bible, "dream" (*chalom*) designates less a form of perception than a state; it is essentially a venue for God or a divine messenger to come and intrude into the human mind and the person's course of action. In this sense, dreams, visions, trances, appearances of angels, and experiences of the spirit are similarly regarded (Sanford 1968: 98).[7] In Genesis, the dreams of Abraham, Abimelech, Jacob, and dreams related to Joseph are all manifestations of God's intention and ways of divine communication. Abraham's story alone is filled with variant forms of divine revelation including visions, direct speeches, and dreams—instruction in a deep sleep.[8] There is also a specific role for the dream interpreters of the Bible. In Gen. 40:8, Joseph makes it clear that dream interpretation is something that belongs to God. This is most interestingly supplemented by Daniel's remark that, with the wisdom of God, the interpretation of a dream is meant to make known the thoughts of the dreamer to him- or herself (Dan. 2:27-30; Sanford 1968: 98–119). In other words, biblical dreams are not only venues for deciphering God's will but also divine tools for revealing the human intention involved in a given situation.

There are quite a few studies on dreams in the Hebrew Bible, including, specifically, the dreams in Genesis.[9] Several scholars have distinguished the different forms of dreams found in the Bible and Genesis, dividing them into two groups: the nonsymbolic message-dreams of the great patriarchs (15:12-16,[10] 20:1-18, 28:10-22, 31:10-13, and 31:24) and the symbolic dreams in Joseph's story (37:5-11, 40:5-22, and 41:1-8).[11] The latter dreams need interpretation and are usually dealt with separately, due to their different literary

---

7. See Num. 12:6: "If there is a prophet among you, I the Lord make myself known to him in a vision, I speak with him in a dream." (English Standard Version)

8. In the books of the prophets, dreams and visions are used almost interchangeably (Joel 2:28).

9. See Diana Lipton's detailed literature review in her introduction to *Revisions of the Night* (1999: 9–25).

10. Although technically the word *dream* is not used in this passage, the context may still be broadly considered a dream. Cf. Lipton 1999: 9.

11. Message-dreams can be passive audition of a divine voice or active dialogue between God and the dreamer. While symbolic or allegorical dreams are also transmissions of messages from God, they come in codes of images, pictures, and events. Because they are coded, these dreams require interpretation. Cf. Husser 1999: 23.

styles, use of words, and theological motifs; therefore, they will not be discussed in this study (Pirson 2002: 41–42). The former are relatively straightforward. Except for Jacob's dream at Bethel, these message-dreams are mostly direct verbal transmission of divine will or verbal exchange between God and the dreamer, and require no interpretation. They are dream-reports mostly about God's appearance and God's talking to those who are dreaming. They serve an important function of divine legitimization for what the patriarchs are about to do.[12]

What I found most interesting in these several message-dreams of the Genesis patriarchs is that they all, in one way or another, deal with the state of migration. For instance, in Abraham's deep sleep (15:12), God announces to him the plight of his descendants after migration, even though he himself would rest peacefully with his ancestors in the end. Abimelech's dream after taking Sarah into his harem takes place when Abraham has just arrived at the Negeb and barely settles down between Kadesh and Shur (20:1). Then there are Jacob's dreams, including the dream of the ladder where the angels of God are ascending and descending right after he flees from Esau and the house of his father and is about to enter Haran, a land unknown to him (28:12). Jacob's dream to depart from Laban's land (31:11) and the latter's dream to let go of Jacob (31:24) are both moments of divine affirmation of Jacob's long overdue return to the land of Esau, a land of a remote "ancestry" and uncertain future. In each of these dreams, the message leads to the same promise of God: that the fathers of Israel would be blessed with offspring "like the dust of the earth," bountiful properties, the possession of all the land of Canaan, and heads of multitude of nations. Each of these dreams foretells a future that flourishes with posterity, wealth, and the prosperity of a nation and its people. Considering these dream-texts in the postexilic context, the significance of God's great promises to the ancestors of a people in a diaspora is not difficult to understand.

---

12. Dreams also serve literary functions as a common thread or device, triggering turns of fate in the biblical narratives. Jacob's dream at Bethel, for example, provides the chief motive for plot development, as it forecasts the plot's outcome, whereas Abimelech's dream belongs to a symmetrical textual organization highlighting the drama of Abraham's giving away of Sarah as sister. Cf. Husser 1999: 103–104.

In Diana Lipton's close reading (1999: 32–33), she suggests six major themes for the five patriarchal message-dreams:[13] (1) each of the dreamers receives the dreams in a state of anxiety from imminent danger, for example, Abraham in 20:1-18 and Jacob in 31:24; (2) each dream relates somehow to a moment of doubt regarding the continuation of an immediate or eventual ancestral line; (3) each dream implicates a change of status for the dreamer; (4) each dream points to some direct divine involvement in the future of the dreamer concerned; (5) each dream deals with the relationship between non-Israelites and Israelites in one way or another; and (6) each dream is connected with migration or absence from the land. In short, the dreams of the patriarchs are also dreams of a migrating people desperately seeking a sense of security, both psychological and material, among people and in a land alien to them. In other words, these patriarchal dreams are also dreams of migration that reach out for divine blessing and promises in the face of uncertain future for the individual, but also the whole clan, in a time of struggle for survival.

My contextual questions are these: What do those dreams tell us about the new immigrants in Hong Kong in the twenty-first century? What are the similarities and differences between these biblical patriarchal dreams and the dreams of Chinese immigrants? And in what ways does the current context—that is, the living dreams of the new immigrants in Hong Kong— enrich our understanding of the biblical narratives in Genesis?

Dreams in the Chinese Tradition

Before we bring these two sets of dream narratives into a cross-textual reading, it is important to understand how the Chinese read their dreams. Obviously, there is a rich tradition of dreams in China, and some commonalities within it can be shared between the two traditions. The most apparent of these commonalities is to be found in the ancient tradition of divination. Much as in the court of the Pharaohs in the Bible, it was common for rulers of each Chinese dynasty to invoke the power of Heaven (*tian*) to grant a good harvest and protect the people from the damages of natural disasters. Rulers in the Zhou Dynasty (1046–711 BCE), for example, would make major

---

13. Excluding those related to Joseph.

policies through divination based on dreams in order to consolidate their ruling authority. In correspondence to such a need was the establishment of a special position entitled *Tai Pu*, founded in the Zhou court and primarily responsible for dream interpretation and various forms of divination.[14] Similar to what Joseph did for Pharaoh, symbols of dreams would be decoded such as "grain" for prosperity, and "rain" and "water" as foretelling natural disasters that necessitate reform measures to be set forth. Influential dreams of ancestral instruction have also been a prominent aspect of the Chinese tradition where the superior, the past, and the powerful could draw their support and justification for action (Fang and Zhang 2000: 11–12). Yet this is not the tradition this paper is drawing on for the comparative readings.

In line with the dream scenes in Xixi's novel, there is a tradition of transgression in the dream literature of China. In this tradition of Chinese literature, dreams have been well developed as metaphors or sometimes function as a vision of utopia and indirect critique of the status quo. *Zhuangzi's* "Butterfly Dream" in the Warring States period (previously mentioned), Pu Songling's *Stories of the Strange*, and Cao Xueqin's *Dreams of the Red Chamber* in the Qing Dynasty (1644–1912) are some outstanding examples. They all express through dreams the authors' concerns, and very often criticisms, of the social realities of their times (Fang and Zhang 2000: 13). Some of the best dream narratives in Chinese literary tradition were developed into four classical Chinese plays by Tang Xianzu (1550–1616), the most gifted playwright in Chinese history. Two of his best-known dream masterpieces are the *Record of Handan* and *Record of Southern Bough*. Both tell of the vanities of life, of how each of the protagonists experiences respective ups and downs, success and failure, and gains and loss of life through dreams, only to wake up and see the world is a different place. All of Tang's plays demonstrate the author's strong belief in the dreams' power of transgression, through which one detaches from as much as engages in life all over at once (Zheng 2008; Li 2002). This is an act of resistance to life as habitual and is an incessant search for life beyond the mundane.

A feature that is most distant from the Genesis dreams is probably the idea of the dreamability of the world, as contended by Wai-yee Li (1999) in her study of the ancient classical texts. This is a notion that often draws on

---

14. A famous dream interpreter named Gu was documented to have played an important role in the court of the Shang Dynasty (1600–1046 BCE).

intellectual contemplation or reflection on one's inability to control in life and the idea of the readability of the world. Rather than the surface renunciations of lives in both the Taoist and Buddhist stories, Li finds that through the brevity of dreams, the dreamers will experience the passions and vicissitudes of life, realize their illusory nature, and be ready to treat them with detachment. The moment of enlightenment by the end of the stories usually "reengages" the dreamer in life, either with the Buddhist idea of "dispassionate compassion" or the Taoist immortals' transcendence of desire. In sum, Chinese dreaming and awakening from it is a way of gaining knowledge and a means to enlightenment (Li 1999: 38–39).

From divination of dreams, where men in power demanded legitimization of their power, to dreams as a critique of status quo and the detachment from and engagement with life through understanding its illusions as a dream, Chinese understanding of dreams has underlined the different states of the struggling human mind with regard to the uncertainty of living, the disillusion and frustration with reality and, at its best, offered a refreshed or enlightened approach to life events with all their unpredictability. I shall, in this study, utilize these insights of Chinese understanding and interpretation of dreams for a feminist intervention into the patriarchal dreams of migration in Genesis.

Dreams of Migration in Genesis

Premonarchic Israel was tribal in character and ran a primarily agricultural economy together with animal husbandry in the land of Canaan. Early theories of Israelite settlement include conquest, immigration, and revolt (Gottwald 1979: 220–24). While there is biblical evidence attesting to a mixed existence of all three models of settlement, I find that a seminomadic tribal background with a gradual settling in over a long period of time explains well the contexts of the Genesis patriarchs' dreams.

The general lifestyles of Abraham, Isaac, and Jacob were those of wealthy clan leaders. They seemed to move often, with their flocks of sheep and goats, while also being attached to semipermanent roots near some major cities. Although they were on the move often, they were never far away from the urban centers of the time. For instance, Abraham settled near Hebron in the south, Isaac in Beer-sheba, and Jacob in the area of Shechem and Bethel, all around the center of Palestine. Among them, Abraham seemed to have made the most extensive journeys, traveling between Haran, Damascus, Shechem, Hebron, and Egypt. He might have taken up a trade in certain goods along with his pasturing and grazing life (Boadt 1984: 134–35).

If we follow Lipton's contention, the patriarchal dreams are narrative moments when God's assurance is sought during the fathers' migration between their native land and a foreign land. A comparison of Abimelech's dream (20:1-18) to the other two sister-wife narratives in Genesis (12:10-20 and 26:1-12) provides a rich textual basis for situating the dream in the context of migration for Abraham and Isaac.[15] With both fathers threatened by famine, their stories are narrated with frequent use of the words *dwell, settled,* and particularly *sojourn(ed)*, describing the state of a guest, a "resident alien" rather than a native. Abimelech's dream, therefore, occurs in the context of Abraham's fear for his survival, hence a threat for the demise of his family line in the foreign land of Gerar. Only after God's intervention through Abimelech's dream are the impotence in Abimelech's house and Sarah's barrenness cured. The dream results in an indirect fulfillment of God's promise to Abraham for progeny and the future prosperity of his house (Lipton 1999: 42–44). In short, the dream tells of a highly anxious Abraham, a sojourner migrating from home, anticipating personal physical danger as well as fear for the end of a clan, who is then assured by God of a future. Despite Abimelech being a foreign king, God intervenes through his dream to ensure Abraham's safety, good treatment, and prospects for the future possession of progeny and land (61–62).

Departing from the dominant interpretation of Jacob's dream at Bethel as a testament of incubation, Lipton contends that the dream functions like Abraham's Covenant of the Pieces as "pivotal events in the spiritual development of the patriarch, occurring at a time of personal crisis" (66). Both dreams, Abraham's (15:1-21) and Jacob's (28:10-22), are responses to uncertainty. Abraham's anxiety and need for reassurance are clear and were just explained. In the case of Jacob, his problem is a little more complicated. He has just fled from Esau, from whom he stole his father's blessing, about to enter a land unfamiliar to him, and is supposed to take a wife and build a

---

15. Lipton (1999: 35–40), drawing on the theories of G. von Rad, J. Van Seters, M. Lichtenstein, H. Gunkel, K. Koch, etc., offers a rich discussion of the various source theories and their relations to the three sister-wife narratives (12:10-20, 20:1-18, 26:1-12).

family among people he has never met. Will God approve of his stolen blessing and follow him into the alien land? Naturally, he is having a great sense of insecurity and badly needs assurance from God. Whereas Abraham seeks confirmation of God's earlier promise of descendants and land through the Covenant of Pieces in Genesis 15, Jacob is anxious for the first sign of God's approval of him here (Lipton 1999: 66–67).

The ladder dream is therefore a sign of God's approval of his link to Abraham and Isaac, that Jacob will be blessed with land and descendants, that the descendants shall be as numerous as "the dust of the earth," and that "all the families of the earth shall be blessed" (28:14) in him and his descendants. The dream is particularly comforting with God's promise to Jacob at the end: "Know that I am with you and will keep you wherever you go, and will bring you back to this land; for I will not leave you until I have done what I have promised you" (28:15). These comforting words are not to be weighed lightly if one considers the continuous plight of Jacob. He will be working with an employer who always outwits him and whose sons resent him. His immediate response to God's promise, with a request for food and clothing, clearly indicates the physical assurance that he badly needs. Needless to say, his eventual escape and success in taking home with him the good fortune he has made depend on God's direct intervention later, through his and Laban's dreams (Lipton 1999: 72). In short, Jacob's dream at Bethel occurs when he is a refugee, empty-handed, going away from home without a family. It is at this particular moment of great insecurity that God's blessing of progeny and land comes to him.

Finally, Jacob's dream of the flocks (31:10-13) deals uniquely with the imagery of sheep and shepherding that characterizes his life. Through a disguise of goatskin, Jacob steals his father's blessing from Esau, and by shepherding, he earns his wives, secures his employment with Laban, invites envy from Laban's sons, and eventually—in his dealings with the flocks—begins to contemplate reconciliation with Esau and plan his return. The message delivered by an angel of God in his dream highlights the imagery of change for Jacob and invokes his last movement from Paddan Aram to his native land. The more than usual presence of angels at various turning points in Jacob's life confirms once again God's blessing for him.

Scholars have largely agreed that the extensive genealogical data, stories, and poetic passages in Genesis were brought together with a specific readership and a purpose in mind. James McKeown (2008: 197) suggests that the three unifying themes of the book are descendants, blessing, and land.[16] In the patriarchal narratives, the theme of land is the most prominent. The concern for assurance of the land cannot be overemphasized, given its persistent recurrence in the patriarchal dreams (McKeown 2008: 255). Yet at the same time, the imagery of journeying is just as central. Migration, just as it has been a prominent feature in human history, is a prominent state of being for the patriarchs. In Genesis, it starts with chapter 11, where the people move to the east (11:2) and closes with Terah's family moving toward Canaan (11:31), which sets the background for the journey of Abra[ha]m (12:1-4). If the emphasis on the land in the patriarchal narratives has to do with the theology of the postexilic Jewish community, the patriarchs' constant moving and journeying reflect a common human experience in history of the search for security, comfort, and good life across territorial borders and cultural boundaries.

Engendering the Migration Stories

In light of Xixi's gendered clock for men and women, and hence the differences in timing and dreaming between them, how would women's dreams differ from men's dreams in the Bible, if there were such dreams? Would women also be dreaming about God's blessing for progeny and land? Carole R. Fontaine (1987: 101) finds Queen Puduhepa of the Hittite empire that flourished during the Late Bronze Age (ca. 1450–1200 BCE) to be the only woman known to have dreamed a message-dream in the Ancient Near East. Yet her dream was mentioned only as part of her husband's "Apology" for dethroning his nephew to become Hattusili III (Fontaine 1999: 170–71). In Genesis, however, Hagar's vision of the angel of God in the desert seems to be the closest to the men's dreams, yet she is "promised" that her son will be living at odds with all his kin (16:7-12), with no mention at all of land. As such, it seems that the revelation of God's vision and blessing implicates a hierarchical relationship on the part of the receivers with regard to their gender (between men and women) and their status (between queens and

---

16. McKeown builds on the themes—land, a relationship with God, and descendants—first suggested by Clines 1997 (originally published in 1977).

women slaves). Excluding the ancient Near Eastern texts of the Hittites, biblical dreams as direct reception of God's message and revelation seem to belong primarily to men such as patriarchs, kings, and prophets. But did women in biblical times not dream, and if they did, what would have been their dreams?

Ilona N. Rashkow makes a very important observation in *The Phallacy of Genesis* (1993: chs. 2–3): women are all silent in the patriarchal dreams of Genesis, even when the dreams are about them. In the parallel narratives in Genesis 12 and 20, for example, Sarah, the supposed protagonist of the men's exchange and present in Abimelech's dream, neither says anything nor acts. She is addressed by Pharaoh only as "she," "your wife," or "her," and by Abimelech as "she, "she herself," and "your wife." In Abimelech's dream, God uses the expression *be'ulat-ba'al* (literally, "possession of a possessor") for Sarah. While the normal word for wife is *'ishah*, the expression *be'ulat-ba'al* is used primarily in the negative sense (Rashkow 1993: 41).[17] It is truly amazing that in the narrative of Genesis 12, Sarah is led into Pharaoh's house and taken as Pharaoh's wife (12:19) while Abraham is enjoying special royal treatments and endowed with luxurious gifts by Pharaoh. The problem is revealed only by a great disaster coming to Pharaoh and his family. In Genesis 20, however, the problem is told by God to Abimelech in a dream that includes a special reference to Sarah as having not been sexually touched.

In both cases, Abraham is presented as showing no concern for the risk of Sarah being caught in the pretense of being his sister or for her situation if this happens. All he is concerned about is the risk associated with surviving in a foreign place. Therefore, when he perceives a potential risk to life, he is prepared to let Sarah be taken as Pharaoh's wife. At the same time, his words, "that it may go well with me because of you" (12:13), indicate that he has anticipated the good treatment and the luxurious gifts that are showered upon him. With regard to such an exchange between Pharaoh and Abraham, Rashkow offers the explanation that both Abraham and later Isaac are threatened by their beautiful childless wives (12:10-20, 20:1-18, 26:1-16). The state of beauty but childlessness has, in fact, caused the respective husbands

---

17. The term *be'ulat-ba'al* is used in Deut. 22:22, referring to the penalty for adultery, and a variant form of *be'ulah* is used negatively in Isa. 54:1 for "sons of the desolate." See Rashkow 1993: 117–18, n. 10.

to have "sexual self-doubts" (1993: 103–104). It is no wonder that God must guarantee Sarah's purity in the dream affirming Abimelech's claim of having not touched her. In short, the exchange between the men affirms that the danger for the man is the issue, not the well-being of the woman; the woman is "a silent object, a pawn, and is effectively suppressed" (43, 46). Even God's reaction to Abraham is dubious here (ch. 20), as God punishes the upright and honest Abimelech but not the deceptive and wife-betraying Abraham.

The case of Jacob is a little different in that the women around him are all actively involved in the turning of his fate. There is similar silence about women in both of Jacob's dreams, in Bethel and about the flocks. However, Jacob's mother, Rebekah, is practically the reason for Jacob's departure from Beer-sheba for Haran, having actively strategized for his place in the family line and his immediate protection from Esau's revenge. In this light, Rebekah is no passive or voiceless woman. In another instance, when Jacob reports his dream regarding the instruction of God's angels for them to leave Laban's land, his two wives, Leah and Rachel, participate in the justification of the move and ally with their husband against their father's interests. Still, what would have been Rebekah's dream for her family and her state of well-being? What would have been Leah's and Rachel's dreams when they competed with each other in bearing sons for Jacob? What would have been Rachel's dreams when she is pregnant and has to move with Jacob from Bethel and Ephrath, when she dies of hard labor after the birth of Benjamin (35:18)? In short, if dreams are visions of God's blessing, what would these women's dreams be with regard to their families in migration? Unfortunately, we have only the male side of the stories in the Bible so far.

If Rashkow is right that there is practically no woman in the dream narratives of Genesis, there is a significant lacuna to be filled in the story of migration in this book. When a patriarch is called to travel to a new land, taking with him his wife/wives, there is no other choice for women except to follow. In the case of Sarah and Rebekah, they have to collaborate with their husbands' stories and allow themselves to be taken into foreign kings' harems. Even though they are delivered to the foreign kings almost like ransom for their husbands' life and luxurious living, they are expected to have preserved their purity. In the case of Leah and Rachel, they are compelled to choose loyalty to their husband against their father. The texts are completely silent about what these women really feel, because their feelings are not important. What is most important is that they can overcome their barrenness and produce bountiful descendants for the patriarchs and be an emblem for the lifting up of the house's hope for future prosperity. Is there a way to postulate what their dreams would be as women constantly on the move with their husbands and families? What would God have painted for them in the future?

I would like to fill this lacuna for women in migration with the stories of Chinese immigrant women in Hong Kong. Chen Xizhi, a Hong Kong journalist, decided to collect stories of new immigrant women in Hong Kong, and these were finally published in *Twelve Women in Tianshuiwei* (2006c). Her project began with a similar observation, that the voice of these marginalized women has been rarely heard, and continued with stories of shattered dreams that pervade the book's pages. Because of the economic disparity between Hong Kong and mainland China, many young women in the mainland dream of marrying Hong Kong men despite the men's low income and class background. Such women have constituted two-thirds of the total new immigrant population to Hong Kong every year (Yui 2008: 6).[18] Furthermore, in the 2001 population census, women constituted 77 percent of new immigrants fifteen years or older, and their average age was twenty-five (Cai 2008: 13). Unfortunately, not only do these women marry into low-income families; they themselves also tend to be less educated and unskilled, so they live in families with income significantly lower than average. They live practically on the edge of the society and suffer much material deprivation. What is worse, cultural and language difference between them and the locals contribute to name calling and labeling them stereotypically as greedy, backward, uncivilized "mainland women" who have to face ostracism on a daily basis within and outside their families (Chen 2008: 27–28). Cai Yuping, who has just finished a study of new immigrant women in Tianshuiwei, finds that their families, when compared with the larger population of Hong Kong, are particularly disadvantaged in having more children and less-educated husbands who have a higher unemployment rate and are mostly concentrated in low-income, unstable jobs. Such women's social capital, including familial and peer support and community and social networks, is comparatively low, which results in a relatively high percentage of domestic

18. Yui is the Permanent Secretary of the Home Affairs Bureau, the Hong Kong SAR Government.

violence. Financially, about 30 percent of these families are running on deficits, with about 14 percent living on heavy loans (Cai 2008).

The following two stories, collected by Chen, were told by two new immigrant women. Sister Yun, whose husband left her in 1997 for another woman in the mainland, is left with the sole responsibility of taking care of her four children and the household at age thirty-nine. Her life has never been easy, either before or after her arrival in Hong Kong. Her typical day in Hong Kong starts with departure for work at seven in the morning. She cycles to work as a domestic helper for one home before lunch, takes a short rest in a nearby library, and then cycles to work at a second home from four to seven in the afternoon. Because of the distance, she ends up cooking for the family at nine at night. She finishes all the housework, including another round of cleaning, ironing, and caring for the youngest children, and then sleeps for about six hours before another day begins. She has the same schedule six days a week (Chen 2006b).

Another woman, Zhang, arrived in Hong Kong in 2003. She began working at a restaurant three days after her arrival. Then the restaurant owner fled without paying her any salary. She experienced discrimination during her search for jobs, due to her unfamiliarity with Cantonese, the local dialect. She finally found a job and now works from seven in the morning to three-thirty in the afternoon for only three thousand Hong Kong dollars, barely enough for her travel between the factory and home. Her husband is unemployed and has become completely withdrawn. Zhang has been taking care of her daughter and the family on her own, the whole time. She has no friends and no time or money for entertainment, but is determined to work through the difficulties. And she has a dream, too. She had education up to high school on the mainland and won a prize for writing. Her dream is to one day go to university for further studies together with her daughter (Chen 2006a).[19] Other women's stories are similar to those of Sister Yun and Zhang.

It has been the norm rather than the exception that people have been on the move from one place to another throughout history. More and more studies have drawn a complex and vibrant picture of the realities of migrant

---

19. Jing Shuying, another new immigrant woman, lived in the same area as Zhang. Unable to cope with the stress in and beyond the family in Hong Kong, she threw herself from the window of her flat together with her two young children, and all plunged to their death.

experiences, as affected by economic, social, and political processes locally and globally. Recent scholarship also shows that there is increased feminization of migration worldwide (Newendorp 2008: 15). Besides migrant workers, women who left home for overseas marriage and family reunion form an important part of world migration. In Hong Kong, an annual quota of 55,000 immigrants from the mainland has been set up since 1995 to facilitate family reunions. The average waiting time for family reunion is five to ten years. Despite the long wait, marriages across the border are on the rise: whereas in 1996 only 2,215 men registered marriages with mainland women, in 2006 this number increased to 18,000—a third of all marriages in Hong Kong (5–6).

Nevertheless, the real story for women begins only after their arrival in Hong Kong. Given the concentration of husbands coming from the low-income group, it is not unusual for wives and children to find themselves trapped by their husbands' and fathers' downward mobility in society, and stuffed into squalid tenement housing or low-cost residences in some old, worn-out districts of the city. To these difficulties, we should add the anxieties of waiting another seven years to become permanent Hong Kong residents (so they can enjoy social welfare and access to government low-cost housing), concerns for the education and well-being of children, disputes with in-laws over living or child care arrangements, conflicts between personal aspirations and the demand for professional qualifications, and competitive job performances in Hong Kong. The reality is that the women have little access to the comfortable, glittering, and modern city life they had imagined (Newendorp 2008: 5–6). In short, family reunions in Hong Kong are anxiety provoking for women from the mainland and highlight the daily difficulties of living in an entirely new environment, as well as the disparity between expectations, privileges, goals and reality (7–8).

Cross-border marriages in Hong Kong involve the women's aspiration to gain access to First World amenities and a better social and economic future for themselves and their children. This is what they imagine, but in reality, they experience truncation of their networks of family, friends, and employers, as well as resentment and hostility from some government officials. As a matter of fact, how each country draws its boundaries on the question of citizenship is a political exercise of inclusion and exclusion, defining who will be "strangers" and who will be "members" of a community (Newendorp 2008: 16–17).

In sum, the stories of the new immigrant women in Hong Kong remind us of the difficult lives of families on the move. While women always follow their husbands and families to where they settle, there is usually little security or social support provided for them. Rather, they are exposed to all kinds of stigmatization, discrimination, and marginalization, and are expected to endure these hardships with superb perseverance and emotional strength.

Women's Dreaming in Migration

What would women be dreaming, then, when they migrate to join their families in a land foreign to them? I started this paper with Xixi's novel *The Flying Carpet*. Her dream is one among many dreams of Hong Kong in the transitional years around 1997. Dreams of Xixi's woman characters represent those of earlier settlers who fled to Hong Kong during and after the war. These settlers faced their biggest challenge when their colonial masters had to return them to their communist "mother country." Their dreams are written in the names of their story's characters: Ye Mousheng (meaning "Prosperous Leaves"), Ye Chongsheng ("Regeneration of Leaf"), Hua Hejiu ("Forever Blooming"), Hua Yanyan ("Splendid Flowers"), and The Flying Carpet. Each name is inscribed with the hope and aspiration of a migrant population that their new life would be ever prosperous and ever growing.

In *The Flying Carpet,* there are several women whose dreams are fulfilled to a degree. Ye Chongsheng's former nursing mother, Zheng Sunu, has persistently looked for her pirate family history and the whereabouts of her grandfather's treasures. Toward the end of the novel, she finally finds the treasures and builds a very successful theme park, "Pirates Paradise," which becomes a major venue for leisure and entertainment in the city (Xixi 1996: 498). Another woman, named Hu Jia, who has never been convinced of the existence of flying carpets, finally steps onto one and strolls through the sky despite her dreamy memories afterward. At least she now realizes that "things that are invisible do not mean that they don't exist" (506–507). Why would the dream of "soaring up high" be one that is so endearing to the city? Hu seems to learn something about the city from her adventure (508).

For years, another woman protagonist, Hua Yanyan, would sleepwalk and ride the flying carpet and enjoy the glittering scenes of the Hong Kong sky and buildings. When her two elder brothers eventually find their dream herbal plants for the cure of sleepwalking and unexpectedly introduce the magic of invisibility, something miraculous happens. One becomes increasingly blended into the environment and turns invisible to others (503). As soon as Hua Yanyan is cured of her frequent sleepwalking, her city and its people increasingly fade into the background. They are eventually lost from sight despite the narrator's efforts to trace, record, and photograph in order to preserve them. They finally go beyond anyone's control (512–13). Ironically, the city that wishes to perpetuate its prosperity and ever-growing importance in history finally disappears. It could be an announcement of the illusory nature of life, that nothing can be kept despite the people's dreams; yet at the same time, the irony could be an act of resistance to giving up hope despite life's unpredictability. Remember Hu Jia's new conviction that "things that are invisible do not mean that they don't exist"?

A film titled *Comrades: Almost a Love Story* (1996),[20] starring Maggie Cheung and Leon Lai and directed by Peter Chan, tells such stories in a touching way. It is a story about the first crop of new immigrants from China after the opening up of the Chinese economy in the early 1980s. Like the story of *The Flying Carpet*, the film starts with two dreams, dreamed by Qiao (Cheung) and Jun (Lai) on the same train as they leave their hometown on the mainland for Hong Kong. Like all Chinese immigrants who first come to Hong Kong, they are isolated from native Hong Kong people and are friendless because of their different languages, living styles, and cultures. Like most new immigrants, they strive to succeed in realizing their dreams of prosperity, making new families, acquiring a modern life, and improving their living standard. Secretly, they may all wish to acquire sufficient material gains so as to shower their relatives in the hometown with lavish gifts and prestigious brands. While Jun's (the man's) dream is to earn enough money

---

20. The film was the first of its kind to attempt to portray the life and the turn of fortune for Chinese new immigrants in Hong Kong. It won nine awards at the sixteenth Hong Kong Annual Film Award, including best picture, best director, best actress, best supporting actor, best screenplay, and others; three awards at the third Hong Kong Film Critics Society Award, including best picture, best director, and best actress; and the best-picture award at the Seattle International Film Festival.

to bring his fiancée to Hong Kong and get married, the dream of Qiao (the woman) is to build up her wealth and climb high on the social ladder. As it turns out, Qiao must make lots of adjustments, including acceptance of the most unwanted jobs—cleaner, McDonald's hourly worker, massage parlor girl, and woman of a triad boss. She largely stays at the bottom rung of the new society despite her university education and professional status at home. Despite Qiao's never-failing spirit to succeed and do well with her business investment, she is never quite satisfied. The film ends with Qiao and Jun (the man) waking up from the train in which they first arrived in Hong Kong, and their dreams start all over again. It is an unfinished dream of migration to a city and a woman's vision of "soaring high."

Both Xixi's *The Flying Carpet* and Peter Chan's *Comrades: Almost a Love Story* elevate the woman dreamers as new immigrants to a new city. We have seen that women in *Twelve Women in Tianshuiwei* are not passive victims of patriarchal families. Although their husbands all failed their family responsibilities, and although the women were not fully informed of the men's poverty before they married, they take charge of the situation and do the best they can to sustain the family and the children. In the case of Qiao in *Comrades*, she is the complete opposite of Jun, the male protagonist. While Jun is quiet, direct, honest, and a good, humble laborer, Qiao is lively, sociable, quick-minded, opportunistic, and determined to reach the top. Because of her ambition, she is willing to swallow hardship, work long hours, brave high-risk investments, and face the consequences. She possesses the courageous spirits that any immigrant would need to survive in an alien environment. She does not reach the top, as she desired in the beginning, but tries her best. After all, she is not married into a Hong Kong family and does not have to join a jobless husband; she comes of her own will and at her own risk. Most of all, in both cases of book and film, women have been making sense of the struggles and meanings of their lives through their dreams.

> Dreams are not only directly connected to divination; they also reflect on other segments of culture. . . . By their very liminality, dreams are at the confluence of theology, cosmology, and anthropology. In a sense, they permit, where other media fail, a way of intracultural communication of great flexibility. In particular, dreams offer a constant balance between the private world of latent images, fears, and hopes, and outside reality, cosmic as well as social. Dreams present the means

to reestablish the constantly shattered equilibrium between these two realms. (Shulman and Stroumsa 1999: 6)

Dreams were primary venues for God and human communication in ancient texts, including the Bible. Interpreters of dreams, whenever they were officials, would be men. While the stories of women and their dreaming and interpretation in history deserve more serious studies, their absence from Genesis is too much of a gap to be missed. The silence of Genesis on women's dreams certainly attests to the patriarchal constitution of the book, so that women's aspirations and desires have never been valued. However, given the richness and complexities of migrant women's experience today, can we not reinscribe their dreams into the patriarchal stories in order to appreciate their presence? And if we can, what will their dreams be?

Xixi's playing with the end of the dream is fascinating. The dreaming people actually become their own subjects. *The Flying Carpet* is then not only a narrative representation of the many stories and people's history of Hong Kong, but also about the dream of a people asserting their subjectivity and finding their space to move on. Picking up again on Xixi's notion of the dream being an act of resistance, if one is to write the dreams of Sarah, Rebekah, Leah, and Rachel, and even Hagar, Zilpah, Bilhah, and the others, I believe they would be dreams to succeed in their roles and better their lives on their own terms. Like the dreams of Xixi, their dreams will bear hopes for the future despite difficulties in their migrating life, adjusting to living between cities. And this will be a project for the future.

Part Three

———

Issues of Gender, Family, and Class

CHAPTER 14

The Case of Judah and Tamar in the Contemporary Israeli Context
A Relevant Interpolation

Yairah Amit

The story of Judah and Tamar (Genesis 38) is planted within the story of Joseph but treats the origins of the clan of Judah from two viewpoints: its connection to the Canaanites and the beginning of its genealogy. Therefore, although the story has some expressions and motifs that are common to the Joseph story, it also has its independent character. Against this background, my discussion is divided into two parts: the first deals with Genesis 38 as interpolation, and the second with the relevance of the story to the contemporary Israeli context. Although the first part belongs to the world of biblical criticism, I am convinced that the need for interpolation in the past is relevant today, too, since past reasons that motivated the interpolation engage Israeli society till this day and are therefore valid also in the present.

Interpolation

The narrative of Judah and Tamar always piqued my curiosity as a youth. Its omission from high school Bible curricula in the State of Israel makes it conspicuous. When the story of Joseph is studied, chapter 38 is skipped for three reasons: firstly, because of the whiff of the erotic; secondly, because this way teachers do not have to confront the problematic levirate law, which is part of juridical life in the modern Israeli state; and thirdly, because it is not seen as an integral part of the plot of the Joseph story, and skipping it does not disturb the plot sequence. In other words, skipping this chapter serves different kinds of interests: literary, didactic, conservative, polemical, and orthodox.

When I embarked on my academic studies, I learned that this chapter is the classic example of *Wideraufnahme* or "resumptive repetition," a phenomenon in biblical texts that is both a technique and proof of interpolation. Using this construct, I could explain to students the approach that sees this chapter as a bracketed interlude that was added by a later redactor between Gen. 37:36 and 39:1.[1]

Viewing the story of Judah and Tamar as having a secondary position in its context is significant, because it immediately raises questions: Who was interested in adding this story, and why was including it so important? Who were the editors willing to pay the price of the illogical chronology that this chapter creates by covering so many events that presumably happened in only twenty-two years?[2] Was it simply in order that the episode would reflect well on Judah and the values that his actions represent?

My initial curiosity led me to take a serious and deep interest in the story when I began to specialize in issues of biblical editing. As you might know, my first book focused on the art of editing in the book of Judges (Amit 1999). Already then, I realized that issues of editing have two facets: the technical side, which deals with the placement of a text, and the conceptual/ideological/tendentious aspect, which deals with questions such as to whom, when, and why was it important to interpolate a specific text.

Studying the issue of placement reminded me of the early comments of the Jewish sages, on which scholars who wish to view the chapter as an integral part of the Joseph story base themselves (Cassuto 1972; Emerton 1975; 1976: see n. 2; Alter 1981: 3–12; and many others). Here is one famous example that the sages used in order to show the close connection between this chapter and its surrounding framework by invoking the concept of "measure for measure." They drew a parallel between the phrase used when the

---

1. The first to discover the phenomenon of "resumptive repetition" was Kuhl (1952: 1–11).
2. This calculation is based on the story's data: twenty-two years elapsed between the sale of seventeen-year-old Joseph (Gen. 37:1) and his reunion with his brothers. He arrived at Pharoah's court at age thirty, thirteen years after the sale (41:46). Add to this seven years of plenty and two more years until he met the brothers (44:11). It cannot be that during that twenty-two-year interval, Judah married and had three sons, married off two of them, and fathered with Tamar two children (Perez and Zerah), and when they went to Egypt, Perez already had two children of his own, Hezron and Hamul (46:12).

brothers ask Jacob to identify signs of Joseph's supposed demise (37:32) and the same phrase in the Tamar episode (38:25): "Rabbi Yohanan said, "The Holy One Blessed be He said to Judah: You used the phrase *Identify this, if you please.* By your life, Tamar will also say to you, *Identify this, if you please,*" (*Genesis Rabbah* 85:11).

However, if scholars assume that editors, like authors, treated the text with sensitivity and sophistication, they may attribute such similarities to the reworking of the text in order to fit it to its new context. Therefore, I am not convinced by the analogies, no matter how many we find. It seems to me that the Tamar and Judah story was inserted into the midst of the Joseph story to meet two editorial considerations:[3]

1. The status of Judah in the immediate context, which is the story of Joseph
2. The issue of intermarriage in the wider context of the book of Genesis and all biblical literature

Immediate Context

This episode contributes to the positive image enhancement of Judah, who is characterized as a concerned father, worried about the fate of Shelah, his last remaining son after the deaths of Er and Onan. Moreover, Judah is described as someone who is willing to admit his mistake and to render a fair judgment. He not only retracts his verdict, but also passes judgment on his own behavior in discouraging his son from the levirate obligation to Tamar. Finally, he admits that Tamar is in the right (v. 26).

This positive portrayal of Judah is critical in the context of emphasizing the achievements of Joseph. We must not forget that Judah already came onstage in the previous story of the sale of Joseph (chapter 37) as a reasonable person who is less cruel than most of his brothers; and thanks to him, Joseph does not die but is rather sold to a caravan of Ishmaelites or Midianites. By interpolating this episode into the beginning of the Joseph story, it will naturally bring the spotlight onto Judah as the story of Joseph unfolds. As it turns out, it is due to Judah's intervention that Joseph is saved and arrives in Egypt (37:39); thanks to Judah's wisdom, Jacob agrees to allow the brothers to bring Benjamin to Egypt (43:3-14); and the speech of Judah to Joseph (44:18-34)

---

3. For a detailed analysis of this story, see Amit (forthcoming).

is so incisive that it persuades Joseph to change course, and he breaks down and reveals himself to his brothers (45:1-15). Therefore, the important role of chapter 38 is to focus on Judah and present him as pivotal in the actualization of God's plans, in which Joseph also is only a vehicle whose purpose is to prepare the background for the migration of Jacob's family to Egypt.

Wider Context

This segment complements the book of Ruth, which contributes the Moabite component to David's family tree (Ruth 4:12, 18-22). It supplies the background for the genealogical connection between Perez and Judah, and even underlines David's Canaanite origins, because Tamar did not come from "there" (Gen. 24:5), which is Abraham's home country, Haran, in contrast to Sarah, Rebecca, Rachel, Leah, and even their maids Zilpah and Bilhah, who came from "there." Rather, Tamar was from a local Canaanite family that lived in Timna or its surroundings.[4] The story of Judah and Tamar contributes an additional voice to the book of Genesis, different and in contrast to the voice we hear, for example, in Genesis 24, where Abraham is against a Canaanite daughter-in-law.[5] We can find these two contending voices in other parts of biblical literature, too: the anti-intermarriage voice in Ezra 9–10; Neh. 9:1, 13:1, 23-30; and Mal. 2:11-12, versus the pro-intermarriage voice in Ruth and in Chronicles 1 and 2.[6] This additional and interpolated voice of Genesis 38 takes us to the contemporary Israeli context.

The Double Relevance in the Contemporary Israeli Context

Intermarriage

The possibility of intermarriage, that is, for a Jew to marry a non-Jew, is extremely relevant to the social reality in Israel today. In the past two decades, over a million immigrants have come to Israel from the former Soviet Union, and up to a third of them are non-Jews according to the *halakha*. We have to know that, according to the *halakha*, identity is determined through matrilineal descent, meaning that a Jew is someone whose mother was Jewish or who

---

4. Emerton (1976: 90; 1979: 405, 412) emphasizes the Canaanite origin of Tamar.
5. See also Gen. 26:34-35, 27:46—28:8.
6. On the different approaches to foreigners and aliens in Chronicles and other writings, see Japhet 1989: 334–51; Dor 2006: 123–50 and bibliography.

converted to Judaism according to the *halakha*. Fifty years ago (1957), Moshe Bar-Yehuda, then minister for interior affairs (under whose jurisdiction fall matters of personal and civic status), instructed ministry registrars to list as "Jew" children born to couples even if the mother was not Jewish whereas the father was Jewish, if the parents so desired. This was a revolutionary step, and the protest in Israel was vociferous. Therefore, David Ben-Gurion, then prime minister, turned to fifty Jewish scholars in Israel and abroad, asking them to clarify the question, "Who is a Jew?" The majority of the responses reflected the matrilineal descent of the rabbinic tradition, rather than the position of the interior minister. The government retracted the minister's ruling and even its own former decision that Jewish identity be recorded according to a person's ("good faith") self-declaration. All this happened fifty years ago.[7] Nowadays halakhic law is enforced in Israel, and therefore intermarriage is a difficult problem. Moreover, everyone who lives in Israel permanently has to carry an identity card issued by the Interior Ministry. Although at this time the identity cards do not explicitly indicate religion (Jewish, Christian, or Muslim) and nationality (Jewish or Arab), all authorities know if you are Jewish, because only in the case of Jews does the document give the Hebrew birth date. Thus, every potential case of intermarriage is known to the authorities.

One could argue that, against the background of the Holocaust, the contemporary rabbinic rulings should take a more lenient, open, and liberal approach and follow the precedent of early biblical editors of the Torah, who accepted not just one view but allowed for many voices to be heard, among them an open one that was not isolationist and not afraid to connect King David with Canaanite origins. For such a purpose, they were even ready to interrupt a story and put in an interpolation. Those early redactors interwove two options concerning "Who is an Israelite?" side by side: the isolationist approach represented by the book of Deuteronomy and the Deuteronomistic School, versus the open option represented by the editing of the Holiness School.[8] Thus, biblical redactors left, for the coming generations, the option to choose. It isn't surprising that Reform Judaism has chosen the lenient

---

7. For more details on this subject, see Corinaldi 2001.
8. See, for example, Deut. 23:1-9 versus Exod. 12:43-49. On Exod. 12:43-49 as part of the Holiness Code and on the principle of the equality for stranger and citizen as a characterization of the Holiness Code, see Knohl 1995: 21, n. 35; Lev. 17:8, 10, 12, 13, 15; 18:26; 19:33, 34; 20:2; 22:18; 24:22.

option, recognizing as Jewish someone whose mother *or* father is Jewish. But this happens abroad and not in Israel. And who knows, maybe the next David will come from a contemporary Reform Tamar.

Levirate Marriage (Yibbum)

The second topic that is relevant today in Israel and in Orthodox communities outside Israel is the issue of levirate marriage. Levirate marriage is presented in detail in the long exposition to our chapter (Gen. 38:1-12)[9] as an actualization of the law in Deuteronomy 25:5-10. According to this law, a childless widow has to marry her husband's brother in order to continue the line of the deceased, because marriage to a stranger, meaning someone outside the family, would diminish the tribe's landholding.

In biblical times, this law implied a major economic advantage for the childless widow who might have been left out in the cold but, through levirate marriage, was able to continue participating in the family circle of her dead husband. Judah, instead of fulfilling the duty of levirate marriage, ordered Tamar to wear a widow's garments and sent her to her father's house. Thus, he made Tamar a social victim. After being removed from her husband's family where she might have shared in the inheritance, she lost her status and became destitute, at the mercy of her father, in his house, and if he passed away, at the mercy of her eldest brother.

Today, to modern sensibilities, levirate marriage seems an archaic relic of the past. However, this law is still alive and well according to Jewish rabbinic law, which today still governs marriage of Jews in Israel and in Jewish Orthodox communities outside Israel.[10] In other words, the brother of a man who died without children has an obligation to marry the widow so that the deceased will have posterity, and if one of the parties refuses to go through with this kind of marriage, both are required to go through a ceremony known as *halitzah* (Heb. taking off), involving a symbolic act of renuncia-

---

9. On the exposition in this story, which is unusually long—over a third of its narrative time—see Amit (forthcoming).

10. On the relevance of levirate marriage in Israel today, see Westrich 2003–04. It is interesting to compare this with the Levirate customs in India that were depicted in the 2005 movie *Water*, set in 1938, where a preteen widow has the choice of throwing herself on her husband's funeral pyre, marrying his younger brother, or living in celibacy with other widows.

tion of their right to take part in this marriage. This ceremony of *halitzah*, after which the widow is free to remarry in a Jewish religious ceremony, takes place in the rabbinic court till this day, just as it is described in Deut. 25:8-10:

> Then the elders of his city [today the rabbis] shall call him [the refusing brother], and speak unto him; and if he stand, and say: 'I like not to take her'; then shall his brother's wife draw nigh unto him in the presence of the elders, and loose his shoe from off his foot, and spit in his face; and she shall answer and say: 'So shall it be done unto the man that doth not build up his brother's house.' And his name shall be called in Israel the house of him that had his shoe loosed.

Now a person's marital status (single, married, widowed, and so forth), number of children, and details about them are indicated in the attachment to the identity card of every Israeli citizen. Therefore, a Jewish childless widow whose dead husband has brothers, and who wants to marry someone other than her dead husband's brother in a religious ceremony, is required to experience the *halitzah* ceremony in order to free herself.

Because Israel is subject to frequent wars and terrorist attacks, there is a relatively large number of childless widows. Orthodox or traditional women will not remarry without *halitzah* and will not engage in common-law marriage or live "in sin" with a man, so they are in limbo not only because in some cases it is hard to convince—or even to force—brothers to marry their widowed sisters-in-law, but also because those widows may not wish for a common-law marriage. To a lesser extent, this legal situation also affects secular widows who want to have a religious marriage ceremony, because they might choose a different alternative, such as common-law marriage (see above). However, the situation is somewhat balanced by the lowered rate of childless couples, due to widely available advanced fertility treatments and the possibility of freezing sperm.

A lawyer from the women's organization *Mavoi Satum* ("Dead End") informed me that the rabbinic courts are not strict in this area and often do not check thoroughly to ascertain the familial relationships of widows wishing to remarry—a kind of "don't ask, don't tell" approach. However, the existence of a brother-in-law can come to the rabbis' attention via someone who sees *halitzah* as an opportunity to extort money or to exact revenge. For example, a brother-in-law will purposely inform the rabbinic court in order to get money from the widow: if she wants to remarry in a religious ceremony she needs the *halitzah* document and the threat of having to obtain it or of not getting it can cause and has led to attempts of such blackmail. When informed, the rabbinic court has to try to persuade or force the brother-in-law to perform *halitzah*. Although, all told, in today's Israel there are probably not many childless widows who cannot remarry. Still, the *halitzah* ceremony has not yet disappeared from Israeli reality.

Since the subject of levirate marriage is still relevant today, one way to minimize possible problems is to make provisions to deal with the situation in prenuptial agreements. In the 1950s, there was such an attempt, but it failed.[11] Today, prenuptial agreements are possible individually to prevent a woman from becoming an *Agunah* (stuck), that is, a woman whose husband is missing and not proved dead, and to prevent a woman from becoming a *mesorevet get*, a woman whose husband refuses to grant her a divorce. But many women do not know about these prenuptial agreements yet. In any event, until now and on a preventive level, the problem of levirate marriage has no official solution.

Conclusion

Genesis 38 serves as a platform for two subjects: marriage with non-Jewish women and levirate marriage. It does so via the portrayal of the character and fate of Tamar, the heroine of the drama, whose behavior is unconventional. Despite her being a Canaanite, she is not criticized at any point in the narrative. Moreover, the fact that she becomes pregnant and even with twins indicates that her origin and initiative have met with divine favor, as pregnancy was considered a sign of heavenly intervention and blessing.[12]

We can conclude that this chapter of Genesis, although an interpolation, is important and relevant to contemporary Israeli society, where there is no separation of religion and state, where most of the population is traditional, and where rabbis, who represent religion, have political clout and play a role in forming and bringing down governments. Genesis 38 presents a positive view of intermarriage and is also an encouragement to women to take their fate into their own hands.

---

11. See n. 10.
12. See, for example, 1 Sam. 1:19-20.

CHAPTER 15

Characterizations, Comedy, and Catastrophe
Divine/Human Relations, Emotions, and Rules of Law

Cheryl A. Kirk-Duggan

The need for my engagement of womanist/feminist sensibilities and scholarship never entered my cosmology until seminary. While I grew up toward the end of segregation and the beginnings of court-ordered integration in the southern United States of America, women experienced equality in my family, and I received tons of support from extended and church families. Mother played classical music all the time; I sang my first solo in church at age four and began piano lessons at age five. Performing is in my DNA, so I have always been comfortable being onstage, being a leader, being in charge—so much so that I have two degrees in music (B.A. in piano and voice; M.M. in voice). When we were children, our teachers believed we could do well, and we did. Most of my classmates, from kindergarten through high school, lived in two-parent homes. As an African American girl, daughter of the first African American deputy sheriff in the state of Louisiana, I knew about racism, though our parents shielded us from a lot of blatant oppression. Reading slave narratives while studying for my master's degree in music was a rude awakening about the depths of racial hatred. I still did not get the impact of sexism until later. Mother and Dad were partners, and God was head of the house, so when Euro-American women were protesting about their rights, initially I did not see the problem. Hearing the stories from women about the abuse, the negation of their selves because they were not male in seminary radically changed my perspective.

During doctoral work, I personally experienced racism and sexism, and subsequently became intrigued with class issues. I knew some people had less and others had more, yet learning about the systemic nature of class issues opened new vistas of research. Seventeen years of teaching in religious and theological education at the undergraduate, seminary, and doctoral levels; my lived experiences in and outside of the classroom; my twenty-six-year interracial marriage to a phenomenal intellectual, loving, compassionate friend; and our large extended multiethnic family have made me more adamant about justice issues: constitutionally, I must ask these questions. Womanist thought, which seeks to name, expose, and transform oppression in all aspects, provides a powerful rubric that allows me to be Professor/Performer/Priest/Preacher/Poet/Prophet, embracing all my rich experiences.

In my reading of the stories found in Genesis 1–9 from a womanist interdisciplinary context, as a scholar, musician, pedagogue, ordained minister, athlete, quilter, and lover of God, rose gardens, and life, I find intriguing characterizations of the divine and of related human couples. This God, as midwife, judge, disciplinarian, and executioner, experiences sensory perceptions expressed in anthropomorphic—i.e., in human—terms. These experiences move this God to know satisfaction, to feel wronged, to retaliate with vengeance, and then to repent. These same stories unfold with two genealogies: of the *adamah* (or earth creature, since God never really names him) and Eve and of Noah and Mrs. Noah. People come into existence, desire divine knowledge, and procreate. One commits murder; others live in covenant and experience blessings and curses, live for hundreds of years, procreate, sometimes worship, and die.

Amid such poetic origins of humanity and civilization, gleaning from the Gilgamesh epic—both Gilgamesh and Genesis are oral stories first reduced to written texts during the Babylonian Exile (beginning in 587/586 BCE)—much of the divine and human engagement from the timing of the events to the results of those engagements is often filled with acts of courage and the comedic, tinged with irony and humor. Human interaction with the earth, beasts, and other human beings often disturbs God, as humanity acts in defiance. The divine countering response exacts tragedy, pain, and suffering.

My essay explores the second creation narrative and the sagas of Adam/Eve and Mr./Mrs. Noah (Gen. 2–3; 6–9) for contexts and dynamics of divine sensibilities, instances of comedy, and the impact of tragedy. I begin

by introducing the life-context and methodological matrix for the interpretation of Genesis, followed by a framing of life context amidst divine–human
relationality, comedy, and tragedy. Next, I provide an overview of the particular Genesis texts and an analysis of the Genesis passages reflecting God,
the two couples, and their environments, framed by how these stories could
inform the lives of a child living in poverty, a person living with sensory disabilities, a person living with domestic violence, and a person labeled as an
illegal immigrant (matters of class, ability, gender, and race). I close with my
overall conclusions.

Life Context Further Mined: Embodied
Womanist Biblical Hermeneutics

Many seek to give the Bible secular and religious authority, both as a spiritual
guidebook and as a political manual. They may confuse the actual texts of
biblical narratives with oral myths and traditions about what is in the Bible,
and disregard the meaning of the literal words of the sacred text. Biblical
scholarship often searches for a privileged reading toward some absolute or
ultimate "Truth" about biblical history and ancient Israel, but biblical stories
often contain multiple and conflictual truths—without certainty, but filled
with irony and ambiguity. Scholarly interpretations of these stories often
engage a psychological need to ascribe infallible authority to church authority and tradition based on alleged inerrant biblical insights. Some biblical
scholarship attempts to reconstruct the sociopolitical and religious history
of ancient Israel and the Near East. The histories within the Bible relate to
stories replete with particular contemporary ideologies, which are then used
to justify the future oppression of others.

Womanist theory invites and insists that one live in the present, while
simultaneously studying history and engaging in radical listening and
discerning to see, know, challenge, analyze, and make a difference. Womanist theory is a field of study and an epistemology that takes seriously the
exposure, analysis, and transformation of societal and personal injustices and
oppressions that affect those who usually matter least in society, as symbol-
ized by poor African diasporan women. Womanist theory is interdisciplinary
and examines experience present in living, written, oral, visual, aural, sensual,
and artistic texts to create its epistemology, hermeneutics, and philosophy.

This involves ongoing intellectual, spiritual dialogue to prepare individuals to experience their own reality in a holistic manner. The term *Womanist,* derived by Alice Walker from the term *womanish* (Walker 1983: xi), refers to women of African descent who are audacious, outrageous, in charge, and responsible. A Womanist emancipatory theory embraces engendering mutuality and community amid the responsibility and stewardship of freedom, and honors the *imago Dei,* the image of God, the essential goodness in all persons, regardless.

Womanist rubrics and fields of inquiry include, but are not limited to theology (divinity, dialogue, identity, sacrality, spirituality, and power), Bible and narratives (texts, authority, characters, rituals, language, and history), ethics (value, behavior, emotions, visibility, integrity, and praxis), and context (autobiography, culture, aesthetics, power dynamics, ecology, and community). Womanist theory as conceptual tool names, questions, interprets, and helps transform the oppression of women, particularly those affected daily by oppressive race and class domination. Womanists champion the struggle for the gift of freedom for all people. Taking the use of language seriously between the divine and the human, and within human community, we engage the politics of language, where words and expressions can inspire or subjugate. This strategy is vital to the analysis of biblical texts.

A Womanist reading of biblical texts requires a hermeneutics of tempered cynicism, creativity, courage, commitment, candor, curiosity, and the comedic.[1] *Tempered cynicism,* occasionally synonymous with reasonable suspicion, invites one to question with a sensitivity that knows the joy of the impossible and the hope of rooted faith, with the scholarship that helps one appreciate and celebrate the complexities of such engagement. *Creativity* provides a context where normative interpretations and traditions do not hinder new, adventurous, perhaps risky exploration of oral or canonical texts. *Courage* provides the cushion for instances when the analysis feels redundant or leads to more mystery, along with the audacity to ask questions and engage comparative analysis of distinctive and seemingly antithetical texts and themes. *Commitment* to in-depth hearing and just, appropriate living of these texts frames the process of significant discovery. *Candor* serves as catalyst to reveal oppression within the texts and the communities that embrace such tenets to

---

1. See my first foray into designing a Womanist biblical hermeneutic: Kirk-Duggan 2000.

produce an oppressive, though mainline faith. *Curiosity* presses one to keep searching the sacred to push toward heightened inclusivity, mercy, justice, and love. And *the comedic* reminds us not to take ourselves so seriously that we cease to grow and respect other modes of interpretation and seeing, despite any disagreement.

Womanist biblical scholars wrestle with the scriptures as they deal with the absurdity of oppression: calling for justice, new kinds of interpretation, accountability, and change. Womanist theology is the study or discipline of God-talk that emerges out of the rich yet oppressive experience of women of African descent (Hayes 1998). Such theology explores individual and social behavior in dialogue with the Divine—a God/Spirit who cares and who looks with disgust on those who dismiss, disregard, or denigrate humanity, all creation. Every person is important and relational. Womanist biblical theology merges the study of theology and exegesis to examine and learn from biblical texts toward the empowerment of all people. Womanist biblical hermeneutics provides a lens for interpreting biblical and living biotexts. Several such texts have had a tremendous impact on how I read scripture.

My life has always been intimately involved with matters of justice, including matters of birth, travel, and inspiration. As already mentioned, my father was the first African American deputy sheriff in the state of Louisiana. People from myriad life experiences came to our door seeking help and information from him. He embodied justice and would often comment that he slept well at night because he had harmed no one that day. During my seminary years, on a trip to Central America during which we met Mothers of the Disappeared, I stood at the foot of the crypt of Archbishop Oscar Romero, who was assassinated while celebrating Mass, and saw a baby running around without a diaper because the only diaper was being washed. This rocked my world. Being invited to share freshly squeezed juice with persons in refugee camps during this Central American study tour, when we knew and they knew that this was the only juice they had, and drinking the juice despite concern about contracting bacteria, became an act of shared hospitality and justice that respected personhood. The tenacity of those refugees and that of people like my parents, extended family, and the numerous communities throughout the world that create a village to support their children and their elders, inspires and often haunts me. Their commitment makes my interrogation of biblical texts even more crucial. My work in justice has expanded to include research and consulting, specifically work on domestic violence and sexual assault.

The space of justice work regarding domestic violence and sexual assault includes teaching courses, engaging workshops, and doing research and performance relating to violence and its transformation. Teaching courses on theology and violence, sexualities and sexual misconduct, and general women's studies informs me of the deadly consequences of oppression, particularly oppression against women. Most aspects of world history and culture, from religion to government to literature and sport, engage violence. Scripture is teeming with divine and human violence. Recent training and work with the FaithTrust institute, dedicated to ending domestic and sexual violence, further presses my interest and commitment to justice.

Justice concerns flow over into my artistic life. A few years ago, I wrote an epic poem, "Mimesis Unbound," using the work of Vern Redekop, which was set to music for voice, strings, and flute. In addition to singing in this seven-movement work, I designed and participated in a plenary, "Reconciliation at the Nexus of Art, Theory and Praxis," which involved three distinct enactments of creative mimesis, including a mini-workshop in religious ethics and social psychology, a multimedia monologue with dance, and a choreopoem with three voices, for the 2006 Colloquium on Violence and Religion (COV&R) in Ottawa, Ontario, Canada. On Easter 2009, I made my liturgical-dance debut to Richard Smallwood's "Healing," and I weekly wrestle with and observe the dynamics of weeds, ants, and weather as I tend my flower beds—a joyous and humbling experience. Being out in creation presses me to ponder its complexities in real time and in scripture.

Lastly, much of my lived and vocational context is that of women's place and space. My first teaching experience in religious studies in higher education was in an all-women's undergraduate liberal arts college. Having to teach from Genesis to Revelation in one semester, for our bread-and-butter course, I committed to mining the roles and places of biblical women out of a concern for the empowerment of young women. I also had the rude awakening that not all women wanted exposure to liberation, challenges, and transformation, despite having selected single-gender education. My next port of call took me to the Graduate Theological Union, a consortium of nine seminaries and ten research centers. There I served as in-residence and core doctoral faculty and director of the Center for Women and Religion. That position and now my position as Professor of Theology and Women's Studies at Shaw University, historically the first Black university in the South, places issues of justice and women's concerns before me daily. Engagement as associate pastor, scholar, and public intellectual places me in pulpits, on the lecture circuit, and in consulting venues where topics are interdisciplinary and varied, including biblical interpretation, theology, ethics, violence, and the arts.

Framing much of life and my rubrics of analysis, my own performance persona is that of comedy. Comedy often illumines the ridiculous, the absurd, and serves as a foil for tragedy. Sometimes people fail to perceive humor because they think it disrespectful of God's majesty, and/or people who employ it do not speak to God, they speak for God. Though often difficult to define, humor involves a gentle acceptance of life's incongruities and allows humans not to take themselves too seriously. Some incongruities are tragic. A prerequisite for holiness, humor helps people experience sanctification, affirms freedom, and allows one to transcend the mundane and not contain the human spirit, freeing one from becoming a false, arrogant, vain self (Donnelly 1992).

The words *humor* and *comedy* are often used synonymously. Comedy, derived from Greek *komodia*, a compound either of *komos* (revel) or *komo* (village) and *ode* (singing), perhaps originally a village reveler, pertains to light and humorous drama, often with a happy or successful conclusion—that which amuses. Comedy, an ironic wrestling with society, involves conflict with particular groups (family, political, religious, etc.), practices, mores, and values, while being a part of that same society. An incapacity to live up to established norms, embodied comedy, often extracts reactions of laughter or smiles. In reacting to societal norms, actualities, and desires, comparatively, the comedic absurd, ridiculous, or naturally improbable character surfaces. Comedy, like tragedy, self-corrects, provides catharsis, and unmasks the foolishness of conformity. Comedy works to adjust the person toward the authentic, or the authentic toward the potential, or both toward the ideal. The comedic brings awareness of irony in human engagement with social evil, in a manner where catharsis involves foolishness exposing foolishness (Ballard 1986a).

Comedy, undergirded by ideology, enhances life, is good, and engages freedom in ambiguous ways, which operates in various ways biblically; it supports propaganda, and sometimes is subversive. David Gunn argues that while comedy can destabilize or ridicule social order, in part or in total, usually comedy trades off one type of imposed convention or values against another, ultimately reinforcing the status quo, making only minor adjustments to peripheral matters. Comedy tends not to yield social liberation. The quest for a happy ending or restoration requires working within the particular social structure the comedy is critiquing, when trying to resolve the plot and reintegrate the protagonist/hero into her or his rightful place in society, which is the same old society, even if characters have changed and learned lessons. When using comedy for biblical analysis, Gunn suggests an agnostic sensibility regarding possible ideological and political positions that may shape Scripture and how a reader's awareness of these sensibilities may affect her/his own perspectives (Gunn 1984: 124).

Humor/comedy, an innate human characteristic, shapes human feelings, relationships, attitudes, and thought. This type of emotional experience can appear paradoxical, as it can signify frivolity yet also maturity and objectivity; it influences perception, and can be elusive yet evokes spontaneous laughter. Arun Wesley (2003: 156–59) notes that some philosophers speak of humor as suggesting incongruity, ludicrousness; a juxtaposition of strained expectation to nothing, a defense against things that hamper life's spontaneity; an experience rooted in joy, which defies human need to inflict somberness on life as if everything is of major import, which then does become funny. Humor influences the broad strokes of human life in myriad ways— reducing tension, balancing one-sided perspectives, nurturing humility, and helping one transcend selfishness.

Scripture contains numerous comedic people, events, and illustrations, notably those that are ridiculous or incongruous and humorous. To grasp the incongruous means that one has to recognize the congruous, the orderly, ordinary expectations of others. Biblical personalities, events, situations, and witty incidents are rife with humor. The blame game in Genesis 3, when the Divine asks who ate of the tree, is an amusing scene. This moment brings to mind the comic strip "Family Circus," where when the parents ask the children who erred, they all say, "Not me!" as a shadowy outline of a child symbolizes the recipient of blame. Relationality between God and humanity, even amidst disobedience, affords an opportunity to experience humor (Wesley 2003: 166–68, 183).

Conversely, tragedy is a serious drama or work of literature that describes a catastrophic experience in the protagonist's life, as she or he must face a superior force (e.g., destiny, the divine, fortune, cosmic values), which usually has disastrous conclusions, often resulting from a character flaw. Usually the protagonist comes to see the impact of her or his acts and accepts the punishment. Thus, the tragic involves a subjective experience of evil that, ironically, may be within oneself. Irony involves ambiguity in human acts of speech amid communicating. When the protagonist wrestles with perceiving evil and a possible creative use of this evil, the matter engages the tragic. Both Aristotle and Hegel see such use of evil functioning as tragedy when pity and terror provide a catharsis *for* pity and terror. Pity awakens our sympathy, where we identify with those caught up in the events; terror repels or overawes amid fate. This struggle with evil often leads characters to question their world and worldviews. When they are pushed to their limits, particularly when the source is nonhuman, the consequences of the struggle result in an avowal of human dignity or self-respect and freedom—a type of triumph, despite the overwhelming power of evil (Ballard 1986b). Thus, I bring an interdisciplinary, performative, critical, and artistic mind and lived reality, cognizant of tensions in the text, using the lens of Womanist thought, comedy, and tragedy as sources for illumination.

Contextual/Thematic Framework for Reading Genesis

All of life involves relationships and communication. Relationships involve an interdependence of characters, communities, and systems as people experience their ontological, existential selves in diverse sociocultural environments. The standards and norms of their encounters, whether intimate or alienating, involve conformity and rebellion, rules and laws, matters of power and authority, and the ways that these elements intersect, empower, and/or oppress. In divine–human and human/personal/communal relationships, levels of connectedness, distance, and interaction vary. Some relationships are deeply personal, others highly public. In the words of Hannah Arendt, all relationships are political, for they all engage negotiations around power (Arendt 1998). With power comes responsibility. Some people multitask and engage on a variety of levels simultaneously, depending upon personal contexts and texts, who one is, what one knows, and what type of access one has to power. Being in a relationship is a contextual process. Who we are and who God is in Genesis, and in the lives of people of faith who adapt this scripture, is an engagement of a divine and human biotexts. We live and exist within a complex societal, spiritual matrix governed by specific laws, conventions, and rituals, all central to what and how we communicate. Communication involves contexts of engaging persons and places and things and processing texts of particular kinds of information. The contexts afford a conduit or connection to support access between people and places, from sender to receiver toward mutual understanding. Communication, using written, verbal, and/or body language, transmits information toward the exchange of ideas. Relationships depend upon communication to exist. Much of Scripture, particularly in Genesis, is the engagement of communication between entities that shape, enhance, or thwart their relationships and ultimately the health of the cosmos.

The Bible, like comedy, involves creation and takes seriously every day, ordinary people engaged in everyday, ordinary things. While the heroic vision exalts, the comedic and biblical visions celebrate a humbling view of human existence and honor human creatureliness. While tragedy omits, comedy embraces details regarding characterization, circumstances, and behaviors, along with the stuff of life—matters of food, sex, and body wastes. Tragedy, in grand fashion and purpose, focuses on vast parameters of injustice, evil, and degeneration. Comedy tackles stew; tragedy tackles haute cuisine. Embracing a sense of basic goodness as natural to humanity, comedy inclusively champions the vast panorama of human reality: forms, fortunes, and faults. In the process, comedy signals our capacity to know awe, pleasure, and delight. Tragedy tends to create a mind/body dichotomy, while comedy tends to help civilize humanity. Comedy can ultimately lead us to joy and an appreciation of God's creation of the world with all of its finiteness, difficulties, repetitions, and cycles. For Hyers (1982), comedy reminds us to appreciate the gift of God's grace embodied within creation, as salvation redeems, fulfills, and completes creation, and does not repudiate it. Ultimately, then, comedy engages irony, satire, and creation, where the mundane balances vanity.

Eugene Fisher (1977: 571) reminds us that Scripture is rife with humor, although readers may lack the capacity to experience the humor: "To be devoid of humor is to lack an awareness of our finitude. It is to make ourselves as gods. . . . Without the capacity to laugh, the bible is cut off from the human condition. Without humor there is no irony, without irony no tragedy. Without tragedy, there is no Good News." Biblical humor includes puns, comedy, trickster figures, riddles, and proverbs, though some of the comedic elements get lost in translation. In Genesis, the irony that the meaning of "Adam's" name relates to his origin from the ground would appeal to Semitic sensibilities. The Hebrew writer may have known of the Mesopotamian creation story, where a mother-goddess heals the rib of a divine hero, when using the pun surrounding Eve being made from Adam's rib. In Akkadian, the term also means "she who makes live." That 'arum means naked and also clever or cunning sets up a pun when the couple is naked ('arum) and feel no shame (Gen. 2:25), over against the serpent who is the most clever ('arum) beast of the field (Gen. 3:1). Considering the pun, the reason for the shame emerges, as the couple's wisdom, which is what distinguishes humanity from other animals, signals that their new awareness means they are 'arum: naked/clever (Gen. 3:7) In the garden scene between the Divine and humans regarding disobedience, God, a master punster with irony, "breaks up the conspiracy for good by placing enmity between the conspirators: woman and serpent, woman and man, man and earth" (Fisher 1977: 574). Tragedy and comedy both emerge in the Genesis creation stories: human finitude; the ironies of talking serpents and embarrassed humans; the simple, everyday dynamics of conversation rife with puns, and questions of *kairos* and *chronos*; and how they affect beginnings, relationships, and the connections between creation and redemption. Hebrew religious sensibilities, steeped in humor, express and unmask divine and human realities (571–74, 578–79).

Peeking into Creation (Genesis 2–3) and Apocalypse (Genesis 6–9)

In Genesis 1, the Bible's ongoing account of God's creation reveals holy space, where God gives people worth and beauty; they are made good, in God's image/shadow, and they have purpose (Moyers 1996: 7–13, 18–29). In the first creation story, God the poet speaks creation into existence. God creates out of God's fullness and wonder, where creation has its own identity, sculpted in freedom and framed by stewardship—not absolute freedom, but freedom to make choices. In the second creation saga, God the potter and giver forms out of dust; God as lover then creates with words and hands. The second account ushers in the dissatisfaction; the "not good" pronouncement of God and the sensibility of "Adam" that he not be alone perhaps trigger an awakening, an awareness of being alone. The two creation stories stand in tension, a complex matrix where the first story champions mutuality and the *imago Dei*. The second creation story focuses on relationships, where male and female find the likeness of themselves in each other: a love poem. Amidst this tension, we find the biblical God and Israel, couched in fidelity and infidelity, not categories of control and sovereignty—texts that make some uncomfortable. Human frailty causes God sadness, anguish, and suffering. Human suffering desires a God who, amidst freedom, will step in. Although most biblical families are dysfunctional, fractured families, there is the gift of carrying the blessing.

Brueggemann states that the second creation story is not decisive, does not assume a fall, and does not explain the emergence of evil in the world, as the text cares more about existential realities and not abstract philosophical thought. Ergo, the text does not pertain to or sustain theological matters of sin, death, evil, and fall, whereas interpreters have objectified these issues, giving them a life of their own, apart from God's purposes and humanity's trust. Undergirding the activity (Gen. 2:15-17) are the call to vocation (tending the garden) and the gift of permission (access to food), balanced and juxtaposed against divine prohibition. Genesis 2:18-25 presents a garden as context for human community, amid God's mystery, which affords a theological critique of human anxiety (Brueggemann 1982: 41–45, 53).

In contrast to Gen. 1:31, where God pronounces created humanity good, the prologue to the flood indicts humans' wickedness in their acts and related consequences. God, as grieving, pained, distressed parent, full of regret, with broken heart announces divine judgment, without exception. Only Noah and his family escape punishment because of his righteousness, being in right relation with God. God will destroy all flesh as the flooding waters cleanse the earth. God gives Noah the blueprint for the ark, and Noah obeys. Noah trusts God, builds the ark, and takes his family and pairs of animals (6:19-20), and seven pairs of clean animals and birds (7:2-3). The flood ensues, the waters rise above the highest mountains, and all living creatures outside the ark die. Once the waters finally abate, the land dries, and God tells everyone to leave the ark. God makes a covenant with Noah and promises not to flood the earth ever again, and that natural order will be restored (Fretheim 1994). Interestingly, Noah does not have dialogue with God or question the fate of the rest of humanity. No one speaks for the condemned, as Abraham intercedes on behalf of Sodom and Gomorrah (Gen. 18:20-33).

The flood story reflects incongruity where God creates the world to be a faithful, covenant partner, framed by harmony, unity, and goodness; but humanity, particularly Israel, refuses God's destiny for them. We must remember that these stories are written after the fact. We may not find the content just or logical, yet we are left with the received text, which presses us to be critical and cautious in assessment and in noting what the text can and cannot yield. In this tale of destruction, amid God's pathos, Brueggemann argues that God grieves human alienation, resistance, and evil. God invites and gives permission, is not authoritarian or coercive. With Noah as a righteous and blameless person, God announces the crisis and divine response of flood, destruction, and death. When the flood ends, God makes a new covenant with Noah and pastorally promises never again to destroy creation with water, signaling that promise with a rainbow (Brueggemann 1982: 73–84). Persons reading from the margins, the underside, and forgotten spaces might not experience such an optimistic reading, if they are willing and have the tools to do a critical analysis of the text.

Bill Moyers's conversation with scholars, artists, journalists, clergy, authors, psychologists, and poets on the Noah apocalypse raises poignant and profound questions. Is the crux of the flood story about a good Creator God punishing totally evil humanity that this God created? Is this about theodicy, or about human accountability and a transformed relationship between the divine and people, where God moves from demanding perfectionism to accepting flawed humanity, toward an irrefutable covenant? Do we read this text historically or as a parable: a parable of divine persistence, one of regret, of God's overreaction? Is this a story of new beginnings—a saga of a marriage gone haywire, the accompanying mistakes, and learning what to avoid amid regret and mistakes? Can this story really be about divine vengeance for human anarchy and sin? Is the God of primeval Genesis growing up? What happens when this apocalyptic story echoes the destructions of the Holocaust, Native American decimated destruction, and diasporan African enslavement? How do we deconstruct God's causing the flood? Is one lesson the reality of catastrophic destruction, which rocks our world and our simplistic views of God, where God is on our side and not that of others? Why does Noah fail to challenge God on behalf of other people's plight? Does the story reflect the difference between perfection and righteousness? With all of the tragedy of Noah, God's errors, human failed empathy, unsound overreaction, how does humanity hold in tension doubt and faith? Does the aftermath of such devastation make a remarkable statement of the human capacity then to choose and love life, to desire relationship with God? Is Noah's relationship one of horrific terror of God, his catalyst for obedience in building an ark, and then he projects his emerging anger on the Canaanites, gets drunk and naked? Is this a story of a too-personalized God? Do we think of God in too-personalized terms? Framed by physical and psychological laws of the universe, would the inclusion of women's voices create a different story? While God is silent yet not absent and swollen bodies are left in the mud, does the covenantal rainbow signal that there is hope within a two-way relationship that reveals things about God and about humanity? (Moyers 1996: 115–34, 140–53).

My commitment to justice issues, the conundrum that theodicy provides for me, and my hermeneutics of engagement move me to let these questions hang in the midst while moving to examine divine–human interactions between God and "Adam"/Eve and between God and Noah and his unnamed, silent, hidden, yet present wife.

Relationships Front and Center: The Divine, "Adam" and Eve, Noah and His Unnamed Wife

Fretheim (1994: 349–50, 354–57) suggests that the redactors of the received second creation story probably intended for it to fill in the gaps of chapter 1, particularly day six. He finds similarities within the two readings regarding God as sole creator, significance of humanity, social functions of female and male, the purpose and goodness of God's world, and cocreativity of divine and human. God's dramatis personae is that of potter, who shapes and forms the man and later the woman; as bellows who breathes divine living breath into all things formed; as farmer/gardener who plants and makes things grow. While we ask questions of this text that its ancient writers did not, Genesis testifies to God's universal, creative activities, which trumps human knowledge about them. God's creativity stands before and with God's redemptive activity. God acts freely to create, and God empowers others with a type of freedom and independence. With this freedom comes human choice, then and today in the twenty-first century. Human choice affects what happens today and for future generations, all of which stands in relation to God.

Arthur Miller (1996: 37) suggests that the God in Genesis is one who has little sentiment for, or cares little about, justice in the sense in which ordinary human beings understand justice. Genesis tells us the reason there has to be a God and the need for the rest of the Bible. Miller's theory again reminds us that the received text may not yield answers we desire, and his theory problematizes the way we use these creation texts in teaching, research, and preaching and as a blueprint for life. Clearly, he is accurate when it comes to the world of women.

Women in Genesis, while signifiers and architects of transition and transformation whose roles reflect patriarchal experiences and attitudes that marginalize women, paradoxically often manage to have critical power from the periphery for the movement of the story line, human progress, and Israelite culture. Eve, the protagonist, as opposed to her husband, engages in a quest for knowledge, challenges the limits of being human, and presses boundaries that require a control on her sensual experiences of taste and seeing. With a trickster serpent speaking truth to power, noting that eating the forbidden fruit affords the ability to tell good from evil, the woman believes the serpent, and the narrator uses a pun to note that the woman indeed sees that the tree is good, a delight to see, and good, for it makes one wise (Gen. 3:6). Both female and male, despite his passive stance, are culpable for the change in the status from a fixed, controlled, well-provisioned world to a world that has discernment, social functions, sexual status, birth, and death (Niditch 1998: 16–17, 29).

Phyllis Trible (1978: 72–81) frames Genesis 2–3 as a love story gone awry, where she sees many of the traditional, patriarchal readings as a violation of the story. Within the erotic creation process, she sees God creating a pun by fashioning *ha-adam* out of the dust of *ha-adama;* "dusty earth and divine breath" form the undifferentiated earth creature, the human being, as God's gift of playful creation. While Fretheim (1994: 353) contends that Trible's notion of *adam* does not have "an explicit linguistic marker . . . that changes from 'earth creature' to 'the man,' [so] this word should be read with the same meaning throughout," and "[when] *adam* becomes the proper name Adam remains uncertain," the turmoil of language and meaning is in itself comedic, for God never names the man, though every other creature including the woman is named by the man.

Kawashima (2006: 46–50) calls into question and refutes arguments by Phyllis Trible and Mieke Bal that Gen. 2:7 indicates creation of a neuter earth creature, "the human" as of yet sexually undifferentiated, as opposed to creation of a man, as he sets out a philosophical realism position to trouble the waters of this debate. Trible and Bal note that "the human" with the definite article signaling a common noun, then later "man," are descriptors for "Adam" to indicate the change from earth creature to male, and the designation of "the human" reappears. Kawashima posits the absence of substantive evidence to support the change in meaning of *ha-adam* from sexually undifferentiated earth creature to man. Given that J signals "the human" twenty-plus times and "man" four times, Kawashima suggests that "the human" operates linguistically as an unmarked term for Adam, and J also uses *ish* when juxtaposing Adam's over against the woman's identity (50). Kawashima's notion that Adam had previously "identified himself as 'man' before the creation of the woman out of his male body . . . and that God retroactively names Adam (*ha-adam*) by revealing his origin and destiny, 'the earth' (*ha-adamah*)" (50), begs a couple of questions: What can we know about "Adam's" epistemology and sense of awareness from scripture and Kawashima's argument? And, when an event occurs retroactively, what type of impact can that have in the previous moment to which it refers, for characters and for readers? Further, if indeed "Adam" begins as an anatomical male but not yet aware of his sexuality, according to Phyllis Bird and Kawashima, then what can we say about differentiation, gender (culturally signified and often prescriptive identities and roles), and sex (biological signification) for the first humans created (Kawashima 2006: 50–51)?

Philosophers, theologians, artists, and authors have demonized Eve, blaming her for human sin and concluding therefore that she and all women must be inferior. Bellis (1994) reviews how several biblical feminists have interpreted Eve. She notes that Phyllis Trible's groundbreaking work, viewing the drama moving from Eros to Eros Contaminated to Eros Condemned, sees judgment as prescriptive, not descriptive punishment. Some feminists focus on other parts of the story; some reject Trible's general approach; and others reject some of her analytical details. Also using literary criticism, Mieke Bal (1987: 112–29) attends to how individuals gradually become characters as they develop capacities to make choices. Of note is the woman eating the fruit in the quest for wisdom, making her *imago Dei*, as opposed to an act of sin. Susan Lanser (1988: 67–72) posits that language operates differently than understood in Trible and Bal's work—that context, not just words, creates meaning. Lanser argues that because the term *Adam* names both the male and humanity, as such he erases the woman and labels her other. With Lanser's reading comes a tension between positive analysis minus inferred meanings and negative readings from using inferred meanings. R. David Freedman (1983: 56–57) translates the term usually translated as "helper" as "strength" or a power equal to Adam, an argument supported by Mary Callaway (1986: 74) and Adrian Bledstein (1977: 200). Lyn Bechtel (1993) interprets the Adam and Eve story as a narrative of maturation, as the two grow from childhood to adolescence with their awareness of their nakedness, as they now have heightened consciousness, maturity, freedom, individualization amidst a group, and socialization. The tree of life encounter is the process of becoming mature and aware of death; the snake has street smarts. Ellen Van Wolde (1989: 217) deals with the problem of disobedience as an experience of independence, as freedom cannot be bestowed, only grasped. Central to the analysis is one's reading of Gen. 2:24, when man leaves his parents to cling to his wife and they become one. If this is a matter of future reality, then the maturation argument works; if this text is about the present, then a fall from grace works. Carol Meyers (1988: 87) argues sin cannot be the central issue in Genesis 3, because there is no explicit mention of sin; rather, she views the story as reflecting why things exist as they are, and the serpent gives wisdom. Meyers's translations and reading of the text show that Genesis 3 does not support male suppression and domination over women. Bellis (1994: 45–63) ultimately suggests that while a "fall from grace" reading is not the original meaning of the story, such a reading can explain how creation and life become so disharmonious. She finds the Adam and Eve story rich and difficult but does not support an argument for roots of evil or for sanctioning women's inferiority coming from within this androcentric story.

Jean Higgins (1976: 639–40) notes that while many commentators blame Eve for tempting Adam, neither Gen. 3:6b nor Gen. 3:17 supports such findings. From early church fathers to the fifteenth-century *Malleus Maleficarum*, a witch hunter's manual, and to German scholarship of eighteenth-century Herder and twentieth-century von Rad, Eve and ultimately all women are scapegoated for evil in the world: allegedly the one the serpent beguiled becomes temptress. Does Eve do what the serpent did? Perhaps this is a matrix of scapegoating, involving human and divine, for Eve gave some fruit to her husband, God gave Eve to "Adam," God gave the garden to Adam to manage, and God created the serpent. Does the serpent speak, and if so, how could it speak in a manner that humans could understand? The text does not explain the beguiling scene, so interpretative integrity requires caution and diligence that often does not occur in religious education, sermons, and commentaries regarding this Genesis text. Higgins notes that even Gen. 3:17 ("Because you have listened to the voice of your wife, and have eaten of the tree about which I commanded you, 'You shall not eat of it,' cursed is the ground because of you; in toil you shall eat of it all the days of your life") is not about Eve—that is, it does not criticize her or condemn her for a sin. Her name is there because Adam excuses himself by blaming Eve. Further, one could read God's words to Eve as prophecy concerning what will happen because of her connection with Adam, who had sinned, and that while Adam is expelled (Gen. 3:22-24), the text does not say Eve has to leave.

Such awareness about Eve leads to the question of where Adam was, since assuming Eve tempted Adam implies that Adam was not present for the conversation with the serpent. However, not only does the serpent use the plural form of *you* when speaking and Eve answer as "we," but Genesis 3 never says Eve ever leaves Adam's presence. If eating the fruit opened their eyes, then Eve's eyes should have already been open. In Gen. 3:6b, the Hebrew indicates that when she takes the fruit, her husband is also with her. Several scholars posit that this section involves a compilation of stories. The notion of the man being there with the woman and never speaking, never trying to stop the temptation, not making any decisions or acting in any way to stop from eating the fruit is comedic—heavily ironic and in a sad way amusing, given the denominations that use Scripture to mandate that women should to not pastor or preach, because they are to be silent. Ultimately, the text does not demonstrate that Eve acts as a temptress (Higgins 1976: 641–47).

In sum, Genesis 2–3 reveals a God who is a compassionate, benevolent, designer, architect, potter, and parent; or at points an egomaniacal deity who cannot stomach youthful rebellion; or the poetry weaves a persona whose mystery will continue to evade us. Depending upon the issues of the day and my context, my sense of it all swings like a pendulum, sometimes landing on a particular point of this triangular axis, sometimes embracing an amalgam of fusion of this matrix. Further, when following Christian tradition where God is omnipresent, omniscient, and omnipotent—is everywhere, knows everything, and has all power—how could God not have known what the couple would do? What does this story of creation and punishment have to say about a familiar adage often recited in many Evangelical and African American churches: "God is good! All the time! All the time, God is good!"?

If Lyn Bechtel is correct and the first couple's story is one of maturation, and they are still in childhood, without parents, did God expect too much of them? By definition, children are curious. Childhood is a time of discovery, of compiling knowledge. How does the childish couple learn? Are they to learn by divine spark? There is no village or community to raise them. Unlike the brief but present parent and crew on the ship in the 1980s remake of the film *The Blue Lagoon* (Kleiser 1980), where two children become sexually aware of each other after being shipwrecked on an island without any adult presence, the first couple has no lineage. How are they to understand the meaning of death? Have they been alive long enough to see anything die? There is a tension between how one learns obedience if it is not juxtaposed over against disobedience. Some children always tend to behave; others have a penchant for misbehaving. The severity of the punishment often tells us more about the one issuing punishment than about the recipients. Regarding language, I tend to side with Trible (1978: 72–81) and her "earth creature" nomenclature, as my mischievous side finds it intriguing how tradition so dismisses "Adam's" culpability, how it tragically blames Eve and no one ever blames "Adam." Naming and the meaning of names are so important in Scripture. Adam's passivity is most amusing, given that the text implies that he was never away from Eve but has no hesitancy in blaming her for their indiscretion.

In addition to the human characters, three other "characters" shape the narrative: the trees, death, and the serpent. The tree of the knowledge of good and evil pertains to possibilities; if someone accessed it, that person might live forever. However, access to the tree of life does not afford possibilities accessible with the breath of life. Fretheim (1994) posits that while God created the couple mortal, access to the tree of life might provide a special blessing in this world. The tree of the knowledge of good and evil pertains to divine knowledge, which human beings cannot handle too well. As divine knowledge, then, it would not indicate "sexual knowledge/experience, which Gen. 2:24-25 [man leaves parents to be with wife, and they become one] and Gen. 1:27-28 [created *imago Dei* and the edict to be fruitful and multiply] already imply, or knowledge of/experience with sin or wickedness" (Fretheim 1994: 350). Further, the expression "good and evil" is not a response to evil's existence; rather, one perceives what is in one's own particular best interests. Together, the role of the tree and the command involves one in seeing human limitations and God's will for actualized human life, with the best intentionality for human well-being (350–52). Yet one's context and access to knowledge would greatly shape one's perception. If one is delusional about self-identity and access to power, one might not appreciate healthy boundaries between divine and human. What is logically apparent to one is not necessarily logically apparent to others. Such matters of interpretation and communication can be quite confusing, perhaps comic and tragic. With interpretation, when one perceives a particular meaning, and when that perception is wrong, what difference does it make?

For example, the death that comes with the disobedience is not physical death, when the couple transgresses the prohibition. Notably, the story of transgression, query, and sentencing does not use a word for sin, though it occurs. Who is the serpent, and what does it symbolize? Does the serpent appear as a literary vehicle to move the story along? Does the serpent in Genesis parallel Balaam's she-donkey (Num. 22:28-30), where the "Lord opens the donkey's mouth," and it inquires as to why Balaam has been beating her: "What have I done to you to make you beat me these three times?" The she-donkey keeps stopping, being resistant, because she can see the angel of the Lord, so the donkey has more discernment than Balaam. The Lord allows the donkey to speak. Are the roles of serpent and donkey similar or in juxtaposition? Is the serpent symbolic and the donkey literal? Do they speak with similar voice pitch and timbre? How would Walt Disney, Pixar, or Stephen Spielberg set the two characters?

Fretheim (1994: 352, 359) suggests that the serpent, introduced abruptly, can metaphorically represent any choices that move humanity from God. The woman responds to the serpent's cleverly stated question by paraphrasing the prohibition and directly quoting God. Both serpent and woman use the plural form of *you*, indicating a silent yet present man, as anxiety and vulnerability around death hang in the air. The serpent says, "God knows," implying that God has not given full disclosure, making access to knowledge a matter of trust. The serpent uses no coercion, force, or intimidation; the woman, in silence, sees, thinks, and eats. The man remains quiet and eats, does not question or contemplate. When they have eaten, their eyes are opened (like Balaam's); they see they are naked, sew fig leaves to cover themselves, and hide from God. God is the only one who can have full knowledge of creation. Following the breach of divine prohibition, God questions the man, asking "Where are you?" What is the root of "Adam's" fear, and how does he now know he is naked? The man blames God; and the woman, though admitting her guilt, blames the serpent as the source of temptation. God then sentences serpent, woman, and man. The divine expulsion stops humanity from having access to the tree of knowledge of good and evil, and from living forever. Though sin never gets mentioned, the wrongdoing, steeped in rebellion and disobedience, is the mistrust of God. Further, there is a disruption, yet there is no definite textual metaphor indicating sin. Fretheim sees the images of "separation, estrangement, alienation, and displacement" that bespeak the past and reflect human life in all times.

Along with the comedic tints of the second creation narrative, there is much tragedy in the text and in its interpretative traditions, beginning with the expulsion. How sad that the couple had to be put out of paradise, and how intriguing that theologians, since the birth of the church, have dubbed this event "the fall." No one falls out of anything, technically. While some argue that the couple experiences "fall from grace," the text states precisely that "Adam" is expelled, put out. The text does not say what happens with Eve. Most such interpreters assume that Eve by implication is also expelled. If one is visiting someone's home and then the visitor is put out of the residence, the feeling and reality of the event are much different than if the visitor fell off of the steps. If the homeowner or God in the garden puts someone out, the action comes from outside of the "injured party"; there is a sense of being acted upon. If a visitor or "Adam" and Eve fall out of the garden, they are engaged in the acting. One could argue that most traditional interpretations collapse being acted upon and acting into their readings. This composite action has been deemed that which produced the so-called original sin. How tragic that this theology allows one to beat up on those deemed "other" and tends to make us forget that all humanity has something of *imago Dei* within. What would happen if all systems assumed that people are made good, and that the responsibility of all leadership is to fashion programming and agendas in ways that enhances that goodness? This becomes particularly problematic in matters of hierarchy, oppression, and greed. Why the emergence of shame? Why not shame about disobedience, rather than connect shame to the first couple's awareness of their nakedness? If God had not mentioned the importance of the two trees in the garden, would the serpent, literally or metaphorically, have been able to tempt the first couple successfully?

Noah's family story also engages the comedic and the tragic. Imagine being told you are righteous, all of your community will die because they are evil, and you have to build an ark to save you and your family, and either two or seven pairs of every kind of animal must accompany you. The thought borders on the absurd and hysterical. Was Noah wealthy? If not, where would he get the resources to build this ark? How in the world could the Noah family deal with the stench and smells of all those animals? What did they do with all the poop? Was the noise devastatingly distracting? How could one have omnivores, herbivores, and carnivores in the same space? Was there some kind of divine blessing that kept natural predator and prey apart for the duration?

In the 2007 comedy film *Evan Almighty* (Shadyac 2007), God hears the desire of a naive junior congressman, Evan Baxter, who campaigned and won on the platform that he wants to change the world, without explaining how. When God (in human form) appears and asks Evan to build an ark, Evan thinks he has gone mad, notwithstanding that his hair and beard grow to heroic lengths even though he shaves, and suits continuously morph into sackcloth. His family thinks he is going through a midlife crisis. But soon Evan discovers mysterious deliveries of wood and tools on his doorstep, animals of every kind come to him two by two, and his self-absorbed life goes from an instant success to an almighty mess; he is suspended from Congress. He sees the number 614 everywhere he goes, and he later learns this is the scripture where God tells Noah to build an ark. Evan's wife, Joan, resists, takes the children, and goes to her mother's house, wanting to leave Evan. Later, God appears to Joan as a server in a diner, telling her that God gives opportunities to get things, not things themselves. Togetherness of families is one such opportunity. Joan goes back to Evan, and the family finishes the ark together. Evan learns that a top congressional representative has commissioned a dam and cut corners in the process, connecting ecology and religion. After a brief rainstorm, Joan tells Evan to leave the ark. Evan remembers the congressional representative's dam, which does burst. Conversely to the biblical account, the flood does not destroy all of the land and people. The spectators and police board the ark. The ark sails down Washington, D.C., streets on the floodwaters of the lake until it lands in the front of the Capitol. The congresspersons present turn against the leading congressional representative when Evan states that his poor design of the dam caused the flood. As investigations transpire, Evan and his family later go on a hiking trip, where God reappears to Evan and tells him that one can change the world by doing one Act of Random Kindness (ARK) at a time. This modern-day ark story is a morality play that does not need to demolish creation and everyone in it. What about the possibility of the actual flood?

Once upon an eon, a catastrophic event occurred: the ice caps and glaciers melted, raising the level of the saltwater oceans 400 feet above the level of an inland freshwater lake now known as the Black Sea. All that held the worldwide sea level was a natural earthen dam now known as the Bosporus. Suddenly, 7,600 years ago, the Aegean/Mediterranean Sea burst this fragile dam, and huge volumes of water poured into the inland lake. As much water poured through in a single day as pours from the Great Lakes over Niagara Falls in a year, and this continued for a year. Was this the flood of Noah and Gilgamesh? Ryan and Pitman (2000) use tools of modern archaeology, geology, linguistics, biblical and Sumerian exegesis, oceanography, and inductive/scientific reasoning to derive this conclusion. Recently, remains of human wooden habitat and tools were found on the preflood lakeshore of this freshwater lake. Most convincing is the flow from the Mediterranean of saltwater into the Bosporus below a contrary flow of freshwater from the Black Sea out. The authors trace the resulting diaspora via archaeology, linguistics, et al., and show how the survivors spread their talents and languages northward and southward from this disaster. They convince the reader of the truths found beneath four thousand years of biblical and Sumerian oral traditions, by wading through the myths and assembling the facts. Science does not displace faith, and faith is made a reassurance for scientific insight. Accepting that the biblical flood actually happened makes it both comic and tragic that such destruction of life and all creation was the by-product.

Reading these texts after Hurricanes Katrina and Rita of 2005, after the terrorist attacks of September 11, 2001, after the tsunamis and global earthquakes of the past decade, one cannot help but see the televised images of homemade signs asking for help and the hundreds of bloated floating bodies; smell the stench; and hear the moans and feel the angst of those waiting to be rescued. Given that hurricane Katrina itself destroyed much of the Gulf Coast but the devastation in New Orleans was caused by a failed levee, human responsibility, like human evil in the text, causes the injustice. Simultaneously, divine edict in the text causes an ecological nightmare.

The environmental tragedy follows with familial ones: an invisible Mrs. Noah and an inebriated Mr. Noah. Why does the text tell us absolutely nothing about the wife of Noah? She is silent and almost invisible. She serves as an incubator for the three sons, yet we learn little else about her character. What did she think, fear, want, or need? Are there any silent daughters? Would she have been a lone, empathetic voice to speak on behalf of those who died? Was she around when God made the covenant with Noah? Did Noah seek her counsel at any time? Has she been codependent and Noah, in reality, a closet alcoholic? Is she unnamed because she's the property of her husband? The name Noah (in Hebrew actually pronounced Noach, from the root nu'ach) means rested, settled (Uittenbogaard 2009). The *Theological Wordbook of the Old Testament* says the root signifies both the nonexistence of movement and being located in a particular place with overtones of victory, finality, salvation. What if Noah's wife embodied the feminine name Noah (similarly pronounced to our protagonist in English but from another root in Hebrew), exuding the feisty determination of Zelophehad's daughter, Noah, in Numbers 27 and 36? This Noah and her four sisters stood up to Moses and demanded that Moses ask God if they should inherit their father's property. The feminine name Noah (from the Hebrew root *nu'a*) means shake, rattle, stagger, or wander (Uittenbogaard 2009). Would such sensibilities, either the persona of Zelophehad's daughter or the meaning of the feminine Noah, place the husband and wife at odds, so the redactors decided to keep the wife out of the picture other than to make legitimate the family's three sons?

How might people today hear or interpret these texts? A child living in poverty might feel even more disconnected from God, for how could an all-powerful being save some of the animals and not all of them? A child who loves animals would know pain at the thought of all those baby animals and their moms dying because God threw a temper tantrum. A person with sensory disabilities might experience feeling overwhelmed when facing so many different types of living beings in a limited, cramped space. S/he would possibly be so distracted by ecological and health concerns that much of the theological implications would be lost. Perpetrators of domestic violence might feel justified in committing domestic violence; victims and survivors of domestic violence might understand how it is that perpetrators attack them. An illegal immigrant might see that others have been displaced before, and that God does not always act positively in a given moment on behalf of the poor and disenfranchised.

Epilogue: Conclusions

Sometimes in theater, people will say, "It's not over until the fat lady sings." I beg to differ. The production is really not over until the custodian turns off all of the lights. And so it is with the story of the first humans and with Noah and wife: how we understand the story is not over, for it continues; various interpreters bring their own context to readings of these primordial texts.

What have I learned about these characters and these texts? Biblical stories are rife with comedy and tragedy. They afford us incredible opportunities for wrestling with texts, traditions, and the ways our own personal contexts and those of others shape how we read. My reading allows me to hold together faith and scholarship, being comfortable with ambiguity. With my Womanist biblical hermeneutic, tempered cynicism pressed me to ask many questions, many of which I did not work to resolve, nor is there space available. Genesis provides a joy of the gift of creation alongside my long-held faith, as I found many complexities, some of which remain in mystery and which the text in its received form cannot answer. Creativity helped me to see these texts through the lens of film and of my life, and to ask questions that are 360 degrees opposite of the Sunday school lessons I learned as a child. Some of my questions were not those we discussed in seminary or my doctoral program. Courage helped me to ask questions that some might consider weird or irrelevant, and allows me to continue to hold what I do know with what I do not know, without becoming heretic or agnostic. Commitment to hearing texts amid contexts allows me to keep room open to see if these texts will ever allow a more just reading than what I sense for women because of how the text and numerous traditions treat Eve and the unnamed wife of Noah. Candor affords me an opportunity to read and reread the texts, and to listen to other scholars in a manner that holds together acceptance, ambiguity, humor, and tragedy. Curiosity frames all of my exegetical process, as I am not yet ready to throw these texts away, even though some readings of them seem empty of inclusivity, mercy, and justice, though the relationality seems to sanction a thought of divine love for humanity. My comedic framing in conversation with tragedy here reminds me not to take myself or these texts so seriously that I cannot respect other modes of interpretation, which, in the final analysis, I incorporated in this study. I walk away with a deeper appreciation for the ancient mind that could weave together these texts, despite the oral traditions that made them available, over against an even deeper commitment to help expose and stamp out injustice, the oppressions of class, race, gender, ability, white privilege, heterosexism, and age, toward a hope that seeks to embody a truly peaceable kingdom.

CHAPTER 16

Reading Hagar in Contexts
From Exegesis to Inter-Contextual Analysis

Kari Latvus

The Working Model

The story of Hagar in Genesis 16 and 21 illustrates both classical exegetical and recent contextual questions.[1] This essay covers the major exegetical results but also aims to read the stories using what is here called *intercontextual analysis*, which aims to offer a tool to connect the text with ancient and present realities in order to read the Hagar story in both contexts. Thus, Hagar, an Egyptian slave and a victim of oppressive acts, is also seen as a forerunner of and companion to all immigrant women who live and work in forced reality.

The contextual view in the article is predominantly European and especially Finnish, but some global aspects will also be brought into the analysis. The working order—to start with the contextual issues—follows the order introduced by liberation theology (Mesters 1989: 90–93; Rowland 1999: 1–16; Latvus 2002: 51–54, 172–86). This means that the description of the current social location will precede the other sections, as well as the exegetical analysis, in order to raise questions and perspectives retained during the analysis.

---

1. I am grateful to several colleagues for their advice during the preparation of this article, and to John Gage for correcting the language.

The second methodological principle is the relations among text, interpretation, and context. The writing process of biblical texts did not occur in a social vacuum, and its current contextual reading invites remembrance of a mixture of actors and sociocultural aspects. The intercontextual analysis aims to bring to the dialogue at least four of those most central views, roles, and actors. They do not exclude other important aspects or ignore the more nuanced division of voices involved in the process of transmission and interpretation. On the contrary, these aspects are chosen on methodological grounds in order to represent the central views, which are as follows:[2]

- Questions of the poor 1: views behind the biblical texts
- Interpreter(s) 1: views of the writer(s) of the Bible
- Interpreter 2: author of this study
- Poor 2: views of persons who are considered poor today

Each actor has his or her own social location, or context. Thus, the working method can also be called a *four-context model*.[3]

Context of Poor and Immigrant Females in Finland

Gender and Poverty

Poverty and social exclusion may look like gender-neutral terms, but in fact they are strongly gender-related. Gender can be described as a key concept in understanding social exclusion. Gender is one of the central questions, and its importance is even greater if we focus on history. In a historical sense, the roles of men and women have been very different, and these ancient models still have great influence. Most of the earlier periods of history (and perhaps even current ones), including the world of the Hebrew Bible, have been marked in many cultures by male dominance, with the patriarchal system dominating the family and society (Gerstenberger 1996: 81–98).

When the phenomenon of poverty is currently, globally observed, there can be no doubt about the significance of gender. According to various UN

---

2. The reality is much more complex, because the approach ignores the possible plurality of voices of poor 1, interpreter 1, and poor 2. Also, the chain of tradents between the ancient text and the modern world is excluded in the model. This does not claim that other tradents did not exist, but their roles are not discussed if not explicitly needed in the analysis.

3. An introduction to the four-context model is available in Latvus, forthcoming.

reports, more women than men are living in poverty. Women lack equal educational opportunities and are more often targets of family violence. Although the imbalance between the genders still clearly exists, there are also trends that indicate gradual, positive developments. Urbanization has occasionally created new threats to women (such as street violence) but has also opened up better chances for education and employment (UNFPA 2007; Aquino 2007: 199–201).

Another recent UN report documents the increasing visibility of female poverty, which is obvious in developing countries (Moghadam 2005). In Europe, the gender issue is significant as well. An example of this is the single-parent family: often a single parent means a single mother. In several European countries, single parenthood is also a probable indicator of living in poverty (Byrne 2006: 99–101).

In a global perspective, Finland and the other Nordic countries can be seen as forerunners in improving and developing the rights of women. Finland in 1906 was among the first nations to give women the right to vote and to be eligible for public office. Not only women's rights issues but also families' economic needs have given women easier access to labor markets outside the family and have forced the development of state and private day care systems. However, although the principle of equal pay for equal work was accepted in 1962, women are still paid less than men, and in some sectors, the difference is remarkable.

A serious question in Finland remains the violence faced by women. According to statistics, about one-fifth of Finnish women have experienced violence at home. In practical terms, this means partner violence. The question of family violence is a global problem, but Finland's ranking in the statistics is the worst among Western nations (Heiskanen and Piispa 1998; Piispa et al. 2005).[4]

Female Immigration in Finland

Another area that must be mentioned is the context of immigrant women; for our topic and in any event, Hagar was an Egyptian living in Israel, who had a history of "immigration." Due to diverse ethnic backgrounds and motivations, immigrant women in Finland do not form a homogenous social group.

---

4. The research data were collected in postal inquiries. The response rate in 1998 was 70 percent (sample size 7,100) and in 2005 was 62 percent (sample size 7,213).

Some (such as those integrated into working life) live well, whereas others (such as unemployed refugees) may be struggling to find their place in society. Among the women in the most difficult situation are those who have no proper knowledge of the Finnish language and who are unemployed. Behind the refugee phenomenon are a variety of reasons such as war and political or religious oppression. Worth remembering is the rather large number of international marriages: about 20,000 Finnish-born males have immigrant spouses, most often from Russia, Estonia, or Thailand. The May 2009 report of the Ministry of the Interior reminds us about the reality of violence and oppression with which hundreds of these women live.[5] In addition, different versions of the sexual abuse of women—and forced sexual abuse can certainly be seen as a form of modern slavery—are still a well-known global problem, and Finland is not free of this phenomenon.

The reality of immigrant women in Finland is documented in the study *Maahanmuuttajanaiset: Kotoutuminen, perhe ja työ* [Immigrant Women, Integration, Family and Work], edited by Tuomas Martikainen and Marja Tiilikainen (2007). This collection of research articles illustrates the reality of female immigrants in Finland, using several methodological points of view. The total (but growing) number of immigrants in Finland is relatively low, about 4 percent (218,626 in 2008) of the population, and their reality as immigrants is well documented. Immigration to Finland has been caused by several reasons such as employment, education, marriage, or seeking asylum. Last but not the least is the group of ethnic returnees from the former Soviet Union. Refugees have come from Europe (the former Yugoslavia), Africa (Somalia, Rwanda, and Sudan), and Asia (Turkey, Afghanistan, Iran, Iraq, and Vietnam).

Noora Ellonen and Kaija Korhonen's article (2007) focuses on violence against immigrant women. In it, they offer a survey of earlier research and analyze the data of physical violence against immigrant women in Finland in 2005. The data are based on 1,254 reports of complaints made to police in 2005. The article describes three different kinds of violence: sexual violence, other forms of physical violence, and threatening to use violence against someone. Under sexual violence, the major issues were acts against children and young women (aged eighteen to twenty-nine). Also, rape, forced sexual

---

5. *Helsingin Sanomat*, May 17, 2009, A5.

acts, and sexual abuse were mentioned on several occasions. In most of the cases, the person accused was a member of the family or another known person. In the category "other forms of physical violence," more than half of the cases involved assault, one-third being simple, or less dangerous, assault. The total number of reports corresponds statistically to the number of immigrant women in Finland. The reality behind the official numbers may be even worse among those who do not know their legal rights, have limited language skills, or accept violence as part of patriarchal culture.

Violence against women is a global phenomenon, but it seems that immigrant women are in an especially vulnerable position because they have often limited access to the needed information, as well as fewer contacts and safety nets. The violence can easily disappear into the cultural differences and be more easily understood as part of a certain culture. According to a UN declaration (1995), violence against women comprises physical, sexual and mental dimensions; intimidation or limiting of freedom are also included under the heading "violence." The Finnish point of view is that cultural background or cultural traditions cannot make violent acts legal or acceptable in any form (Ellonen and Korhonen 2007: 164–66, 183–85).

An Exegetical Analysis of the Hagar Stories (Gen. 16; 21:8-21)

The Hagar stories have been read and studied well and from various perspectives.[6] The following exegetical analysis offers historical and diachronic perspectives to Genesis 16 and 21. This is needed before we are ready to enter the intercontextual analysis. The exegetical analysis follows the classical methods of observing the text, and reminds us that seldom are there shortcuts to contemporary contextual interpretation; especially in chapters 16 and 21, there are good reasons to believe that the diachronic view will enhance the understanding of the plot. This approach reveals the differences between the chapters and, moreover, clarifies the development process, especially in chapter 16, thus giving a more logical explanation to the different attitudes toward

---

6. A bibliography and evaluation of earlier (especially sixteenth-century) and recent history of the (especially feminist) interpretation of the Hagar stories is offered by J. L. Thompson (1997). About Hagar in art, see Kramer (1998).

Hagar (especially in Gen. 16:9-12).[7] For readers who are more interested in contextual analysis and do not wish to follow a full discussion of diachronic research history but are satisfied with the results, skipping to "Summary and Conclusions: The Growth Process of the Text" is recommended.

General Frames

Texts about Hagar (Gen. 16 and 21:8-21) are interwoven with the story of Abram/Abraham[8] in Genesis 12–25. There are some obvious features in the plot: a genealogical framework, itineraries, and the theme of divine promises (Van Seters 1999: 123). Abraham is the key figure, but Sarah, Isaac, Hagar, and Ishmael also play important roles. The plot is based on the tension between the promise of offspring and reality running against the promise. In this context, Hagar, an Egyptian slave, represents both a threat and a chance: she is able to give a son to Abraham but still seems to be a deviation. She gives the son but is expelled. She is given to Abraham as a second wife (אשה) but is treated as a concubine (שפחה). Abraham agrees to take the Egyptian as a wife although marriage with a foreigner is forbidden (Gen. 24:2). From Sarah's point of view, Hagar represents a person who is able to help her barrenness: "it may be that I shall obtain children by her (אבנה ממנה)."

Two major issues create the cultural and social frames of the Hagar story: marriage and slavery. According to Hebrew custom, a man was supposed to "take" (לקח) a wife, and a father to "give" (נתן) his daughter to the other man. These expressions, here used by Sarah, reflect ownership. Sarah gives Hagar to Abraham, and Abraham takes Hagar as his wife. Still, Hagar is treated as a slave with no authority over her own life. This was possible because Hagar was owned by Sarah. Similar occasions are mentioned also in the Code of Hammurabi:

> If a man take a wife and this woman give her husband a maid-servant, and she bear him children, but this man wishes to take another wife, this shall not be permitted to him; he shall not take a second wife. (CH 144)

---

7. A synchronic approach is offered by Reis 2000; and Jacobs 2007: 129–55. See also the study by Fretheim 2007, which analyzes Genesis as a (canonical) narrative.
8. The names Abram and Sarai are changed to Abraham and Sarah in Genesis 17. This analysis will use the latter names.

> If a man take a wife and she give this man a maid-servant as wife and she bear him children, and then this maid assume equality with the wife: because she has borne him children her master shall not sell her for money, but he may keep her as a slave, reckoning her among the maid-servants. (CH 146: trans. King 1915)

Slavery, forbidden in Western countries only since the middle of the nineteenth century, was generally known, used, and accepted in the ancient Near East. Common reasons for being sold into slavery were wars, debts, and being left without the protection of an extended family.

The basic structure in Genesis 16 and 21 follows the same plot with some variation. In both chapters, Abraham is left more or less as a bystander in a competition between two women; Hagar struggles in the wilderness but receives divine help at the last moment. Among the variations between the chapters are different divine names (יהוה - אלהים) and different expressions of the word *slave* (שפחה - אמה), just to mention two examples. Such doublets belong to the core evidence used when the Documentary hypothesis was introduced into biblical studies (Westermann 1981: 413).

The following analysis will summarize the three most central theories explaining the origin and meaning of the Hagar story: the traditional source critical view (JEDP), which for a long time represented the majority opinion but is now also strongly challenged; newer theories about the origin of the text (a diachronic view); and the analysis of the final text (a synchronic or rhetorical view). A good summary of the research history related to the relevant chapters as well as a bibliography up to the 1980s is given by Westermann (1981: 276–81, 411–14).

The Traditional View: The Documentary Hypothesis

Based on the classical analysis presented by Julius Wellhausen (1899: 19–27), Martin Noth (1972: 17–35) modified the source-critical solution to understand the origin and relation of Genesis 16 and 21:8-21. Following this research tradition, Noth attributed chapter 16 to the Yahwist (J), excluding the Priestly (P) texts in 16:1a, 3, 15-16, and a later editor's insertion in 16:9-10. As a doublet to the J version, the passage 21:8-21 belongs to Elohist source (E). Based on this source-critical division, von Rad (1972: 10, 148, 152, 186) located the texts as follows: J reflected the reality of the early Judean period, the Solomonic monarchy around 950 BCE, whereas

E belonged to one or two centuries later, and P was dated to the postexilic period (538–450 BCE).

According to this analysis, P did not pay much attention to Hagar but was active in creating the chronological frames of the story. According to those (16:6; 21:5), Ishmael must have been already sixteen or seventeen years old during the expulsion, although chapter 21 assumes that a baby was carried (von Rad 1972: 183).

In his analysis (149, 152–253), von Rad described the Hagar story as a strange sidetrack in a wrong direction (*ein höchst merkwürdiges Zwischenspiel*), which created a complex situation. Although the practice of taking a second wife followed Ancient Near East legislation and contemporary customs, it was still a great wrongdoing (*eine grosse Verfehlung*) based on the mistrust of Abraham and Sarah. The whole episode was caused by lack of faith in God's promise about offspring. From this point of view, Ishmael did not represent the line of promise but a sidetrack.

Following the same research paradigm, Claus Westermann (1981: 279–82, 412–14) offered an analysis, monumental in length and detail, based on mostly the same source-critical research line as in his commentary. He attributed chapter 16 to J, excluding the P verses in 16:1a, 3, 15-16, and later insertions in 16:9 and 10. In a source-critical point of view, the obvious difference between von Rad and Westermann is that the latter hesitated to attribute 21:8-21 to E. Instead, he assumed that the origin of the story was in the oral patriarchal tradition.

Von Rad and Westermann differ greatly in their attitudes toward Hagar. Westermann clearly argued against interpreting Hagar as an error (*Verfehlung*) and said that such an idea was a strange theological reflection not belonging to the patriarchal stories. Instead, Westermann interpreted the Hagar stories as conflicts belonging to normal human behavior. Thus, in chapter 16, Hagar expressed normal maternal pride without showing disrespect for her mistress, while Sarah was behaving in the framework of existing legal practices. Conflict between the women was a human episode (284, 286–87). Furthermore, Westermann described the escape of Hagar as a sign of emancipation. The escape from the hands of Sarah was also an escape from power that may have contained violence. The escape from "the legal oppression" to the threats of the wilderness was an expression of the human need for liberty (288).

The Quest for J

John Van Seters's study *Abraham in History and Tradition* (1975), published six years before Westermann's commentary,[9] signaled the new quest triggered by T. L. Thompson's (1974) study. Van Seters offered a fully new model to evaluate patriarchal stories both in what he described as the literary activity of J—the identification of the texts belonging to J—and also in the late (exilic) dating of J. The analysis underlined the character of patriarchal stories as literature (often against the forms of oral tradition) and expressed severe criticism of the stories' historicity. Van Seters also questions the entire existence of E (Van Seters 1999: 310–11).

In the analysis of the Hagar stories, Van Seters identified chapter 16 as a source of J and 21:8-21 as a text also written by J. Chapter 16 in itself was not understood as a literary unity but as a text with several redactional additions, such as verses 10 and 13-14, and also some additional words supplemented by P in verses 1 and 3. Verses 16:10, 13-14 were actually added by J to prepare a larger redactional insertion in 21:8-24 (Van Seters 1999: 192–96).

Based on form-critical observations, Van Seters argued that the expulsion of Hagar could not be an independent story, because of several details. At the beginning of the story, people are not introduced but are expected to be known. Hagar is mentioned as a slave (אָמָה) and as a mother of the son of Abraham, but without a reference that she was a wife of Abraham. Actually, Hagar is described as slave of Abraham (v. 12). Furthermore, Ishmael is supposed to be the main figure but is *never* mentioned by name in the entire story. All these details would have been needed if the story had been transmitted in the oral tradition (1999: 196–97). As a conclusion based on his analysis, Van Seters summed up, "Since there are no elements of folklore in 21:8-21 or any indications of real tradition variant, these facts can only point in one direction: 21:8-21 must be a literary composition drawing its material from chap. 16, but written for its own distinctive purpose and concern" (200). The writer of verses 21:8-21 was J in the analysis of Van Seters, although the use of word אֱלֹהִים is traditionally not connected with Yahwistic authorship (200–202).

---

9. Westermann (1981: 73–74) partly accepts the criticism of the new quest expressed by Van Seters and T. L. Thompson but rejects doubts of the historical value of the patriarchal stories and their exilic dating.

In the content of 21:8-21, Van Seters underlined the expulsion motive. Sarah's order to "expel" (גרשׁ) Hagar and Ishmael so that Ishmael would not "inherit" (ירשׁ) with Isaac (v. 12) is a reflection on how to treat non-Israelites. Unlike in Deuteronomy, foreigners are not annihilated as subject to *herem* (annihilation devoted to God), but are sent away with the idea that God will help them. The expulsion of foreigners representing other people is connected to Israel's election, the theme represented also by Deutero-Isaiah (200–201).[10]

The study by Christoph Levin, *Der Jahwist* (1993), also built on the traditional documentary hypothesis but modified it greatly. Levin agreed with Van Seters about the late date of J and the relative chronological order of chapters 16 and 21, but disagreed about the identification of the texts. For Levin, chapter 16 was a text written by J (the source text of J and the Yahwistic redaction), excluding some later additions.[11]

According to Levin (1993: 147–52), the Yahwist wanted to give an explanation for the previously known information about the marriage of Abraham with an Egyptian. The redactional work of J underlined the connection between the stories in Genesis 3 and 16. In both cases, the woman (Eve/Sarah) was active, and the man accepted the act. The verbal connections to the story of the fall (see 3:17 and 16:2b) may thus reflect the accusations against marrying an Egyptian. As a secondary theme in chapter 16, Levin underlined the Yahwist's intention to show how God has a special concern for strangers and the lonely, but only if they remain outside of the Israelite family circle. Hagar is accepted and taken care of by God only after she runs away. Further, the escape of the oppressed connected the Hagar story with the Exodus motive in Exod. 1:11-12. Levin concluded that the original part of the J story could be found in the passage 16:1-15 (excluding vv. 3aβ, 7b, 9-10, 12, 13b, 14). To the sources of the Yahwist belonged only meager information about persons, and most of the story belongs to J.

In the analysis of Genesis 21, Levin followed the observations of Van Seters and E. A. Knauf (1985: 16–25)[12] about the literary dependency on chapter 16, and concluded that the text is a kind of midrash, a later expli-

---

10. "But above all the Yahwist must be viewed in the light of the history of Israel's sacred traditions of election" (Van Seters 1999: 310).

11. See also Levin 2007.

12. Knauf gives a detailed analysis of intertextuality. According to Knauf, 21:8-21 is a post-P insertion, a kind of midrash based on earlier texts.

cation of earlier traditions. Consequently, Levin (1993: 151, 177) identified 21:8-21 (with 16:9) as a very late stratum, as an addition to the Pentateuch's final redaction (*Nachendredaktionelle Ergänzungen*). The function of
Genesis 21 was to connect to a broader theological theme, articulated especially in the book of Joshua: the expulsion of non-Israelites (Van Seters 1975:
196–202).[13]

Both analyses, by Van Seters and Levin, abandoned the preexilic dating
of the earliest layer of the Pentateuch. Both also agreed about the literary and
redactional or midrashic character of Genesis 21. This underlines the special
nature of chapter 21 among the M/Patriarchal stories: the chapter was not an
accidental case collected from oral tradition and a doublet to chapter 16 but,
rather, a conscious literary structure intended to re-articulate how Israelites
were expected to behave in non-Israelite family relations. The question was
not about personal experience but a theological illustration. Both Van Seters
and Levin called to mind the theological connections to land inheritance in
Joshua. If the very late dating of chapter 21 is taken into consideration, there
might not only be allusions to the stories in Joshua but also even a reflection
of the mentality articulated in Ezra 9–10.

The recent debate has challenged strongly the JEDP theory (see Kratz
2005; Dozeman and Schmid 2006). The present analysis does not offer a
broad basis to evaluate the theory, but two aspects are worth noting. Based
on the preceding analysis, the criticism against E is reasonable, and 21:8-21
can be explained much more easily as a literary creation based on chapter 16.
However, there seem to be good grounds to support the existence of J as the
earliest literary layer in the non-P material in Genesis. This leaves the door
open to support the existence of J (at least in Genesis).

Other Views: Rhetorical and Postcolonial Analysis

A fully different methodological view was offered by Phyllis Trible in her
analysis in *Texts of Terror* (1984) and in another version of the analysis in
2006.[14] Using a special view of gender, Trible focuses on the final text—its
rhetorical forms (skillfully used also in her own texts) as well as its contents.

---

13. Van Seters argues that J wrote 21:8-21 based on chapter 16, which belongs to the source
of J.
14. For further bibliography on this topic, see J. L. Thompson 1997: 213–33.

The method also aims to be *intertextual* and to pay attention to the connections with other parts of the Hebrew Bible and New Testament.

Trible (2006: 38) noted in her analysis how Genesis 16 strongly plays with conflicting sociological positions. Sarah, the Hebrew, was married, rich, old, and with power, but also suffered from barrenness. Hagar, the Egyptian, represented the opposite, being single, poor, and a slave, thus powerless, but also had a chance because she was young and fertile. According to Trible (38–40), the language of the text contains references to the story of the Garden of Eden but also to the Exodus. Like the Israelites in Egypt, Hagar in her social setting in the family of Abraham was afflicted by a harsh treatment: "Instead, this tortured woman claims her own exodus, thereby becoming the first person in the Bible to flee oppression, indeed the first runaway slave. The power to flee counters the power to afflict" (40).

According to Trible (46–47), Genesis 21 contains various aspects. Abraham gave freedom to the slave but also expelled her. As well, Hagar became the first woman in the scriptures to be a divorced wife, "banished by her husband at the command of his first wife and God" (46). Even though Abraham seemed to be a wealthy person (based on passages like Gen. 12:16 and 13:2), he did not use his resources in the expulsion but simply sent Hagar and Ishmael away, giving them only bread and water.

As a conclusion to her analysis, Trible pointed out the viewpoint of the narrator. The narrator's core ideas are related to patriarchy and covenant. This androcentric bias is not created by the narrator but seems to hold him captive. The major outcome of this view can be seen in the expulsion of Hagar and Ishmael: "Patriarchy and covenant produce the outsider and the insider, the superior and the inferior, the accepted and the rejected" (58). This can also be seen in the way God is described. God both allows Hagar to be afflicted and provides for her rescue, excludes Ishmael from the covenant but gives him a blessing, and favors the rich (Abraham and Sarah) instead of the poor (Hagar and Ishmael) (57–58).

Finally, it is very much worth briefly referring to the postcolonial approach applied to the Hagar story in Genesis 16 by Boyung Lee (2007).[15] Her perspective focuses on the analysis of the biblical text, which is ethically

---

15. The article aims to apply exegesis and especially the postcolonial approach to the educational field.

problematic and may not be a tool for "justice and peace" for those who live on the margins of society. The answer to this is the postcolonial perspective, which aims not only to analyze the text but also to give attention to critical voices, "to see the Bible as both liberating and outlandish." The postcolonial view seeks to "emancipate the Good News from imperialism" (50).

Lee observed that, in the exegesis, the role of Hagar was often neglected or mainly described as that of a concubine or rebellious slave. This happened even though in the biblical story, Hagar was the first person who named God and the first female to receive a promise from God concerning offspring. Based on feminist interpretations, Lee noted that Hagar opposed abuse and claimed equality but was also subject to the legal customs of her time. Thus, the postcolonial view allows more emphasis on Hagar without ignoring the reality of the ancient context (Lee 2007: 55–59).

Compared with earlier researchers, both Trible and Lee paid special attention to Hagar's role. They wanted to connect the biblical text and the ethical questions in it to related contemporary issues. They did not view the text as existing "alone" but as connected to both the ancient and current contexts. This became obvious when they noted the ethical problems in the text and in its current interpretation. This approach clearly enhances the perspective but also creates a need to articulate the use of contextual methodology: how can we read an ancient story as a part of a feminist interpretation or pedagogical framework without assimilating the current and ancient perspectives? The question is ignored by Trible and dealt with only briefly in Lee's article.

Summary and Conclusions: The Growth Process of the Text

The Hagar stories in Genesis 16 and 21 offer a classical challenge by the Pentateuch, with inconsequence in the plot and repetition in the storytelling. Most obviously, this can be seen when Hagar is twice threatened in the wilderness: first when pregnant and later when she is with the child. Hagar is twice treated harshly, expelled, then receives mercy and blessing from God. Can these characteristics be explained by diachronic exegetical analysis? A positive answer seems to be possible.

The traditional answer based on the documentary hypothesis, as represented especially by von Rad and Westermann, explained several of the peculiarities. The theory was, however, based on an assumption that both stories existed independently in either literary (JE hypothesis) or oral (Westermann) versions. Severe critics (Van Seters, Knauf, and Levin) of this traditional view argue that the expulsion of Hagar and Ishmael in Genesis 21 is more likely a later exposition based on the story in chapter 16. The literary dependency of 21:8-21 on chapter 16 implies a rather late dating of 21:8-21 and 16:9.

According to a wide consensus, the Hagar story in Genesis 16* belongs to the earliest literary non-P layer of Genesis named J or Yahwist (according to Van Seters, the sources of J). Some verses or parts of verses (16:1a, 3) probably come from P, but, in a wider sense, Hagar is not an issue in P. Furthermore, it seems obvious that in chapter 16 there are some other minor additions like 16:9 and 16:10, both inserted with exactly similar introductions to the oracle of the angel: "and the angel of the LORD said to her" (וַיֹּאמֶר לָהּ מַלְאַךְ יְהוָה).

The J story in Genesis 16 contained a version about Abraham's son with an Egyptian slave and counted Hagar and Ishmael as part of the family. Actually, the marriage with an Egyptian slave already belonged to the pre-Yahwistic tradition. Similarly, the preexilic (early) layer of the laws of Deuteronomy accepted marriage with a foreigner (Deut. 21:10-14; Preuss 1982: 56).[16] J's attitudes toward foreigners in Genesis 16 may thus refer not so much to an exilic dating, as supposed by Van Seters and Levin, but to the preexilic period. The major arguments for the late dating given by Van Seters actually refer to chapter 21, not chapter 16. According to Levin, the pre-J layer (sources of J) already contained the information that Abraham had an Egyptian slave as a wife. The Yahwist seemed to have a dual attitude toward Hagar: on the one hand, the text emphasizes the power and affliction used by Sarah; but, on the other hand, it also pays attention to the divine blessing received by Hagar.

The literary character and the bias in chapter 21 do not allow locating it as a part of the same storytelling layer as chapter 16, but clearly locate it in the later literary layer.[17] The origin of 21:8-21 can be best explained as a midrash that aims to clarify the foreign woman's position in Abraham's family—and,

---

16. Cf. Deut. 20:14.
17. Cf. Carr 1996: 197–99. Carr argues that chapters 21 and 22 are literarily related to each other and are built on the compositional layer beginning in Gen. 12:1-8. These arguments do not exclude the possibility that 21:8-21 is a later insertion based on chapter 16.

moreover, as a way to be separated from her.[18] By using different terminology, building on the information given in Genesis 16, and introducing a more hostile attitude toward the poor Egyptian slave, the writer of chapter 21 expelled the foreign woman but allowed her to live in her own milieu. The writer partially shared the need of the early Deuteronomistic writer to take *all* the land as inheritance but disagreed with the need to destroy other inhabitants in war (Deut. 7:1-6; Josh. 24) and, especially, disagreed with the later Deuteronomistic aim of annihilating the "other" living nearby (Deut. 20:10-14; *herem*; Rofé 1985).

A further interesting parallel to Gen. 21:8-21 is in Ezra 9–10.[19] Both texts represent a policy against marrying non-Israelites and a way to solve the problem: expel foreign women and children (10:3) in order to gain full possession of the land (9:10-13). However, unlike Ezra 9:10-14, Gen. 21:8-21 does not mention purity or uncleanness as a major problem.

The similarities and dissimilarities between the Deuteronomistic texts and Ezra 9–10 do not allow locating Gen. 21:8-21 precisely in one certain moment or connecting them to a single theological Hebrew Bible tradition. The rejection of the foreign slave gives, however, some clues for preferring a dating of Genesis 21 to the postexilic rather than preexilic period and to supporting Knauf's late dating. This raises the question of whether the expulsion story in 21:8-21 was actually a reaction to the real and acute postexilic inheritance debate.

Finally, it is also worth underscoring the radical shift in attitudes. The earliest level, the sources of J, probably knew the tradition about the Egyptian slave who gave birth to Abraham's son. In the next layer, J described the oppression, conflict, escape, and return. Without the follow-up in 21:8-21, Hagar and the son would have stayed with Abraham and would have been ignored in the story. Ultimately, in the last layer, the later (postexilic) writer created a new version, a midrash that describes how Hagar was expelled. The last version was a pure historical fiction that exposed the changed attitude

18. For a modern version of the midrash of Genesis 16 and 21, see Fewell 1998: 182–94.

19. Ezra 9–10 seems to be dependent on Deut. 7:1-6, but the prohibition of intermarriage in Deut. 7:3-4a may also be a later insertion (Preuss 1982: 49). According to Veijola (2004: 193–99), the denial of mixed marriages (Ezra 9–10) was introduced by the late Deuteronomistic group (DtrN) in the exilic/postexilic period.

toward other ethnic groups. Even marriage with a foreigner was no longer allowed, and the semi-Israelite offspring had to go.

An Intercontextual Analysis

The exegetical analysis focused on the writers' points of view (context 2). The results follow more or less the conventional exegesis (if it still exists) and are valuable in themselves. The sphere is, however, limited and mostly ignores the issues of the ancient and present poor.

The following intercontextual analysis continues the text analysis from different perspectives, especially those of the poor 1 and poor 2. The dialogue between different views is introduced by the researcher (context 3). Due to different perspectives on the same story, and in the interests of methodological clarity, a certain overlapping with the exegetical analysis cannot be avoided.

Reading with Hagar: The Position of Poor 1

Do we have possibilities to analyze the poor *behind* the biblical story (context 1)? We can say that there is a difference between the Hagar described in the text and the Hagar beyond the text. The Hagar described in Genesis is a literary creation based on earlier tradition. Behind the tradition of Hagar there may well exist a historical Hagar, although mostly she is hidden from our eyes. In saying this, I do not mean that the stories in Genesis happened as described. It seems even too much to say that the stories somehow described a history of existing families somewhere in the second *or* first millennium. By saying that the historical Hagar may have existed, I simply refer to the fact that the earliest layer of tradition knew her as a person. We may conclude that the marriage with an Egyptian slave called Hagar actually happened in the preexilic period, but should be careful to take further steps. Drawing a detailed family line or trying to date the century when Hagar lived goes far beyond the facts confirmed.

What we certainly have is the figure in the text. When we strive to go behind the text, we are still mostly restricted to the information given by the biblical writer(s). Also, the narrative about Hagar is written from the point of view of the rulers ("oppressors"; Jebakani 2000: 35). The poor (in context 1) behind the text (in context 2) do not have their own and independent voice. Indirectly and on a general level, however, we are also able to have complementary information about slaves' social location in the Ancient Near East. Remembering these limitations, it seems to be highly valuable to try to see and read the story *from* Hagar's viewpoint and to read the text *with* an Egyptian slave called Hagar.

The poor behind the text do not speak but need an advocate. Thus, the researcher has the role of supporting the weak and silent voices of the text in order to make them audible. In this role, the researcher can speak on behalf of the poor (Hagar) to make her position real and visible (Bird 1997: 65–66). This requires that we must also be ready to reinvestigate biblical traditions critically and to reread them, because "the Bible continues to be an unsafe and a problematic text" for those on the margins either in the ancient or in the modern world (Sugirtharajah 2002: 100). According to the perspective of gender, "the Old Testament is a collection of writings by males from a society dominated by males," and even "prophetic concern for the 'poor' should be understood essentially as concern for a poor man, and more particularly a 'brother'" (Bird 1997: 13, 78).

The fixed starting point for us is the text of Genesis, which includes the stories of Hagar. The general background of the Ancient Near East knows the reality of slavery as a part of normal and accepted behavior. The Code of Hammurabi, Egyptian laws, and the laws of the Hebrew Bible acknowledged the existence of slavery. Slaves were mostly seen as objects of trade and means of labor. In the legislation, the main interest was to secure ownership questions or responsibility in case of injuries. Usually, it was a question about damaging other persons' property. Legislation did not protect the rights of slaves but the interests of owners.[20] Slavery was taken for granted by all without any call for its abolishment (Cardellini 1981; Dandamayev 1992).

Thus, the stories told in Genesis 16 and 21—the experience of a young woman who was sold as a slave in a foreign country, to be used as a concubine and facing mental and/or physical violence—is not an exceptional story but quite the opposite: probably a normal and realistic description of the ancient world through the centuries. The current critical evaluation against slavery reflects the reality that slavery has been forbidden in most Western countries

---

20. For a good illustration of legal documents, see Baker 2001.

since the first half of the nineteenth century.[21] From the modern perspective, slavery in itself includes a negative and doubtful essence.

In the stories of Genesis, Hagar has a key role but an extremely passive one. She is practically an object in the decision making. In chapter 16, her pregnancy triggers the overall development and changes the power relations in the family.[22] Hagar is a slave of Sarah but also a wife of Abraham. In any event, Sarah, who was first willing to use Hagar to have a child, does not allow these changes. After gaining permission from Abraham and God, in Gen. 16:5-6, Sarah "dealt harshly with her." Actually, the Hebrew expression (ותענה) refers to violent and aggressive behavior. The same verb is used concerning national oppression (Gen. 15:13; Exod. 1:11) and also sexual violence and rape (Gen. 34:2; Judg. 19:24). The question is, did Hagar earn this because of raised self-respect and lowered respect toward Sarah? Did Sarah have a right to violate and punish Hagar?

Physical violence against slaves was not forbidden in biblical law. For example, the Covenant Code[23] does not penalize the use of the rod on slaves but does not allow the killing of a slave. The use of physical violence is thus at least partly accepted, but causing injuries created a need for compensation, even from the owner to the slave:

> When a slaveowner strikes a male or female slave with a rod and the slave dies immediately, the owner shall be punished. But if the slave survives a day or two, there is no punishment; for the slave is the owner's property. . . . When a slaveowner strikes the eye of a male or female slave, destroying it, the owner shall let the slave go, a free person, to compensate for the eye. (Exod. 21:20-21, 26)[24]

The legislation of the Covenant Code thus authorizes the use of violence but clearly adheres to the value of the slave as a person. The slave is part of the property, but the value of a human being is recognized because a slave

---

21. Among the wide variety of scholarly works about the history of slavery is Rodriguez 1997.

22. For a detailed synchronic analysis of power relations, see Jacobs 2007: 129–55.

23. The Covenant Code (CC) is conventionally seen as preexilic and the earliest legislative document in ancient Israel. Late-dating of the CC is, however, argued for by Van Seters (2007).

24. Cf. Code of Hammurabi: "If he put out the eye of a man's slave, or break the bone of a man's slave, he shall pay one-half of its value" (CH 199).

may become a free person as compensation for severe injury. Using mild violence against slaves was mainly understood as part of property management,
which helped maintain the status quo and suppression of a slave's too strong
or rising self-confidence.

Whatever the concrete form of the violence used by Sarah and whatever
the cultural and legal standards, the act of affliction caused Hagar to become
a runaway in Genesis 16. Although Sarah's behavior seems to be culturally
acceptable, it needed to be legitimized by Abraham and God. This is a clear
indicator that Sarah acted in an area where the legal or moral codes were
not clear. Whatever the legal or moral status of the punishment, it was such
wrongdoing against Hagar that she fled.

Hagar's situation is supported in the divine message. The message confirms that Yahweh has heard of the wrongdoing (כי שמע יהוה אל עניך).
The affliction in itself was an oppressive act against a vulnerable human
being, a foreigner without full rights compared with Israelites. The slave was
dominated by the owner, and the pregnant young woman became an object
in a power game: "Read in the light of contemporary issues and images, the
story depicts oppression in three familiar forms: nationality, class and sex"
(Trible 1984: 27).

The other version of the use of power is told in Genesis 21. In the earlier
story in chapter 16, the reason for the conflict was the emancipation of Hagar,
and here the process is triggered by the play (מצחק) of Hagar's son. The
expression צחק (pi). does not have negative implications in itself, although it
is often translated as "mocking."[25] Actually, the plain play and existence of Ishmael seem to threaten Sarah because Ishmael, as Abraham's older offspring,
challenges the inheritance order (Gen. 21:11). Although, in an earlier passage,
Ishmael is mentioned as a child of Abraham and his second wife (16:3), Ishmael is now only a son of *Abraham's female slave* (21:10, 12).

From Hagar's point of view, chapter 21 repeats the same themes as chapter 16:

- The foreigner has a new existence (Hagar has raised her self-esteem/
  Ishmael is growing up).
- The result is violent behavior or expulsion.
- Sarah is the real actor.

---

25. Among many others, the translation "mocking" is favored by Wenham (1994: 82).

- Hagar is in the wilderness.
- Hagar meets an angel of Yahweh.
- Yahweh is the one who hears the affliction or the cry.
- Ultimately help for Hagar comes from Yahweh.

Both chapters explore a story in which Abraham had an Egyptian slave as a wife/concubine who reached a remarkable position in the family but was finally expelled. Through the whole story, one perspective focuses on the survival of Hagar. It is finally Yahweh who helps the Egyptian runaway/castaway to resist the use of power and violence. Hagar and Ishmael are expelled but not annihilated, oppressed but not abandoned, and finally guided to settle down.

Hagar's story can be read also as an oppression story (Trible 1984; Williams 1993: 1–4). From this point of view, Hagar is a victim, a foreigner, and a female slave. This means that she belongs to the margins of the support system and safety net provided by an extended family. This becomes obvious in the story's plot, which explores her status as vulnerable and without rights. Hagar is used as a child-making machine, oppressed, and expelled, as motivated by power relations and inheritance questions.

Through the whole story, Hagar is described as a person who lives in a marginal area. She is from Egypt, but her background is not explained. She is treated as a slave who is not appreciated and is forced to go into exile. Through her escape and expulsion, she is emancipated due to her personal will and divine help. She overcomes the violence and power over her, which gives her the possibility to be free. In the end, she stays in the border area between Egypt and Palestine, in the margins but no longer marginalized. Based on the help and promise given by God, Hagar becomes a person of success.

Option for the Insiders and Concern for the Others: Reading with Interpreter 1

The Hagar stories in Genesis 16 and 21 describe the family of Abraham in two episodes. The chapters do not have similar views on how to deal with a poor and foreign slave. The writer of chapter 16, the Yahwist (J), treated Hagar with a much more positive attitude than the later writer in chapter 21. The Yahwist let Hagar stay in Abraham's family and described her as a woman met and helped by God. Hagar's credo is short: God sees me (אֵל

וֹרַאִי). The reality of the poor (Hagar) was seen by God, and the poor one (Hagar) herself was aware of this—a major issue in awareness building (Freire 1993: 68–105; 1990).

The later insertion in Gen. 16:10 interpreted the event against a wider horizon. Hagar's credo was connected to the promise of multiple offspring. Beside these positive attitudes, J also told about the punishment Sarah gave Hagar. J even allowed Sarah to treat Hagar harshly without any critical comments. These observations do not give us permission to go further and presume that J had a negative attitude toward Hagar, even if certain verbal connections with the fall story exist, and it is certainly beyond the limits of the story to see Hagar as an error (von Rad; cf. Levin).

The writer of 21:8-21 (probably also the writer of 16:9) represented harsh opinions toward the poor Egyptian slave married to Abraham. The passage was built on earlier information given in chapter 16, but the views are sharpened. As noted in the exegetical analysis, chapter 21 is a literary creation based on earlier texts, especially on chapter 16. Chapter 21 is a piece of narrative theology, a midrash, explaining the division between those who belong to the family and those who are outsiders. According to the writer, it was not sufficient that Hagar was kept under strict control, including harsh treatment. Hagar also had to be excluded from the family in order *not* to give her son the chance to share the inheritance (21:12).

The way the expulsion is articulated emphasizes that Hagar and Ishmael did not receive even a small part of the inheritance. In 21:14, Abraham gave Hagar nothing but bread and a skin full of water (לֶחֶם וְחֵמַת מַיִם), which is in sharp contrast to other biblical texts. For example, compared with the laws of Deuteronomy, the contrast is clear: Deut. 15:12-18 gave an order to release a Hebrew slave and give the slave plenty of gifts. By mentioning bread and water, the writer implies that Hagar and Ishmael did not take any of the material resources belonging to Abraham but left with "empty hands" (cf. Deut. 15:13).[26]

When Hagar and Ishmael are driven from the midst of Abraham's family, the writer is free to return to the divine help and promise to Hagar. At the moment of near death, God intervenes and repeats the earlier promise

---

26. The contrast between rich Abraham and poor Hagar is emphasized by Fewell (1998: 189–92).

about Ishmael's offspring—which means not only survival but the growth of a large nation. The last theme already requires the existence of 16:10, which is later than J but earlier than chapter 21.

The latter Hagar story represents ambiguous attitudes toward the foreign slave and concubine. This can be noticed also in the changed terminology: Hagar is not articulated as a servant (שִׁפְחָה) of Sarah and wife (אִשָּׁה) of Abraham but rather the slave of Abraham (אָמָתְךָ) and a concubine. The use of power against Hagar is accepted by the divine authority. The best explanation for the strict views in chapter 21 is the altered social setting. In the exegetical analysis, chapter 21 was dated to the postexilic period. That period forced Israelites to protect their identity against colonial powers and also against other ethnic groups. At such a time, the formulations about circumcision (P), Sabbath legislation (still later in P), and the idea of annihilation of the other nations (Dtr) as part of the nation's earlier history were developed. These aimed to protect identity and support the struggle of survival against outer pressure. The expulsion of Hagar and Ishmael can be seen as an expression of a similar bias—a tendency toward hostility against other ethnic groups and to protect one's own group.

In the preexilic period, endogamy (marriage within one's own people) was not a rule, as a variety of examples show (Deut. 21:10-14; 2 Sam. 11; 2 Kings 11:1).[27] The open criticism against exogamic marriages was reasonable only in the exilic/postexilic period. Despite all the problematic tones, the episodes in chapters 16 and 21 have also a clear and at least partly positive message for the foreign poor: they are accepted among the Israelites and blessed, but not unconditionally. Chapter 21 in particular makes this obvious. The poor are taken care of by Yahweh, but they are socially excluded from the inner circle of Israelite society. How can this obvious tension be explained?

Actually, there seem to be two lines to follow, and the tension is between these basic lines. The main story line appeals to the exclusive promise concerning offspring made to Abraham and Sarah. This major theme of the story is an explanation about the promise and blessing given exclusively to the chosen insiders. The patriarchal mainstream view of the story describes

---

27. For further examples, see Brenner 1985: 115–18; Hamilton 1992.

how Yahweh keeps his promise to Abraham and makes him a large nation. Beside the mainstream is a side story that pays attention to Hagar, the poor in the margin. The core of this story is based on oppression of the poor and Yahweh's reaction to it. The importance of the relation between Yahweh and Hagar is described in chapter 16 with several verbs. Yahweh heard (שׁמע) the oppression and spoke (דבר) to Hagar. Finally, the last aspect described is Hagar's experience of having been seen by God: "You are the God who sees me" (אתה אל ראי). The concern for the poor, the "other" who do not live in the inner circle of society and family institutions, is evident especially in chapter 16. In the later layer of the texts (16:9 and 21:8-21), the scene has been modified. The promise made to Hagar is not canceled, but the expulsion guarantees that the offspring of Isaac—the insiders—will not have to compete for the land with Ishmael's offspring. According to the writers of Genesis 16 and 21, it was God who helped the poor in their survival struggle. Hagar is expelled but also empowered and enabled to have her own growing family. Hagar is blessed but left outside, according to the Israelite point of view.

Values of the Hagar Stories: Ethical Comments of the Contemporary Reader (Interpreter 2)

What is the researcher's role in the intercontextual analysis? On the one hand, the researcher may be an outsider having no direct contact with either poverty in the ancient world or current poverty. Conventionally, exegesis has tried to be as neutral as possible, nearly invisible, as if the researcher (with his or her own social location) does not exist at all. On the other hand, this entire study would not have its shape without my questions, analysis, and conclusions. Thus, the neutrality or invisibility is an illusion. Without being poor, an immigrant, or a woman (I am white, middle class, and male), I still have an obligation to aim to recognize, hear, and analyze all the variety of dimensions related to poverty.

For the current researcher (interpreter 2), one of the most difficult questions is how to evaluate the views of the writers of the Bible. Their attitudes were exclusive and hostile to poor people. This was articulated clearly in the affliction and expulsion of Hagar. Still, the writers also represented the positive understanding that Yahweh is the one who helps those who are in trouble, who are in need of divine help because of oppression.

If these ideas are brought together, they create an obvious tension between excluding social actions and an inclusive theological understanding of God. How is it possible that the same God contains such a strong circle of contradiction: God is the one who takes care of those who are excluded by the people guided by the same God? In the story, "the Deity is on the side of the oppressors" (Jacobs 2007: 154).

This particularistic behavior makes God schizophrenic or a double-faced Janus figure that allows affliction but also heals the wounds of the oppressed. To accept the story as divine guidance leads to an illusory world where wrong acts are too easily accepted and made divine.[28] The implications of this can be severe and lead to the reality where the poor, the "other," are not really empowered but only helped and doomed to remain the targets of charity. To avoid this, it is important to see that the real promise of a future blessing includes a social dimension, too, for a blessing without justice hides original wrong acts.

Other Contextual Voices: Reading with the Poor 2

"As a symbol of the oppressed, Hagar becomes many things to many people. Most specifically, all sorts of rejected women such as black women and *dalit* women find their stories in her" (Jebakani 2000: 41). When the Hagar stories are read with the current voices of the poor, several observations and questions arise, showing both similarities and differences between these two contexts, that is, social locations. The reality of women in Finland is largely very different from the life setting of women in ancient Israel, but the poverty theme opens views that are worth noting.

An example is international marriages in Finland. Mostly, immigrants are fine and are happily married. However, the report by the Ministry of the Interior in May 2009 served as a reminder of the reality of violence and oppression in which hundreds of Thai women live in Finland. One Thai female, "Naan," age thirty-three, told her story of life in Finland:

---

28. This was conventional in precritical interpretation during the Reformation (Cajetanus, Luther, Calvin) (J. L. Thompson 1997: 213–33). Reis (2000: 106–109) explains the oppressive action only as human failures that were later requited to the Israelites during their stay in Egypt. In the concept of God, nothing seems to be problematic for Reis. In a similar way, Williams (1993: 20–22) wondered if God did "not know about Sarai's brutal treatment" when Hagar asked to return (Gen. 16:9). In her analysis, Williams (following Tamez) tried to find a point of view that would make God's acts justified and right.

"I met my husband in a restaurant in Thailand. He guaranteed my visa. We never married. When I came here, it appeared that my husband already had a wife. I was sad. They lived in the same house but like friends in separate rooms. I had to do all the work and serve the man, but he treated me like a slave. He was violent and did not give money. I ate potato peels.

I escaped and met another man. Also he hit me. Now I am sick and broke. The social workers give me 100 euros in a week. Children are with the man, and because of them, I do not want to move away, but I cannot live here either. Who will help me?" (*Helsingin Sanomat,* May 17, 2009, A5; my translation)

In many cases, poverty is caused by external reasons and not by one's own choices, as seems to be obvious in Hagar's case. A poor person often is unable to make decisions about him- or herself. Problems are linked to the different layers of economics, society, and culture far beyond the choices of an individual. As with Hagar, also the contemporary poor have only a limited number of possibilities for decisions about their lives.

A fairly central question related to poverty in the modern world is that of mentality: how are the poor seen, and how do they see themselves? In contemporary descriptions of poverty, one of the main themes is shame and lack of self-esteem. Poverty gives a label that saps energy and excludes from social arenas. For the poor to avoid exclusion and deprivation, special support is often needed, as well as personal strength. Using contemporary terms, the Hagar stories can be seen as an empowerment story where the foreign female slave, an object of other people's decisions, finds self-esteem, survives, and is able to create her own social world with her son.

The present reality of immigrant women in Finland, briefly described earlier in this article, contains aspects of a difficult reality. Major difficulties are connected with the new role in the new society, questions of living conditions, and also questions of violence. According to the existing definition of violence, we have good reasons to say that the story of Hagar fulfills the criteria. Hagar was forced to face physical and mental violence, expelled, and then pushed almost to the point of death. According to the modern knowledge of law, we notice that her rights as a member of an extended family, as a human being, and as a wife were not respected—not even according to the ancient criteria.

Another example of a socially oriented contextual interpretation is offered by Nicole M. Simopoulos (2007), who collected different readings of Genesis 16 in socially and geographically varying female groups. One such group of South African black women had lived in the middle of a "dehumanizing system of Apartheid [and] were [the] poorest of South Africa's poor." For them, Hagar was an Egyptian slave girl, perhaps a case of child abuse. For them, the central themes of the story were abuse, misuse of power, corruption, sexual and economic exploitation, and slavery. The women reacted especially strongly to 16:9. The oppressive image of God was linked in their attitudes to the rich and powerful. The women concluded, "The author of the Gen. 16 story is clearly mistaken in his or her understanding of God" (69–71).

According to an intercontextual interpretation, these readings have special value as authentic and genuine current interpretations. These women represent the current poor (poor 2) as described above (context 4). With good grounds, the group of South African women can identify themselves as poor. The current voices cannot be understood as equal to or the same as the voices in the biblical story but, rather, are new interpretations and versions of ancient voices.

The following lines written by Phyllis Trible sum up well the reason why Hagar has become a symbol for many other oppressed persons:

> She is the faithful maid exploited, the black woman used by the male and abused by the female of the ruling class, the surrogate mother, the resident alien without legal recourse, the other woman, the runaway youth, the religious fleeing from affliction, the pregnant young woman alone, the expelled wife, the divorced mother with child, the shopping bag lady carrying bread and water, the homeless woman, the indigent relying upon handouts from the power structures, the welfare mother, and the self-effacing female whose own identity shrinks in service to others. (Trible 1984: 28)

Final Remarks

The method used in this article illustrates how a four-context model works. With this method, it is possible to combine contextual and exegetical working processes and avoid a possible one-sidedness of approaches. Conventional exegesis has all too often ignored contextual viewpoints and tried to act as if the biblical *text* were the only dimension of analysis, even if, in such cases too, scholars and their studies are not free from their social reality. If contextual reality is ignored, the perspective for understanding the essential dimensions of the story becomes all too narrow. Similarly, if the results of conventional exegesis are not studied carefully, the contextual approaches are in danger of being one-sided and of assimilating the ancient to the contemporary readings. Thus the four-context model aims to introduce a more balanced reading of biblical texts.

The position of poor 1 behind the text is mostly a way of looking at the text, an optional view on the same text analyzed normally. But even as such, it seems to be a valuable point of view. The position of poor 2 evokes the hard reality that still exists but that remains a methodological challenge. The four-context model is a helpful way of formulating questions, but it can and must still be developed in the future.

What are the central findings? The writers of the Bible do not describe Hagar's feelings and words in detail. Often Hagar is a plain bystander with regard to the decisions related to her. Mostly the text describes acts done and words said *to* her. In the story, Hagar is taken from her homeland and sold as a slave, abused, and made an object of mental and physical violence, but most of all, she is the person who has no opportunity to make decisions about her own life. As a slave, Hagar was not in an equal position but had to fight for herself and even for her survival. The culmination is in the expulsion story, because it contains the possibility of total destruction but leads to an experience of empowerment. At the end, Hagar is able to also make her own decisions: to find her own place and to take a wife for her son. This means that she has, at least partially, a power position similar to that of Sarah's earlier in the story. No further details about the rest of her life are given, but the story contains the possibility of her finding a future acknowledged position and social protection in Ishmael's growing family. Is the God who heard and saw Hagar, the poor slave, and who spoke to Hagar and saved her from "suffering premature and unjust death," the God who also has a preferential option for the poor (Gutierrez 1999)?

The first interpreter(s) of the Hagar story, the writer(s) of the Bible, did not agree that Hagar is the one to be first and foremost protected.[29] For them, the existence of the Israelite nation, embodied in Abraham and Sarah, was the priority concern that represented the main target of God's protection and blessing. Within these national limits, they wanted, however, also to call to mind that God paid special attention to the foreigner and the poor.

The current social location of many poor immigrant females reminds one that Hagar's story has not yet been closed. The voices in the margin still cry for refuge and protection and are still in danger of being expelled. The question of the ancient writers' moral is actually a current one and requires both ethical and practical actions.

The methodology introduced in this article aims to offer a broader and more adequate contextual reading of the Hagar stories. One of the confirmed results is that both exegetical and contextual approaches are needed, in order to complement each other. Limited interest in either of these will increase the danger of one-sided views: either pretending that present reality does not affect exegesis or, all too fast, assimilating biblical texts to current issues.

An intercontextual analysis creates an ongoing discussion between texts, contexts, and different voices. None of those positions has priority in the end, however: all dimensions are invited to be critically heard and evaluated. A singular final view of Hagar is an illusion that does not exist. Nevertheless, Hagar's story offers inspiration and challenges in new contexts—as long as her contemporary companions are still in danger of being (ab)used, dealt with harshly, and expelled.

---

29. The treatment of Hagar was probably the major reason for the later explanations in the postbiblical Jewish tradition as well as in the Christian writings. About later Jewish, Christian, and Muslim tradition, see articles in Trible and Russell 2006.

CHAPTER 17

The African Wife of Abraham
An African Reading of Genesis 16:1-16 and 21:8-21[1]

David Tuesday Adamo and
Erivwierho Francis Eghwubare

Introduction

The tendency of Euro-American Old Testament scholars has been to deny or dilute African influence upon Scripture, that is, to de-Africanize it. For example, according to Rogers (1998), Eurocentric artists and Bible commentators of the past several centuries have painted and described all biblical characters, even God, as White.

This approach does not seem to have taken into account the positive references to Africa, the land of Moses' birth, Israel's infancy, the prophet Jeremiah's last days, and Jesus' childhood. In fact, many scholars, especially those of the past three centuries, have studied the Old Testament from the perspective that it does not mention people of color (Rogers 1998).

Their writings have been based on Eurocentrism and academic prejudice. Little wonder that their views have been used to biblically justify black slavery and the subjugation of black people.

In recent years, the efforts of Afrocentric scholars have helped to establish the African presence in the Bible (see, for example, Dunston 1974; Felder 1989; Copher 1991: 146–64). Charles B. Copher (1993) and David Tuesday Adamo (2001; 2006) have also contributed immensely to the subject,

---

1. This article was originally published in a different version in *Old Testament Essays* (18/3 2005).

focusing especially on contributions made by Africans to Old Testament history and literature.

Even so, existing literature on the Old Testament in relation to Africans seems to pay inadequate attention to the status and role of African biblical women. Besides, the cast of African female characters in the Old Testament includes a parade of prostitutes, princesses, queens, as well as abused, single, and married women. How can African people hear the stories of courage, perseverance, and faith that earned African biblical women a place in salvation history if African biblical women are not identified?

The purpose of this study is to examine the Hagar story to demonstrate that African women are present in the Old Testament. It will also examine the position of Hagar, an African woman, in the biblical text. This study examines Hagar in the light of Urhobo[2] customary marriage law and thus relives one of the stories about African biblical women with the hope that contemporary African women will find in it a useful resource as they are confronted with a myriad of religious, social, and cultural problems in their faith and life journeys.

The study recognizes that God's option is for the oppressed and disinherited and so points to the work of God in the world to all of humanity, male and female, Hebrew and non-Hebrew. Thus, its basic premise is that because God is the God of all nations, the chosen Hebrew people were able to tap into the surrounding cultures as these cultures had also formulated praise and thanksgiving to the God who had performed miracles in their lives.

Name and Nationality of Hagar

The story of Hagar, which appears in both J (Yahwist; Gen. 16: 1-16) and E (Elohist; 21:8-21) strands, falls under what have become known as the African texts of the Old Testament. Lavik (2001) defines African texts as "those texts that refer to areas and/or individuals from the continent of Africa."

Capoccia (2000) says Hagar is an Egyptian name meaning "flight," or "fugitive or immigrant." Jones (1990: 136) and Poole (1981) state that the

---

2. The Urhobo people, who are linguistically counted among the Edo-speaking peoples, live in Delta State, Nigeria, and spread across twenty-two identifiable and exclusive sociopolitical units. See Ilega 2003. According to Onigu Otite (1993), a renowned sociologist, this people might have come from Egypt and Sudan, a claim that has yet to be substantiated.

name is from the Hebrew root הגר (*hgr*), meaning "flee or be fugitive." Incidentally, this is the same as the Arabic word "to flee," hence *Hejirah*, the flight of Muhammad. Some claim that the name signifies "the south," in which case Hagar may have received the name in reference to her coming out of Egypt. The Hebrew root *gur* means "to tarry," "be a sojourner" (Jones 1990: 137) Indeed, this fits Hagar's condition as a stranger and sojourner in Abraham's household, for she was an Egyptian (Jones 1990:137).

Yet others say that הגר means "rocky," referring to a mountain in Arabia, which they suppose agrees with the words of Paul in Gal. 4:25. This passage allegorically refers to הגר as Mount Sinai in Arabia. We agree with Jones (137) that the name points to the sojourner or stranger, who may be under bondage. This position corresponds both to the condition of Hagar and to that of the children of Israel at Sinai.

Concerning Hagar's nationality, both the J and E sources state that she was an Egyptian. The treatment of Egypt is a good example of the inclination of Western scholars to downplay African influence on the Old Testament. One strategy that has been employed to achieve this is to deny that the ancient Egyptians were black people. For instance, Kuntz (1974: 60–63) discusses Egypt under a chapter titled, "The Ancient Near East during the Patriarchal Period." A more graphic example is found in volume 1 of *The Image of the Black in Western Art,* which treats the portrayal of blacks in Egyptian art (Desanges et al. 1976).

It should immediately strike one as strange to see Egyptian art depicted as *Western.* But this initial bewilderment is removed by the author's maintaining throughout the article that there is a classic differentiation between Egypt and Africa (Felder 1989: 157). Of course, his message is clear: ancient Egypt should be considered Western, and the existence of blacks there was an aberration. Ninian Smart (1992) has achieved the same objective, using religion. He discusses Egyptian religion under the chapter titled "The Ancient Near East," alongside Mesopotamian, Canaanite, and Israelite religions, instead of treating it under the chapter titled "Classical African Religions" (193–208).

The argument against the Africanness of the ancient Egyptians may be countered. In the Old Testament, several terms are used to refer to Africa and Africans. They include *Ham, Cush, Egypt, Put,* and *Canaan.* As used in the Table of Nations in Genesis 10 (hereafter "Table"), *Hamitic* refers to peoples who descended from Ham. This is the usage adopted in this study. In other words, we do not use the term to denote a classification of ancient peoples based on their linguistics affinity. Thus, it is unfortunate to postulate, for example, that Semitic people (descendants of Shem, Noah's first son; Gen. 10:1) were, or are, all White. Such a linguistic usage does not facilitate the process of identifying Africans in the Bible. Semitic languages include Akkadian, Arabic, Aramaic, Ethiopic, Hebrew, and Phoenician (McCray 1990: 72). But not all Semitic-speaking people are non-Hamitic people. For instance, the Ethiopians and Phoenicians are defined as descendants of Ham (Gen. 10:6, 15), although their languages are Semitic (McCray 1990: 4).

As McCray (15) rightly observes, Genesis 10 is unique in the sense that most of the peoples we see in the world today may be traced back to a person or people identified by name in the Table, which is ethnographic in character. Thus, the Table is crucial for our study of the presence of an African woman in the Old Testament. It provides for us, says McCray, an identifiable African Family Tree and other genealogical, geographical, and political data by which Africans can trace the roots of their biblical brothers and sisters.

Ham was the second son of Noah (Gen. 5:32; 6:10; 7:13; 9:18; 1 Chron. 1:4). The name *Ham* means "hot/dark, coloured, swarthy" (Lockyer 1958: 134) or "warm/hot" (Copher 1991) and by implication black. At any rate, the consensus of opinion about the survivors of the flood, whether real or imaginary figures, is that Ham is the ancestor of black people. Ham, besides being a patronymic designation for Egypt (e.g., Pss. 78:51; 105:23; 106:22), is also used to refer to a place in Canaan's Transjordan (Gen. 14:5; 1 Chron. 4:40). It may also be the designation of a people who were the most ancient core group of the people of Egypt (cf. Gen. 10:6: "The sons of Ham . . . Egypt"). Concerning this last point, Mokhtar (1981: 62) writes, "The Egyptians used only one word to describe themselves: *KMT* (my emphasis), the strongest term existing in the language of the Pharaohs to indicate *blackness*. This hieroglyphic was written with a piece of charcoal. The word *KMT* gave rise to the term *Hamite* which has been much used subsequently. It is also found in the Bible in the form *Ham.*"

Ham was the ancestor of Cush, Egypt, Put, and Canaan (Gen. 10:6). These nations are listed geographically from south in Africa to north in

Canaan. The Old Hamitic Hypothesis, which is based on the Table, considers the descendants of Ham therein listed (Cushites/Ethiopians, Egyptians, Putites/Libyans, and Canaanites) as black.

The Bible makes no mention of racial differences among the ancestors of humankind. It is much later that an idea of race appears with reference to the sons of Noah, which concerns Ham's descendants. The Babylonian Talmud, a collection of the Jews' oral traditions, states that the descendants of Ham are cursed by being black, and depicts him as a sinful man and his progeny as degenerates (quoted in Sanders 1969). Thus, early tradition identified the Hamites with Negroes and endowed them with both certain physiognomic attributes and an undesirable character. This notion persisted in the Middle Ages, when fanciful rabbinical expansions of the Genesis stories were still being made. Some of them held that Ham was supposed to have emasculated Noah, who consequently cursed him thus: "Now I cannot beget the fourth son whose children I would have ordered to serve you and your brothers! Therefore, it must be Canaan, your firstborn, whom they enslave. And since you have disabled me . . . doing ugly things in blackness of night, Canaan's children shall be borne ugly and black! . . . Men of this race are called Negroes" (521). Some scholars claim that these Hebrew oral traditions grew out of a need of the Israelites to rationalize their subjection of Canaan, a historical fact validated by the myth of Noah's curse (523).

The idea of a Negro-Hamite was not universally accepted. Some considered the blackness of Negroes to be due to the soil on which they lived together with the extreme heat of the sun. Others doubted that either the climate theory or the efficacy of Noah's curse was responsible for Negroes' physiognomy; rather, they reasoned that "their colour and wool are innate or seminal, from their first beginning" (523).

By and large, however, the Negro was seen as a descendant of Ham, bearing the stigma of Noah's curse. This view was compatible with the various interests extant at that time. For instance, it allowed exploitation of the Negro for economic gain to remain undisturbed by any Christian doubts as to the moral issues involved. "A slave of slaves shall he be to his brothers" (Gen. 9:25b) clearly meant that the Negro was preordained to slavery. Thus, neither individual nor collective guilt was to be borne for a state of the world created by God. Similarly, Christian cosmology could remain at peace, because identifying the Negro as a Hamite—thus, as a brother—kept him in the family of man in accordance with the biblical story of the creation of humankind.

The Western world, which was growing increasingly rich on the institution of slavery, grew increasingly reluctant to see the Negro slave as a brother under the skin. The rational and scientific White man was impatient to find some definitive proof for the exclusion of the Negro from the family of man and for ultimate denial of common ancestry.

The catalyst that made this possible was a historical event, namely, Napoleon's invasion of Egypt in 1798. The scientists who accompanied him discovered treasures that led them to found the new science of Egyptology. These discoveries were to revolutionize history's view of the Egyptians and lay the basis for a new Hamitic myth.

Napoleon's scientists discovered that the beginnings of Western civilization were earlier than the civilizations of the Greeks and Romans. Mysterious monuments, evidence of the beginnings of science, art, and well-preserved mummies were uncovered in Egypt. Attention was drawn to the population that lived among these ancient splendors and was presumably descended from the people who had created them. It was a mixed population, just as it is today, with physical types ranging from light to black and with many physiognomic variations. The French scholars concluded that the Egyptians were Negroid. It must be noted that the view that the Egyptians were Negroid and highly civilized had apparently existed before the French expedition to Egypt. Sanders reports that Count Volney affirmed so in 1787, after his visit to the land of the Pharaohs (Sanders 1969: 525).

Nevertheless, the Egyptian expedition made it impossible to hide the seeming paradox of a population of Negroids who were, once upon a time, originators of the oldest civilization of the West. Such a notion upset the main existing tenets; it could not be internalized by those on both sides of the Atlantic who were convinced of the innate inferiority of the Negro, or by those who religiously stuck to the biblical explanation of the origin of races. To the latter group, such an idea was blasphemous, as Noah's curse condemned the Hamites to misery and precluded high original achievement.

Shortly after Napoleon's Egyptian expedition, there appeared a large number of publications dealing with Egypt and Egyptians. Many of them attempted to prove in some way that the Egyptians were not Negroes.

W. G. Browne, for instance, insisted that the Egyptians were white (Sanders 1969: 526).

The new Hamitic theory was propounded early in the nineteenth century. If the Negro was a descendant of Ham, and Ham was cursed, how could he be the creator of a great civilization? It follows logically that the theologians had to take another look, both at the Bible and at its explanation of the origin of human races. The veracity of Scriptures obviously could not be challenged. Hence, new interpretations of the meaning of biblical texts were offered. The Egyptians, it was now recalled, were descendants of Egypt, a son of Ham. Noah had cursed only Canaan, son of Ham, so that only Canaan and his progeny suffered the malediction. Ham, his other sons, and their children were not included in the curse.

So it came to pass that the Egyptians emerged as Hamites, Caucasoid, uncursed, and capable of high civilization. This view became widely accepted and is reflected in the theological literature of that era. A survey of Bible dictionaries published during this period is quite revealing. For instance, the *Encyclopedia of Biblical Literature,* published by John Kitto in 1846, has a long article under the title "Ham." It stressed that the curse of Noah was directed only against Canaan. Thus, the early decades of the nineteenth century created a new Hamitic myth, this time with a Caucasoid protagonist!

We observe that the attribution of the name *Ham* to one of Noah's sons as indicative of black color is inconsistent with his having been made black. Anyhow, despite a long tradition of perverted exegesis in some quarters, there is nothing to connect the curse of Ham with a permanent divinely instituted malediction on the Negroid peoples; it is explicitly applied to the Canaanites (Vos 1975: 57). Geerhardous Vos is emphatic on this: "It should be noticed that not all the descendants of Ham are cursed but only the Canaanites; the others receive neither curse nor blessing" (57).

The African origin of the Egyptian people is attested in the inscriptions of Queen Hatshepsut of Egypt. The records show that during her reign, the Egyptians embarked on several expeditions to Punt, which she considered as the place of origin of the Egyptians (Adamo 2005: 14). Adamo (17) quotes E. A. Wallis Budge as affirming that Punt can be located nowhere else but in Africa and that Puntites were the ancestors of the Dynastic Egyptians. McCray (1990: 115) is more specific, for he says that *Punt* has been found in an Egyptian inscription in Somalia.

Punt may well be an alternate spelling of the biblical *Put*. If that is correct, then another location has been suggested for it. According to Flavius Josephus, the Jewish historian, Put was the founder of Libya, and its inhabitants were called Putites (McCray 1990: 112), just as the Septuagint identified Put with Libya. Incidentally, the region of Cyrenaica along the Mediterranean coast of Libya is called *Puita* in the inscriptions of Darius the First, the Persian Emperor (112). Thus, Put refers to all or a part of Libya.

We notice that the character of Put described in the Bible accords more with Libya than Somalia. In six out of the eight passages where Put is mentioned in Scripture (Isa. 66:19; Jer. 46:9; Ezek. 27:10; 30:5; 38:5; Nah. 3:9), its people are pictured as warlike, providing mercenaries for foreign rulers. And four passages (2 Chron. 12:3; 16:8; 30:5; Dan. 11:43) out of the six references to Libya in the Bible give the same impression. Some scholars, including K. A. Kitchen, believe that the Libyans actually played this role in the first millennium BCE (McCray 1990: 113).

If the Pu(n)tites and the Somalis/Libyans are not identical, then they must be related. And concerning the exact location and identity of Pu(n)t, its relationship with African countries suggests that it was situated in the same geographical area and possessed a black population akin to that of her neighbors.

Many scholars have argued in favor of the blackness of the ancient Egyptians. Two of them are Glenn Usry and Craig Keener (1996). The duo states emphatically, "Most ancient Egyptians were black Africans by anyone's definition" (61). As to why the Egyptians of today are generally more fair-skinned than the Africans in the rest of the continent, Adamo says this was due to long periods of "the infiltration of many nationalities such as the Hyksos, Assyrians, Babylonians, Greeks, Romans, Syrians, and Palestinians" (Adamo 2005: 16). Of course, there were later intermarriages, and the offspring were mulattos. Means (1978: 54) admits the fact that the ancient Egyptians were full-blooded Negroes, and belonged to the same race of Negroes that you find in America and Africa today. In fact, he says, "I take great pride to introduce them to the world as a nation of Black men" (Means 1978: 54). He goes on to describe them as "black with woolly hair and thick lips" (54).

However, he claims that those living in Upper Egypt were darker than those in Lower Egypt, and offers a curious explanation: "(because of) the vertical rays of the sun" (54).

The preceding discussion is an attempt to affirm, beyond doubt, the Africanness of the ancient Egyptian people. Hence, Hagar can safely be described as an African and is a black African woman.

Hagar's Role in Salvation History

Hagar stands between Hebrew and Islamic traditions. The child she bore for Abraham has a heritage that is part Egyptian and part Mesopotamian. In her encounter with God, she uses the Canaanite divine *El* to name the God that she meets in the wilderness (*El Roi,* the God who sees). Transcending the Hebrew scriptures, Hagar's story becomes the basis for a new culture, a new people, and a new religion. The Arabs celebrate their heritage as descendants of Ishmael, the son of Abraham and Hagar. They consider the duo as the patriarch and matriarch of their people and the Islamic faith.

Within the context of God's plan for salvation for all humankind, a new perspective on the Hagar story emerges. She is treated in the Bible as few women and men are treated. She is put in a relationship with God that only the patriarchs enjoy. Like Abraham, she is given a promise of a child who will father a nation. Like Moses, she sees and even names God. Like the Hebrews fleeing from Egypt, she is met in the wilderness by God, given sustenance, and delivered from starvation. And like the Hebrews during their oppression, she utters a cry heard by God, who knows of her affliction.

The Hagar story gives meaning to God's plan for deliverance of humankind, not just the Israelites. This is evident in the uniqueness of her story and the introduction of other cultural practices that emerge from the encounter with God. They include the naming of God, the matriarchal implications in the Bible, and the unique role she plays as a woman who arrests God's attention and benefits from God's justice. Hagar is one of the few women in the Old Testament who has a recorded theophany. She is also a recipient of the promise for possession of land and uncountable descendants (Gen. 16:10; 21:18). The other woman who experiences a theophany in the Hebrew Bible is the mother of Samson (Judg. 13:2-25). But unlike Hagar, Samson's mother does not become a recipient of the promise of land and descendants. This explains why Hagar is portrayed as "the first genuine matriarch in the Old Testament." This North African woman thus demonstrates that the divine promise could be given to a non-Israelite or a woman.

As Waltke (1995: 2) has correctly remarked, "The roles played by godly women in ancient Israel are due to his [God's] design, not to chance." This applies to Hagar. This is because God's sovereignty extends even to assigning the Gentiles their gods and their cultures (Deut. 4:19). The angel of the Lord said, "Hagar, maid of Sarai" (Gen. 16:8). This address is very significant. This is the only instance in all of the many thousands of ancient Near Eastern texts where a deity, or his messenger, calls a woman by name and thereby invests her with exalted dignity (5).

Why does Hagar obey God's command to return to the same household where she had been persecuted? Even where divine demands seem to be outrageous and in conflict with socially responsible authorities, or where the demands seem unrealistic in light of human limitations, they are to be fulfilled. As Streng (1976: 8) explains, people often consider the degree that they hold to religious beliefs and practices despite abuse and ridicule as a measure of the power by which a religious experience has transformed and regulated their lives. What seems strange to the secular mind is exactly the reflection of the "wholly other." Thus, various extraordinary activities such as glossolalia, trembling, or uncontrollable shouting and singing are taken as indications of being in contact with the Divine. Hagar was probably involved in one or more of these. The Bible testifies that, under divine influence, she gave God an enduring name.

Henceforth, the awareness of a holy presence became the center of Hagar's life. Ideally, all human functions, abilities, and decisions are informed by the special impact of such an experience. Thus, Hagar's choice of an African wife for Ishmael might have been divinely guided, just as her decision to settle in that part of the Sinai Peninsula called the Wilderness of Paran.

In the first Hagar episode (Genesis 16), we meet for the first time the symbol of the well (Hooke 1976). Hagar and her son may lie outside the mainstream of promise, yet they are not beyond the activities of divine mercy. The well in the wilderness is revealed to Hagar in her distress by divine agency ("God opened her eyes"; Gen. 21:19). In the earlier episode she named it *Beer lahai-roi* (באר לחי ראי), which Spangler and Syswerda (1999: 34) understand to mean "the well of the Living One who sees me." Hooke (1976: 192) suggests that behind this name, with its doubtful Hebrew etymology, there probably lies an ancient name of Canaanite origin indicating the occupation of the well by a local deity. Indeed, Blenkinsopp and Challenor (1971: 93) hold that at this sacred spring, "the high god El was worshipped under yet another designation which in the course of time came to be identified with Yahweh, 'the god of Abraham, Isaac, and Jacob.'"

The Yahwist had already represented Yahweh as interested in the destiny of Ishmael's descendants. The insertion of a fragment of P material containing Ishmael's genealogy in the regular form of the Priestly genealogies (Gen. 25:12-17) brings the Arab tent dwellers within the ambit of the divine purpose.

In Hagar's first encounter with God, she sees God and lives. She also names God *El-roi* (Gen. 16:13). She thus becomes the only woman in the Bible given the chance to name God. Nowhere else does this name appear in the Old Testament, although the naming convention does. (For instance, *el shaddai* means "God Almighty" [Gen. 28:3, 35:11, 43:14, 48:3; Exod. 6:3; Ezek. 10:5], and *el elyon* "The Most High God" [Gen. 14:18-20, 22]. We also have *immanu el*, meaning "God is with us" [Isa. 7:14, 8:8]).

The Hagar texts are set apart from others in the Hebrew Bible in other ways, too. One is the fact that Hagar is the only non-Israelite female to receive a blessing and a visit from God. Another is that God's compassion and promises extend beyond the Israelites and that God's justice includes equality for women. In other words, a caring God exhibits compassion, promise, and presence in the world outside the chosen Israelites and their patriarchal system.

Hagar, as the mother of Ishmael, is celebrated for her role as the matriarch of the Arab people and Islam. Where the Hebrew text leaves her in the wilderness, the Arab historical and sacred writings follow her through to her death and maintain her memory by honoring her as the matriarch of a nation.

The writers of the Qur'an and the history of the Arabs have various versions of the Hagar/Sarah/Abraham narrative. This is evident in *The History of al-Tabari*, which Brimner considers the "most important universal history produced in the world of Islam" (Gill 2000). Among other things, it elaborates on the extrabiblical stories that intersect with the Hebrew scriptures. Prominent among these narratives is the story of Abraham and Hagar, the patriarch and matriarch of the Arab people.

This narrative differs in many respects from the biblical story because it serves as the foundation for the origin of the Islamic religion and the parentage of the Arab race. To illustrate, in the Islamic tradition, Abraham is said to have left Egypt for Syria and settled in what is now Palestine with Sarah, Hagar, and Ishmael. Considered as one of the pre-Islamic prophets, Abraham is said to have established a place of worship in Syria before being called by God to go to Mecca to build another house of worship for God. Abraham took Hagar and Ishmael with him and went to the land of the present-day Mecca to build a place of worship. As he leaves to build the house, he leaves Hagar and Ishmael behind without food or drink. Hagar asks him, "O Abraham! To whom are you entrusting us?" He replies, "To God." She says, "Then go! He will not lead us astray" (Gill 2000: 23).

While Hagar and Ishmael wait for Abraham, they become thirsty, and Hagar climbs a mountain, looking for water. As she searches for water, the angel Gabriel calls her, saying, "Who are you?" She answers, "Hagar, mother of the son of Abraham." To the question, "To whom did he entrust you?" she responds, "He entrusted us to God." The angel concludes, "He has entrusted you to One who is sufficient." When Hagar returns to Ishmael, he has scraped the land and found water (23).

According to Hughes (n.d.: 154), Abraham sent Hagar and Ishmael away in the direction of Mecca, and at Mecca, God produced for them the spring Zamzam. Zamzam is the sacred well within the precincts of the mosque of Mecca. Islamic tradition says it is identical with the spring from which Hagar and Ishmael drank while they were in the wilderness (Poole 1981: 978). This same tradition claims that Hagar was buried at Mecca (Poole 1981: 977–78).

The picture of Hagar that emerges from the history of the Arab people is that of a formidable figure in the life of Abraham and a fellow traveler in faith, rather than an interloper with an alien faith and a different God. Thus, there is a clear distinction between the Hagar of the Hebrew Bible and that of the Arab tradition. In the latter, she is empowered and liberated. Her identity as the mother of Ishmael is one of pride, not of shame.

Hagar's Marriage in the Context of Urhobo Customary Law

Genesis 16:3 (RSV) reads, "Sarai, Abram's wife, took Hagar the Egyptian, her maid, and gave her to Abram her husband as a wife."

What is the position of Hagar? Is she a wife or a concubine? The following versions of the Bible translate *ishshah* here as *wife*: KJV (1611/1769),

Webster Bible (WEB, 1833), Young's Literal Translation (YLT, 1862/1898), the Derby Bible (DBY, 1884/1890), the Douay–Rheims (DR, 1899), American Standard Version (ASV, 1901), Bible in Basic English (BBE, 1949/1964), RSV (1952), NKJV (1982), NIV (1984), NRSV (1989), Revised Webster Bible (RWB, 1995), New American Standard Bible (NASB, 1995), New International Version (NIV, 1978), LXE LXX English Translation (Brenton; 1851), the New American Bible (NAB, 1991), New Living Translation (NLT, 1996), and the New Jerusalem Bible (NJB, 1985). However, the New American Bible and the Catholic Study Bible render the Hebrew word as *concubine.*

There are some problems with the translation of the word *ishshah* as *concubine,* because there is an actual Hebrew Bible word, *pilegesh,* for concubine (such as in Judg. 19), and that word is not used in the Hagar text. The translation of *ishshah* as "wife" is therefore more appropriate than "concubine."[3]

Considering that every translation is contextual, the rendering of this Hebrew word as *concubine* accords more with Western culture, which recognizes monogyny as the norm. Thus, since Abraham is seen by Christians as the symbol of righteousness, it would be absurd to make Abraham a polygamist. It was Hagar's bid to assume an air of equality with her mistress (Gen. 16:4) because she is a wife and trying to exercise her legal right that led to her expulsion from the household.

In ancient Near Eastern culture, the marriage institution is based on two fundamental principles: procreation and companionship (Gen. 1:27-28, 2:20-24). Section 146 of the Hammurabi Code provides that a maidservant's status in the household is changed once she becomes pregnant by the head of the household: "If later that female slave has claimed equality with her mistress because she bore children, her mistress may not sell her" (Pritchard 1961: 172). Hagar's attitude to her mistress may have been fostered by her knowledge of such or a similar code, especially if she was one of "the persons that they [Abraham and Sarah] had gotten in Haran" (Gen. 12:5).

---

3. Among the Urhobo, *Osen eje* (concubinage) is a friendship, usually between a married man and an unmarried woman, that provides for a sexual relationship and some responsibilities on the part of the man. This friendship does not confer the status of a wife on the woman, but it may, in due course, graduate into marriage, just as it can be terminated unceremoniously.

The patriarchal stories in Genesis often stress that a foreign wife is inferior to and less desirable than a woman of the man's clan or ethnic nationality. For instance, Abraham (24:3-8, 37-41) and Rebekah (27:46) insisted on endogamy, at least for the favorite son, the carrier of the divine promise. The Hebrew polemic against foreign wives may be summarized as viewing them as immoral, corrupt. In Malachi, a foreign woman is explicitly called a "daughter of a foreign god" (2:11), that is, a foreign cult worshipper. She can easily lure her Judean husband to her cult (cf. Neh. 13:23-30). Ironically, the book of Ruth, also a product of the Persian period, is a counterexample of the faithfulness of non-Jewish women and their importance in the life of Israel. The disdain for intermarriage assumed alarming proportions by the mid-fifth century BCE, when Ezra and Nehemiah struck an official blow against the practice and excommunicated families that refused to expel the foreign women in their midst (Ezra 9–10; Neh. 13).

Warnings against the foreign woman, a stranger who does not seem to see herself as bound by the social conventions of the place she resides in, are also found in extrabiblical sources. For example, we read in *The Instruction of Ani*, from Egypt, which Athalya Brenner (1994: 43) tentatively dates between the eleventh and eighth centuries BCE, "Be on thy guard against a woman from abroad" (Pritchard 1961: 420). In Urhobo society, parents tend to dissuade their sons from marrying outside the tribe. The most common explanation for this seems to be that a non-Urhobo woman would introduce strange elements into the matrimonial home and, by extension, into the extended family. Concerning customary law, Nnaemeka Agu (1975) says it is "a blanket expression embodying several principles hammered together, and still growing, out of different systems of 'native customs' which are essentially tribal in origin and the operation of which is often limited to particular areas and some of which have matured into principles of general and notorious customs and indigenous laws."

Now, what would have been Hagar's fate if she were married under Urhobo customary law? Among the Urhobo, where the matrimonial home boasts of more than one wife, the first one is the head wife. All the others rank in seniority from the dates of their marriages. The head wife is highly respected by the rest, even where she is not the oldest among them.[4] In Hagar's case, she was doubly inferior to Sarah: she became a member of the household as a maid, and her wifehood postdated Sarah's. The head wife occasionally enjoys the last word. In Abraham's household, Sarah had the last word, at least on one occasion, and the issue at stake was whether or not Ishmael, the firstborn, should inherit. It might well be that Abraham granted Sarah the privilege to have the last word in this matter because of the degree of consanguineous affinity between Sarah and himself. They had the same father but different mothers (Gen. 20:12).

What Taylor says of matrimonial relationships under Sierra Leone customary family law is applicable also to the Urhobo. Usually, the head wife is next in command to the head of the household. Other wives are subject to her direct supervision (Taylor 1975). Barring petty jealousies caused by the husband's favoritism or some other friction caused by children or childlessness of one of the wives, the co-wives in a polygamous setup treat each other as friends. The degree of harmony may be such that the wives club together against the husband to demand better conditions from him.

In Urhoboland, seniority of children in a polygynous family is determined by their dates of birth, not the dates of their mothers' marriages to the father. However, seniority of children begins to affect the mothers' status only at the demise of the father. The status of the mother of the eldest son, no matter how junior she is in the family setup, is automatically affected by her son's elevation, and she begins to enjoy more prestige and recognition in the family.

The importance the Urhobo attach to procreation may be gleaned from such personal names as *Omohwo* (meaning "A Man without a Child Is Nothing") and *Omonefe* ("Wealth Is Nothing Compared to a Child") (Ubrurhe 2003). In ancient Urhobo society, a barren woman who died usually had her stomach slit and was buried facedown because she had failed to fulfill her primary task in life.

Under Urhobo customary law, intestate succession does not reckon with a wife. She does not inherit any portion of her late husband's estate. As Ovie-Whisky (1975) points out, whatever she gets at her husband's death intestate

---

4. However, Sarah's action has its parallel among some customs in Nigeria. For instance, one of the basic features of the social system of the people of Umuahia in Abia State is the institution of "women's marriage." Under it, a housewife who has attained the age of menopause and is childless may marry a woman and give her to her husband as a wife. All the children borne by this woman treat the head wife as their grandmother (Nwoko, personal interview, August 15, 2004).

comes indirectly through her children. If she is childless, then no matter how long she may have been married to the deceased husband, she gets nothing if he dies intestate (141).

There can be no doubt that Abraham died intestate. What is not certain is whether Hagar's son, Ishmael, eventually shared in the inheritance. Under Urhobo marriage law, all the children of the deceased father are entitled to a portion of the inheritance; that is, the children born by an *Ose* are treated equally with those of the wife (Odje 1995: 101). This is only logical, considering that the two categories of children are expected to participate in the funeral rites without discrimination. In fact, in Urhobo custom, there is no illegitimate child.

One important fact is clear from this discussion. An African reader of Hagar's story is in an advantageous position to understand this story because African culture is close to the biblical culture.

Conclusion

God made a way in the wilderness for an African single mother without friends, family, or resources in order to help her and her son. In all of Hagar's story, only God, whether in person or through a messenger, speaks to her. Only God calls her by name. (Sarah and Abraham consistently call her "maid/servant.") It is God who sees this woman as a person, hears her, sends a message to her, and makes her mother of a nation. Hagar in turn sees God as a person and names him.

Tamez et al. (1983) read the Hagar story from the perspective of the poor and oppressed of the Third World. Like many women in Africa, Hagar is thrice oppressed: because of her class (she is a maid), because of her race (she is an African, an impure race according to the Hebrews), and because of her sex (she is a woman). However, Hagar's theophany points to liberation, for it shows that God is in solidarity with (1) the poor and oppressed, wherever they may be found; (2) the despised races and ethnic minorities; and (3) women (Tamez et al. 1983: 184).

Africans must appropriate the Bible in such a way that emphasis is placed on God's response to black people's situation, rather than on what would appear to be hopeless aspects of their lives. Hagar's story shows that she meets hopelessness with hope and promise when God is revealed to her in her time of need and destitution. African women can relate to her prayer for sustenance in the wilderness, because their faith journeys reflect God's presence in their time of trial. Today's African woman ought to find her own life mirrored in the stories of her black biblical counterparts who experienced God's blessing on them.

The Bible identifies many virtues; chief among them are justice, faith, hope, charity (love), perseverance, wisdom, and courage. What are the virtues that qualify Hagar to become a citizen in the realm of God? Hagar may be held up as a paradigm for contemporary black women in terms of faith, trust, courage, perseverance, and justice. Hagar must have learned from Abraham about Yahweh, the God of Israel. Therefore, when she and her son are face-to-face with death in the desert, she cries not to her Egyptian deities but to Yahweh. She must be aware that this God is the liberator who promised to free Abraham's descendants from bondage (Gen. 15:13-14). Paradoxically, the land of enslavement will be Egypt, the country of her birth.

Her status as maid notwithstanding, Hagar makes herself useful and proves herself trustworthy. Sarah must have some confidence in, and perhaps even affection for, Hagar to want her to be the surrogate mother of her son. The same goes for Abraham, for he believes what Hagar tells him concerning the theophany—at least as it relates to the name to be given to the unborn child.

Felder (1989: 140) affirms that "many of the female personalities in the Bible are progenitors of many black women today, in terms of their 'low estate' in ancient society, and their enormous faith." Hagar played a vital role as an instrument of God in the history of salvation. Notwithstanding her social position, this woman, who at first appeared to be of a very low status, later attained theological significance by liberating herself from her circumstances and participating dramatically in God's redemptive scheme. All this happened despite her being a Gentile, a servant, and a woman—a triple jeopardy in the context of ancient Israelite society.

Simpson (1952) sees an important point of interest in the first Hagar narrative (Genesis 16). It derives from her expulsion from her matrimonial home. Though she has been driven out by Sarah, with Abraham's consent, yet God follows her. The lesson here is that though human relationships may go sour, divine mercy does not fail. The words with which Hagar responded to that mercy, "I flee from the face of my mistress Sarai" (Genesis 16:9) have an enduring quality. As Simpson reports, "In old houses of the stern Puritan tradition those words embroidered could be seen framed upon the wall, and usually they were taken to mean the watchful eyes of God's increasing judgment" (607). But that is not their meaning in the Hagar story. Rather, they are the joyful acknowledgment of God's grace that beholds our human needs. As the Psalmist sang, "He that keepeth Israel shall neither slumber nor sleep" (Ps. 121:4 KJV). To be sure, many lonely souls for whom the world has seemed desolate, as it seemed to Hagar, have sought solace in the faith that there is One who always sees their sorrow and will come with compassion and help.

Many African women today are in a position similar to Hagar's. Each aspect of her condition has its parallel among them. They may not be actual servants, but they are in a position of weakness, with no one to defend them. No one except God. The same God who defended Hagar and heard the cries of Ishmael in the wilderness hears their cries and those of their children even today.

While the sacred Hebrew story is the foundation for the Judeo-Christian faith, it does not preclude the presence of God in the lives of other peoples. God's salvation plan has the whole world in view. When we employ this strategy of God's presence among African people, African biblical women are lifted out of the footnotes of biblical history and placed in the mainstream of the salvation plan.

BIBLIOGRAPHY

Abravanel, Isaac. 1960. *Commentary on the Prophets and Writings, Sefer Ma'yenei ha-yeshu'ah* [*Fountains of Salvation*; Commentary on Daniel]. Jerusalem: Abravanel [Heb.].

————. 1964. *Commentary on the Torah*, 3 vols. Jerusalem: Benei Arbal [Heb.].

————. 1979. *Commentary on Last Prophets*. Jerusalem: Benei Arbal [Heb.].

Adamo, David Tuesday. 2001. *Exploration in African Biblical Studies*. Eugene, Ore.: Wipf & Stock, 95–106.

————. 2001. *Africa and the Africans in the Old Testament*. Eugene, Ore.: Wipf & Stock. (Orig. pub. San Francisco: Christian University Press, 1998.)

————. 2006. *Africa and Africans in the New Testament*. Lanham, Md.: University Press of America.

Aderibigbe, G. 1999. "Yoruba Cosmology as a Theory of Creation: Limits and Assets." *Asia Journal of Theology* 13, no. 2: 328–38.

Agu, Nnaemeka. 1975. "The Dualism of English and Customary Law in Nigeria." In *African Indigenous Laws: Proceedings of Workshop*, eds. T. O. Elias, S. N. Nwabara, and C. O. Akpamgbo, 251–67. Nsukka: Institute of African Studies, University of Nigeria, Nsukka.

Ahiamadu, Amadi. 1982. "Executive-Legislative Relations in Nigeria 1900–1980." M.Sc. Thesis, University of Ibadan.

————. 2003. "Living with Oil Exploration, Exploitation and Exportation in Niger Delta: A Case Study of Oil Mining Lease 57, 58, 100–101." Paper presented to the Postgraduate Seminar of Environmental Ethics Department, University of Stellenbosch.

————. 2006. "Stakeholders and Human Rights: Implications for a Responsible and Accountable Land Ownership and Use in the Niger

Delta (Nigeria)." Paper presented at Amnesty International Business Group, Stockholm, Sweden.

Aichele, G., et al. (The Bible and Culture Collective). 1995. *The Postmodern Bible*. New Haven and London: Yale University Press.

Alshekh, Moshe. 1876. *Sefer Havaszelet hasharon*. Repr. Warsaw: Goldman, 1961 [Heb.].

Alston T. M., et al., eds. 1993. *Dream Reader: Psychoanalytic Articles on Dreams*. Madison, Conn.: International Universities Press.

Alter, R. 1981. *The Art of Biblical Narrative*. New York: Basic.

Amadi, Elechi. 1982. *Ethics in Nigerian Culture*. Ibadan, Nigeria: Heinemans.

Amit, Y. 1999. *The Book of Judges: The Art of Editing*. Leiden: Brill.

———. Forthcoming. "The Story of Judah and Tamar: Meaning, Context and Affiliation." *Society of Biblical Literature*. Petersen Festschrift, eds. J. M. LeMon and K. H. Richards.

Amnesty International Report 2005—the State of the World's Human Rights. London: Amnesty International Publications, 199–200.

Amnesty International. 2006. "Nigeria—Ten Years On: Injustice and Violence Haunt the Niger Delta." http://web.amnesty.org/library/print/ ENGAFR440222005.

Anderson, A. 1991. *Moya: The Holy Spirit in an African Context*. Pretoria: University of South Africa.

Aquino, Maria Pilar. 2007. "The Feminist Option for the Poor and Oppressed in the Context of Globalization." In *The Option for the Poor in Christian Theology*, ed. Daniel Groody, 191–215. Notre Dame, Ind.: University of Notre Dame Press.

Arama, Isaac ben Moses 1961. *Sefer 'Aqedat Yitzhak*, 2 [*The Sacrifice of Isaac*]. Jerusalem: Offset Israel_America [Heb.].

Arendt, Hannah. 1998. *The Human Condition*. 2nd edition. Chicago: University of Chicago Press.

Asha Forum. 2008. "Mobilizing Churches." Viva Network Web site, http:// www.asha.viva.org/involve_churches.htm (accessed September 29, 2008).

Atkinson, David. 1990. *The Message of Genesis 1–11*. Downers Grove, Ill.: InterVarsity.

Avorti, Solomon. 1999. "Genesis 11:1-9: An African Perspective." In *Return to Babel: Global Perspective on the Bible*, eds. Priscilla Pope-Levison and John R. Levison, 17–23. Louisville: Westminster John Knox.

Ayandele, E. A. 1969. *The Missionary Impact on Modern Nigeria, 1842–1914.* London: Macmillan.

Bailey, C. Randall. 1991. "Beyond Identification: The Use of Africans in the Old Testament Poetry and Narratives." In Felder 1991: 165–84.

Baker, H. D. 2001. "The Degrees of Freedom: Slavery in Mid-First Millennium BC Babylonia." *World Archeology* 33:18–26.

Bal, Mieke. 1987. *Lethal Love: Feminist Literary Readings of Biblical Love Stories.* Bloomington: Indiana University Press.

———. 2008. *Loving Yusuf: Conceptual Travels from Present to Past.* Chicago: University of Chicago Press.

———. 1993. "Myth à la Lettre: Freud, Mann, Genesis and Rembrandt, and the Story of the Son." Repr. in *A Feminist Companion to Genesis*, ed. A. Brenner, 343–78. Sheffield: Sheffield Academic. (Orig. pub. in *Discourse in Psychoanalysis and Literature*, ed. S. Rimon-Kenan, 57–89. London: Methuen, 1987.)

Ballard, Edward G. 1986. "Sense of the Comedic." In *Dictionary of the History of Ideas: Studies of Selected Pivotal Ideas* 1:467–70. New York: Scribner's Sons.

———. 1986. "Sense of the Tragic." In *Dictionary of the History of Ideas: Studies of Selected Pivotal Ideas* 4:411–17. New York: Scribner's Sons.

Barr, James. 1962. *Biblical Words for Time.* London: SCM.

Barret, D., ed. 1996. *Trauma and Dreams.* Cambridge, Mass.: Harvard University Press.

Bechtel, Lyn M. 1993. "Rethinking the Interpretation of Genesis 2.4b—3.24." In *A Feminist Companion to Genesis*, ed. Athalya Brenner, 17–117. Sheffield, England: Sheffield Academic.

Beckwith, Roger T. 1988. "The Vegetarianism of the Therapeute, and the Motives for Vegetarianism in Early Jewish and Christian Circles." *RevQ* 13:407–410.

Bellis, Alice Ogden. 1994. *Helpmates, Harlots, Heroes.* Louisville, Ky.: Westminster John Knox.

Benhabib, S. 2002. *The Claims of Culture: Equality and Diversity in the Global Era.* Princeton: Princeton University Press.

Bennet, Chris. 1998. "Marijuana and the Goddess." *Cannabis Culture* (Aug. 31), http://www.cannabisculture.com/articles/1374.html.

Berman, Louis A. 1982. *Vegetarianism and the Jewish Tradition.* New York: Ktav.

Bietak, Manfred. 1995. *Avaris: The Capital of the Hyksos; Recent Excavations.* British Museum Publications.

———. 1997. "The Center of Hyksos Rule: Avaris (Tell el-Dab'a)." In *The Hyksos: New Historical and Archaeological Perspectives*, ed. Eliezer D. Oren, 87–140. Philadelphia: University Museum, University of Pennsylvania.

Binger, Tilde. 1997. *Asherah: The Goddess in the Texts from Ugarit, Israel and the Old Testament.* Sheffield: Sheffield Academic.

Bird, Phyllis. 1997. *Missing Persons and Mistaken Identities: Women and Gender in Ancient Israel.* Minneapolis: Fortress Press.

Bledstein, Adrien Janis, 1977. "The Genesis of Humans: The Garden of Eden Revisited." *Judaism* 26, no. 2: 187–200.

Blenkinsopp, Joseph, and John Challenor. 1971. *The Pentateuch.* London: Sheed & Ward.

Blum, Lawrence. 1998. "Recognition, Value and Equality: A Critique of Charles Taylor's and Nancy Fraser's Accounts of Multiculturalism." *Constellations* 5, no. 1: 3–99.

Boadt, Lawrence. 1984. *Reading the Old Testament: An Introduction.* New York: Paulist.

Bodde, Derk. 1953. "Harmony and Conflict in Chinese Philosophy." In *Studies in Chinese Thought*, ed. A. F. Wright. Chicago: University of Chicago Press.

———. 1961. "Myths of Ancient China." In *Mythologies of the Ancient World*, ed. Samuel Noah Kramer. Garden City, New York: Doubleday.

Bosman, Hendrik L. 2002. "Appropriating the Decalogue according to African Proverbs." *Scriptura* 81: 354–61.

———. 2006. " 'What Is Humankind?' Both King and Slave: Job 7:17-21 as Ironic Parody of Human Identity in Psalm 8:4-6." *Paper delivered at the Old Testament Society of South Africa Conference*, Pretoria: University of South Africa, 1–6.

Bottéro, Jean. 2001. *Religion in Ancient Mesopotamia.* Trans. Teresa Lavender Fagan. Chicago: University of Chicago Press.

Braner, Baruch, and Eli Freiman, eds. 1993. *The Rabbinic Pentateuch with Commentary on the Torah by R. Levi ben Gershon*, 5 vols., Jerusalem: Maaliyot [Heb.].

Brenner, A., and F. van Dijk-Hemmes. 1993. *On Gendering Texts: Female and Male Voices in the Hebrew Bible.* Leiden: Brill.

Brenner, Athalya. 1985. *The Israelite Woman: Social Role and Literary Type in Biblical Narrative.* Sheffield: JSOT. 2nd ed. 1994.

Brenner, Athalya, and F. H. Polak, eds., *Performing Memory in Biblical Narrative and Beyond.* Sheffield: Sheffield Phoenix, 2009.

Brett, M. G. 2000. *Genesis: Procreation and the Politics of Identity.* London: Routledge.

Brichto, Herbert Chanan. 1998. *The Names of God: Poetic Readings in Biblical Beginnings.* Oxford: Oxford University Press.

Brown, Francis S., R. Driver, and Charles A. Briggs, eds. 2003 ed. *The Brown-Driver-Briggs Hebrew and English Lexicon.* Peabody: Hendrickson (*BDB*).

Brown, P. 1988. *The Body and Society: Men, Women, and Sexual Renunciation in Early Christianity.* New York: Columbia University Press.

Brueggemann, Walter. 1982. *Genesis.* Interpretation, A Bible Commentary for Teaching and Preaching. Atlanta: John Knox.

———. 2002. *The Land: Place as Gift, Promise and Challenge in Biblical Faith,* 2nd ed. Minneapolis: Fortress Press.

———. 2003. *An Introduction to the Old Testament: The Canon and Christian Imagination.* Louisville: Westminster John Knox.

Bryant, D. J. 2000. "*Imago Dei,* Imagination, and Ecological Responsibility." *Theology Today 57,* no. 1: 35–50.

Buber, Shlomo, ed. 1900. *Midrash Sekhel Tov on Genesis and Exodus of Rabbi Menachem Ben Shlomo.* Berlin: Itzkowski [Heb.].

———. 1960. *Midrash Lekach Tov by Rabbi Tobiah b. Eliezer on the Pentateuch.* 2 vols. Jerusalem: Offset Monzon [Heb.].

Butler, J. 1993. *Bodies That Matter: On the Discursive Limits of "Sex."* New York: Routledge.

Butler, Mark, Thulani Ndlazi, David Ntseng, Graham Philpott, and Nomusa Sokhela. 2007. *Learning to Walk: NGO Practice and the Possibility of Freedom.* Occasional Paper No. 3. Pietermaritzburg: Church Land Programme.

Butler, T. C., ed. 1991. *Holman Bible Dictionary.* Nashville: Broadman & Holman.

Byrne, David. 2006. *Social Exclusion,* 2nd ed. Maidenhead: Open University Press.

Cai, Yuping. 2008. "'Newly Arrived' Women: Personal Background, Family Situation and Social Capital." In Lou and Lo 2008: 10–19.

Callaway, Mary. 1986. *Sing, O Barren One: A Study in Comparative Midrash.* SBL Dissertation Series 91. Atlanta: Scholars.

Capoccia, Kathryn. 2000. "A Woman Who Raised a Wild Donkey of a Man." http://www.scribd.com/doc/14524799/A-Woman-Who-Raised-a-Wild-Donkey-of-a-Man.

Cardellini, Innocenzo. 1981. *Die biblischen "Sklaven"-Gesetze im Lichte des keilschriftlichen Sklavenrechts: Ein Beitrag zur Tradition, Überlieferung und Redaktion der alttestamentlichen Rechtstexte* ["The Biblical "Slave"-Laws in the Light of Cuneiform Slavelaws: A Study of Tradition, Transmission and Redaction of Old Testament Lawtexts"]. BBB 55. Bonn: Hanstein.

Carr, David. 1996. *Reading the Fractures of Genesis: Historical and Literary Approaches.* Louisville, Ky.: Westminster John Knox.

Cassuto, Umberto. 1972. "The Story of Tamar and Judah." In *Studies on the Bible and Ancient Orient.* Vol. 1, *Biblical and Canaanite Literatures.* Jerusalem: Magnes.

———. 1978. *A Commentary on the Book of Genesis, 1—6:8 (Adam to Noah).* Jerusalem: Magnes.

Chavel, Charles B., trans. and annot. 1971. *Ramban (Nachmanides): Commentary on the Torah.* 5 vols. New York: Shilo.

Chen, Jian Xian. 1994. "Women and the Earth: New Interpretation of Nu Kua's Forming Human Beings." *Journal of Hua Zhong Normal University (Humanities and Social Sciences)* 2:78–79.

———. 1996. "Types and Distributions of Chinese Flood Myths." *Forum on Folk Culture* [《民間文化論壇》] 3:2–10.

———. 2005. "The Research of China's Circle of Deluge Story: An Analysis of 568 Versions." Ph.D. diss., Central China Normal University.

Chen, Robert Shanmu. 1992. *A Comparative Study of Chinese and Western Cyclic Myths.* New York: Peter Lang.

Chen Xizhi. 2006a. "If Only Jing Shuying Knew Me." In Chen 2006c: 44–49.

———. 2006b. "The Little Giant on the Bicycle." In Chen 2006c: 38–41.

———. 2006c. *Twelve Women in Tianshuiwei.* Hong Kong: Bluesky [Chin.].

———. 2008. "The Experience of Interviewing 'New Immigrant' Women." In Lou and Lo 2008: 20–31.

Childs, B. S. 1960. *Myth and Reality in the Old Testament.* London: SCM.

Chiu, M. M. 1984. *The Tao of Chinese Religion*. Lanham, Md.: University Press of America.

Church Land Programme (CLP), n.d. CLP Web site, www.churchland .org.za.

Clifford, Richard J. 1985. "The Hebrew Scriptures and the Theology of Creation." *Theological Studies* 46:507–23.

———. 1993. "The Unity of the Book of Isaiah and Its Cosmogonic Language." *CBQ* 55:1–17.

Clifford, R. J. 1994. *Creation Accounts in the Ancient Near East and in the Bible*. Washington, D.C.: Catholic Bible Association of America.

Clines, David. 1997. *The Theme of the Pentateuch*. 2nd ed. JSOTSup 10. Sheffield: Sheffield Academic. (Orig. pub. 1977.)

Coats, G. W. 1983. *Genesis* 1. Trans. by William Heynen. Grand Rapids: Eerdmans.

———. 1983. *Genesis, with an Introduction to Narrative Literature* 1. Grand Rapids: Eerdmans.

Cochrane, James R. 1999. *Circles of Dignity: Community Wisdom and Theological Reflection*. Minneapolis: Fortress Press.

Cohen, Alfred S. 1981. "Vegetarianism from a Jewish Perspective." *Journal of Halacha and Contemporary Society* 1, no. 2: 38–63.

Cohen, Joseph, and Uriel Simon, eds. 2007. *R. Abraham Ibn Ezra: Yesod mora' ve-sod Torah [The Foundation of Piety and the Secret of the Torah]* Ramat Gan: Bar-Ilan University [Heb.].

Cohen, Menachem, ed. 1996, 1997, 1999. *Mikra'ot Gedolot 'Haketer': A Revised and Augmented Scientific Edition of 'Mikra'ot Gedolot' Based on the Aleppo Codex and Early Medieval MSS, Isaiah*. Ramat Gan: Bar-Ilan University Press [Heb.].

Cohen, N. J. 1995. *Self, Struggle and Change: Family Conflict Stories in Genesis and Their Healing Insights for our Lives*. Woodstock, Vt.: Jewish Lights.

Confucius. 1983. *The Analects* [論語, Lun Yu]. Trans. D. C. Lau. Hong Kong: Chinese University Press.

Cook, Roger. 1974. *The Tree of Life*. London: Thames & Hudson.

Copher, Charles B. 1991. "The Black Presence in the Old Testament." In Felder 1991: 146–64.

———. 1993. *Black Biblical Studies: Biblical and Theological Issues on the Black Presence in the Bible*. Chicago: Black Light Fellowship.

Corinaldi, M. 2001. *The Enigma of Jewish Identity: The Law of Return—Theory and Practice.* Sarigim, Israel: Nevo [Heb.].

Cox Miller, P. 1994. *Dreams in Late Antiquity: Studies in the Imagination of a Culture.* Princeton: Princeton University Press.

Crawford, Christa Foster, and Mark Crawford. 2005. "Human Trafficking: Children and the Sex Trade." *Theology News & Notes* (Fuller Theological Seminary) 52, no. 3: 17–19.

Cronjé, Johan M. 1982. *Born to Witness: A Concise History of the Churches Born out of the Mission Work of the Dutch Reformed Church (Nederduitse Gereformeerde Kerk).* Pretoria: NG Kerkboekhandel.

Dandamayev, Muhammed A. 1992. "Slavery, Ancient Near East." In *ABD* 6:58–65. New York.

Demarchi, Franco, and Riccardo Scartezzini. 1996. *Martino Martini: A Humanist and Scientist in the Seventeenth Century.* Trento: Università degli studi di Trento.

Desanges, Jehan et al. 1976. *The Image of the Black in Western Art,* 1. New York: Morrow & Co.

DeWitt, C. B., ed. 1996. *The Just Stewardship of Land and Creation.* Grand Rapids: Eerdmans.

Dibeela, P. B. 2001. "A Setswana Perspective on Genesis 1:1-10." In Gerald O. West and Musa W. Dube, eds. *The Bible in Africa: Transactions, Trajectories and Trends,* 384–99. Leiden: Brill.

Ding, W. D. 1988. *100 Chinese Myths and Fantasies.* Hong Kong: Commercial.

Donnelly, Doris. 1992. "Divine Folly: Being Religious and the Exercise of Humor." *TT* 48, no. 4 (January): 385–98.

Dor, Y. 2006. *Have the "Foreign Women" Really Been Expelled? Separation and Exclusion in the Restoration Period.* Jerusalem: Magnes [Heb.].

Dozeman, Thomas B., and Konrad Schmid, eds. 2006. *A Farewell to the Yahwist? The Composition of the Pentateuch in Recent European Interpretation.* Atlanta: SBL.

Dube, Musa W. 1996. "Reading for Decolonization (John 4:1-42)." *Semeia* 75:37–59.

Dubs, Homer H., trans. 1966. *The Words of Hsuntze.* Taipei: Ch'eng-wen.

Dumbrell, William J. 1975. "Midian: A Land or a League?" *VT* 25:323–37.

Dunston, Alfred G. 1974. *The Black Man in the Old Testament and Its World.* Philadelphia: Dorrance & Co.

Dutch Reformed Church. 1976. *Human Relations and the South African Scene in the Light of Scripture.* Cape Town: National Book Printers.

Du Toit, H. L. 2005. "'n Kort Filosofiese Besinning oor Waarheid in die tyd van Aardverwarming en die Godin." *Diskoers* 33, no. 2: 35–40.

Dyrness, W. 1979. *Themes in Old Testament Theology.* Downers Grove: InterVarsity.

Eagleton, Terry. 1996. *Literary Theory: An Introduction.* 2nd ed. Minneapolis: University of Minnesota Press.

Eichel, W. 1986. *In the Heart of the Tiger: Art of South Africa [Azaria Mbatha].* Wuppertal: Hammer.

Eilberg-Schwartz, H. 1990. *The Savage in Judaism: An Anthropology of Israelite Religion and Ancient Judaism.* Bloomington: Indiana University Press.

———. 1995a. "Introduction: The Spectacle of the Female Head." In Eilberg-Schwartz and Doniger 1995: 1–13.

———. 1995b. "The Nakedness of a Woman's Voice, the Pleasure in a Man's Mouth: An Oral History of Ancient Judaism." In Eilberg-Schwartz and Doniger 1995: 165–84.

Eilberg-Schwartz, H., and W. Doniger, eds. 1995. *Off with Her Head: The Denial of Women's Identity in Myth, Religion, and Culture.* Berkeley: University of California Press.

Ellonen, Noora, and Kaija Korhonen. 2007. "Maahanmuuttajanaiset väkivallan kohteena" ["Immigrant Women as a Target of Violence"]. In *Maahanmuuttajanaiset: Kotoutuminen, perhe ja työ* [Immigrant Women, Integration, Family and Work], ed. Tuomas Martikainen and Marja Tiilikainen. Väestöliitto. Väestöntutkimuslaitoksen julkaisusarja D 46/2007. Helsinki [Fin.].

Emerton, J. A. 1975. "Some Problems in Genesis xxxiii." *VT* 25:338–61.

———. 1976. "An Examination of a Recent Structuralist Interpretation of Genesis xxxviii." *VT* 26:79–98.

———. 1979. "Judah and Tamar." *VT* 29:403–415.

Empowering Dalit Women of Nepal (EDWON). 2006. Personal communication (March).

Ertürk, Yakin. 2003. "Integration of the Human Rights of Women and the Gender Perspective: Violence against Women; Towards an Effective

Implementation of International Norms to End Violence against Women."
Available at http://www.unhchr.ch/Huridocda/Huridoca.nsf.

Evuleocha, Stephenas U. 2003. "Managing Indigenous Relations: Corporate Social Responsibility in a New Age of Activism." *Corporate Communications: An International Journal* 10, no. 4: 328–40.

Exum, J. Cheryl. 1993. *Fragmented Women: Feminist (Sub)versions of Biblical Narratives.* Valley Forge, Pa.: Trinity Press International.

Eze, E. C. 1997. "The Color of Reason: The Idea of 'Race' in Kant's Anthropology." In *Post-colonial African Philosophy: A Critical Reader,* ed. E. C. Eze, 103–140. Cambridge: Blackwell.

Fager, J. A. 1993. *Land Tenure and the Biblical Jubilee: Uncovering Hebrew Ethics through the Sociology of Knowledge.* Sheffield: Sheffield Academic.

Fang, Jing Pei, and Zhang Juwen. 2000. *The Interpretation of Dreams in Chinese Culture.* New York: Weatherhill.

Felder, Cain Hope. 1989. *Troubling Biblical Waters.* Maryknoll, N.Y.: Orbis.

———, ed. 1991. *Stony the Road We Trod: African American Biblical Interpretation.* Minneapolis: Fortress Press.

Fewell, Dana Nolan. 1987. "Feminist Reading of the Hebrew Bible: Affirmation, Resistance and Transformation." *JSOT* 39:77–87.

———. 1998. "Changing the Subject: Retelling the Story of Hagar the Egyptian." In *Genesis: A Feminist Companion to the Bible,* ed. A. Brenner, 182–94. Sheffield: Sheffield Academic.

Fidler, R. 2005. *"Dreams Speak Falsely"? Dream Theophanies in the Bible: Their Place in Ancient Israelite Faith and Traditions.* Jerusalem: Magnes [Heb.].

Finkelstein, Israel. 1988. "Arabian Trade and Socio-Political Conditions in the Negev in the Twelfth–Eleventh Centuries, B.C.E." *JNES* 47: 241–52.

Fishbane, M. 1998. *Biblical Text and Texture: A Literary Reading of Selected Texts.* Oxford: Oneworld.

Fisher, Eugene J. 1977. "The Divine Comedy: Humor in the Bible." *RelEd* 72, no. 6 (November–December): 571–79.

Fokkelman, J. P. 1975. *Narrative Art in Genesis.* Assen: Van Gorcum.

Fontaine, Carole R. 1987. "Queenly Proverb Performance: The Prayer of Puduhepa." In *The Listening Heart: Essays in Wisdom and the Psalms in*

Honor of Roland E. Murphy, O. Carm., ed. Kenneth G. Hoglund et al., 95–126. JSOTSup 58. Sheffield: Sheffield Academic.

———. 1999. "A Heifer from Thy Stable: On Goddesses and the Status of Women in the Ancient Near East." In *Women in the Hebrew Bible: A Reader*, ed. Alice Bach, 159–78. New York: Routledge.

———. 2002. *Smooth Words: Women, Proverbs and Performance in Biblical Wisdom*. JSOTSup. 356. Sheffield: Sheffield Academic.

———. 2008. *With Eyes of Flesh: The Bible, Gender and Human Rights*. Sheffield: Sheffield Phoenix.

———. Forthcoming. "The Sharper Harper (1 Sam 16:14-23): Iconographic Reflections on David's Rise to Power." In *The Fate of King David: The Past and Present of a Biblical Icon*, ed. Claudia Camp et al. Library of Hebrew Bible/Old Testament Studies 500. New York: T&T Clark.

———. 2008. Artist and Director. "Combat Art in the Ancient Near East." Greenheart Studio. http://www.youtube.com/greenheartstudio (accessed September 29, 2008).

Freedman, H., and Maurice Simon, eds. 1939. *Midrash Rabbah, Genesis*. London: Soncino.

Freedman, R. David. 1983. "Woman, A Power Equal to Man: Translation of Woman as a 'Fit Helpmate' for Man Is Questioned." Biblical Archaeological Review 9, no. 1 (January/February): 56–58.

Freire, Paulo. 1990. *Education for Critical Consciousness*. London: Sheed & Ward.

———. 1993. *Pedagogy of the Oppressed*, 20th anniv. ed. New York: Continuum.

Fretheim, Terence E. 1994. "The Book of Genesis: Introduction, Commentary, and Reflections." In *NIB* 1:389–94. Nashville: Abingdon.

———. 2007. *Abraham: Trials of Family and Faith*. Columbia: University of South Carolina Press.

Freud, S. 1976. *The Interpretation of Dreams*. Trans. J. Styachley. London: Penguin.

Frieden, K. 1990. *Freud's Dream of Interpretation*. Albany: State University of New York Press.

Fung, Yu Lan. 1952. *A History of Chinese Philosophy*, 1. Trans. D. Bodde. Princeton, N.J.: Princeton University Press.

Gad, C. J. 1981. "The Invasion of Agade and the Gutian Invasion." In *Cambridge Ancient History* 1, part 2A. Cambridge: Cambridge University Press, 417–463.

Gaebelein, Frank E., ed. 1990. *The Expositor's Bible Commentary*, 2. Grand Rapids: Zondervan.

Garr, D. M. 1996. *Reading the Fractures of Genesis: Historical and Literary Approaches*. Louisville: Westminster John Knox.

Gericke, J. W. 2004. "Does Yahweh Exist? A Philosophical-Critical Reconstruction of the Case against Realism in Old Testament Theology." *OTE* 17 (1): 30–57.

Gersonides (R. Levi ben Gershon). 2001. *Mikraot Gedolot (HaMaor): Prophets and Writings*. Jerusalem: Hamaor [Heb.].

Gerstenberger, Erhard S. 1996. *Yahweh the Patriarch: Ancient Images of God and Feminist Theology*. Minneapolis: Fortress Press.

———. 1997. "The Paternal Face and the Maternal Mind of Yahweh." *WW* 17, no. 4: 365–75.

———. 2002. *Theologies in the Old Testament*. London: T&T Clark.

Gill, Laverne McCain. 2000. *Daughters of Dignity: African Women in the Bible and the Virtues of Black Womanhood*. Cleveland, Ohio: Pilgrim.

Gimbutas, Marija. 1991. *The Language of the Goddess*. San Francisco: HarperCollins.

Gitau, S. K. 2000. *The Environment Crisis: A Challenge for African Christianity*. Nairobi: Acton.

Gollnick Lewiston, J. 1987. *Dreams in the Psychology of Religion*. New York: Mellen.

Goodenough, E. R. 1965. *Jewish Symbols in the Greco-Roman Period*. Bollingen Series 37. Toronto: Pantheon.

Gordon. R. G. Jr. 2005. *Ethnologue: Languages of the World*. 15th ed. Dallas: Summer Institute of Linguistics.

Gottlieb, Ze'ev, ed. 1980. *Rabbi Obadiah Sforno Commentary to the Pentateuch*. Jerusalem: Mossad Harav Kook [Heb.].

Gottwald, Norman K. 1979. *The Tribes of Yahweh: A Sociology of the Religion of Liberated Israel, 1250–1050 B.C.E.* London: SCM.

Graham, Angus C. 1981. *Chuang-tzū: The Seven Inner Chapters and Other Writings from the Book Chuang-tzū*. London: Allen & Unwin.

Greenstein, Edward L. 1999. "Reading Strategies and the Story of Ruth." In *Women in the Hebrew Bible,* ed. Alice Bach, 211–31. New York: Routledge.

Gu, Jiegang. 1982. *Debates on Ancient History.* Shanghai: Shanghai Ancient Books.

Gu, Jiegang, and Tong Shuye. 1982. "The Legend of Kun and Yu." In *Debates and Critiques of Ancient History* [《古史辯》] 7, part 11: 142–72. Shanghai: Guji.

Gu, Zhizhong, trans. 1992. *Creation of the Gods.* Beijing: New World.

Gunkel, Hermann. 1922. "Die Komposition der Joseph-Geschichten." *ZDMG* 76:55–71.

———. 1984. "The Influence of Babylonian Mythology upon the Biblical Creation Story." In *Creation in the Old Testament,* ed. Bernhard W. Anderson, 25–52. Philadelphia: Fortress Press.

———. 1997. *Genesis.* Macon: Mercer University Press.

Gunn, David M. 1984. "The Anatomy of Divine Comedy: On Reading the Bible as Comedy and Tragedy." *Semeia* 32:115–29.

Gutierrez, Gustavo. 1999. "The Task and Content of Liberation Theology." In *The Cambridge Companion to Liberation Theology,* ed. Cristopher Rowland, 19–38. Cambridge: Cambridge University Press.

Habel, N., ed. 2000. "Introducing the Earth Bible: Readings from the Perspective of the Earth" in *The Earth Bible,* vol. 1. Sheffield: Sheffield Academic.

Habel, Norman et al., eds. 2000. *The Earth Bible.* 5 vols. Sheffield: Sheffield Academic.

Hadley, Judith M. 2000. *The Cult of Asherah in Ancient Israel and Judah: Evidence for a Hebrew Goddess.* Cambridge: Cambridge University Press.

Hamilton, Victor P. 1990. *The Book of Genesis, Chapters 1–17.* Grand Rapids: Eerdmans.

———. 1992. "Marriage (OT and ANE)." In *ABD* 4:559–69. New York.

Hamlin, E. John. 1979. *A Guide to Isaiah 40–66.* London: SPCK.

Hammer, Reuven, ed. 1986. *Sifre: A Tannaitic Commentary on the Book of Deuteronomy.* New Haven: Yale University Press.

Harris, R. Laird, Gleason L. Archer and Bruce Waltke. 1980. *Theological Wordbook of the Old Testament.* Chicago: Moody.

Hattingh, Johan. 1997. "Shell International and the Ogoni People of Nigeria: Toward a Better Understanding of Environmental Justice in Africa." Paper presented at the University of Melbourne, Australia Conference on Environmental Justice, "Global Ethics for the 21st Century," October 1–3.

Hayes, Diane. 1998. "And When We Speak: To Be Black, Catholic, and Womanist." In *Taking Down Our Harps,* ed. Diana L. Hayes and Cyprian Davis, 102–19. Maryknoll, N.Y.: Orbis.

Hays, J. Daniel, and Donald A. Carson. 2003. *From Every People and Nation: A Biblical Theology of Race.* New Studies in Biblical Theology. Downers Grove: InterVarsity.

He, Ning, ed. 1998. *A Commentary of Huai Nan Zi.* Beijing: Chinese Publishing House.

He, Shihua. 2007. *The Three Kings and Five Emperors and the Ancestry of Naxi.* Kunming: Yunnan People's.

He, Zonghua, and Yang Shiku, eds. 1992. *History of Naxi Literature.* Xichuang: Xichuang National Minorities Publication.

Heyndricks, Jerome, ed. 1990. *Philippe Couplet (1623–93): The Man Who Brought China to Europe.* Nettetal: Steyler-Verlag.

Hiebert, Theodore. 1996. "Rethinking Dominion (sic) Theology." *Direction* 25, no. 2: 16–25.

Heiskanen, Markku, and Minna Piispa. 1998. *Faith, Hope, Battering: A Survey of Men's Violence against Women in Finland.* Helsinki: Statistics Finland.

Higgins, Jean M. 1976. "The Myth of Eve: The Temptress." *JAAR* 44, no. 4: 639–47.

Hirsch, Samson Raphael. 1971. *The Pentateuch, Translated and Explained,* 2nd ed. 6 vols., English trans. Isaac Levy. New York: Judaica.

Ho, Craig Y. S. 2006. "The Cross-Textual Method and the J Stories in Genesis in the Light of a Chinese Philosophical Text." In *Congress Volume Leiden 2004,* ed. Andre Lemaire, 419–39. Boston: Brill.

Hooke, S. H. 1976. "Genesis." In *Peake's Commentary on the Bible,* ed. Matthew Black and H. H. Rowley, 175–207. Nairobi: Thomas Nelson.

Huang, Shou Qi, and Tong Sheng Mei. 1998. *A Commentary of Chu Ci.* Taipei: Taiwan Ancient Books.

Hughes, Thomas Patrick. n.d. *A Dictionary of Islam.* Lahore: Premier.

Human Smuggling and Trafficking Center (HSTC). 2005. "Distinctions between Human Smuggling and Human Trafficking." http://www.usdoj .gov/crt/crim/smuggling_trafficking_facts.pdf (accessed September 24, 2008).

Hunt, H. T. 1989. *The Multiplicity of Dreams: Memory, Imagination, and Consciousness.* New Haven: Yale University Press.

Husser, Jean-Marie. 1999. *Dreams and Dream Narratives in the Biblical World.* Trans. Jill M. Munro. Sheffield: Sheffield Academic.

Hyers, Conrad. 1982. "Comedy and Creation." *TT* 39, no. 1 (April): 17–26.

Ibn Ezra, Abraham. 1992. *Nevi'im and Ketubim with all the Commentaries of the Mikraot Gedolot (Orim Gedolim): Commentary on Daniel, Ezra and Nehemiah.* Jerusalem: Even Israel [Heb.].

Idowu, E. B. 1962. *Olodumare God in Yoruba Belief.* London: Longmans.

———. 1969. "Introduction." In *Biblical Revelation and African Beliefs,* ed. K. Dickson and P. Ellingworth. Maryknoll, N.Y.: Orbis.

Ilega, I. Daniel. 2003. "Marriage among the Urhobo." In *Studies in Art, Religion and Culture among the Urhobo and Isoko People,* ed. G. G. Darah, E. S. Ekama, and J. T. Agberia, 113–30. Chobo, Port Harcourt: Pam Unique.

Interfaith Committee for the Support of Protected Persons in Ashraf, Iraq (ICSPPAI). 2008. http://professorfontaine.com/HumanRightsResources .html.

Iran Focus. 2006. "U.S. Cites Iran as Human Trafficking Hub." Iran Focus Web site (June 6), http://www.iranfocus.com/en/index.php?option=com _content&task=view&id=7488 (accessed September 24, 2008).

Isaac, Jacqueline R. 2006. "Here Comes This Dreamer." In *From Babel to Babylon: Essays on Biblical History and Literature in Honor of Brian Peckham,* ed. Joyce Rilett Wood, John E. Harvey, and Mark Leuchter, 237–52. New York: T&T Clark.

Jacobs, Mignon R. 2007. *Gender, Power, and Persuasion: The Genesis Narratives and Contemporary Portraits.* Grand Rapids: Baker Academic.

Jacobsen, Thorkild. 1946. "Mesopotamia." In *The Intellectual Adventure of Ancient Man,* ed. Henri Frankfort et al. Chicago: University of Chicago Press.

Japhet, S. 1989. *The Ideology of the Book of Chronicles and Its Place in Biblical Thought.* Frankfurt am Main: Lang.

Jastrow, M. Jr. 1914. *The Religion of Babylonia and Assyria.* New York: Scribner's Sons.

Jebakani, Jasmine. 2000. "Hagar: The Misery of Rejection." *Black Theology in Britain* 5:33–42.

Jeffery, Anthea J. 1997. *The Natal Story: Sixteen Years of Conflict.* Johannesburg: South African Institute of Race Relations.

Ji, Yun, ed. 1986. *Complete Library in Four Branches of Literature,* 7. Taipei: Commercial.

Jones, Alfred. 1990. *Jones' Dictionary of Old Testament Proper Names.* Grand Rapids: Kregal.

Jung, C. G. 2002. *Dreams.* Trans. R. F. C. Hull; foreword, K. Raine. London: Routledge.

Kalechofsky, Roberta, ed. 1995. *Rabbis and Vegetarianism: An Evolving Tradition.* Marblehead, Mass.: Micah.

———. 1998. *Vegetarian Judaism: A Guide for Everyone.* Marblehead Marblehead, Mass: Micah.

Kappah, J. D., ed. 1981. *Daniel with the Translation and Commentary of Rabbenu Saadia b. Joseph Fayumi [of Blessed Memory].* Jerusalem: Committee to Publish the Works of Saadia Gaon [Heb.].

Kawashima, Robert. 2006. "A Revisionist Reading Revisited: On the Creation of Adam and then Eve." *VT* 56, no. 1: 46–57.

Keel, Othmar. 1998. *Goddesses and Trees, New Moon and Yahweh: Ancient Near Eastern Art and the Hebrew Bible.* JSOTSup 261. Sheffield: Sheffield Academic.

Kelly, Mary B. 1999. *Goddess Embroideries of the Balkan Lands and the Greek Islands.* McLean, N.Y.: StudioBooks.

Klein, Daniel A., ed. 1998. *The Book of Genesis: A Commentary by ShaDal (S. D. Luzzatto).* Northvale, N.J.: Jason Aronson.

King, L. W., trans. 1915. *The Code of Hammurabi.* http://sacred-texts.com/ane/ham/index.htm.

Kirk-Duggan, Cheryl A. 2000. "Hot Buttered Soulful Tunes and Cold Icy Passionate Truths: The Hermeneutics of Biblical Interpolation in R&B (Rhythm and Blues)." In *African Americans and the Bible: Sacred Texts and Social Textures,* ed. Vincent Wimbush, 782–803. New York: Continuum.

Kleiser, Randal. 1980. *Blue Lagoon*. VHS. Sony Pictures, ASIN: 6303451489.

Klopper, F. 2002. "Women, Monotheism and the Gender of God." *IDS* 36:421–37.

Knauf, Ernst Axel. 1983. "Midianites and Ishmaelites." In *Midian, Moab and Edom: The History and Archaeology of Late Bronze and Iron Age Jordan and North-West Arabia*, ed. John F. A. Sawyer and David J. A. Clines, 147–62. JSOTSup 24. Sheffield: JSOT.

———. 1985. *Ismael: Untersuchungen zur Geschichte Palästinas und Nord-arabiens im 1. Jahrtausend v. Chr.* [Ishmael: Studies about the History of Palestine and Northern Arabs in the First Millennium BCE] 2nd ed. Wiesbaden: ADPV.

Knohl, I. 1995. *The Sanctuary of Silence: The Priestly Torah and the Holiness School*. Minneapolis: Fortress Press.

Kook, Abraham Isaac. 1983. *The Vision of Vegetarianism and Peace from a Torah Perspective*. Ed. David Hakohen. Jerusalem: Nezer David [Heb.].

Kramer, Phyllis Silverman. 1998. "The Dismissal of Hagar in Five Art Works of the Sixteenth and Seventeenth Centuries." In *Genesis: A Feminist Companion to the Bible*, ed. A. Brenner, 195–217. Sheffield: Sheffield Academic.

Kramer, S. N. 1970. *The Sumerians*. Chicago: University of Chicago Press.

Kratz, Reinhard Gregor. 2005. *The Composition of the Narrative Books of the Old Testament*. Trans. John Bowden. London: T&T Clark.

Kretzmann, John P., and John McKnight. 1993. *Building Communities from Inside Out: A Path towards Finding and Mobilizing a Community's Assets*. Evanston: Center for Urban Affairs and Policy Research, Northwestern University Press.

Ku Chieh-kang [顧頡剛] and T'ung Shu-yeh [童書業]. 1982. "The Legend of Kun (鯀) and Yu (禹)." In *Debates and Critiques of Ancient History* [《古史辨》] 7, part 11, pp. 142–72. Shanghai: Guji.

Kuhl, C. 1952. "Die 'Wiederaufnahme'—ein literar-kritisches Prinzip?" ["'Resumptive Repetition'—A Literary-Critical Principle?"]. *ZAW* 64:1–11.

Kuntz, J. Kenneth. 1974. *The People of Ancient Israel: An Introduction to Old Testament Literature, History and Thought*. New York: Harper & Row.

Lackner, Michael. 1991. "Jesuit Figurism." In *China and Europe: Images and Influences in the Sixteenth to Eighteenth Centuries,* ed. Thomas H. C. Lee, 129–51. Hong Kong: Chinese University Press.

Lanckau, J. 2006. *Der Herr der Träume: Eine Studie zur Funktion des Traumes in der Josefsgeschichte der hebräischen Bibel* [The Dreamer: A Study of the Function of Dreams in the Joseph Narrative of the Hebrew Bible]. Zurich: Theologischer Verlag Zürich.

Laniado, Samuel. 1996. *Isaiah with the Commentary Keli Paz,* part 1. Jerusalem: Haktav Institute [Heb.].

Lanser, Susan. 1988. "(Feminist) Criticism in the Garden: Inferring Genesis 2–3." *Semeia* 41: 67–84.

Last, Isaac HaLevi, ed. 1905. Joseph Ibn Kaspi, *Tirat kesef (Silver Battlement)* (*Mishneh kesef [Double Portion of Silver],* 1). Pressburg, Slovakia: Alkalay; repr. Jerusalem: Mekorot, 1970 [Heb.].

———. 1906. Joseph Ibn Kaspi, *Mitzraf le-kesef (Refining of Silver)* (*Mishneh kesef,* 2). Pressburg, Slovakia: Alkalay; repr. Jerusalem: Mekorot, 1970 [Heb.].

Latvus, Kari. 2002. *Arjen teologia: Johdatus kontekstuaaliseen raamatuntulkintaan* [Theology of Every Day: Introduction to Contextual Hermeneutics]. Helsinki: Kirjapaja [Fin.].

———. Unpublished. "Reading the Hebrew Bible Poverty Texts: Some Proposals for a Method."

Lau, D. C., trans. 1970. *Mencius.* Middlesex: Penguin.

Lauterbach, Jacob Z., ed. 1933. *Mekilta de-Rabbi Ishmael* [*Mekilta of Rabbi Ishmael*], 2. Philadelphia: Jewish Publication Society of America.

Lavik, Marta Hoyland. 2001. "The 'African' Texts of the Old Testament and Their African Interpretations." In *Interpreting the Old Testament in Africa: Papers from the International Symposium on Africa and the Old Testament in Nairobi, October 1999,* ed. Mary Getui, Knut Holter, and Victor Zinkuratire, 43–53. New York: Lang.

Le Blanc, Charles. 1985. *Huai Nan Tzu: Philosophical Synthesis in Early Han Thought.* Hong Kong: Hong Kong University Press.

Lee, Archie C. C. 1989. "The Dragon, the Deluge and Creation Theology." In *Doing Theology with People's Symbols and Images,* ed. Yeow Choo Lak and John C. England, 101–23. Singapore: The Association for Theological Education in South East Asia.

———. 1993. "Biblical Interpretation in Asian Perspective." *AJT* 7, no. 1: 35–39.

———. 1993a. "Genesis 1 from the Perspective of a Chinese Creation Myth." In *Understanding Poets and Prophets: Essays in Honour of George Wishart Anderson,* ed. A. Graeme Auld, 186–98. Sheffield: JSOT.

———. 1993b. "Theological Reading of Chinese Creation Stories of P'an-ku and Nu Kua." In *Doing Theology with Asian Resources: Ten Years in the Formation of Living Theology in Asia,* ed. John C. England and Archie C. C. Lee, 230–37. Auckland, New Zealand: Pace.

———. 1993c. "The Unity of the Book of Isaiah and Its Cosmogonic Language." *CBQ* 55:1–8.

———. 1994. "The Chinese Creation Myth of Nu Kua and the Biblical Narrative in Genesis 1–11." *BibInt* 2/3: 312–24.

———. 1995. "Death and the Perception of the Divine in *Qohelet* and *Zhuang Zi.*" *Ching Feng* 38, no. 1: 69–81.

———. 1997. *Interpreting the Old Biblical Texts: The Time Meaning of the Old Testament.* Hong Kong: Hong Kong Christian Study Society.

———. 2002. "Cross-textual Interpretation and Its Implications for Biblical Studies." In *Teaching the Bible: Discourses and Politics of Biblical Pedagogy,* ed. Fernando F. Segovia and Mary Ann Tolbert, 247–54. Maryknoll, N.Y.: Orbis.

———. 2005. "Asians Encountering Jesus Christ: A Chinese Reading of Jesus in the Wisdom Matrix." *Quest: An Interdisciplinary Journal for Asian Christian Scholars* 4, no. 1: 41–62.

———. 2008. "Cross-textual Hermeneutics and Identity in Multi-textual Asia." In *Christian Theology in Asia: Emerging Forms and Themes,* ed. Sebastian Kim, 179–204. Cambridge: Cambridge University Press.

Lee, Boyung. 2007. "When the Text Is the Problem: A Postcolonial Approach to Biblical Pedagogy." *RelEd* 102, no. 1: 44–61.

Levin, Christoph. 1993. *Der Jahwist.* FRLANT 157. Göttingen: Vandenhoeck & Ruprecht.

———. 2007. "The Yahwist: The Earliest Editor in Pentaeuch." *JBL* 126:209–30.

Lewis Herman, J. 1992. *Trauma and Recovery.* New York: Basic.

Li, Fengmao [李豐楙]. 2004. *A Glimpse into Baopuzi: Quest for Immortality* [《抱朴子快读: 不死的探求》]. Haikou: Hainan.

Li, Lin-ts'an, ed. 1957. *Translations and Annotations of Mo-so Classics.* Taipei: China Series Publishing Committee.

Li, Shuping. 2002. "The Role and Function of 'Dream' in Handanji and Nankeji." *Journal of Fujian Institute of Education* 4:26–28 [Chin.].

Li, Wai-yee. 1999. "Dreams of Interpretation in Early Chinese Historical and Philosophical Writings." In Shulman and Stroumsa 1999: 17–42.

Liao, W. K., trans. 1959. *The Complete Works of Han Fei Zi.* London: Arthur Probsthain.

Lincan, Li, Zhang Kun, and He Cai. 1957. *Translations and Annotations of Mo-so Classics in Six Volumes.* Taipei: Zhonghua Cong Shu.

Lipton, Diana. 1999. *Revisions of the Night: Politics and Promises in the Patriarchal Dreams of Genesis.* Sheffield: Sheffield Academic.

Liu, Ts'u Yan. 1962. *Buddhist and Taoist Influences on Chinese Novels.* Wiesbaden: Kommisociousverlag.

Lockyer, Herbert. 1958. *All the Men of the Bible.* London: Pickering & Inglis.

Long, Asphodel. 1996. "Asherah, The Tree of Life and the Menorah." http://www.asphodel-long.com/html/asherah.html. Repr. in *Patriarchs, Prophets and Other Villains*, ed. Lisa Isherwood. Gender, Theology and Spirituality. London: Equinox, 2007.

Lou, Weiqun, and Lo Jiayong, eds. 2008. *Migrant Women from China: Annual Gender Role Workshop 2008.* Hong Kong: Hong Kong Institute of Asia-Pacific Studies.

Loubser, J. A. 1987. *The Apartheid Bible: A Critical Review of Racial Theology in South Africa.* Cape Town: Maskew Miller Longman.

Löw, Judah ben Bezalel. 1972. *Be'er ha-golah* [*Well of the Exile*]. Jerusalem: [Heb.].

Lu, Hsun. 1979. *Old Tales Retold.* Beijing: People's Literature.

Lukhero, M. B. 1985. *Ngoni Nc'wala Ceremony.* Lusaka: National Educational Company.

Luntshitz, Shlomo Ephraim, ed. Avraham Rabinovitch. 2001. *Keli yaqar hashalem 'al ha-Torah* [*Precious Vessel (Com. on the Pentateuch)*]. Jerusalem: Orot Hayim [Heb.].

Luo, Zhu Feng. 1998. *Chinese Dictionary Concise Edition.* Vol. 1. Shanghai: Chinese Dictionary Publication House of Zambia.

Lust, John. 1987. *Western Books on China Published up to 1850 in the Library of SOAS.* London: Bamboo.

Lzo Zi. 1982. *Tao Te Ching.* Trans. D. C. Lau. Hong Kong: Chinese University Press.

Major, John S. 1993. *Heaven and Earth in Early Han Thought: Chapters Three, Four, and Five of the Huai Nan Zi.* Albany: State University of New York Press.

Malbim (Meir Leibush ben Yechiel Michel). 1992. *Nevi'im and Ketubim [Prophets and Writings] with all the commentaries of the Mikraot Gedolot (Orim Gedolim), Commentary on Daniel, Ezra and Nehemiah.* Jerusalem: Even Israel [Heb.].

———. 2008. *Commentary on the Torah,* vol. 1: *Genesis.* Jerusalem: Horev. [Heb.].

Malina, Bruce J. 1993. *The New Testament World: Insights from Cultural Anthropology.* Louisville: Westminster John Knox. Western Books on China published up to 1850 in the Library of SOAS.

Malul, M. 2002. *Knowledge, Control and Sex: Studies in Biblical Thought, Culture and Worldview.* Tel Aviv/Jaffa: Archaeological Center.

Martikainen, Tuomas, and Marja Tiilikainen, eds. 2007. *Maahanmuutta-janaiset: Kotoutuminen, perhe ja työ* [Immigrant Women: Integration, Family and Work]. Väestöliitto. Väestöntutkimuslaitoksen julkaisusarja D 46/2007. Helsinki [Fin.].

Mbiti, J. S. 1970. *Concepts of God in Africa.* London: SPCK.

McCray, Walter Arthur. 1990. *The Black Presence in the Bible and the Table of Nations.* Chicago: Black Light Fellowship.

McKenzie, J. L. 1954. "The Literary Characteristic of Genesis 2–3." *TS* 15:491–572.

McKeown, James. 2008. *Genesis.* Grand Rapids: Eerdmans.

McKinley, Judith E. 1996. *Gendering Wisdom the Host: Biblical Invitations to Eat and Drink.* JSOTSup 216. Sheffield: Sheffield Academic.

Means, Sterling M. 1948. *Black Egypt and Her Negro Pharaohs.* Repr. Baltimore, Md.: Black Classic, 1978. (Orig. pub. as *Ethiopia and the Missing Link in African History.*)

Meng Zi. 1970. *Mencius.* Trans. D. C. Lau. New York: Penguin.

Mesters, Carlos. 1989. *Defenseless Flower: A New Reading of the Bible.* Maryknoll: Orbis.

Meyers, Carol L. 1976. *The Tabernacle Menorah.* Missoula, Mont.: Scholars.

Meyers, Carol. 1988. *Discovering Eve: Ancient Israelite Women in Context.* New York: Oxford University Press.

Middleton, J. R. M. 2005. *The Liberating Image: The* Imago Dei *in Genesis 1.* Grand Rapids, Mich.: Brazos.

Miller, Arthur. 1996. "Adam and Eve." In *Genesis: As It Is Written; Contemporary Writers on Our First Stories,* ed. David Rosenberg, 37. San Francisco: Harper San Francisco.

Miller, Lucien, ed. 1994. *South of the Clouds: Tales from Yunnan.* Seattle: University of Washington Press.

Moghadam, Valentine M. 2005. "The 'Feminization of Poverty' and Women's Human Rights." SHS Papers in Women's Studies/Gender Research, no. 2 (July). UNESCO http://portal.unesco.org (accessed September 1, 2008).

Mokhtar, G. 1990. "Introduction." In *General History of Africa,* vol. 2, *Ancient Civilizations of Africa,* ed. G. Mokhtar. Los Angeles: University of California Press.

Moore, S. D. 1996. "Gigantic God: Yahweh's Body." *JSOT* 70:87–115.

Moyers, Bill. 1996. *Genesis: A Living Conversation.* New York: Doubleday.

Mungello, David E. 2005. *The Great Encounter of China and the West, 1500-1800.* Lanham, Md.: Rowman & Littlefield.

Munk, Eliyahu, trans. 2001. *Akeydat Yitzchak: Commentary of Rabbi Yitzchak Arama on the Torah.* Jerusalem: Lambda.

Newendorp, Nicole. 2008. *Uneasy Reunions: Immigration, Citizenship, and Family Life in Post-1997 Hong Kong.* Stanford: Stanford University Press.

Ngada, N. H., and K. E. Mofokeng. 2001. *African Christian Witness: The Movement of the Spirit in African Indigenous Churches.* Pietermaritzburg. Cluster.

Niditch, Susan. 1998. "Genesis." In *The Women's Bible Commentary, Expanded Edition,* ed. Carol A. Newsom and Sharon H. Ringe, 13–29. Louisville, Ky.: Westminster John Knox.

Noebel, D. A. 1999. *Understanding the Times: The Religious Worldviews in Our Day and the Search for Truth.* Eugene: Harvest House.

Nolan, Albert. 1996. "Work, the Bible, Workers, and Theologians: Elements of a Workers' Theology." *Semeia* 73:213–20.

Noth, Martin. 1972. *A History of Pentateuchal Traditions.* Trans. B. W. Anderson. London: Prentice Hall.

Obi, C. A. 2006. "Biblical Perspective on Suffering in African Context." *African Journal of Biblical Studies* 22, no. 1: 91–122.

Odje, S. J. 1995. *Kokori People: Ancient and Modern*. Benin: Assembly Printers.

Oduyoye, Mercy Amba. 2003. *Daughters of Anowa*. New York: Orbis.

Olley, John. 2000. "Mixed Blessings for Animals: The Contrast of Genesis 9." In Habel and Wurst 2000: 2:130–39.

Olyan, S. M. 1988. *Asherah and the Cult of Yahweh in Israel*. Atlanta: Scholars.

Onyewuenyi, I. 1991. "Is There an African Philosophy?" In *African Philosophy: The Essential Readings*. New York: Paragon.

Oren, Eliezer D. 1997a. *The Hyksos: New Historical and Archaeological Perspectives*. Philadelphia: University Museum, University of Pennsylvania Press.

———. 1997b. "The Hyksos Enigma: Introductory Overview." In *The Hyksos: New Historical and Archaeological Perspectives*, ed. Eliezer D. Oren, xix–xxvi. University Museum Monograph 96. Philadelphia: University of Pennsylvania Press.

Otite, Onigu. 1993. "A Profile of Urhobo." In *Some Nigerian Peoples,* ed. W. Bassey, A. Andah, Ikechukwu Okpoko, and C. A. Folorunso, 195–212. Ibadan: Rex Charles.

Ovie-Whisky, V. E. 1975. "Some Aspects of the Law of Domestic Relations in Nigeria." In *African Indigenous Laws: Proceedings of Workshop,* ed. T. O. Elias, S. N. Nwabara, and C. O. Akpamgbo, 137–44. Nsukka: Institute of African Studies, University of Nigeria, Nsukka.

Oyediran, Oyeleye. 1979. *Policy-Making in the Nigerian Political System*. Research Report. Ibadan: University Press.

Pardes, I. 1992. *Countertraditions in the Bible*. Cambridge, Mass.: Harvard University Press.

Patte, Daniel, et al., eds. 2004. *Global Bible Commentary*. Nashville: Abingdon.

Patte, Daniel, Teresa Okure, et al. 2005. *Global Bible Commentary*. Nashville: Abingdon.

Parry-Davis, D. 2004. *The Enviropaedia*. Simonstown, South Africa: Ecologic.

Penner, Todd, and Caroline Vander Stichele, eds. 2005. *Her Master's Tools? Feminist and Postcolonial Engagements of Historical-Critical Discourse*. Global Perspectives on Biblical Scholarship. Atlanta: SBL.

Philpott, Graham. 1993. *Jesus Is Tricky and God Is Undemocratic: The Kin-Dom of God in Amawoti*. Pietermaritzburg: Cluster.

Piispa, Minna, Markku Heiskanen, Juha Kääriäinen, and Reino Sirén. 2005. *Naisiin kohdistunut väkivalta* [Violence against Women]. OPTL: N Julkaisuja. Publications of the National Research Institute of Legal Policy, 225 [Fin.]. Helsinki.

Pirson, Ron. 2002. *The Lord of the Dreams: A Semantic and Literary Analysis of Genesis 37–50.* Sheffield: Sheffield Academic.

Polak, F. 1994. *Biblical Narrative: Aspects of Art and Design.* Jerusalem: Mosad Bialik, [Heb.].

Poole, Edward Stanley. 1981. "Hagar." In *Smith's Dictionary of the Bible,* ed. H. B. Hackett, 2:977–78. Grand Rapids: Baker.

Preuss, Horst Dietrich. 1982. *Deuteronomium.* Ertäge der Forschung 164, Darmsadt: Wissenschaftliche Buchgesellschaft.

Primavesi, Anne 2000. "Ecology." In *The Oxford Companion to Christian Thought,* ed. A. Hastings. Oxford: Oxford University Press.

Pritchard, James B., ed. 1961. *Ancient Near Eastern Texts Relating to the Old Testament,* 3rd ed. Princeton: Princeton University Press.

Pritchard, James Bennet, and W. F. Albright. 1969. *Ancient Near Eastern Texts Relating to the Old Testament.* Princeton, N.J.: Princeton University Press.

Qu Yuan [屈原]. 1959. "Tian Wen" [天問, The Heavenly Questions]. In *The Songs of the South,* trans. and ed. David Hawkes. Oxford: Clarendon.

Rashkow, Ilona N. 1993. *The Phallacy of Genesis: A Feminist-Psychoanalytic Approach.* Louisville: Westminster John Knox.

Rathbone, Mark. 2006. "Interaction of Scholarly and Non-Scholarly Readings of Genesis 11:1-9 in the South African Context." D.Th. diss., University of Stellenbosch.

Rawlinson, George. 1875. *History of Herodotus,* Book I. Trans. H. Rawlinson, with Essay VI in its appendix. 3rd ed. London: John Murray.

Read, Margaret. 1956. *The Ngoni of Nyasaland.* New York: Holt, Rinehart & Winston.

Redford, D. B. 1970. *A Study of the Biblical Story of Joseph.* VTSup 20. Leiden: Brill.

Reis, Pamela Tamarkin. 2000. "Hagar Requited." *JSOT* 87:75–109.

Rendtorff, Rolf. 1990. *The Problem of the Process of Transmission in the Pentateuch.* Sheffield: JSOT.

Rhoads, David, et al., eds. 2005. *From Every People and Nation: The Book of Revelation in Intercultural Perspective.* Minneapolis: Augsburg Fortress.

Rimmon-Kenan, S., ed. 1987. *Discourse in Psychoanalysis and Literature*. London: Methuen.

Rodriguez, Junius P., ed. 1997. *The Historical Encyclopedia of World Slavery*. Santa Barbara: ABC-CLIO.

Rofé, Alexander. 1985. "The Laws of Warfare in the Book of Deuteronomy: Their Origin, Intent and Positivity." *JSOT* 32:23–44.

Rogers, Dan. 1998. "The Evidence of Black People in the Bible." Worldwide News (Grace Communion International [formerly Worldwide Church of God]), available at http:www.wcg.org (accessed September 22, 2003).

Rooke, D. W., ed. 2009. *Embroidered Garments: Priests and Gender in Biblical Israel*. Sheffield: Sheffield Phoenix.

Rosenbaum, M., and A. M. Silbermann, eds. 1973. *Pentateuch with Rashi's Commentary*, 5 vols. Jerusalem: Silbermann.

Rosenblatt, Samuel, ed. 1948. *Saadia Gaon: The Book of Beliefs and Opinions*. Trans. from Arabic and Hebrew Samuel Rosenblatt. New Haven: Yale University Press.

Rousselle, A. 1988. *Porneia: On Desire and the Body in Antiquity*. Oxford: Basil Blackwell.

Rowland, Christopher. 1999. "Introduction: The Theology of Liberation." In *The Cambridge Companion to Liberation Theology*, ed. Christopher Rowland. Cambridge: Cambridge University Press.

Ruether, R. R. 1982. "Feminism and Patriarchal Religion: Principles of Ideological Critique of the Bible." *JSOT* 22, no. 1: 54–66.

Runzo, J. M. N., and A. Sharma, eds. 2003. *Human Rights and Responsibilities*. Oxford: Oneworld.

Ryan, William, and Walter Pitman. 2000. *Noah's Flood: The New Scientific Discoveries about the Event That Changed History*. New York: Simon & Schuster.

Rycroft, C. 1972. *A Critical Dictionary of Psychoanalysis*. London: Penguin.

Sanders, Edith R. 1969. "The Hamitic Hypothesis: Its Origin and Functions in Time Perspective." *Journal of African History* 10, no. 4: 521–32.

Sanford, John A. 1968. *Dreams: God's Forgotten Language*. Philadelphia: Lippincott.

Sawyer, D. F. 2002. *God, Gender and the Bible*. London: Routledge.

Schebesta, P. 1936. *Revisiting my Pygmy Hosts*. London: Hutchinson.

Schochet, E. J. 1984. *Animal Life in Jewish Tradition: Attitudes and Relation-ships*. New York: Ktav.

Schrey, H. H. 1979. "Ist Gott ein Mann: zur Forderung einer feministischen Theologie." *TRu* 44:227–38.

Schroer, S., and T. Staubli. 2001. *Body Symbolism in the Bible*. Collegeville, Minn.: Liturgical.

Schroer, Silvia. 1987. *In Israel gab es Bilder: Nachrichten von darstellender Kunst im Alten Testament*. OBO. Freiburg: Universitätsverlag.

———. 2005. *Die Ikonographie Palästinas/Israels und der alte Orient: Eine Religionsgeschichte in Bildern*. Vol. 1, *Vom Ausgehenden Mesolithikum bis zur Fruehbronzezeit*. Freiburg: Universitätsverlag.

———. Ed. 2008. *Images and Gender: Contributions to the Hermeneutics of Reading Ancient Art*. Freiburg (CH)/ Göttingen: Freiburg Universitätsverlag.

Schuele, A. 2005. "Made in the Image of God: The Concept of Divine Images in Genesis 1–3." *ZAW* 117: 1-20.

Schwartz, Richard H. 1988. *Judaism and Vegetarianism*. Marblehead, Mass.: Micah.

Scott, James C. 1990. *Domination and the Arts of Resistance: Hidden Transcripts*. New Haven: Yale University Press.

Segovia, Fernando F., ed. 1995. *Reading from This Place*. Vol. 1, *Social Location and Biblical Interpretation in the United States*. Minneapolis: Augsburg Fortress.

Segovia, Fernando F., and Mary Ann Tolbert, eds. 2000. *Reading from This Place*. Vol. 2, *Social Location and Biblical Interpretation in Global Perspective*. Minneapolis: Augsburg Fortress. (Orig. pub. 1995.)

———. eds. 2004. *Teaching the Bible: The Discourses and Politics of Biblical Pedagogy*. Repr. Eugene, Ore.: Wipf & Stock. (Orig. pub. 1997.)

Shadyac, Tom. 2007. *Evan Almighty*. DVD. Universal Studios: ASIN: B000UNYK4E.

Shavel, H. D., ed. 1996. *Perushey ha-tora le-rabenu moshe ben nahman* [The commentary on the Pentateuch by our rabbi Nachmanides]. Jerusalem: Mossad Harav Kook [Heb.].

Shemesh, Yael. 2008. "Compassion for Animals in Midrashic Literature and Traditional Biblical Exegesis." *Studies in Bible and Exegesis* 8:677–99 [Heb.].

Shi, Junchao. 1995. "The Flood and Symbolism of the Gourd (〈洪水與葫蘆的象征系統〉)." *Forum on Folk Culture* 1:30–41.

Shulman, David, and Guy G. Stroumsa, eds. 1999. *Dream Cultures: Explorations in the Comparative History of Dreaming.* New York: Oxford University Press.

Simoons, Frederick J. 1994. *Eat Not This Flesh: Food Avoidances from Prehistory to the Present.* 2nd ed. Madison: University of Wisconsin Press.

Simopoulos, Nicole M. 2007. "Who Was Hagar? Mistress, Divorcée, Exile, or Exploited Worker: An Analysis of Contemporary Grassroots Readings of Genesis 16 by Caucasian, Latina, and Black South African Women." In *Reading Other-wise: Socially Engaged Biblical Scholars Reading with Their Local Communities,* ed. Gerald O. West, 63–72. Semeia Studies 62. Atlanta: SBL.

Simpson, Cuthbert. 1952. "Genesis." In *IB,* ed. George Arthur Buttrick et al., 1:465–829. Nashville: Abingdon.

Sliw, Yitzchok. 1993. "Meat: The Issues; An Analysis of Vegetarianism in the Light of Biblical, Talmudic and Rabbinic Teachings," *Le'Ela* 36:25–29.

Smart, J. D. 1952. *The Old Testament in Dialogue with Modern Man.* Philadelphia: Westminster.

Smart, Ninian. 1992. *The World's Religions: Old Traditions and Modern Transformations.* Cambridge: Cambridge University Press.

Smith, M. A. 1987. "God Male and Female in the Old Testament: Yahweh and His 'Asherah.'" *TS* 48:333–40.

Smith, Mark S. 1990. *The Early History of God: Jahweh and the Other Deities in Ancient Israel.* San Francisco: Harper & Row.

Spangler, Ann, and Jean E. Syswerda. 1999. *Women of the Bible.* Grand Rapids: Zondervan.

Speiser, E. A. 1979. *Genesis.* Anchor Bible 1; Garden City, N.Y.: Doubleday.

———. 1986. *Genesis.* New York: Doubleday. (Orig. pub. 1964.)

Sproul, Robert Charles, ed. 1995. *New Geneva Study Bible.* Nashville: Nelson.

Steiner, Franz. 1954. "Enslavement and the Early Hebrew Lineage System: An Explanation of Genesis 47:29-31." *Man* 54:73–75.

Sternberg, M. 1987. *The Poetics of Biblical Narrative: Ideological Literature and the Drama of Reading.* Bloomington: Indiana University Press.

Streng, Frederick J. 1976. *Understanding Religious Life,* 2nd ed. Belmont, Calif.: Wadsworth.

Strickman, H. Norman, trans. and annot. 1995. *The Secret of the Torah: A Translation of Abraham Ibn Ezra's Sefer Yesod Mora Ve-Sod Ha-Torah.* Northvale, N.J.: Aronson.

Strickman, H. Norman, and Arthur M. Silver, trans. and annot. 1988. *Ibn Ezra's Commentary on the Pentateuch.* Vol. 1. *Genesis [BERESHIT].* New York: Menorah.

———. 1996. *Ibn Ezra's Commentary on the Pentateuch.* Vol. 2. *Exodus [SHEMOT].* New York: Menorah.

Stuhlmueller, Carroll. 1970. *Creative Redemption in Deutero-Isaiah.* Rome: Biblical Institute.

Sudarkasa, Niara. 2005. "The Status of Women in Indigenous African Societies." In *Gender in Africa,* ed. Andrea Cornwall, 25–31. London: International African Institute.

Sugirtharajah, R. S. 2002. *Postcolonial Criticism and Biblical Interpretation.* Oxford: Oxford University Press.

Sutskover, T. 2007. "The Semantic Field of Seeing and Oral Communication in the Joseph Narrative." *JNSL* 33, no. 2: 33–50.

Tamez, Elsa, Sun Ai Park, et al. 1983. "Worship Service: This Hour of History." In *Irruption of the Third World: Challenge to Theology,* ed. Virginia Fabella and Sergio Torres, 181–87. Maryknoll, N.Y.: Orbis.

Tao, Yang, and Xiu Zhong. 1989. *Chinese Creation Myths.* Shanghai: Shanghai People's.

Taylor, P. Olive. 1975. "The Position of Women under Sierra Leone Customary Family Law." In *African Indigenous Laws: Proceedings of Workshop,* ed. T. O. Elias, S. N. Nwabara, and C. O. Akpamgbo, 195–231. Nsukka: Institute of African Studies, University of Nigeria, Nsukka.

Thompson, John L. 1997. "Hagar, Victim or Villain? Three Sixteenth-Century Views." *CBQ* 59:213–33.

Thompson, Stith. 1993. *Motif-Index of Folk-Literature: A Classification of Narrative Elements in Folk Tales, Ballads, Myths, Fables, Medieval Romances, Exempla, Fabliaux, Jest Books and Local Legends.* Bloomington, Ind.: University of Indiana Press.

Thompson, Thomas L. 1974. *The Historicity of Patriarchal Narratives: The Quest for the Historical Abraham.* BZAW 133. Berlin: de Gruyter.

Towner, W. Sibley. 1996. "The Future of Nature." *Interpretation* 50:27–35.

———. 2001. *Genesis.* Louisville: Westminster John Knox.

Trible, Phyllis. 1973. "Depatriarchalizing in Biblical Interpretation." *JAAR* 41:30–48.

———. 1978. *God and the Rhetoric of Sexuality.* OBT. Philadelphia: Fortress Press.

———. 1984. *Texts of Terror: Literary-Feminist Readings of Biblical Narratives.* Philadelphia: Fortress Press.

———. 1988. *God en Sekse-Gebonden Taalgebruik* [God and Sexual Language]. Hilversum: Gooi & Sticht.

———. 2006. "Ominous Beginnings for a Promise of Blessing." In *Hagar, Sarah and Their Children: Jewish, Christian, and Muslim Perspectives,* ed. Phyllis Trible and Letty M. Russell, 33–69. Louisville: Westminster John Knox.

Trible, Phyllis, and Letty M. Russell, eds. 2006. *Hagar, Sarah and Their Children: Jewish, Christian, and Muslim Perspectives.* Louisville: Westminster John Knox.

Tutu, Desmond. 1983. "Christianity and Apartheid." In *Apartheid Is a Heresy,* ed. John W. de Gruchy and Charles Villa-Vicencio, 39–47. Cape Town: David Philip.

Ubrurhe, J. O. 2003. "Polygyny and African Christianity: The Urhobo Experience." In *Studies in Art, Religion and Culture among the Urhobo and Isoko People,* ed. D. G. Darah, E. S. Ekama, and J. T. Agberia, 100–112. Chobo, Port Harcourt: Pam Unique.

Uittenbogaard, Arie. 2009. "Meaning, Origin and Etymology of the Name Noah." Abarim Publications' Biblical Name Vault, www.abarim-publications.com/Meaning/Noah.html (accessed May 14, 2009).

United Nations Commission on the Status of Women (UNCSW). 2008. http://www.un.org/womenwatch/daw/csw/ (accessed September 29, 2008).

United Nations Economic and Social Commission for Asia and the Pacific (ESCAP). 2003. *Combating Human Trafficking in Asia: A Resource Guide to International and Regional Legal Instruments, Political Commitments and Recommended Practices.* http://www.unescap.org/esid/GAD/Publication/index.asp.

United Nations Educational, Scientific and Cultural Organization (UNESCO). 2008. "Data Comparison of Trafficking Estimates." http://www.unescobkk.org/index.php?id=1963 (accessed September 29, 2008).

United Nations Office of Drugs and Crime (UNODC). "UNODC Launches Global Initiative to Fight Human Trafficking." n.d. http://www.unodc .org/newsletter/en/perspectives/no03/page009.html (accessed September 29, 2008).

United Nations Population Fund (UNFPA). 2007. *State of World Population 2007: Unleashing the Potential of Urban Growth.* http://www.unfpa.org (accessed October 1, 2008).

Usry, Glenn, and Craig S. Keener. 1996. *Black Man's Religion.* Downers Grove, Ill.: InterVarsity.

Uwane, Henry, Personal Interview, April 15, 2004.

Van Heerden, W. 2005. "Norman Habel se Interpretasie van Genesis 1:1— 2:4a binne die Raamwerk van die Earth Bible Project" ["Norman Habel's Interpretation of Genesis 1:1—2:4a within the Framework of the Earth Bible Project"]. *OTE* 18, no. 2: 371–93.

van Huyssteen, J. W. 2004. *Alone in the World? Human Uniqueness in Science and Theology.* Cambridge: Eerdmans.

Van Kley, Edwin J. 1971. "Europe's 'Discovery' of China and the Writing of World History." *American Historical Review* 76: 358–85.

Van Seters, John. 1975. *Abraham in History and Tradition.* New Haven, Conn.: Yale University Press.

———. 1992. *Prologue to History: The Yahwist as Historian in Genesis.* Louisville: Westminster John Knox.

———. 1999. *The Pentateuch: A Social-Science Commentary.* Trajectories 1. Sheffield: Sheffield Academic. Repr. 2004.

———. 2007. "Law of the Hebrew Slave: A Continuing Debate." *ZAW* 119:169–83.

Van Till, H. J. 1990. *Portraits of Creation: Biblical and Scientific Perspectives on the World's Formation.* Grand Rapids: Eerdmans.

Van Wolde, Ellen J. 1989. *A Semiotic Analysis of Genesis 2¬3: A Semiotic Theory and Method of Analysis Applied to the Story of the Garden of Eden.* Studia Semitica Neerlandica. Maastricht, The Netherlands: Van Gorcum/Assen.

———. 2000. "The Earth Story as Presented by the Tower of Babel Narrative." In *The Earth Story in Genesis,* ed. N. C. Habel and S. Wurst, 147–76. Sheffield: Sheffield Academic.

Veijola, Timo. 1972. *Das 5. Buch Mose: Deuteronomium. Kapitel 1,1—16,17.* ATD 8, no. 1. Göttingen: Vandenhoeck & Ruprecht.

Venter, P. P. 2006. "Vroulikheid by die Skeppergod? 'n Liggaamskritiese Ontleding van geselekteerde Skeppingstekste in die Ou Testament" ["Femininity within God the Creator: A Body Critical Analysis of Selected Texts of Creation in the Old Testament"]. D. Litt. et Phil. thesis, University of Johannesburg.

Von Rad, Gerhard. 1966. *The Problem of the Hexateuch, and Other Essays.* Trans. E. W. Trueman Dicken. New York: McGraw-Hill.

———. 1972. *Genesis: A Commentary,* rev. ed. Philadelphia: Westminster.

———. 1972. *Das Erste Buch Mose: Genesis.* ATD 2/4, 9, rev. ed. Göttingen: Vandenhoeck & Ruprecht.

Vorster, J. N. 2002. "A Rhetoric of the Body, Praxis and Wisdom." Unpublished Lecture at the OTSSA Annual Congress in Stellenbosch, 2000.

Vos, Geerhardus. 1975. *Biblical Theology.* Edinburgh: Banner of Trust.

Walker, Alice. 1983. *In Search of Our Mother's Gardens: Womanist Prose.* New York: Harcourt Brace Jovanovich.

Wallace, H. N. 1985. *The Eden Narrative.* Atlanta: Scholars.

Waltke, Bruce. 1995. "The Role of Women in Worship in the Old Testament." Peninsula Bible Church (Palo Alto, Calif.) http://www.raystedman .org/misc/waltke.html.

Waters, W. John. 1991. "Who Was Hagar?" In Felder 1991: 187–205.

Watson, Burton. 1963. *Mo Tzu, Basic Writings.* New York: Columbia University Press.

Webb, S. H. 1996. "Ecology vs. the Peaceable Kingdom." *Sounding* 79:239–52.

Wegerif, Marc, Bev Russell, and Irma Grunding. 2005. *Still Searching for Security: The Reality of Farm Dweller Evictions in South Africa.* Polokwane North: Nkuzi Development Association.

Weiser, Asher, ed. 1976. *R. Abraham Ibn Ezra's Torah Commentaries,* 2. Jerusalem: Mosad Harav Kook [Heb.].

Wellhausen, Julius. 1899. *Die Composition des Hexateuchs und der historischen Bücher des Alten Testaments* ["The Composition of the Hexateuch and Historical Books of the Old Testament"]. 4th ed. Berlin: de Gruyter, 1963.

Wen, Yi Duo. 1947. *Yi Duo Wen's Complete Works.* Beijing: SDX Joint.

Wenham, Gordon J. 1987. *Genesis 1–15.* WBC 1. Waco, Tex.: Word.

———. 1994. *Genesis 16–50.* WBC 2. Dallas: Word.

Wenwaipo. 2005. http://paper.wenweipo.com/2005/12/28/CF0512280005
.htm (accessed November 10, 2008 [Chin.]).

Wesley, Arun Kumar. 2003. "Mere Frivolity: An Analysis of Humour for a
Theological Enterprise." *AJT* 17 (April): 156–96.

West, Gerald O. 2003. *The Academy of the Poor: Towards a Dialogical Reading
of the Bible*. Pietermaritzburg: Cluster.

———. 2006. "Contextual Bible Reading: A South African Case Study."
Analecta Bruxellensia 11:131–48.

———. 2009. "The Not So Silent Citizen: Hearing Embodied Theology in
the Context of HIV and AIDS in South Africa." In *Heterotopic Citizen:
New Research on Religious Work for the Disadvantaged*, ed. Trygve Wyller,
23–42. Göttingen: Vandenhoeck & Ruprecht.

Westermann, Claus. 1969. *Isaiah 40–66*. Philadelphia: Westminster.

———. 1981. *Genesis*. Biblisher Kommentar I/2. Neukirchen-Vluyn:
Neukirchener.

———. 1984. *Genesis 1–11: A Commentary*. Trans. John J. Scullion. Minneapolis: Augsburg.

———. 1987. *Genesis 37–50: A Commentary*. Trans. J. J. Scullion. London:
SPCK.

Westrich, E. 2003–04. "Levirate Marriage in the State of Israel: Ethnic
Encounter and the Challenge of a Jewish State." *Israel Law Review* 37,
nos. 2–3: 427–500.

White, Lynn. 1967. "The Historical Roots of Our Ecological Crisis." *Science*
155, no. 3767: 1203–1207.

Williams, Delores. 1993. *Sisters in the Wilderness: The Challenge of Womanist
God-Talk*. Maryknoll, N.Y.: Orbis.

Women Advancing Freedom and Equality (WAFE). www.wafe-women.org
(accessed September 29, 2008).

Women's United Nations Report Network (WUNRN). 2008a. "Preference
for Boys." http://www.wunrn.com/factual/aspects/fa1.htm (accessed
September 29, 2008).

———. 2008b. WUNRN http://www.wunrn.com/ (accessed September
29, 2008).

Wright, Christopher H. J. 1990. *God's People in God's Land*. Grand Rapids:
Eerdmans.

Wybrow, C. 1991. *The Bible, Baconianism and Mastery over Nature: The Old Testament and Its Misreading.* New York: Lang.

Xixi. 1979. *Wo Cheng.* Hong Kong: Suye.

———. 1996. *Feizhan* [The Flying Carpet]. Taipei: Hongfan.

Yakubu, M. G. 1985. *Land Law in Nigeria.* London: Macmillan.

Yang, Kuan. 2003. "Four Seasons God Idols of Chu Bo Shu and Its Creation Myths." In *Kuan Yang's Selected Essays on Ancient History.* Shanghai: Shanghai People's.

Yee, Gale A. 2003. *Poor Banished Children of Eve: Women as Evil in the Hebrew Bible.* Minneapolis: Fortress Press.

Yu, David. 1981. "The Creation Myth and Its Symbolism in Classical Taoism." *Philosophy East and West* 31:481.

Yuan, Ke. 1998a. *Chinese Myths and Tales.* Beijing: People's Literature.

———. 1998b. *A Commentary of Shan Hai Jing.* Taipei: Taiwan Ancient Books.

Yui, Zheng Jiali. 2008. "Keynote Address: An Overall Review of New Immigrant Women." In Lou and Lo 2008: 4-8.

Yusuf Ali, A., trans. and com. 1934. *The Holy Qur'an.* Lahore: Islamic Propagation Centre International.

Zheng, Yanling. 2008. "The Mundane Content and Intellectuals' Sentiment in Handan Dream." *Journal of Hebei University of Science & Technology (Social Sciences)* 8, no. 2: 66–70 [Chin.].

Zucker, Moshe, ed. 1984. *Saadya's Commentary on Genesis, with Introduction, Translation and Notes.* New York: Jewish Theological Seminary of America [Heb.].

Zulu, Edwin. 1999. "A Ngoni Assessment of the Role of Ancestors within Ancient Israelite World Views and Religion in Genesis 11:28—50:1-26." Doctoral thesis, University of Stellenbosch.

CONTRIBUTORS

David Tuesday Adamo is Professor of Religion in the Department of Philosophy and Religious Studies and Deputy Vice Chancellor at Kogi State University, Anyigba, Kogi State, Nigeria. He has published books including *Africa and Africans in the Old Testament, Africa and Africans in the New Testament,* and *Biblical Interpretation in African Perspective,* and articles including "The Problem of Translating the Hebrew Old Testament Book Titles into Yoruba Language of Nigeria," "Psalm 109 in African Context," "The African Wife of Moses," "The African Queen," "The Concept of Peace in the Old Testament and in Africa," "Ancient Africa and Genesis 3," "African Cultural Hermeneutics," and "The Black Prophet in the Old Testament."

Amadi Ahiamadu trained as a political scientist in the late 1970s and 1980s before converting to the Reformed Faith. Since then, he has served as ordained minister of the Reformed Church in Nigeria. His theological training began from the grassroots in Nigeria and continued at the University of Stellenbosch, South Africa, where he completed his research on biblical stewardship with a special focus on land ownership and use in Nigeria. He is currently Lecturer in Old Testament and African Religion and Culture at the Department of Religious and Cultural Studies, University of Port Harcourt, Nigeria. His two books, *Responsible and Accountable Stewardship* and *Biblical Hermeneutics,* are nearing completion.

Yairah Amit is Professor of Biblical Studies in the Department of Hebrew Culture Studies at Tel Aviv University. Her main fields of interest are the poetics of biblical narrative, historiography, and aspects of ideological criticism. Among her publications are *The Book of Judges: The Art of Editing* and *Hidden Polemics in Biblical Narrative.*

Athalya Brenner is Professor Emerita of Hebrew Bible/Old Testament at the University of Amsterdam, The Netherlands, and Professor in Biblical Studies at the Department of Hebrew Culture Studies at Tel Aviv University, Israel. She holds an honorary Ph.D. from the University of Bonn, Germany. She edited the first and second series of *A Feminist Companion to the Bible* (Sheffield Academic, 1993–2000). Among her other publications is *I Am: Biblical Women Tell Their Own Stories* (Fortress Press, 2005).

Erivwierho Francis Eghwubare is Lecturer in the Department of Religious Studies, Kogi State University, Abraka, Nigeria. He is completing his Ph.D. in Old Testament at Delta State University, Abraka, Nigeria. He has published many articles.

Carole R. Fontaine is the Taylor Professor of Biblical Theology and History at Andover Newton Theological School, and was a Henry Luce III Fellow in Theology (2008–09). She is interested in diversity hermeneutics and human rights, feminist criticism and historiography, folk traditions, and iconography, especially with reference to texts about females. Her most recent books are *Smooth Words: Women, Proverbs and Performance in Biblical Wisdom* (Sheffield Academic, 2002) and *With Eyes of Flesh: The Bible, Gender, and Human Rights* (Sheffield Phoenix Press, 2008).

The Rev. Cheryl A. Kirk-Duggan, Ph.D., is Professor of Theology and Women's Studies, Shaw University Divinity School, Raleigh, N.C., and an ordained elder in the Christian Methodist Episcopal Church. She has written and edited over twenty books, including *The Sky Is Crying: Racism, Classism, and Natural Disaster, in response to Katrina* (Abingdon, 2006). Kirk-Duggan is the 2009 recipient of the Excellence in Academic Research Award, Shaw University. With degrees in music and religious studies, Kirk-Duggan conducts interdisciplinary research spanning religious and women's studies, culture, pedagogy, spirituality and health, justice, violence, and sexuality.

Kari Latvus is University Lecturer of Biblical Studies and Hebrew at the University of Helsinki (in 2009–11; on leave from the Diaconia University of Applied Sciences, Finland). He is also Docent of Old Testament Exegesis at the Helsinki University and Visiting Professor of Diaconia at the Theological Institute (Tallinn). Before his current positions, he worked at the Lutheran

Theological Seminary in Hong Kong as an Old Testament professor (1992–94). His main fields of interest are Deuteronomistic theology, Hebrew Bible poverty texts, *diakonia*, and postcolonial and contextual analysis. Among his publications in English are *God, Anger and Ideology: The Anger of God in Joshua and Judges in Relation to Deuteronomy and the Priestly Writings* (Sheffield Academic, 1998) and several articles about the origin of *diakonia* and diaconal ministry.

Archie Chi Chung Lee is Professor of Religious Studies at the Chinese University of Hong Kong. His major field of research is the Hebrew Bible and Chinese biblical interpretation. He is interested in how the Bible is translated and read in the Chinese context and interpreted cross-textually with Chinese scriptural texts. His recent publications include "Cross-textual Hermeneutics and Identity in Multi-textual Asia," in *Christian Theology in Asia* (ed. Sebastian Kim, Cambridge, 2008); "Mothers Bewailing: Reading Lamentations," in *Her Master's Tools? Feminist Challenges to Historical-Critical Interpretations* (ed. Tod Penner and Caroline Vander Stichele, SBL, 2005); and "The Book of Lamentations," *NIDB* (2008). He is an associate editor of the *Global Bible Commentary* (Abingdon, 2004) and *Cambridge Dictionary of Christianity* (Cambridge, 2010).

The Rev. Thulani Ndlazi is a Ph.D. candidate at the School of Religion and Theology, University of KwaZulu-Natal, South Africa. He earned a Master of Arts in Religion (MAR) from Lancaster Theological Seminary (Pennsylvania) in 2002. Currently he is Program Manager at the Church Land Programme (CLP), Pietermaritzburg, South Africa. The CLP is a nongovernmental organization (NGO) established to work with churches, people, and land, with particular attention to women and the poorest people on land redistribution issues (in the context of the apartheid legacy).

Meira Polliack is Professor of Bible at Tel Aviv University. Her main field of research is Jewish Bible interpretation, particularly in the medieval Islamic world. Among her books are *The Karaite Tradition of Arabic Bible Translation* (Brill, 1997); *Karaite Judaism: A Guide to Its History and Literary Sources* (Brill, 2003); and *Yefet ben 'Eli's Commentary on Hosea, Annotated Edition, Hebrew Translation and Introduction* (with E. Schlossberg [Hebrew]; Ramat Gan: Bar-Ilan University Press, 2009).

The Rev. Mark Rathbone is a minister of the Dutch Reformed Church, involved in intercultural ministry. He obtained his Doctorate of Theology in 2006 with the title "The Interaction between Scholarly and Non-Scholarly Readings of Genesis 11:1-9 in the South African Context." His main fields of interest are postcolonialism, hermeneutics, ethics, ideology critique, and the role of nonscholarly readers of the Bible in biblical interpretation. He was involved in an international, intercultural reading project entitled *Through the Eyes of Another* from 2000 to 2002. He contributed the article, "Intercultural Biblical Interpretation: Toward a Global Ethic," in the subsequent publication released in 2004.

Yael Shemesh is Senior Lecturer of Bible at Bar-Ilan University. Her main fields of interest are the poetics of biblical narrative, prophetic stories, measure for measure in the Bible, feminist interpretation to the Bible, and animal ethics. Among her publications are "Punishment of the Offending Organ in Biblical Literature," *VT* 55 (2005): 343–65; and "Rape Is Rape Is Rape: The Story of Dinah and Shechem (Genesis 34)," *ZAW* 119 (2007): 2–21. She is currently preparing a study on mourning in the Bible.

Philip Venter is a full-time pastor of the Dutch Reformed Church in Fairland, Johannesburg, and a research associate of the Faculty of Theology at the University of Pretoria. His research interests include ecotheology, body criticism, and evolutionary theology. Recently published articles include studies on Psalm 74, embodied realism, and Proverbs in *Old Testament Essays, Verbum et Ecclesia* and *Hervormde Teologiese Studies.*

Gerald West teaches Old Testament/Hebrew Bible and African Biblical Hermeneutics in the School of Religion and Theology at the University of KwaZulu-Natal, South Africa. He is also Director of the Ujamaa Centre for Community Development and Research, a structural formation that enables collaboration between socially engaged biblical scholars, organic intellectuals, and local communities. He has published extensively in the area of African biblical hermeneutics.

Wai Ching (Angela) Wong is Associate Professor of Cultural and Religious Studies at the Chinese University of Hong Kong. Her main fields of interest are gender studies, postcolonial studies, and culture. Among her publications is *"The Poor Woman": A Critical Analysis of Asian Theology and Contemporary Chinese Fiction by Women* (Peter Lang, 2002).

Yan Lin is Lecturer on Hebrew Bible at Shenzhen University. Her main fields of research are Hebrew Bible, biblical literature, and Western literature, especially literary texts influenced by biblical texts. Her first published book is *Re-reading Genesis 1–3 in the Light of Creation Myths from Ancient Chinese Texts* (Lanzhou University Press, 2008; in Chinese). She is currently preparing studies on "The Daughters of Eve and Nu Kua: Cross-Textual Readings on Women in the Hebrew Bible and in Ancient Chinese Literature" and "The Influence of Biblical Texts on Medieval Heroic Epics."

Gale A. Yee is Nancy W. King Professor of Biblical Studies at Episcopal Divinity School, Cambridge, Mass. She is the author of *Poor Banished Children of Eve* (Fortress Press, 2003), editor of *Judges and Method: New Approaches in Biblical Studies* (Fortress Press, 2007), and General Editor of Semeia Studies.

Edwin Zulu, from Zambia, was formerly Senior Lecturer in Old Testament and Hebrew at Africa University, Mutare, Zimbabwe. He is now the rector of Justo Mwale Theological University College, Lusaka, Zambia. His main fields of interest are Bible and culture, contextual Bible interpretation, and biblical narratives. He has published in these areas.

AUTHOR INDEX

SCRIPTURE INDEX

ANCIENT AND OTHER EXTRA-BIBLICAL SOURCES INDEX

Also from Fortress Press

Teaching the Bible
The Discourses and
Politics of Biblical
Pedagogy
Fernando F. Segovia and
Mary Ann Tolbert, Editors

Paperback
384 pages
978-0-8006-9698-6

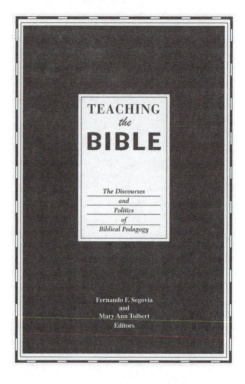

"Although the field of biblical studies is bursting with new methods and fresh interpretations, there has been surprisingly little discussion of what these changes mean for the actual task of teaching the Bible. Happily, this volume takes significant first steps in addressing the shifts in classroom pedagogy that the new day in biblical studies urgently demands."
Norman K. Gottwald, Author of *The Hebrew Bible: A Brief Socio-Literary Introduction*

"An absolutely indispensable compendium of resources for charting the changes in the discipline of biblical studies, for exposing the operations of power in past and present interpretations and uses of the Bible, and for discovering a variety of postmodernist and postcolonial pedagogies in the reading and teaching of the Bible in a radically pluralistic age."
Abraham Smith, Perkins School of Theology, S.M.U.

Also from Fortress Press

Reading from This Place, Volume 1
Social Location and Biblical Interpretation in the United States
Fernando F. Segovia and Mary Ann Tolbert, Editors

Paperback
336 pages
978-0-8006-2812-3

Reading from This Place, Volume 2
Social Location and Biblical Interpretation in Global Perspective
Fernando F. Segovia and Mary Ann Tolbert, Editors

Paperback
336 pages
978-0-8006-2949-6

Also from Fortress Press

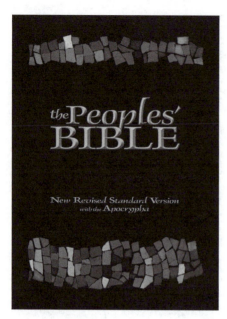

The Peoples' Bible

New Revised Standard Version, with the Apocrypha

Curtiss Paul DeYoung, Wilda C. Gafney, Leticia Guardiola-Sáenz, George E. Tinker, and Frank Yamada, Editors

Hardcover
1786 pages
978-0-8066-5625-0

The Peoples' Companion to the Bible

Curtiss Paul DeYoung, Wilda C. Gafney, Leticia Guardiola-Sáenz, George E. Tinker, and Frank Yamada, Editors

Paperback
320 pages
978-0-8006-9702-0

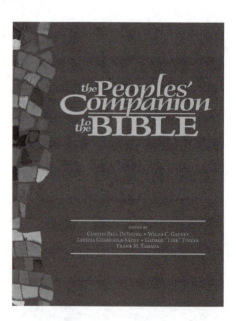